Drinking from the (
How Amos Tutuola Can Change Our Minds

Francis B. Nyamnjoh

Langaa Research & Publishing CIG
Mankon, Bamenda

Publisher:
Langaa RPCIG
Langaa Research & Publishing Common Initiative Group
P.O. Box 902 Mankon
Bamenda
North West Region
Cameroon
Langaagrp@gmail.com
www.langaa-rpcig.net

Distributed in and outside N. America by African Books Collective
orders@africanbookscollective.com
www.africanbookscollective.com

ISBN-10: 9956764655

ISBN-13: 9789956764655

© Francis B. Nyamnjoh 2017

All rights reserved.
No part of this book may be reproduced or transmitted in any form or by any means, mechanical or electronic, including photocopying and recording, or be stored in any information storage or retrieval system, without written permission from the publisher

Praise for this Book

"Twenty years after his death, valued by some scholars and writers but discounted by others, Amos Tutuola here finds a compelling advocate. Nyamnjoh reveals a voice that both embraces a range of African communal experience beyond 'lettered' reach and challenges commonplace aesthetic and philosophical constructs of African knowledge. And he shows why Tutuola matters, in his own time and now." **Milton Krieger, Emeritus Professor, Western Washington University, USA**

"Francis Nyamnjoh invites us to rethink contemporary cosmopolitanism through strange encounters and marvellous episodes recounted in the stories of Amos Tutuola, a mid-twentieth century Nigerian Yoruba author. This might seem an endeavour more implausible than the tales themselves, but reading will change your mind." **Richard Fardon, Professor of West African Anthropology, School of Oriental and African Studies (SOAS), University of London, UK**

"Francis Nyamnjoh's book argues that Tutuola's work provides a theoretical tool kit for conceptualising and understanding what it means to be African at the contemporary moment. Tutuola's tales of frontiers, of incompleteness, of crossroads and conviviality advance profound epistemological perspectives on being and knowledge that we will do well to acknowledge. Nyamnjoh positions Tutuola as a vernacular theorist whose narratives are a fount of hermeneutical and epistemological insight. Much is often made of the idea of vernacular theory but this book is an exemplary instance of putting that idea into practice." **Harry Garuba, poet and scholar, University of Cape Town**

"The book is an important contribution to African intellectual history. It offers a fresh and original interpretation of the life and work of Amos Tutuola, but at the same time marks a substantial advance in the ongoing epistemological debates on the study of Africa. Moving beyond the restrictions of the Eurocentric/anti-colonial dichotomy, Nyamnjoh presents a more creative alternative for an African epistemology. Based on his concept of the incompleteness of human existence, he opts for an inclusive, dialogical and interdisciplinary approach. Of special interest is the way in which he relates ethnography to fiction and his focus on the real life experiences of ordinary people. This is a seminal work which no doubt will have a significant impact on current epistemological thinking." **Professor Bernard Lategan, Founding Director, Stellenbosch Institute for Advanced Study (STIAS)**

"Weaving varied ethnographic accounts together with richly textured historical perspectives, Nyamnjoh traces and rehabilitates the checkered career of an unusual and often controversial literary icon." **Sanya Osha, author of** *African Postcolonial Modernity: Informal Subjectivities and the Democratic Consensus*

About the Book

In this book, Amos Tutuola's unusual writing style firmly rooted in African storytelling is used to refute the common misconception that there is only one type of scholarship and set of experiences worth writing about. The issues faced by African intellectuals and scholarship who seem to have to abandon their African identities in search for international recognition at the expense of local relevance by reiterating dominant colonialist scopes of knowledge are explored. This is especially relevant in light of the wave of protests at universities all over South Africa where students demanded the "fall" of Eurocentric education standards, calling for a more Afrocentric curriculum, more grounded in African traditions and experiences, and thus more relatable to the African students in the ivory towers of Africa.

The idea of the West as the centre of knowledge and civilisation is challenged by pointing out that this number one status achieved was only possible by borrowing bits and pieces from all over. Rather than just a simple dismissal of Western ideals, an alternative to these Eurocentric dualisms is offered – an acquiescence of incompleteness as a way of being. A number of stories from Tutuola's works are used to illustrate the importance of conviviality. We are urged to accept that one's independence will always be thwarted by one's dependency on others and to see debt and indebtedness as a normal way of being human though relationships with others.

Acknowledgements

Writing this book has been a questing journey of many enriching encounters. I would like to express my most sincere gratitude to all those who in one way or another contributed with humbling generosity their ideas, insights, time, suggestions, and intellectual and related energies to kindle and rekindle my efforts in putting together this book on African epistemologies of incompleteness and conviviality inspired by Tutuola and the cosmologies of his existence and creative imagination.

Of special mention are all those who read and commented various drafts and sections of this book, pointing me as they did to sources and resources for further enrichment of my argument and its substantiation. These include, in alphabetical order, Richard Fardon, Ntonghanwah Forcheh, Divine Fuh, Malizani Jimu, Milton Krieger, Bernard Lategan, Ayanda Manqoyi, Louis Herns Marcelin, Motoji Matsuda, Dirk Moons, Artwell Nhemachena, Anye-Nkwenti Nyamnjoh, Sue Bih Nyamnjoh, Itaru Ohta, Elsemi Olwage, Sanya Osha, Michael Rowlands, Nanna Schneidermann, Kathryn Toure, Jean-Pierre Warnier, Joanna Woods, and Wafule Yenjela. They include as well, the reviewers for *Journal of Asian and African Studies* and *Stichproben. Wiener Zeitschrift für kritische Afrikastudien*, which respectively published "Incompleteness: Frontier Africa and the Currency of Conviviality" and "Amos Tutuola and the Elusiveness of Completeness," essays which highlight some of the ideas developed in this book. I acknowledge the opportunity to present and discuss aspects of my thoughts on Amos Tutuola at graduate conferences and doctoral seminars at the University of KwaZulu Natal, Stellenbosch University and UNISA in South Africa, and at Kenyatta University in Kenya. I cherish my Japanese editions of *The Palm-Wine Drinkard* and *My Life in the Bush of Ghosts*, a special gift from Itaru Ohta, and I look forward to reading them the day I acquire the juju to activate my competency in Japanese.

I am most grateful for three fellowships, one from the Stellenbosch Institute for Advanced Study (April – June 2015), a second from the Graduate School of Asian and African Area Studies of Kyoto University (June – July 2015), and a third from the Rockefeller Foundation Bellagio Center Residency Program (25 August – 22 September 2016), which fellowships enabled me to write sections of the book. I benefitted enormously from the generosity, both intellectual and social, of fellows and staff of the three institutions. I am in their debt. I am also grateful to Steve Howard and his colleagues of Ohio

University, for a visiting scholarship (August – September 2015), which enabled me to develop some of the themes in this book.

Special thanks go to Richard Fardon who generously agreed to do the Foreword, and to Harry Garuba, Milton Krieger, Bernard Lategan and Sanya Osha for their commendations. I acknowledge with profound gratitude the editorial contributions of Kathryn Toure. I am equally indebted to Manya van Ryneveld and Sue Bih Nyamnjoh for assistance with proofreading.

Last but not least, my sincere gratitude flows out to all the palm-wine tapsters and drinkards of Africa and the worlds beyond.

Table of Contents

Acknowledgements... vi

Foreword... xi
by Richard Fardon

Chapter 1: A Preview.. 1

Chapter 2: Dominant and Dormant
Epistemologies of Africa... 33

Chapter 3: Tutuola and the Extravagant
Illusion of Completeness... 61

Chapter 4: Keeping Alive Popular
Ideas of Reality.. 125

Chapter 5: *The Palm-Wine Drinkard*
and the Challenge of Dichotomies........................... 141

Chapter 6: Activation, Potency and
Efficacy in Tutuola's Universe................................ 159

Chapter 7: Tutuola in Conversation
with the Cameroon Grassfields and Beyond.............. 199

Chapter 8: Conclusion: Tutuola's Legacy................... 255

References.. 277

Foreword

I am unsure which tense – past, present or future – best addresses the discerning reader you must be. You will soon find, if you don't already know, that Francis Nyamnjoh is not a thinker who marches in straight lines or turns at right angles; he prefers to explore meandering bush paths where a traveller might encounter strange companions and other wonders. Perhaps you read similarly and so are coming to this Foreword finally, or not at all (in which case my choice of tense won't matter). But let me assume that you are holding a book you have yet to read and are wondering what awaits you. I can tell you it will be an expansive and inclusive read; we are all addressed, wherever or however we find ourselves.

Francis has taken a companion on this intellectual journey which is for him both a setting forth and looking back. The Yoruba author Amos Tutuola was among the earliest Nigerian fictional writers of English, and he piques Francis's curiosity in two related but different ways. Tutuola's imagination re-envisioned classic themes of African, particularly West African, story-telling and published them from the mid-twentieth century onwards in a written English that remains uniquely his. By doing so, Tutuola attracted so wide a range of assessments that his work became a chamber of opinions: approved and disapproved in equal strength; the grounds for approval were frequently no more sustaining than those for disapproval. Some Nigerian intellectuals, particularly student expatriates, disparaged his unconventional use of English, suspecting his prestigious London publishers, Faber & Faber, might be encouraging a quaint view of Nigerians' capacities to express themselves grammatically, a view of which they were themselves the living disproof. By the same token, some of the ringing endorsements by western commentators now ring as patronizing as the rejections in their assumption that this mid-twentieth century writer had channelled some timeless collective African imagination not of his own era. This mirroring, often distorted, has continued as each new development has found its own Tutuola – recently as a magical realist and pathfinder for Ben Okri's generation of Nigerian writers.

Amos Tutuola accompanies Francis both as a fellow writer of fiction and as a reflection of the state and status of writing. As writer, Tutuola's stories expand 'what is out there'; put more formally, through them he makes ontological claims about everyday African worlds. His protagonists' experiences show us how they 'find out what is out there'; or more formally, they suggest practical epistemologies for understanding this given world that has been expanded beyond the mundane. Their knowing both 'that' and 'how and why', Francis Nyamnjoh argues, are correctives to colonial or western ontologies and epistemologies, and particularly to the forms in which these have been embraced as ideologies by African intellectual elites. The focus of his interest, however, lies less in those ideologies, which he is content to treat in shorthand, than it does in everyday African knowledge practices (or for that matter everyday western practices). To these, Francis brings an anthropologist's ability to derive middle-range generalizations from grounded local circumstances, including their fictional representation.

I have room to touch upon the generalizations you are about to read only incompletely, which happily is a virtue in this context because the first of them is precisely about the matter of incompletion. Drawing on Tutuola's story-telling, Francis notes the principled incompletion of agents, both individual and collective. This quality has two aspects: that they consist of assemblages of more or less completely fused elements that are hence more or less susceptible to decomposition; and that these incomplete entities seek to complete themselves through extension. These are characteristics compatible with a number of others: an emphasis upon conviviality and a capacity, even compulsion, for living together, supplemented by an openness to frontier experience in its various forms. Paradigmatically, the frontier will involve encounters with the bush, both in a narrower and more literal sense of the word, and in the geographically wider sense of the migrant's world, particularly as these expand the possibilities of interaction with powers and forms beyond the mundane, local world. Such experiences, which have been documented primarily by creative artists and by anthropologists, who happen sometimes, as in Francis's case, to be the same people, are the source of embarrassment to the carriers of modernizing ideologies. Artists can be dismissed as fiction makers, but what of anthropologists?

Other than in South Africa, where Francis Nyamnjoh works now, anthropologists are thin on the ground in Africa south of the Sahara. It takes a brave African scholar to argue that anthropology which, like a character from one of Tutuola's tales, has been fated to drag a reputation tarnished since imperial and colonial times behind it, can be a liberatory discipline. But Francis encourages us to think about the variety of conversations an anthropological sensibility invites. Over several years, I was struck to see my students captivated by an essay of his which brought a cool ethnographic eye to his lived experience in order to dissect the ambivalence of belonging. Titled after a saying popular in his Grassfields Cameroon home, that 'A child is one person's only in the womb', Francis's essay is partly about the ways an individual is supplemented by belonging to family and community. Supplemented but never entirely completed, since frontier experiences are always available. The reader might begin to sense a familiar cosy nostalgia, but before this condition is allowed to seem too rosy, Francis presents us with the other, coercive face of connection, composed of entreaties and more or less veiled threats that cajole any 'bushfallers' who seem to have prospered to recognize the obligations due connection (including connections they might never have known of). Connection is ambivalent, so some disown it and choose a social death. For only the socially dead, and perhaps the chiefs maintained by immense collective effort to be perfect symbolic containers, can aspire to completion. The rest must live imperfectly but, as Francis suggests, convivially and hopefully. This argument enlarged is at least part of the ontological condition he figures for us here by drawing insights from fictions, both his own and Tutuola's, as well as from the ways these stories provoke their readers.

Richard Fardon
SOAS, University of London

Chapter One

A Preview

African intellectual history has been a struggle. A struggle of how to reconcile international recognition with local relevance ever since the publication of Amos Tutuola's *The Palm-Wine Drinkard* in 1952. African intellectuals' quest for distinctively African ways of interpreting African life and thought has taken many forms and provoked lively cross-disciplinary debate and literature. The results are, however, mixed. Students still decry curricula that do not satisfactorily reflect, if at all, their African context and lived realities. Their professors complain about a geopolitics of knowledge production and consumption skewed in favour of the West or the global north. While students and professors of African universities are having a raw deal at the global marketplaces of the production and circulation of ideas, ordinary Africans outside of the academy, a high proportion of whom have pursued little or no formal education, are equally complaining and challenging their universities to prove their relevance to the wider society. To many, universities are indeed ivory towers (sometimes perched on hilltops or hillsides like deities, spirits or gods), notorious for talking academic gibberish and for talking without listening, even when claiming that no social knowledge is of much import if not immersed in and distilled from the lived realities of those it purports to be knowledge about.

This is a book on the epistemological dimensions of how research is conceptualised and practiced in African universities caught betwixt and between the tensions and possibilities of interconnecting global and local hierarchies. These hierarchies shape relations and structure knowledge production in and on Africa. Inspired by Amos Tutuola, the late Nigerian writer, and his novels and short stories, the book is a contribution to the unfinished business of the transformation of colonial and apartheid ideologies on being human and being African that continue to shape how research is conceptualised, taught and practiced in universities across Africa. The book also examines how such resilient colonial and apartheid ideologies continue to shape the attitudes and behaviour of African intellectuals towards ordinary Africans and vis-à-vis popular understandings of reality. The book discusses Amos Tutuola and his works and argues the following main points.

First, it is argued that popular ideas of what constitutes reality in Africa are rich with ontologies of incompleteness. Such conceptions of incompleteness could enrich the practice of social science and the humanities in Africa and globally. The book suggests that incompleteness as a social reality and form of knowing generative of and dependent on interconnections, relatedness, open-endedness and multiplicities is both exciting and inspiring, at personal, group and collective, political and scholarly levels. Incompleteness harbours emancipatory potentials and inspires unbounded creativity and hopefully a reclamation of more inclusionary understandings of being human and being in general. Incompleteness is not a unidirectional concept. Every social organisational category – be it race or ethnicity, place or geography, class or status, gender or sex, generation or age, religion or beliefs, etc. – is incomplete without the rest of what it takes to be human through relationships with other humans, as well as with non-humans – or what Munyaradzi Mawere (2015) perhaps more appropriately terms "other beings" – in the natural and supernatural worlds. Africa is incomplete without the rest of the world, and the world is incomplete without Africa; and both are incomplete without the natural and supernatural worlds.

Social sciences and humanities steeped in the dualisms of colonial ways of knowing and producing knowledge in Africa are ill-prepared to midwife the renaissance of African ways of knowing and knowledge production that have been victims of unequal encounters with Western colonialism and its zero-sum games of completeness and winner takes all. To achieve such an epistemological turn, African social scientists (practicing and aspirant) and practitioners of the humanities would have to turn to and seek to be cultivated afresh by ordinary Africans immersed in popular traditions of meaning making. As Tutuola's experiences as a writer illustrate, these people in rural areas and urban villages are the very same Africans to whom the modern intellectual elite in their ivory towers tries to deny the right to think and represent their realities in accordance with the civilisations and universes they know best. Many scholars schooled in Western modernity push away or even run from these worldviews and conceptions of reality. Instead of creating space for the fruit of "the African mind" as a tradition of knowledge, they are all too eager, under the gawking eyes of their Western counterparts, to label and dismiss (however hypocritically) as traditional or superstitious the creative imagination of their fellow Africans.

The full valorisation of African potentialities in future social scientific endeavours depends on the extent to which scholars in the social sciences and humanities in or of Africa are able to (re)familiarise themselves with and encourage these popular modes of knowing and knowledge-making in the production of relevant, inclusive, negotiated, nuanced and complex social knowledge. There is a clear need to decentre social sciences and the humanities from their preponderantly parochial or provincial, not to mention patriarchal, Eurocentric origins and biases and from illusions of completeness (Amin 2009[1988]), and for African researchers and scholars to (re)immerse themselves and be grounded in endogenous African universes and the interconnecting global and local hierarchies that shape and are shaped by these universes.

Second, the book argues that Africans who are able to successfully negotiate change and continuity and bring into conversation various dichotomies and binaries qualify as frontier Africans. Their frontierness comes from their continual straddling of myriad identity margins and bridging of various divides. This encourages them to recognise and provide for the interconnections, nuances and complexities in their lives made possible or exacerbated by technologically inspired and enhanced mobilities and encounters. In this regard, there is an interesting conversation to be had between forms of mobility and the capacity to tame time and space inspired by jujus or spells and charms in Tutuola's universe and the forms of mobility and presence made possible by new information and communication technologies such as the television, internet, cell and smart phones.

Popular ideas of reality and the reality of frontier Africans suggest an approach to social action in which interconnections, interrelationships, interdependencies, collaboration, coproduction and compassion are emphasised, celebrated and rewarded. Within this framework of conviviality, intricate entanglements and manglements, if hierarchies of social actors and actions exist, it is reassuring to know that nothing is permanent or singular about the nature, order and form of such hierarchies. Agency is available and affordable to humans as singular, plural and composite beings – whole or dis(re)membered – and in human or non-human forms, apparent or virtual, tangible and intangible alike.

Third, the book argues that commitment to crossroads[1] conversations across divides makes frontier Africans express discomfort with suggestions or ambitions of absolute autonomy in action and reject ideas that humans are superior to any other beings and that a unified and singular self is the only unit of analysis for human action. In the absence of permanence, the freedom to pursue individual or group goals exists within a socially predetermined frame that emphasises collective interests at the same time that it allows for individual creativity and self-activation. Social visibility derives from (or is facilitated by) being interconnected with other humans and the wider world of nature, the supernatural and the imaginary in an open-ended communion of interests. Being social is not limited to familiar circles or to fellow humans, as it is expected that even the passing stranger (human or otherwise, natural or supernatural) from a distant land or from out of this world should benefit from the sociality that one has cultivated on familiar shores. The logic of collective action that underpins the privileging of interconnections and frontier beings is instructive in a situation where nothing but change is permanent, and where life is a currency in perpetual circulation. The tendency towards temporality, transience or impermanence calls for social actors to de-emphasise or domesticate personal success and maximise collective endeavours. It calls for humility and the interment of mentalities and practices of absolutes and conquest.

Fourth, it is argued that scholars interested in rethinking African social sciences and humanities could maximise and capitalise upon the currency of conviviality in popular African ideas of reality and social action. Conviviality is recognition and provision for the fact or reality of being incomplete. If incompleteness is the normal order of things – natural, human and supernatural – conviviality invites us to celebrate and preserve incompleteness and mitigate delusions of grandeur that come with ambitions and claims of perfection. Conviviality emphasises the repair rather than the rejection of human relationships. It is more about cobbling and less about ruptures. It is fundamental to being human – biologically and socially – and necessary for processes of social renewal, reconstruction and regeneration. As noted in Nyamnjoh (2015b), conviviality depicts diversity, tolerance, trust, equality, inclusiveness, cohabitation, coexistence, mutual accommodation, interaction, interdependence, getting along, generosity, hospitality, congeniality, festivity, civility and privileging peace over conflict, among other forms of sociality.

Fifth, the book argues that granted the intricacies of popular conceptions of reality, and in view of the frontier reality of many an ordinary African caught betwixt and between exclusionary and prescriptive regimes of being and belonging, nothing short of convivial scholarship would do justice to the legitimate quest for an epistemological reconfiguration of African universities and the disciplines, a reconfiguration informed by popular agency and epistemologies. A truly convivial scholarship is one which does not seek a priori to define and confine Africans into particular territories or geographies, particular racial and ethnic categories, particular classes, genders, generations, religions or whatever other identity marker is ideologically en vogue. Convivial scholarship confronts and humbles the challenge of over-prescription, over-standardisation, over-routinisation, and over-prediction. It is critical and evidence-based; it challenges problematic labels, especially those that seek to unduly oversimplify the social realities of the people, places and spaces it seeks to understand and explain.

Convivial scholarship recognises the deep power of collective imagination and the importance of interconnections and nuanced complexities. It is a scholarship that questions assumptions of a priori locations and bounded ideas of power and all other forms of relationships that shape and are shaped by the socio-cultural, political and economic circumstances of social actors. It is a scholarship that sees the local in the global and the global in the local by bringing them into informed conversations, conscious of the hierarchies and power relations at play at both the micro and macro levels of being and becoming. Convivial scholarship is scholarship that neither dismisses contested and contrary perspectives a priori nor throws the baby out with the bathwater. It is critical scholarship of recognition and reconciliation, scholarship that has no permanent friends, enemies or alliances beyond the rigorous and committed quest for truth in its complexity and nuance, and using the results of aspirations for a common humanity that is in communion with the natural and supernatural environments that make a balanced existence possible.

Convivial scholarship does not impose what it means to be human, just as it does not prescribe a single version of the good life in a world peopled by infinite possibilities, tastes and value systems. Rather, it encourages localised conversations of a truly global nature on competing and complementary processes of social cultivation through practice, performance and experience, without pre-empting or foreclosing particular units of analysis in a world in which the messiness of encounters and relationships frowns on binaries, dichotomies and dualisms. Indeed, like Tutuola's universe, convivial scholarship challenges us, however grounded we may be in our disciplines and their logics of practice, to cultivate the disposition to be present everywhere at the same time. It is a scholarship that cautions disciplines, their borders and gatekeepers to open up and embrace the crossroads culture of presence in simultaneous multiplicity and concomitant epistemologies of interconnections. With convivial scholarship, there are no final answers, only permanent questions and ever exciting new angles of questioning.

What exactly does Tutuola – renowned for his highly creative effervescent imagination and for writing in acrobatic brushstrokes – have to offer ongoing epistemological debates on the study of Africa, especially in the social sciences and humanities? This is the central question addressed in this book. As evidenced in the pages that follow, Tutuola's writings and the universe he depicts are a proliferation of ethnographic accounts of popular understandings of reality in Africa. Reality that is fluid and flexible, and that is as amenable to reason, logic and sensory perceptions as it eludes them. In his writings we see the frontierness of ordinary Africans in how they collapse dichotomies and build bridges of conviviality between nature and culture, the visible and invisible, tradition and modernity,

Africa and Europe, gods, spirits, ghosts, animals and kindred creatures of the bushes, and humans.

This book is also an account of how the heated debates provoked by Tutuola's writings offer a compelling case for convivial scholarship on the continent and beyond. If only scholars and scholarship could borrow a leaf from Tutuola's imaginative inventiveness and the flexibility of his characters, big and small, human and non-human, they would discover the infinite richness, virtues, merits and humility in striving less for sweeping, neutralising victories and more for living and letting live through genuinely inclusive pursuits and participatory articulations of success. For, in Tutuola's universe, sooner or later, it dawns on a creature consumed with the quest for total victories through conflictual relationships, that they are much better off working together, striking deals and reaching compromises, given the contingency of their victories and in light of the nimble-footedness of their power. Most importantly, the book explores how instructive to anthropologists Tutuola's rich ethnographic insights and *manière de faire* are in making a case for so-called "native" non-professional, university trained ethnographers in mitigation of the resilient prevalent tendency towards white-male dominated lone-rangerism (Clifford and Marcus 1986; Tsing 1993; Visweswaran 1994; Gupta and Ferguson 1997; Abu-Lughod 2008; Harrison 2008; Nyamnjoh 2012a).

Amos Tutuola was born in Abeokuta, Nigeria, in 1920. He benefitted from only "six years of frequently interrupted" formal education, and died on 7 June 1997 desperately seeking completeness in a world of binary oppositions and obsession with winning (Larson 2001: 2). Within the framework of colonial education and its hierarchies of credibility, Tutuola was seen by some as an accidental writer (Lindfors 1970; Larson 2001: 1-25) or "the unlettered man of letters" (Lindfors 1999a: 109), as if others are born with a mission to write and a pen in hand. Never wholly endorsed as a writer at any given time away or at home, Tutuola's literary career went from "foreign enchantment and local embarrassment" to "universal but qualified acceptance" through "foreign disenchantment and local reappraisal" between 1952 and 1975 alone (Lindfors 1975: xiii).

Tutuola's parents – Charles Tutuola and Esther Aina Tutuola – were cocoa farmers and also Christians – a significant mention, as Christianity, its symbols, morality and beliefs feature prominently in Tutuola's books, where not even the bush of ghosts is able to escape its ubiquitous grip, and are a clear illustration that Tutuola is far from stuck in a frozen African past filled with fear and terror, as some of his critics have suggested. In his works, Tutuola seeks to reassure his readers that it is possible to be what Charles Taylor terms "open and porous and vulnerable" to a world of spirits, powers and cosmic forces, and still be "disenchanted" enough to have the confidence of Taylor's "buffered self," exploring one's own "powers of moral ordering" (Taylor 2007: 27). Equally noteworthy is the fact that Tutuola did not allow his embrace of Christianity to serve as an ideological whip to flog him and his Yoruba cultural beliefs into compliance with the one-dimensionalism of colonial Christianity and the dualistic prescriptiveness of European missionaries, vis-à-vis their African converts. His Christianity simply afforded him an opportunity to add another layer of complexity to his toolkit of personal identification (adopting the name "Amos" for example, without giving up "Tutuola") and to his Yorubaness of being. In this connection, the following observation by Judith Tabron is worth keeping in mind, as we read and seek to understand the nuanced complexities of Tutuola the writer:

> Amos Tutuola was born Olatubusun, son of Tutuola, son of the *Odafin* Odegbami of the town of Abeokuta in Nigeria. His name is an example of the way in which his life was to straddle the transition from traditional Africa to colonized Africa to independent Africa, a complete index of the twentieth century of Africa's history His grandfather was a spiritual leader and administrator of a large section of the town, and Olatubusun grew up watching the ceremonies of the *orishas* in his town, listening to the orature of Yoruba religion in his compound, and seeing the art celebrating this belief in his grandfather's house.
> When the family Europeanized their name, after years of work on the part of Christian missionaries in Akeobuta and the death of the *Odafin* and his son, the rest of the family took the surname Odegbami, for the leader of their clan; Olatubusun took his father's name, Tutuola,

the gentle one, as his surname, and chose or was given the name Amos, his Christian name in every respect, for he had converted by this time, as had his parents (though his grandfather never had) (Tabron 2003: 43-44).

As a Christian named Amos, Tutuola, "the gentle one," was resolute in turning down an invitation to break with his past and to disown the gods, beliefs and traditions of his land, even as these were reduced to screaming silence, often with the complicity of purportedly enlightened Africans. He was at odds with the hypocrisy of some Africans who harkened to Christianity by day and succumbed by night to endogenous African religions disparaged as superstition, yet would not own up in broad daylight to being more than just Christians. Studies in contemporary African religions and religiosities attest to the tensions and frustrations felt by many an African with a Christianity unyielding in its preference for conversion over conversation and determined asphyxiation of endogenous religions and belief systems in Africa (Ela 1986[1980]; Boulaga 1984[1981]; Olupona 2004; Bongmba 2012; Adogame et al. 2013; Soyinka 2013; Echtler and Ukah 2015).

Tutuola served as a servant for a certain Mr F. O. Monu, an Igbo man, from the age of seven. Mr Monu sent him to the Salvation Army school of Abeokuta in 1934. He also attended the Anglican Central School in Abeokuta. Following the death of his father in 1939, Tutuola left school to train as a blacksmith, a trade he practised from 1942 to 1945 for the Royal Air Force in Nigeria (Owomoyela 1997: 865). Again, the significance of Tutuola's employment by the Royal Air Force is worth bearing in mind, as some critics have tended to express surprise at how Tutuola is able to make reference to aeroplanes, bombs and other technological gadgets usually assumed European. As if Europe, in exporting itself and its technologies of power had, by some strange logic, hoped that these would somehow not ignite the imagination and sense of appropriation of those it sought to conquer, humble and, *à la* Frederick Lugard, pacify, through the creation of native authorities and a system of indirect rule, or what Mahmood Mamdani has termed "decentralised despotism" (Mamdani 1996). As we read Tutuola, it is worth bearing in mind that not only has there never been or can there ever be a "completely un-British Nigeria," given the territory's colonial origins and continuities, but also that Tutuola's work "reflects the coexistence of English and Yoruba influences in both his cultural past and present" (Tabron 2003: 37). Indeed, his work in Yorubanised English, contributes to the building blocks of the materialisation of the imagined community known as "Nigeria." As a *lingua franca*, English (domesticated and otherwise) provided Tutuola and continues to provide other "Nigerian" writers a chance of bridging ethnic divides communicatively and exploring the possibilities and challenges of nationhood, and seeking recognition and relevance in an interconnected and dynamic world (Tabron 2003: 73; Adebanwi 2014a).

Tutuola tried his hand at several other vocations, including selling bread, as a metal-worker and as a photographer (which again features in his books, *The Palm-Wine Drinkard* (Tutuola 1952: 65)[2], for example), as well as serving as a messenger for the Nigerian Department of Labour, which he joined in 1948. From 1956 until retirement, he worked as a storekeeper for the Nigerian Broadcasting Corporation in Ibadan while continuing to write. He married Victoria Alake in 1947 and had eight children with her, four sons and four daughters. In 1967 he published *Ajaiyi and his Inherited Poverty*, with a dedication that read: "In memory of my Mother Mrs. Esther Aina Tutuola who died on 25th November 1964" (Tutuola 1967)[3] (see also Arthur Calder-Marshall, reprinted in Lindfors 1975: 9; *West Africa*, May 1, 1954, reproduced in Lindfors 1975: 35-38; Owomoyela 1997: 865-866).

Tutuola's first published novel, *The Palm-Wine Drinkard* (Tutuola 1952), through the controversy it generated, exposed both the possibilities and limitations of colonial education and the civilisation it represented and sought to enshrine through racialized, evolutionary ideas of humanity, culture and cultivation. In his review of the book in the *Observer* newspaper on 6 July 1952, Dylan Thomas, the famous Welsh poet to whom "Tutuola may owe much of his early notoriety" (Lindfors 1975: 1), talks of "a brief, thronged, grisly, and bewitching story" and nothing was "too prodigious or too trivial to put down in this tall, devilish story" (Dylan Thomas, reprinted in Lindfors 1975:

7-8; Soyinka 1963: 391; Lindfors 1970: 311; Larson 2001: 4).[4] Dylan Thomas's review turned out as the precursor of initially "extremely favourable" reactions in Europe and North America to Tutuola's first two published novels (Lindfors 1975: xiii), where "the first reviewers greeted Tutuola's unusual tale with wide-eyed enthusiasm, hailing the author as a primitive genius endowed with amazing originality and charming naiveté" (Lindfors 1975: 1).

While many non-African readers (English and Americans in the main) were ambivalent but fascinated by Tutuola's young English and "unhinged imagination,"[5] Nigerians who had drunk profoundly from the wells of colonial education were angered by the book. "They had learned that dexterity in handling language was a necessity for a literary career, and they found Tutuola's critical reception befuddling" (Owomoyela 1997: 868). They considered it a spanner in the works of their ambitions for and dedicated pursuit of colonial modernity. To Yemi Ogunbiyi, for example, Tutuola was "the one-time store-keeper-turned writer whose rather limited knowledge of the grammar and rather tedious syntax of the English language became something of an advantage in his attempt to tell his many stories" (Ogunbiyi, quoted in Larson 2001: 20). Lindfors captures this contrast as follows: "To native speakers of English Tutuola's splintered style was an amusing novelty; to educated Nigerians who had spent years honing and polishing their English it was a schoolboy's abomination" (Lindfors 1970: 331). To the colonially educated Nigerians, for Tutuola's European readers to display such open fascination with his exotic subject matter and his atrocious English grammar was nothing short of suspect (Lindfors 1975: xiii).

Writing under the African sounding pseudonym of "Akanji" Ulli Beier, a German refugee who had trained in linguistics in London and worked at University College, Ibadan (Currey 2008: 41), was one of those critical of the decision by Faber and Faber to allow even spelling mistakes to go uncorrected. Akanji remarked disapprovingly:

> Tutuola's language will lose none of its poetry, his style will not lose character if he is told that "gourd" is not "guord." It is mere sensationalism on the part of the publisher not to correct a mistake like the following: "I thank you all for the worm affection you have on me."

The publishers are in this case no longer interested to preserve Tutuola's originality, they are inviting the readers to have a good laugh at his expense. I wonder whether the publishers realise how much harm they do to Tutuola's reputation in West Africa through this kind of thing? There has been a great deal of opposition to Tutuola on the part of young West Africans. They suspect that his success in Europe is not based on literary merits but on his curiosity value. They feel that Europeans merely laugh at the "funny" language and the "semi-literate" style of Tutuola. The publisher's attitude confirms their suspicions in the eyes of the younger generation and helps to blind them to Tutuola's genuine literary merits (Akanji, reprinted in Lindfors 1975[1958]: 84-85).

The merit of this criticism must not be dismissed in a hurry, especially when seen in light of other well known experiences of how Europeans have in the past imported and paraded Africans as freak shows. Examples of such displays of Africans for the entertainment of and ridicule by European audiences include Sara Baartman "the Hottentot Venus," who was paraded as a freak show or as a caged tigress (Crais and Pamela 2009), and El Negro – whose body was stolen by two French taxidermists from a grave beyond the Cape Colony frontier in 1830-31 (Parsons 2002). So Africans critical of the uncritical endorsement of Tutuola in Europe were not without worrying precedence to draw on.

Further support to the complaining West Africans came from other colonial or former colonial subjects in Britain. One of them was Trinidadian Indian writer, V. S. Naipaul, who, in a brief review in April 1958 in the *New Statesman* of Tutuola's fourth novel *The Brave African Huntress*, criticised Tutuola's persistent schoolboy imperfections thus:

> Tutuola's English is that of the West African schoolboy, an imperfectly acquired second language. In what other age could bad grammar have been a literary asset? And how has it preserved its wonderful badness? These queries are unavoidable when one reads The Brave African Huntress. It is Tutuola's fourth, the most straightforward and the thinnest. …. Were it not for the difficult

language, the book could be given to children (V. S. Naipaul, reprinted in Lindfors 1975[1958]: 87).

V. S. Naipaul's critical opinion of the persistence of Tutuola's schoolboy English demonstrates a frustration with Tutuola's subsequent books, after the sensational enthusiasm that greeted his first two publications in Europe and North America. As an unattributed review published in *The Times Literary Supplement* in May 1962 remarked, those initially dazzled and intoxicated by the combination of "the strangeness of the African subject matter, the primary colours, the mixture of sophistication, superstition, and primitivism and above all the incantatory juggling with the English language" of his first two novels were disappointed in Tutuola's subsequent writings, which came across as flat and repetitive[6]. Quoting Gerald Moore, Paul Neumarkt describes the later Tutuola as a writer whose magic had leaked away, and who could no longer use "the lures of the bush" to which he so easily "succumbed" to dazzle his European readers and embarrass his fellow Africans who were desperately seeking escape from the fear and terror of the very same African bush which Tutuola celebrated (Neumarkt 1975[1971]: 188-189]. This fluctuation between attraction and repulsion experienced by Tutuola and his writing is in consonance with Lindfors' observation that Tutuola's "reputation as a writer suffered a sharp decline in the late fifties and early sixties but rose again in the middle and late sixties" (Lindfors 1975: 71). It speaks as well of the discomfort and unease of being anything less than perfect under a colonising civilisation that demands nothing short of completeness on the part of those it co-opts into its ideology and rhetoric of individual autonomy and personal success.

As a winner takes all project, colonialism and colonial education encouraged the adoption of the *colonial language* in its purest authentication – English, in the case of Yorubaland and the rest of colonial Nigeria – which was generally perceived to be superior to the languages (often referred to condescendingly as vernaculars and dialects) of the colonised. As we gather from anthropologist and writer Okot p'Bitek's epic poem *Song of Lawino* (p'Bitek 1989[1966]), which I bring into conversation with Tutuola's works here and there in this book (given that the colonially illiterate narrator Lawino has much in common with the barely colonially literate Tutuola and is treated in the same condescending manner by the "fully" or marginally better educated African in colonial terms), the tendency was for schools to punish grammatically incorrect English such as Tutuola's. As Pido attests, it was a punishable offense in the 1950s when Okot p'Bitek was in school to speak the Acholi language in the school compound (Pido 1997: 674). This was meant to discourage teaching and learning in indigenous African languages, and to stunt the sort of creative use of language which passes for award-winning genius.[7] Notwithstanding, in certain cases, some overly enthusiastic converts adopted the colonial language in their families to the exclusion and detriment of their own mother tongues.

Such trends persist. Adaobi Tricia Nwauban, a 21st century Nigerian novelist, admitted in a BBC interview as recently as November 2016 how she grew up in a context where the English language was privileged to the detriment of her mother tongue, the Igbo language – so eloquently celebrated by Chinua Achebe in his sumptuous menus of proverbs –, which was banned at home and treated as a punishable offence if spoken at school. Nwauban puts it thus:

> My parents forbade my local language, Igbo, from being spoken in our home when I was a child.
> Unlike the majority of their contemporaries in our hometown of Umuahi in south-east Nigeria, my parents chose to speak only English to their children.
> They also conversed between themselves in English, even though they had each grown up speaking Igbo with their own parents and siblings.
> On the rare occasion my father and mother spoke Igbo with each other, it was a clear sign that they were conducting a conversation in which the children were not expected to participate.
> Guests in our home adjusted to the fact that we were an English-speaking household and conformed, with varying degrees of success.
> Our live-in domestic staff were equally compelled to speak English.

Many arrived from their villages unable to utter a single word of the foreign tongue, but as the weeks rolled by, they began to string complete sentences together with less contortion of their faces.

Over the years, I endured people teasing my parents, usually behind their backs, for this decision. 'They are trying to be like white people,' they said (Adaobi Tricia Nwauban, interviewed by the BBC).[8]

Rigid expectations of linguistic purity and regimes and rituals of language purification are rife even in present day Nigeria, where one would expect a measure of confidence and pride in legitimate recognition of and representation for popular creative appropriation and domestication of the English language, as analysed by Farooq A. Kperogi[9]. These attitudes surrounding English as a colonial language, Tutuola and the universe he depicts are discussed at length throughout this book, as are the epistemological implications for studying and representing Africa and Africans.

Until action accompanies the desperate cry of the *vast majority of African people* who continue to be sidestepped by a colonial and colonising education that pretends to be complete, and unlike the Skull in Tutuola's *The Palm-Wine Drinkard*, is portrayed as needing no enhancements by means of creative borrowings. *Endogenous epistemologies* such as depicted by Tutuola, despite their popularity with ordinary Africans *and with elite Africans especially in settings away from the scrutinising prescriptive gaze of their colonising and colonised counterparts*, are mainly dormant or invisible in scholarly circles. They are often ignored, caricatured or misrepresented through colonial and colonising epistemologies that are actively and uncritically internalised and reproduced by a Eurocentric modern African intellectual elite. Africans immersed in popular traditions of sense- and meaning-making find themselves denied by such colonising epistemologies and their African facilitators the right to think and represent their realities in accordance with the dynamic civilisations and universes of their everyday existence stripped of pretence. Often, the ways of life cherished by ordinary Africans are labelled and dismissed too eagerly in broad daylight (even if not consistently under the cover of darkness as well) as traditional knowledge by some of the very African intellectual elite they tend to look up to for development as a process of bringing change and continuity into creative conversations.

The book makes a case for space to be created for sidestepped traditions of knowledge such as those depicted in Tutuola's books and shared as anthropological and sociological realities across a culturally dynamic Africa. It draws attention to Africa's possibilities, prospects and emergent capacities for being and becoming in tune with its creativity and imagination. It speaks to the nimble-footed flexible-minded frontier African at the crossroads and junctions of myriad encounters, facilitating creative conversations and challenging regressive logics of exclusionary claims and articulation of identities and achievements. This book makes the case, to quote a Tutuola reviewer, Desmond MacNamara, for "a tolerant coexistence between fearful monsters and oil refineries" in modern day Africa (Desmond MacNamara, reprinted in Lindfors 1975[1967]: 97). It argues that an African literature shy of and embarrassed by its mythical and folkloric past, even if this past were indeed barbaric and primitive, impoverishes itself through such an uncritical and elitist embrace of the one-dimensionalism of colonial education and its palatability regimes. African literature has much catching up to do with African filmmakers and musicians in this regard. Makers of African movies have already navigated this path, and the popularity of their films suggests that indeed there is no longer shame in telling the stories of their past and present, no matter how "backward" these may seem (Barlet 2000[1996]; Gugler 2003; Okwori 2003; Tcheuyap 2005, 2011; Şaul, and Austen 2010; Krings and Okome 2013; Meyer 2015). Many African musicians have for years been comfortable going to their home villages to shoot videos in houses that would shame the majority of their Eurocentric elite. If anything, Tutuola confidently teaches by example, that Nigerians and Africans by extension "must not be ashamed of their old way of life, if they are to produce a literature worthy of their own aspirations" (Harold R. Collins, reprinted in Lindfors 1975a[1961]: 66-68). This book uses Tutuola's stories to question dualistic assumptions about reality and scholarship all too present in the absolutistic colonising epistemologies of European origins and ancestry, and to call for conviviality, interconnections and interdependence between competing knowledge traditions in Africa and globally.

The need for this book on Amos Tutuola has become more urgent with recent and surging student protests across universities in Africa seeking decolonisation and transformation of higher education. In South Africa, for example, intensifying student protests for the transformation of an alienating, often racialized, higher education system currently across universities – symbolised by the "Rhodes Must Fall" movement initiated by students of the University of Cape Town, as well as the "Fees Must Fall" and related movements – is an indication that even so-called privileged African students in first-rate African universities feel just as unfulfilled and alienated by an overly Eurocentric index of knowledge and knowledge production in Africa and globally. There is an almost total discontinuity between the idea of knowledge in African universities and what constitutes knowledge outside the universities and in African art and literature. The student-driven ferment seeks recognition and integration in teaching and research on popular and endogenous forms of knowledge and ways of knowing informed by African experiences and predicaments (Gibson 2016; Nyamnjoh 2016), and especially by the continent's frontier realities. As a frontier author of frontier stories with little interest in zero-sum games of dominance and conquest, Tutuola is best placed to point us in the direction of more truly inclusive, solidly Africanised systems of higher education on the continent.

Once despised, exoticised, primitivised and ridiculed as a relic of a dying and forgotten past of a dark continent awakening and harkening to the call of the floodlights of a colonising European civilisation, Tutuola is increasingly influencing younger generations of storytellers and filmmakers, especially following his death in 1997. His brushstrokes are gaining in popularity. New editions of his works are surfacing, and if the talks I have given at universities and research institutions across the continent on Amos Tutuola are anything to go by, scholars of different disciplinary backgrounds, students and intellectuals of other walks of life who hear of him are keen to locate and read his books. As Wole Soyinka has suggested in an introduction to the latest edition of Tutuola's first published novel,

The Palm-Wine Drinkard, Tutuola appears to be enjoying a "quiet but steady revival" both "within his immediate cultural environment, and across America and Europe" (Soyinka 2014: viii). In the pages that follow, I explore what might account for such growing interest in someone who was for a long time summarily dismissed by elite African intellectuals as an embarrassment and an expensive distraction.

A closer look at the universe depicted by Tutuola suggests it has far more to offer Africa and the rest of the world than was initially provided for by the one-dimensional logic of conquest and completeness championed by European imperialism and colonialism. Tutuola's universe is one in which economies of intimacy go hand in hand with a market economy, and where pleasure and work are expected to be carefully balanced, just as balance is expected between affluence and poverty, nature, culture and supernature. Tutuola draws on popular philosophies of life, personhood and agency in Africa, where the principle of inclusive humanity is celebrated as a matter of course, and the supremacy of reason and logic are not to be taken at face value. Collective success is emphasised, and individuals may not begin to consider themselves to have succeeded unless they can demonstrate the extent to which they have actively included intimate and even distant others: family members and friends, fellow villagers and even fellow nationals and perfect strangers, depending on one's stature and networks – in the success in question (Nyamnjoh 2015b, 2015c, 2016). This book argues that despite his unconventional English domesticated by his Yoruba syntax, modest and less than intellectual education in elite African terms, Tutuola has contributed significantly to the resilience of ways of life and worldviews that could easily have disappeared under the weight of extractive colonialism, globalisation and the market economy. His are stories of an accommodating resilience against a tendency towards metanarratives of superiority and conquest championed by the aggressive zero-sum games of the powerful. Tutuola's stories emphasise conviviality and interdependence, including between market and gift economies.

For an African who saw himself as written out of active agency by the colonial education and civilisation he was being co-opted into body, mind and soul (Nyamnjoh 2012c), Tutuola saw his writing as therapeutic personally. Responding to a question on the extent to which Tutuola's writings were biographical, one of his son's, Yinka Tutuola, speaking after his father's death, had this to say:

> There is basically no autobiography in his works for they are mainly based on Yoruba folktales. Except to say that like the heroes in his works, he passed through many ordeals in life. His education and literary ordeals are well known, but there were personal ones like ulcer, which strongly deprived him of enjoying many kinds of food and drinks throughout his adult life. It was when he went for an award in Italy that his publishers took him to the hospital there and he was greatly relieved. Generally, he did not write himself into his books (Yinka Tutuola, interviewed by Jeff VanderMeer).[10]

Tutuola's writing also serves as an *archive for endangered ways of life and of the possible* as a result of colonialism and its zero-sum games of exclusive and exclusionary victories. Driven by his determination to keep the past alive and protect Yoruba culture, to resist being forced to choose between the ways of others and the ways of his own people, Tutuola did not allow his lack of higher formal education – his incompleteness – to stand in the way of his mission to preserve an African way of being human. His desire to write was informed and justified by a deep unease with the blazing lights of colonial civilisation – lights as dazzling and blinding as the flood of light from one of his characters in *My Life in the Bush of Ghosts* (Tutuola 1954), the Flash-Eyed Mother. Aware of the corrosive and infectious nature of colonial education, Tutuola felt he might have become a worse writer or not written at all had he embraced colonial education uncritically, or had he the opportunity to be duped completely and blunted by its pretensions. His imperfection in this connection was a blessing. Because he had no pretensions to sophistication in the mother of all civilisations which colonial education was supposed to bring about, Tutuola was able to write his books in a way that today offers Africans a rare window of opportunity to see how current asphyxiating and impoverishing epistemologies championed by reductionist Cartesian rationalism raised to an ideology could be enriched by complementary traditions of knowledge production initially disqualified and inferiorised under colonialism and its metanarratives of conquest.

As Robert Armstrong observes in his review essay on *The Palm-Wine Drinkard*, "to the Yoruba the bush has traditionally been a place of mystery and often of fear," and much fiction from the region represents the awe with which Yoruba people regard the bush (Armstrong 1975[1970]: 217). At the heart of many of Tutuola's stories are bushes, both tamed and wild, into which humans venture for sustenance and sometimes get lost and are subjected to gruelling encounters with strangers, and often larger or smaller than life creatures. Hunting and hunters are significant in this relationship between the town and the bush, and are often instrumental in the sort of conversations that develop between the two. *There are always new bushes to be imagined, invented and found* by Tutuola's quest-heroes. It is imagination gone wild that produces new bushes open to exploration by the questers of his universe. His bushes are not as confined to a spatial reality, as they are zones of possibilities and activation. This is another key theme in the book, buttressed by a discussion of similarities drawn from Cameroon, where it is common for villagers and youth to consider urban and transnational migration as a hunting expedition. This discussion offers an opportunity to ponder interconnections and interdependencies in a sweet- and nimble-footed world of flexible mobilities and encounters of various types and intentionalities. Such mobilities and encounters provide added meaning to an African saying that until the lions [prey] produce their own historian, the story of the hunt will glorify only the hunter. No one has the monopoly of defining what constitutes a hunting ground and of who may or may not hunt. As amply illustrated in Tutuola's bush of ghosts, the story of the hunt is open to the hunter and the hunted, and hunting is not confined to professional hunters. Tutuola suggests ways for vulnerable Africans to challenge victimhood. In his stories very ordinary Africans are quite simply extraordinary in their capacity to challenge victimisation and the brutal and brutish games of power and conquest. His stories challenge the illusion of the autonomous, omnipotent, omniscient and omnipresent individual, by inviting the reader to embrace and celebrate incompleteness as the normal order of being and of things. They suggest an epistemology of conviviality in which interdependence is privileged and delusions of grandeur and completeness discouraged. Rich and poor are co-implicated and mutually entangled in Tutuola's universe of the elusiveness of completeness.

The book explores and builds on the idea of *incompleteness* inspired by Tutuola and his writings (Nyamnjoh 2015b, 2015d). It delves into how the flexibility and fluidity of reality depicted in Tutuola's universe challenge a social science founded narrowly on dichotomies, dualisms and bounded identities (Mudimbe-Boyi 2002) in favour of flexible and nimble-footed identities as fluid osmotic envelopes for consciousness (Salpeteur and Warnier 2013; Warnier 1993a, 1993b; 2006, 2007, 2009, 2013c; Amadiume 1987, 1997; Sanders 2008). It examines the extent to which Tutuola's writings provide popular ontological insights that could contribute significantly to the reconstruction and recalibration of a decolonised social science in Africa. This book argues that the universe depicted by Tutuola in his novels is one of infinite possibilities where nothing is ever complete, and where to seek or claim completeness is to ignore, to one's peril, the reality of imperfection or impurity as the normal order of things and being. Humans, ghosts, spirits, monsters, freak creatures, death and the dead, and gods are far from seeking completeness as a permanent state of being – an ultimate and extravagant illusion in a context where categories acquire meaning only through action and interaction. To achieve greater efficacy in actions and interactions, Tutuola's creatures seek creative ways and technological enhancements to activate themselves to commensurate levels of potency. This is achieved through relationships of interdependence with incomplete others, as well as through technologies of self-extension, juju (spells and charms) and magic, which can be acquired and lost with circumstances. Tutuola himself epitomises the universe he depicts, not only through his own cunning and trickery, prankishness and elusive quest for completeness in a world of zero-sum games of civilisations founded on exclusionary violence, but also by pointing a critical finger at the modern African intellectual elite who have unquestioningly yielded to a narrow Eurocentric index of civilisation and humanity (Tobias 1999).

Of especial relevance to this objective are *The Palm-Wine Drinkard* and *My Life in the Bush of Ghosts*, Tutuola's first two published novels. In an article published in 1963, just over ten years following its publication, Wole Soyinka describes *The Palm-Wine Drinkard* as Tutuola's best and least impeachable novel. "This book," apart from the work of Chief Daniel Olorunfemi Fagunwa "who writes in Yoruba, is the earliest instance of the new Nigerian writer gathering multifarious experiences under, if you like, the two cultures [Yoruba and English] and exploiting them in one extravagant, confident whole" (Soyinka 1963: 390, parenthesis inserted by me). According to Arthur Calder-Marshall, who reviewed *The Palm-Wine Drinkard* in *The Listener* in November 1952, Tutuola credits "a very old man" on his father's farm for inspiring him with the initial story of the palm-wine drinkard, after feeding him with palm-wine to a point where "it was intoxicating me as if I was dreaming." Of this revelation by Tutuola, Calder-Marshall remarks: "How much was due to the very old man, how much to the influence of palm-wine and how much to the poetic imagination of Amos Tutuola, it is impossible to say" (Arthur Calder-Marshall, reprinted in Lindfors 1975: 9; see also Eric Larrabee, reprinted in Lindfors 1975: 13). Following Tutuola's death, Yinka Tutuola, one of his sons, reiterated this in an interview, and provided additional sources of inspiration to his late father.[11]

This book thus explores *what Tutuola offers ongoing epistemological debates on the study of Africa more broadly*, especially in social science disciplines and the humanities. It highlights and discusses elements from Tutuola's novels that emphasise the logic of inclusion over the logic of exclusion and the violence of conquest often uncritically internalised and reproduced by practicing social scientists and humanities scholars in Africa fixated with text without context, micro categorisations, abstractions, appearances and metanarratives of permanence and superiority. The book argues that Tutuola's novels offer *comprehensive depictions of endogenous universes* in Africa wherein *reality is more than meets the eye* and the world an experience of life beyond sensory perceptions. These are universes where existence or being and becoming materialises through the consciousness that gives it meaning. Tutuola's contribution to understanding epistemologies endogenous to Africa is in his elusive quest to be a "complete gentleman" of letters and of the world – through publication of his stories inspired by his native Yoruba universe in its dynamism and mobility – and to be recognised by and relevant to Yoruba, Nigerian and African readers as well as to the rest of the world (Lindfors 1970, 1999a; Larson 2001: 1-25) of diasporic Africans and beyond.

As evident from the frontier existence of the "born and die"[12] babies common throughout Tutuola's writings (see for example, Tutuola 1954: 40-45; Tutuola 1981: 65), and from the often double or multiple consciousness of his beings who assume various natures and forms contingent on the challenges or exigencies at hand, consciousness is something bigger than the physical body a human being or creature of the wild (creepy crawlies included) assumes, and is in continuous interconnection and conversation with the consciousness of relatives and related others – visible and invisible – such as ancestors or the community one may have left behind, such as happens often with the "born and die" babies and with many a Tutuola narrator preoccupied with and tested by questions of origins, nature and destiny of humanity from the vantage point of Yoruba culture, belief systems and agency (Fadipe 1970: 261-329; Soyinka 1976; Verger 1989; Peel 1968, 2002; Clarke 2004; Adebanwi 2014a; Guyer 2015a, 2015b). The complex truth and reality of the Yoruba world, requires, among others, sociologists, anthropologists and historians in intimate conversations with cultural producers who, like Wole Soyinka in *Aké*, (1981) and *Ìsarà* (1990), demonstrate a creativity with history, chronology, story, structure and language that are exemplary of how African writers have gone about making intimate strangers of and negotiating the tensions and attractions between fact and fiction, literature and ethnography, tradition and modernity, competing traditions of religiosity, change and continuity (Peel 2002).

A key contribution of Tutuola's is in how he *brings essence and consciousness into conversation* that evidences their complementarity. Consciousness opens a window to the world in its tangible and intangible, visible and invisible multiplicities, by means of which it constantly enriches itself. Tutuola introduces us to the complexity of consciousness not only through the transcendental capacity for presence in simultaneous multiplicities, but also through the reality of intricate interconnections and interdependencies. While the former attribute is abundantly obvious in every one of his works, the latter is especially extensively developed in *The Witch-Herbalist of the Remote Town*, through the idea of the interconnections and interdependencies between the "First Mind," the "Second Mind," the "Memory" and the "Supreme Second" of the brave hunter of the Rocky Town (Tutuola 1981: 270-279). I discuss and illustrate this point later in the book.

In Tutuola's universe, consciousness works in intricate and often circular ways, compressing time and space in manners that defy the logic of the senses and its fixation with linearity, chronology and unity of form – body, mind and soul. Tutuola's universe (especially through the "born and die" babies and their experiences) suggests that consciousness is there in an out-of-body sort of way before humans enter the bodies with which they are apparently saddled for most of their lives as human beings on earth, and consciousness remains after humans leave these bodies, as exemplified, yet again, by the death of "born and die" babies – an issue equally discussed further in the course of the book. To anthropologists, Tutuola brings home in compelling ways Todd Sanders epistemological challenge to think beyond bodies when seeking to understand rainmaking and sense making in Tanzania – a reality too easily corrupted by a Eurocentric modernity and its obsession with evolutionary thinking and binary oppositions (Sanders 2003, 2008). Tutuola also provides for fascinating conversations with contemporary efforts to create humanoid robots as virtual receptacles of uploaded consciousness of [deceased] humans.

Indeed, thinking beyond bodies – as Nigerian anthropologist and gender scholar Ifi Amadiume has richly demonstrated in her pacesetter study of gender in Africa and African feminism – unlocks and situates the often misunderstood intricacies and apparent contradictions in African worldviews, beliefs, social systems and privileged relationships of interconnection and interdependence (Amadiume 1987, 1997). Amadiume reiterates not only the social construction of identities, but more importantly, disrupts the dualism that insists on a priori distinctions between male and female as bounded and discrete biological entities, which is implicit even in the most radical Eurocentric articulations of gender and power. Far from all being subordinates to men, as is often erroneously claimed in studies informed by Western-inspired orthodoxies, women in precolonial Africa, Amadiume argues, were structurally allowed to play roles usually monopolised by men, even if that meant becoming classified as "men" in the process. Sex and gender did not necessarily coincide, as the dualistic thinking in dominant Western orthodoxies suggests, where roles tend to be rigidly, narrowly and blindly masculinised or feminised in abstraction. This made precolonial Africa a place where "masculinity" was possible without men – "female masculinity" – as women assumed positions or characteristics usually regarded as the preserve of men. Amadiume challenges gender scholars to do more than embrace the multiple and ambiguous dimensions of masculinities and femininities, by contesting a narrow idea of reality characterised by dualisms and the primacy of the mind, the purportedly autonomous individual and a world of sensory perceptions. Amadiume's understanding of gender is ultimately an invitation to challenge thinking by dichotomies and to problematize a tendency to be wedded to appearances and the implicit or explicit unilinear rationality of the mind even among those who provide for other forms of rationality (Amadiume 1987, 1997). Some prominent gender scholars, evidenced for example by Oyeronke Oyewumi's *African Gender Studies* reader (Oyewumi 2005), have built on this thinking, and it would be a missed opportunity not to identify and engage this body of literature in a study of masculinities and femininities, especially in a context yearning for an infusion of epistemologies and perspectives silenced, misrepresented or caricatured by the overwhelming dominance of resilient colonial and colonising epistemologies.

Tutuola is a fascinating precursor to these debates on *flexible and fluid categories,* social and biological bodies, and of how usefully to bring essence and consciousness into fruitful and innovative conversations. He may not have been to the university, but many in universities today would need to pass through him for intellectual re-imagination. If in Tutuola's universe biological bodies are mindful vehicles or containers or envelops (Scheper-Hughes and Lock 1987; Shilling 2012[1993]; Warnier 1993a, 1993b, 2006, 2007, 2009, 2013c; Salpeteur and Warnier 2013), and men and women are always subjects in context of the relationships and material possibilities that shape and are shaped by them, then consciousness becomes more important than the particular containers that house them and power as the capacity to activate one's potency for efficacious action is not as predictable and permanent as often imagined. This is all the more significant, as Jean-Pierre Warnier argues with reference to the container kings of the Cameroon Grassfields, in contexts where, due to various afflictions, containers as "vital piggy banks" are known to suffer various "leakages" (Warnier 1993a, 1993b, 2013c). Herein lies the danger of instinctively conflating a particular container with a particular consciousness, however practiced we have become in seeing and having containers and contents conterminous in their presence. Within this framework and understanding of reality – *a framework that is very popular across Africa* – "in-betweenness" or "incompleteness" of masculinities and femininities anywhere, far from being an inadequacy in the Levi-Straussian logic of binary opposition between anthropophagic (inclusive) and anthropoemic (exclusive) societies, is a reflection of the normal order of what it means to be male or female as an open-ended frontier reality (Kopytoff 1987). Instead of seeing "frontier masculinities or femininities" as the absence of fulfilment in belonging, I suggest that it be seen as the normal state of things in a context where every masculinity or femininity (housed by men or women as biological categories), is necessarily "incomplete" or "frontier," constantly needing to be activated into degrees of potency for efficacious action through relationships with others (equally incomplete).

In Tutuola's universe, consciousness is responsible for choosing the body a human is born into. As the example of the brave hunter in *The Witch-Herbalist of the Remote Town*, an adult who as a "born and die" baby was prevented from returning to the bush of ghosts by his earthly father's powerful juju, shows, a ghost trapped in the body of an earthly, must resume the body of a "born and die" baby to re-enter the ghostly community of "born and die" babies, even if only in transit. The brave hunter does this, in order to assume the consciousness of the "born and die" to be able to tap into the network of consciousness to which he belongs as a source of knowledge about how to overcome obstacles on his way to the "Witch-Herbalist who was also called the Omnipotent, Omnipresent and Omniscient Mother" (Tutuola 1981: 190).

In a review of Tutuola's *Ajaiyi and His Inherited Poverty* in 1968, Ola Balogun highlights Tutuola's capacity to draw his readers "into a magical world in which events occur exactly as the subconscious mind would represent them in a dream," adding that the universe of Tutuola's creative imagination is "a world where real and imaginary meet on equal terms" (Ola Balogun, reprinted in Lindfors 1975: 101). Dreams are an important medium through which all the different "consciousnesses" can converse, and nothing, it seems, is ever a coincidence to be explained purely in terms of sensory perception or rationalised away. Free floating consciousness see in dreams able vehicles for downloading themselves into human bodies and flowing through them in rhizomic delta fashion. To J. K. Rowling, a world renowned writer who thrives on the world of dreams and the possibilities it opens up to her as an author, "When you dream, you can do what you like" (J. K. Rowling, quoted in Shapiro 2004: 6). Examples of creative and imaginative dreaming by the science fiction film industry alone, include movies and TV series such as Star Wars, Star Trek, Battlestar Galactica, Caprica, The Matrix, Alien, The Martian, Avatar, E. T. The Extra-Terrestrial, Back to the Future, Invasion of the Body Snatchers, The Wizard of Oz, Pinocchio and District 9. Interconnections, interdependencies and entanglements, even when not evident to our senses and the logic of the mind, are the language of conviviality cherished by the multiple consciousnesses that people the world with their infinity of possibilities.

Tutuola's universe invites his readers not to seek to confine the richness and possibilities of consciousness through single factor approaches to fathoming reality. He provides us with a *basket of possibilities for exploring and entertaining conversations with consciousness*, and without seeking to prioritise, a priori, some to the detriment of others. These approaches include, inter alia, perception, experience, memory, sensation, impression, evidence, reason, reflection, intention, intuition, introspection, imagination, doubt, faith, humility, mind, body, self, language, symbolism, values, myth, belief and speculation. As repeatedly demonstrated in Tutuola's universe, *consciousness matters more than the containers* that house it. Consciousness can inhabit any container – human and non-human, animate and inanimate, visible and invisible – regardless of the state of completeness or incompleteness of the container in question, and irrespective of the capacity of a juju, a spell or charm to influence and control the physical nature, form, action and activities of the container in accordance with the bidding of an external agent. These universes celebrate what it means to be a *frontier being*, at the crossroads and junctions of multiple influences and possibilities, mixing and blending to forge a vision where certainties are never too rigid and the prospect of innovation a constant source of hope. The disposition of these universes to the reality of crossroads as points of confusion, contradiction, competition and transit, and as meeting points and neutral grounds highlight their potential to welcome, accommodate and enable activation for myriad forms of potency for the efficacy of those – humans and non-humans – who inhabit them, however temporarily. If confusion is a nimble-footed recurrent danger to established sociality in Amos Tutuola's universe, as Jane Guyer points out, "amenable to momentary containment and expulsion, and recognisable when it returns … as it certainly will" in the person of the Slanderer (Guyer 2015a: 71), then the crossroads, with its infinite capacity to entertain and accommodate contradictions and incommensurability, and to provide for those frustrated by or frustrating to various heartlands of birth, citizenship, certainty and certitude, are the best location for bringing myriad confusions into creative and innovative conversations bearing on frontier cosmopolitanism, inclusive belonging and conviviality (Nyamnjoh 2006a, 2012b).

In its quest for retainers, interpreters and advocates, *consciousness and its repertoire of memory* are extendable, projectable, downloadable, transportable and outsourceable through embodiment, sensation, action and interaction as material and social realities (Piaget 1972; Senghor 1977; Stoller 1989, 1997). Seen in terms of Pierre Bourdieu's self-awareness through habitual practice and creative improvisation – *habitus*, consciousness is at the origin and also at the end of the rules and regulations which humans and other creatures of habit, as part of a field or fields, internalise, embody and reproduce almost effortlessly (even if creatively and with improvisation), as if these were second nature, or as nature as a continuum into culture. Consciousness as *habitus* is produced and reproduced through the embodiment and enactment of social action, not simply as a system of rules, but determined as well by the resources, practical dispositions and strategies available to the social agents involved in its daily translation, interpretation and articulation (Bourdieu 1991, 1996).

Furthermore, the book argues that Tutuola's novels are not just works of fiction. They are *founded on the lived realities of Yoruba society* – realities shared with many other communities across the continent – and depict endogenous epistemologies that are very popular in Africa. The stories he recounts are commonplace across the continent. However, despite their popularity with ordinary Africans and with elite Africans when not keeping up appearances with the rationalist expectations of their Western and Westernised counterparts, such epistemologies are largely silent and invisible in scholarly circles because they are often ignored, caricatured or misrepresented in derogatory and ideologically loaded categories of "magic," "witchcraft," "sorcery," "superstition," "primitivism," "savagery" and "animism" inspired by the origins and dominance of homogenising Eurocentric modernity and its traditions of meaning making (Sanders 2003, 2008; Jeater 2007). Like the narrators in his books, Tutuola is unapologetically and actively part and parcel of the universe that fascinates him.

Like the storytellers of First Nations peoples of northern Canada who, according to anthropologist Julie Cruikshank use "optimistic stories about the past" to "draw on internal resources to survive and make sense of arbitrary forces that might otherwise seem overwhelming," subvert administrative ambitions and official orthodoxies, "challenge imperial conceptions of time and space," "make meaningful connections and provide order and continuity in a rapidly changing world" through interweaving information, moral content and philosophical guidance (Cruikshank 1998: xii-xvii), Tutuola invites his readers to challenge superiority syndromes and zero-sum games of potency and dominance. His stories are contributions to his mission of keeping alive and relevant African ways of knowing and knowledge production, and fending off the one-dimensionalism of resilient colonialism and the ambitions of purity and completeness which it claims and inspires.

This study compares Tutuola's Yoruba universe and cosmology to Chinua Achebe's Igbo dancing masquerade, the truth of which is dynamic, constantly on the move and in need of nimble-footedness to appraise and keep track of. Its complexities, ambiguities and ambivalences call for nuanced and multiple angles of appreciation. Hence, the idea of approaching Tutuola's work from different perspectives in the different chapters is meant to break open the richness of his work and to illustrate the layered complexity of the universe of his creative imagination of which he is an active participant. This strategy, however, also has a downside. It results inevitably in some measure of repetition, like retelling the basic storyline of various episodes from different Tutuola books several times, the arguments regarding decolonisation, Cartesian rationalism, and incompleteness. It is hoped that such repetition is worthwhile, instructive and very much in tune with repetition as the mother of all learning.

Notes

[1] In Yoruba language, the term for crossroads would be "*orita,*" which means "where three ways meet." For example, named "Orita," the Ibadan Journal of Religious Studies, indicates that "every effort will be made to give equal coverage to African traditional religion, Christianity and Islam," the three ways at the crossroads of religiosity in Africa
(see, https://www.cambridge.org/core/journals/africa/article/orita-ibadan-journal-of-religious-studies/D9246A531D1416C27F78A742253A5E44, accessed 7 March 2017. This book returns again and again to the significance of crossroads in Tutuola's works, and the importance of crossroads dispositions among Africans keen to bring in and domesticate outside influences, in the course of their journeys and encounters with other universes, humans and other beings. I am grateful to Afeosemime "Afe" Adogame, Professor of Christianity and Society at Princeton

Theological Seminary, USA, for drawing my attention to *Orita: Ibadan Journal of Religious Studies*.

[2] When the palm-wine drinkard and his wife come by a big tree in their journey through the bush, Tutuola makes him refer to a photographer thus: "As we were about forty yeards away from it, there we noticed that somebody peeped out and was focusing us as if a photographer was focusing somebody" (Tutuola 1952: 65).

[3] See https://en.wikipedia.org/wiki/Amos_Tutuola, accessed 1 November 2016.

[4] See also www.theguardian.com/books/interactive/2013/oct/05/dylanthomas-wales, accessed 16 May 2015.

[5] This expression is by Charly Ndichia, a carpenter turned journalist, former editor of *The Post* and current editor of *The Rambler*, both newspapers in Cameroon. He used this categorisation of Tutuola's imagination during a discussion we had on 10 January 2017 in Buea.

[6] See "The Mixture as Before," first published in *The Times Literary Supplement*, May 25, 1962, and reprinted in Lindfors 1975: 91.

[7] This is exemplified in the 2015 Man Booker Prize winning book by Marlon James, *A Brief History of Seven Killings*. One reviewer states "The story is told in a cacophony of voices from gangsters to ghosts, drug dealers to CIA agents and in dialects ranging from American English to Jamaican patois." http://www.jamaicaobserver.com/news/Jamaica-s-Marlon-James-wins-Booker-Prize-for-fiction, accessed 31 December 2016. I recall one of the judges making specific mention of the fact that the book captured the use of different variants of English across the Commonwealth

[8] See http://www.bbc.com/news/world-africa-38069481, accessed 30 November 2016.

[9] See "Top 10 Words That Trended in Nigerian English in 2016," by Farooq A. Kperogi, http://www.farooqkperogi.com/2017/01/top-10-words-that-trended-in-nigerian.html, accessed 3 January 2017. See also his "Politics of Grammar Column," http://www.farooqkperogi.com/p/politics-of-grammar-column.html, accessed 3 January 2017.

[10] Yinka Tutuola, interviewed by Jeff VanderMeer, http://weirdfictionreview.com/2013/01/amos-tutuola-an-interview-with-yinka-tutuola-by-jeff-vandermeer/, accessed 1 November 2016.

[11] Yinka Tutuola, interviewed by Jeff VanderMeer, http://weirdfictionreview.com/2013/01/amos-tutuola-an-interview-with-yinka-tutuola-by-jeff-vandermeer, accessed 1 November 2016.

[12] As discussed later, these are babies from the bush of ghosts or world of spirits, who insituate themselves into the wombs of pregnant earthly women, replacing the earthly babies of the pregnancies with themselves, so they can be born as if they were normal children. This is a ploy by the "born and die" babies to dispossess their earthly parents of their material wealth, which they then repatriate to their hometowns in the bush of ghosts, for their personal enjoyment when they die a few years or less after they are born to their earthly mothers.

Chapter Two

Dominant and Dormant Epistemologies of Africa

This chapter reiterates the following: (i) there is a dominant colonial epistemology characterised by dogmatic positivism, dualisms, a posture of universalism, violence and alienation of alternative epistemologies; (ii) it is limited in its ability to help us understand the world and ourselves in it, because of these characteristics and its disposition toward the centrality of "what" versus "why" questions in understanding the world; (iii) we should therefore seek alternatives to this colonial epistemological order by understanding and embracing popular epistemologies of inclusivity, interconnection, and interdependence; (iv) Tutuola's themes of interconnectedness, fluidity and conviviality point us in the right direction; (iv) disrupting colonial epistemologies is difficult but can in part be achieved through cross-disciplinary conversations and joint initiatives between natural and social scientists, and between scholars and academics in university institutions and actors involved with alternative and complementary traditions and practices of knowledge production, circulation and consumption.

Amos Tutuola and the universe he depicts in his writings do not have a place in a colonial order of things. The very idea of a colonial civilising mission was meant to invite and indeed force the colonised to abandon their universe of interconnections, interdependencies, mobilities and flexible and fluid identities. Tutuola and others committed to the popular systems of being and becoming inspired by the universes of the colonised were/are determined to defend them at all costs. Even in the 21st century, Africa remains prey to a dominant colonial and colonising epistemological export, ideologically labelled as "Western" despite its gross insensitivity not only to popular African epistemologies but even to popular epistemologies in Western societies and lack of empirical authentication in the lives of ordinary Westerners. It is a colonising export that reduces science to nineteenth-and-twentieth century preoccupations with theories of *what* the universe is, much to the detriment of theories of *why* the universe is. By rendering science "too technical and mathematical," and by prioritising scientific knowledge over all other forms of knowing this parochial epistemological export or reductionist theory of knowledge has made it difficult for those interested in questions of why to keep pace with developments in scientific theories (Hawking 1990: 171-175). The technicisation of science has also increased the risk of branding as "intellectual imposture" the appropriation and extension of scientific concepts by philosophers and other "non-scientists" (Sokal and Bricmont 1998) interested in redefining and popularising science and the academy.

Such dogmatism or positivism in science or what Austin Hughes has termed "the folly of scientism" promotes the erroneous idea that competence in natural science, however modest, empowers one to pontificate knowingly on almost any and all subjects, and encourages an overbearing tendency to behave as though natural science and scientists were better at answering even philosophical and metaphysical questions than philosophy and philosophers (Hughes 2012). A consequence is that not enough conversation is taking place between scientists and the wider public, and developments in and changing understandings and practices of science – revolutionary or not (Kuhn 1970[1962]) – are not disseminated much beyond the often narrow confines of professional scientists and scientific institutions. Little wonder that some accommodating, less presumptuous and pretentious scientists are likely to find certain categorisations – even if and when done in good faith – of their work by non-scientists in the academy and wider society overly caricatural. Practising natural scientists who do not interact much with practitioners of the social sciences and humanities are likely to be as prone to errors and conceptual confusion about the social and the human, as are social scientists and scholars of the humanities who seek to appropriate natural scientific knowledge and concepts from the safe distance of ignorance or by claiming to share a common ancestry in positivism and Cartesian rationalism with the natural scientists, however farfetched in terms of Karl Popper's criterion of falsifiability as a central determinant of scientificity. Scientism as an uncritical adherence to the universal competence and superiority of science is little different from popular beliefs and popular ideas of reality, which scientists readily dismiss as superstition and as lacking supporting evidence (Hughes 2012).

Austin Hughes (2012) insists that scientism among natural scientists is equitable to superstition and blind faith in its stubborn insistence that science and science alone can answer longstanding questions even in fields such as philosophy, metaphysics, epistemology and ethics (Hughes 2012). When such blind faith in science is handed down to the masses or appropriated by arms of the academy other than the natural sciences, this can become even more recklessly dangerous. An example of such appropriation is Darwin's evolutionism translated into Social Darwinism, to serve ideologies aimed at justifying ambitions of dominance by certain groups in society or by some countries and regions. This is tantamount to superstition and the misappropriation of science at the service of power and the powerful. It is often those least endowed with science and the scientific spirit that are most emphatic and evangelical about science as the ultimate answer to questions, big and small. Such people are most likely to resort to claims without substantiation on what science can and has resolved, and why certain cultures are more amenable to a scientific approach to issues than others. This instrumentalised variant of scientism is science raised to an ideological whip to be used to flog divergent or dissenting itineraries of quest into submission and subservience.

Such scientism and narrow views of science in the hands of promoters and disciples of the colonising and colonial epistemological export have tended to separate the universe into the physical and the metaphysical or the religious, and to ignore the fact that people – non-Western and Western, in the global north and global south alike – are ordinarily "not content to see events as unconnected and inexplicable." Scientism is an elite and elitist epistemological order with little room for popular cravings to understand "the underlying order in the world" (Hawking 1990: 1-13). By taking "little notice of the mystical and the metaphysical dimensions of human existence," this dominant epistemological order has "made such matters appear trivial and unworthy of attention" (Rosenau 1992: 10). And in the rare occasions that scientism has shown interest, the tendency has been to claim, erroneously, that science has already resolved questions that are clearly inherently beyond its ability to answer (Hughes 2012). Although science has significantly moved beyond this limited version of scientism to contemplate "the big bang and black holes," and "a quantum theory of gravity" (Hawking 1990), its narrow and hegemonic "certainties" of the nineteenth and twentieth centuries continue to make waves and to inform the social sciences, attitudes, policies and relations in general, especially between the purportedly civilised West and the emerging rest. The Tutuolas of this world and the realities of complex interconnections and nuance which they represent, continue to be excluded from what is thought and taught and/or researched as viable complements in the quest for legitimate theories of knowledge, even at the risk of such theories passing for highly parochial and Eurocentric (Chinweizu 1987[1975]; Amin 2009[1988]; Mudimbe 1988; Diop 1991; Rosenau 1992; Depelchin 2005, 2011; Obenga 2004; Connell 2007; Connell et al. 2016).

If, in what some have termed the "kingdom of knowledge" (Niiniluoto et al. 2004: vii), epistemology is about what constitutes knowledge (certainty and truth) and the place of perception, experience, memory, sensation, impression, evidence, reason, reflection, intention, intuition, introspection, imagination, doubt, faith, humility, mind, body, self, critical self-awareness, language, symbolism, values, myth, belief, common sense, speculation, action, fact and method in knowledge claims (Ogden and Richards 1923; Freud 1957; Gulley 1962; Levi-Strauss 1966; Piaget 1972; Polanyi and Prosch 1975; Senghor 1977; Ruch and Anyangwu 1984; Shweder and Levine 1984; Ruthven 1990[1984]; Mudimbe 1988; Fine 1993; Stoller 1989, 1997; Allen 1997; Eze 1997; Ramose 1999; Hountondji 1980[1976], 1997, 2002, 2007; Losambe 2005; Okolo 2007; Wolenski 2004; Tschemplik 2008; Masolo 2010; Diagne 2013; Mbembe 2013a), and if reason and the senses are both shaped by nature and nurture, then history, encounters, interconnections, power relations and context (natural, political, economic, social and cultural) matter critically in what constitutes knowledge, how knowledge is produced and legitimated, and who is involved or not in knowledge production, dissemination and consumption (Ruthven 1990[1984]; Shweder and Levine 1984; Tsing 1993; Visweswaran 1994; Behar 1993; Lennon

2004; Abu-Lughod 2008; Harrison 2008; Clifford and Marcus 1986; Gupta and Ferguson 1997; Magubane 2004; Losambe 2005; Dieng 2006; Mamdani 1996, 1998, 2009; Mbembe 2008, 2010; Ntarangwi 2010; Lauer and Anyidoho 2012a, 2012b; Ndlovu-Gatsheni 2013a, 2013b; Willems 2014; Ndi 2015).

As demonstrated throughout this book by my discussion of Amos Tutuola's writings and the universes they depict, the dominant so-called "Western" epistemological export from the imperial and colonising Europe and its North American extensions, in view of its insensitivities to contextual specificities and real life human predicaments, has serious weaknesses, especially when compared with the popular and more traditional epistemologies of ordinary people in Africa and elsewhere. Unlike Tutuola's epistemologies, this elitist import and imposition paraded as Western for hegemonic purposes tends to limit reality to appearances, which it then seeks to justify (without explaining) with meta-narratives claiming objectivity and a more epistemologically secure truth status. Under this kind of epistemological order, reality is presented as anything whose existence has, or can be, established in a rational, objective manner, with universal laws operating only in perceived space and time. In the social sciences, such a perspective has resulted in an insensitive pursuit of a *physique sociale*, informed almost exclusively by what the mind (reason) and/or the hierarchy of senses (sight, taste, touch, sound, smell) tell us about society and social relationships.

The science inspired by such an epistemological order has tended to celebrate dichotomies, dualisms, teleologies and analogies, dismissing anything that does not make sense in Cartesian or behaviourist terms, confining to religion and metaphysics what it cannot explain and disqualifying as non-scientific and indeed primitive more inclusive epistemologies. The world is perceived and presented as dichotomous: there is the real and the unreal. The real is the rational, the natural, the physical and the scientific; the unreal is the irrational, the supernatural, the religious, the metaphysical and the subjective. The logic of this colonising and colonial epistemological order is simple: if truth is one and universal, then there should be a one best way of attaining it[1]; and those who have been there before are the best guides of the rest still in search of truth.

It sounds like Okonkwo's father in Chinua Achebe's *Things Fall Apart*, who insists, to a debtor to whom he owes a small debt compared to what he owes many others, that it is only natural for the sun to shine on those standing before it can shine on those sitting. This evokes the image of a Jacob's ladder to Heaven, where those highest up the rungs are best placed to tell everyone else what paradise is or could be, or even what the rays of the sun truly feel like. We may all be animated by partial theories – like "the six blind men and the elephant," – but some are more likely to claim authority and to silence others about the nature of the universe and the underlying order of things, thanks to the hierarchy of cultivated blindness made explicit in this epistemological order (Lindfors 1999d; Nyamnjoh 2012a).

This dominant colonial epistemological order has engendered theories and practices of social engineering capable of justifying without explanation almost everything, from colonialism to neoliberalism and globalisation, through racism and imperialism. Whole societies, countries and regions have been categorised, depending on how these "others" were perceived in relation to Cartesian rationalism and empiricism as a conquering and governing ideology. The order has resulted in disciplines and fields of studies that have sacrificed interconnections and interdependencies, humanity and the social on the altar of a false objectivity, while at the same time claiming a scholarship of the highest ethical standards. In other words, it has allowed the insensitivities of power and comfort to assume the moral high ground, dictating to the marginalised and the disabled, and preaching salvation for individuals and groups who repent from "retrogressive" attitudes, cultures and practices such as those some have accused Tutuola of peddling to the embarrassment of the "authentic" modern and "certified" writers of Africa.

As an epistemological order that claims the status of a solution, there is little room for introspection or self-scrutiny, since countervailing forces are invariably to blame for failure. The assumption is made here that such messianic qualities have imbued disciples of this colonial epistemological prescription with an attitude of arrogance, superiority and intolerance towards creative difference and the value of appropriation. The zeal in them to convert creative difference has not excluded violence as an option, for the epistemological order from which they draw knows neither compromise nor negotiation, nor conviviality. To paraphrase Lawino in Okot p'Bitek's *Song of Lawino*, the ways of the ancestors of the colonised may be good and solid with roots that reach deep into the soil, their customs neither hollow, nor thin, nor easily breakable or blown away by the winds; but this does not deter the colonial epistemology and its disciplinarians and propagators from inviting the colonised subject to despise these ancestral customs and worldviews, in favour of imported and imposed foreign customs they may not even understand or admire (p'Bitek 1989[1966]: 19). Closely entangled with ideology and hegemony as the colonial epistemological order is, it leaves little room for critical thinking, paradoxically, even as it celebrates Cartesian rationalism and freedom of thought and action. The result, again quite paradoxically, is an emphasis on doing than on thinking, and all attempts at serious questioning are rationalised away or disciplined to the point of obscurity and acute invisibility.

Popular epistemologies in Africa such as depicted by Amos Tutuola in his novels and short stories are different. They create room for why questions, and for "magical interpretations" where there are no obvious explanations to "material realities" (Moore and Sanders 2001). To them, reality is more than meets the eye; it is larger than logic. Far from subscribing to the rigid dichotomies of the dominant epistemological import from a colonising and imperial external agent (be this the West, the Orient or whatever other conquering force), the popular epistemologies of Africa build bridges between the so-called natural and supernatural, physical and metaphysical, rational and irrational, objective and subjective, scientific and superstitious, visible and invisible, real and unreal, explainable and inexplicable; making it impossible for anything to be one without also being the other. They constitute an epistemological order where the sense of sight and physical evidence has not assumed the same centrality, dominance or dictatorship prescribed by the "hierarchies of perceptual faculties" in the streamlined Cartesian export (van Dijk and Pels 1996: 248-251). They thrive on balances, and have space for all the senses, just as they do for the visible and the invisible, the physical and metaphysical. The real is not only what is observable or what makes cognitive sense; it is also the invisible, the emotional, the sentimental or the inexplicable, and not simply the yet to be explained. In these inclusive, expansive, open-ended popular epistemological orders, emphasis is on the whole, and truth is negotiated consensually rather than resulting from artificial disqualification, dismemberment, atomisation or mutilation by a science of exclusionary superiority syndromes. There is room in them even for popularised variants of colonial epistemologies and pretensions.

In this popular system of knowledge which Tutuola champions, the alternative or complement of presence is not necessarily absence, but invisibility, inaudibility, insensitivity and odourlessness. Thus, as Mbembe (1997) argues with regard to visibility and its lack, understanding the visible is hardly complete without investigating the invisible. We misunderstand the world if we "consider the obverse and the reverse of the world as two opposite sides, with the former partaking of a 'being there' (*real presence*) and the latter as 'being elsewhere' or a 'non-being' (*irremediable absence*) or, worse, of the order of unreality" (Mbembe 1997: 152). The obverse and its reverse are also linked by similarities which do not make them mere copies of each other, but which unite and at the same time distinguish themselves according to the "principle of *simultaneous multiplicities*" (Mbembe 1997: 152). In others words, far from merely being the other side, or the mask or the substitute, of the visible, the invisible is in the visible, and vice versa, "not as a matter of artifice, but as *one and the same* and as external reality simultaneously – or as the image of the thing and the imagined thing at the same time" (Mbembe 1997: 152). A question here is, what role could less restrictive popular epistemologies play in the recalibration of higher education in Africa, if the continent's intellectual elite were to take seriously the call to bring recognition and relevance together in the interest of social transformation and development imperatives of the African continent (Nyamnjoh 2012c)?

Given the persistent indifference to what the likes of Tutuola and their purportedly "genuine primitive simplicity"[2] have to offer in terms of popular epistemologies, the highly extraverted nature of education in Africa and the global south has tremendously favoured the knowledge industry of Europe and North America. Even as popular voices and popular knowledge systems in the West continue to have a raw deal as well, the colonial and colonising epistemology, acting in the name of the West in general, has facilitated the intellectual traditions and practitioners it promotes and protects in order to write themselves into the past, present and future of Africa as civilisers, saviours, initiators, mentors, and arbiters (Fonlon 1967; Ngugi wa Thiong'o 1997; Chinweizu 1987; Mudimbe 1988; Schipper 1990a, 1990b; Comaroff and Comaroff 1997a; Crossman and Devisch 1999, 2002; Mbembe 2000a: 7-40, 2001: 1-23; Magubane 2004; Grinker et al. 2010), in the same manner that facilitated the penetration and control of the working classes of Europe by its cultural and intellectual elite (Bourdieu 1984; Elias 2000; Magubane 2004). Europe and North America have for generations dominated the rest of the world with their academic products and canons of knowledge production and consumption (Ake 1979; Amin 2004, 2009[1988]; Gareau 1987; Achebe 1988, 2000, 2012; Zeleza 1997; Quijano 2000; Canagarajah 2002; Nyamnjoh 2004b; Connell 2007; Mama 2007; Harrison 2010; Ntarangwi 2010; Lauer and Anyidoho 2012a, 2012b; Ndlovu-Gatsheni 2013a, 2013b).

In the social sciences and humanities under which much of African studies falls, the West, in its multiple hierarchies, has been consistently more "advanced" and expansionist than the underdeveloped and dependent regions of the world it has sought to penetrate and humble with its military and epistemological prowess (Amin 1980, 2004, 2006, 2009[1988], 2010; Mentan 2010a, 2010b). In the late 1980s, Frederick Gareau remarked that American social science, positioning itself at the apex of Western social scholarship, in its "unrelenting one-way traffic," was able to penetrate countries with cultures as different from its own as those of France, Canada, India, Japan and the Republic of Korea. This penetration has given American social science a "privileged position" with "a very favourable export balance of communications" or "talking without listening" (Gareau 1987: 599). Thus, not only is Africa, for example, disadvantaged by the a priori exclusion of its popular traditions of knowledge, but even its own intellectual elite, readily or reluctantly subscribing to the colonial and colonising theories of knowledge spearheaded by the West and epitomised by the USA, are equally sidestepped or treated with callous indifference. The recognition these African elite seek to the detriment of relevance is hard to come by even for the most willing disciples of Western colonial credentialism among them (Ake 1979; Nyamnjoh 2004b; Nwagwu 2015; Nwagwu and Ojemeni 2015).

According to Gareau, not only is there little importation, but American social scientists also ensure that any "incoming messages are in accord with American socio-cultural norms." This approach and practice to scholarship demonstrates American power to define and determine the knowledge systems of the world. It also "betrays [even today] an ethnocentric, inward-looking fixation," with little preference for anything foreign: "if foreign, a preference for the Anglo-Saxon world; little concern for Continental Europe, and indifference or hostility towards the Second and the Third Worlds" (Gareau 1987: 598–599; see also Amin 2009[1988]; Connell 2007; Comaroff and Comaroff 2012; Santos 2014; Rosa 2014; Cooper and Morrell 2014; Guyer 2015a, 2015b; Connell et al. 2016). This must indeed be frustrating to African scholars seeking recognition and inclusion in American intellectual and academic circles. Yet, as mentioned earlier and as discussed in subsequent chapters, it does not deter them from acting condescendingly to what Tutuola and popular epistemologies on the continent have to offer.

In a study focusing on international relations as a subdiscipline of political science, Kim Richard Nossal reached conclusions similar to those of Gareau. Nossal notes that textbooks in this area: "portray the world to their readers from a uniquely *American* point of view: they are reviewed by Americans; the sources they cite are American; the examples are American; the theory is American; the experience is American; the focus is American; and in… [some cases], the voice is also explicitly American" (Nossal 1998: 12). And many an African political scientist continues to swear by the study of international relations inspired by American theories and theorists. Their publications suggest there is no better anywhere, and that Africa has little to offer that could possibly challenge, let alone enrich current theories. African scholars seem to be mere potted plants in greenhouses in the face of such resilient colonialism and their education and logic of practice as scholars and intellectuals (Nyamnjoh 2004b, 2012a, 2012c, 2013b, 2015a, 2016).

Even in death, Tutuola waits patiently in the wings, refusing to give up, determined to keep hope alive about the potentials and prospects of Africa, Africaness and African thinking, and African values in knowledge production on the African condition, and on what it means to be human as a universal pursuit. Alive, his resilience kept him writing undeterred, looking forward to a future disabused of obsessions with completeness, indeed, a future where scholars and intellectuals are schooled to detect and celebrate interconnections and intimacies, even when surfaces, essences and aggressive ambitions of dominance might tend to suggest otherwise.

In addition to the accounts on American dominance in the social sciences by Gareau and Nossal, similar "single story" (TED Conferences 2009) observations could be made of almost all other disciplinary, academic, scholarly, and intellectual production and consumption. Despite proclaimed independence, dependency reigns, much to the detriment of interdependence, and right into the 21st century (Amin 2004, 2009[1988]; Connell 2007; Lauer and Anyidoho 2012a, 2012b; Ndlovu-Gatsheni 2013a, 2013b). Yet, all what Africans like Tutuola really want is not to be defined and confined in an arbitrary manner and with callous indifference by a colonising external agent from the bush of ghosts and its hired local customs clearing officers at the frontiers fronting as authentic African voices. When African intellectuals and leaders prefer to identify themselves by their colonial heritage to the exclusion of their indigenous and endogenous cultural heritages, there is little chance of Africans succeeding to tell African stories and to celebrate African achievements in science and history.

As Achebe sums it up, speaking of the West in general, "Europe's reliance on its own experts would not worry us if it did not, at the same time, attempt to exclude African testimony. But it often does" (Achebe 1988: 26). And often succeeds, I should add, because, like Count Dracula, the colonising epistemologies of the West have their activators, propagators, intermediaries and disciples ready to caricature and misrepresent Africa and African reality with impunity.

Such unequal encounters and unequal exchanges in the sphere of knowledge production and consumption are still characteristic of the 21st century, a reality that has driven some concerned scholars to seek a global theory of knowledge by balancing the equation with theories and epistemological insights from the global south (Connell 2007; Comaroff and Comaroff 2012; Santos 2014; Rosa 2014; Cooper and Morrell 2014; Guyer 2015a, 2015b; Connell et al. 2016).

This book is emphatic in its suggestion that we will still be nibbling at the exterior of resilient colonial education by the 22nd century, if we, yet again, bypass the cosmologies of the Tutuolas of Africa and of elsewhere, and the ontologies they have to offer in terms of popular epistemologies. Scholarship calls for southern theories or theories from the south. Limiting ourselves yet again only to what is within the ivory tower, would be a huge missed opportunity to re-embrace the complexity of reality and thus contribute to scholarship and knowledge production globally. Tutuola may be dead, but his writings live on, and so do the popular realities which he depicted meticulously – for those who care to accord him the seriousness he has always deserved. Increasingly, however, academic institutions and academics can ill-afford to continue to delude themselves and seek to convince the rest of the world that they are the sole or even main drivers of information. Tutuola-like universes of popular African beliefs in supernatural forces are not only alive but thriving and driving African entertainment in film and music. What is challenging African beliefs in African films are Christian Evangelists with their "Be filled with the fire of the Holy Spirit!" alternatives. Even so, it is the same belief in the supernatural and unknown that drives millions of Africans to these churches, irrespective of education and political power. In some cases, as the subsequent example of occult practices in Cameroon reveal, some powerful Africans couple such attractions with belief in the use of human body parts as protective charms and sources of material enrichment.

Perspectives sympathetic to the predicaments and resiliencies of Africa have suffered a great rejection rate by university curricula, reviewers for publishers, and academic peers who stick to their conceptual and methodological spots however compelling arguments to the contrary (Ake 1979; Nyamnjoh 2004b; Nwagwu 2015; Nwagwu and Ojemeni 2015). Given that recognition as knowledge is very much a function of the power to define and prescribe (Bourdieu 2004: 18-21), European and North American scholars are only too aware that they can ignore with impunity work conducted in peripheral sites like the African continent, while any African scholar who similarly ignores Western scholarship puts his or her professional competence at issue (Gupta and Ferguson 1997: 27). While a little semblance of knowledge about Africa might go a long way in Europe and North America, African scholars are often expected to bend over backwards to demonstrate their knowledge of and sophistication in the theories, theorists and scholarly practices of the colonising West, to be visible even marginally. Little wonder therefore that disciplinary debates even in the 21st century can be so uneven across geographies and among various racial and social categories. A common way of shooting down an African debate is to claim that it is *passé*, that it took place in the West a long time ago, and that the discipline has since moved on in terms of its menu and debate agenda.

The advent of the internet and its purported equalising potential for the developing world does not seem to be achieving much in *significantly* redefining unequal flows of information and cultural products between the West and the rest, the internet's remarkable impact and opportunities notwithstanding. Cultural creativity and innovation made possible by accelerated mobility under globalisation are both liberating and confining, with "no absolute winners and losers" as the cultural field continues to be an uneven playing field (Hall 2010). Could this be an opportunity to creatively explore, foreground and actively promote what popular epistemologies in Africa have to offer? This book on Tutuola's ideas and his universe are a modest affirmation on my part that this, indeed, is a possibility and opportunity for Africans to re-visit, redefine and re-engineer their scholarly contribution to a global ecumen of scholarship and knowledge production where even the best of them have been passive participants reduced to hired customs clearing officers for imported colonising ideas, theories, theorists and practices.

Even those Africans ready to research and understand and enrich their scholarship with what Tutuola and others in the realm of popular epistemologies have to offer, continue to encounter phenomenal hurdles. Their intellectual dependence, for example, is further exacerbated by very limited resources for research, and the fact that even the available resources can be wasted, underused, or badly used. Without serious investments in research, curricula informed by prejudiced and racialized assumptions about the continent are recycled, and teaching and learning remain void of African perspectives and ignorant of in-depth understandings of African realities. African scholars and Africans in general are doomed to consume not books and research output of their own production or choice, but, what their affluent counterparts in North America and Europe produce and enforce.

While some, the elite in the main, may not warm up to Tutuola because of his persistent capacity to embarrass them, others, especially among the younger generation, simply know very little about the likes of Tutuola because libraries are unlikely to stock his works, and even worse, lecturers are unlikely to recommend his books. Cooperation takes the form of North American and European universities calling the tune for the African pipers they have paid. Collaborative research has often worked in the interest of European and North American partners who, armed with assumed theoretical sophistication and economic resources, often reduce their African collaborators to data collectors, research assistants (Amadiume 1997: 183-198) and token citations or inclusion in course syllabuses (Nnaemeka 2005: 55). It is all too common for a single phrase by an African scholar, cited out of context, to do its rounds among non-African scholars. Handed down through the ranks and generations, few ever bother to read the book or article for themselves, to see whether or not there is much more to Africa and Africans than the merry-go-round phrase they are using to endorse or dismiss Africa and Africans as they see fit or unfit. As Arjun Appadurai has nicely summed up, the tendency remains to relate to scholars from "more marginal regions of the world" as if they were "simply producers of data for the theory mills of the North" (Appadurai 2001: 5).

African Studies as a field that brings together different disciplines in the social sciences and humanities is no exception, as Africanists appear as gatekeepers and Africans as gatecrashers (Berger 1997; Mkandawire 1997; Zeleza 1997; Prah 1998; Mama 2007; Lauer and Anyidoho 2012a, 2012b). Some Africans, as I have argued and illustrate abundantly in the pages which follow with reference to Tutuola, are equally actively gatekeeping against popular forms of knowledge on their continent. With the leading journals and publishers based in Europe and North America and controlled by academics there, African debates and perspectives, in tune with or at variance with the dominant colonising epistemologies, find it very difficult getting fair and adequate representation. When manuscripts by Africans are not simply dismissed for being "uninformed by current debates and related literature," they may be turned down for challenging conventional scholarly wisdom and traditional scholarly assumptions about their continent (Mkandawire 1997; Cabral et al. 1998). African academics who succeed in penetrating such gate-keeping mechanisms have often done so by making serious sacrifices in terms of the perspectives, methodologies and contextual relevancies of their publications and scholarship (Prah 1998: 27-31), or by co-authoring with "experts" from North America or Europe.

It is akin to Tutuola's narrator surviving his bush of ghosts, and related strange creatures only by means of charms, spells, juju and trickery. While some have followed Tutuola in his resilience and sensitivity to a dynamic sense of African cultures and in crusading for a complex and nuanced idea of what it means to be African, others have single-mindedly followed the prescriptive gaze of a colonising idea of knowledge, and have often done so in zombie-like fashion. Fela Kuti, who decries zombie mentalities, had the courage to make his music popularly relevant. Afrobeat, as the music is known, is, according to Sanya Osha, "a deft assortment of diverse styles and traditions notably West African highlife, jazz, funk and indigenous West African drumming amongst others," the distinctly spiritual dimensions of which Kuti intended to facilitate "a communion with Yoruba deities."[3] Steve Biko, who strove for a marriage of essence and consciousness informed by his experiences as a black person under an apartheid regime, courageously stuck to writing what he liked in an audacious quest for "self-actualisation" and "a radical refusal to be a willing accomplice" in his own oppression (Pityana et al. 1991; Malusi and Mphumlwana 1996; Mngxitama et al. 2008a, 2008b: 1-20). Unlike Tutuola and the likes of Fela Kuti and Steve Biko, many an African intellectual and scholar has had to conform rather than lose internationally-mediated visibility by daring to defend what Achille Mbembe (2000b) has provocatively termed "African modes of self-writing," even at the risk of appearing like Ocol and Clementine in *Song of Lawino*[4], belittled and belittling in their xenophilia and craving for whiteness (p'Bitek 1989[1966]).

Ocol and Clementine – the "modern" colonial educated man and woman in p'Bitek's (1989[1966]) *Song of Lawino* – are incapable of producing or reproducing anything of substance, preoccupied as they are with ostentatious consumption (ballroom dances, white people's foods and hair, dressing and speaking like whites, naming themselves after and following the religion of whites) to demonstrate the value of so-called "modern education." The "thirst for ease," "craving for luxury," and "itch to get rich quick" are still "running riot everywhere" (Fonlon 1965: 23-26), despite herculean needs for social transformation and in spite of renewed calls for decolonisation and decoloniality (Ndlovu-Gatsheni 2013a, 2013b; Gibson 2016; Nyamnjoh 2016). Few cases of radical nationalism have survived neutralisation after independence (Fanon 1967a: 118-165), as colonialism has always succeeded in staying on despite its formal ending. This is not dissimilar to slavery and enslavement. Through various practices including imprisonment, some countries are able to extract slave labour from those whose humanity they have actively and strategically devalued.

In South Africa, the achievements of Steve Biko and his Black Consciousness movement in using the popular creativity of everyday life (music, song, poetry, etc.) in classrooms, churches, neighbourhoods and townships, in anti-apartheid struggles, the promotion of knowledge of protest history, and the affirmation of the integrity and humanity of marginalised black masses and their cultures (Pityana et al. 1991; Malusi and Mphumlwana 1996; Mngxitama et al. 2008a) seem to have suffered a major reversal under the new, negotiated post-apartheid dispensation (Ramose 2003, 2004,

2010; Mngxitama et al. 2008a, 2008b; Gumede and Dikeni 2009). This is a fate not dissimilar to that of other anti-colonial and resistance movements in Africa and beyond, where aspirations for liberation and self-determination have almost invariably been watered down to accommodate continuity for the value system and interests of the dominator, who, as abundantly evidenced in the unending debate among Nigerians and other Africans around Tutuola and his writings, champions divide and rule to compound the predicaments of the marginalised masses and their systems of knowledge, sense- and meaning-making. The situation is hardly facilitated by the infighting amongst senior and well-connected scholars, who indulge in backstabbing and delight in frustrating others and using them as stepping stones. It is common for academism to pave the way to political activism, not necessarily to advance knowledge but rather to fan the flames of ambitions of dominance outside the academy. Within the logic of divide and rule and infighting, it is hardly surprising that Tutuola was recognised and celebrated much more, and paradoxically, in Europe and North America than in Africa or his home country, Nigeria.

A pilgrimage to the West might bring desired international recognition and exhibition as "Hottentot Venus of the Academy," but often does not help, and could indeed exacerbate the problem of the irrelevance of the knowledge produced and consumed. The tendency is for African scholars in the diaspora to shop "up" for northern sources, not "down" for local scholarship, not even when such scholarship, like theirs, seeks conformation with and embraces the colonial template without question. Little wonder, therefore, that the most prominent voices in African studies are "diasporic intellectuals" whose inspiration is most likely to come from what Richard Werbner has described as "nicely subtle readings of fashionable European theorists" than from "current local knowledge of the cultural politics of everyday life in the postcolonial hinterlands" (Werbner 1996: 6), which the likes of Tutuola have dangled in their faces since the early 1950s. And little wonder that the study of Africa continues to be dominated by perspectives that privilege analogies to a nebulous, generic and homogenous "West" over the historical processes that should qualify Africa as a unit of analysis on its own terms (Mamdani 1996: 12-13; Amadiume 1997; Imam 1997; Nnaemeka 2005; Oyewumi 2005; Mama 2007; Lauer and Anyidoho 2012a, 2012b; Ndlovu-Gatsheni 2013a, 2013b).

Despite bending over backwards for recognition, many an African elite in European and North American universities, continue to feel invisible and thoroughly ignored. They would readily share the following frustration of Paul Gilroy, a black British professor of sociology, who as a faculty member at Yale University, never ceased to wonder why he seemed so invisible to his white colleagues: "I recall a kind of quiet racism in the meetings of the Yale Professoriate where nobody would speak to me and many looked at me – even in my best suit – as if I had come in there on the bottom of somebody's shoe."[5]

Confusing, conflating and sweeping generalisations are the order of the day, and Africans are invited to see themselves in the image of a purported "West" with which few amongst ordinary citizens of the different countries which fall under this canopy or category of "the West" can identify. As Tutuola repeatedly demonstrates through his sweet-footed boundary crossing quest-heroes, if a frozen or bounded Africa exists nowhere empirically, why should Africans uncritically subscribe to a mind-numbing abstract idea of the West with which every purported Westerner is assumed to identify? Why can Africans or Westerners, often presented as extreme binary opposites, not simply be like Tutuola's quest-heroes, who do not have to belong to the worlds of their adventures from the beginning to claim and be claimed as part and parcel of these worlds? There is much to inspire scholarly imagination in creative and innovative ways by taking a closer look at the capacity by Tutuola's quest-heroes to take the inside out and the outside in, and to acknowledge the value of debt and being indebted. Until the freedom to wander and be recognised becomes common currency for all and sundry without exception, African researchers, even in relation to endogenous knowledge systems in Africa, will continue to prioritise theories and theorists from elsewhere, because the empirical realities that shaped their theorising were everything but African, but the relevance of those theories can at best be indirect. The suggestion to study and understand Africa first on its own terms will continue to be easily and uncritically dismissed as an invitation to celebrate African essentialism and exceptionalism, even as the imported colonising theories and theorists are nothing but essentialist and bounded as "Western," as are the assumptions they make of Africans, their communities and identities.

Without the humility to acknowledge debt and indebtedness on the part of the West and its African acolytes, it is hardly surprising that there is little patience with anything African, even by Africans, as the story of overwhelming rejection of Amos Tutuola tells us. There is little discourse on Africa for Africa's sake, and the colonising West has often used Africa as a pretext for its own subjectivities, fantasies and perversions. And no amount of new knowledge or insistence on sidestepped old knowledges seems challenging enough to bury for good the ghost of simplistic assumptions about Africa (Schipper 1990a, 1990b; Comaroff and Comaroff 1997b: 86-125, 1997b: 236-322; Mbembe 2000a: 10-21, 2001: 3-9; Magubane 2004; Nnaemeka 2005; Oyewumi 2005; Mama 2007; Lauer and Anyidoho 2012a 2012b; Ndlovu-Gatsheni 2013a, 2013b). Even in the 21st century, representations of Africa as a necessarily negative trope in the language of Eurocentric modernity perfected in the era of imperial imagination and conquest continue to be re-actualised in a manner that defies the very logic and science by which they are purportedly inspired.

Given its remarkable ability to reproduce and market itself globally, the colonial and colonising epistemology has emptied academia of the power and impact of competing and complementary systems of knowledge (Mudimbe 1988: x-xi) such as Tutuola's universe. "Even in the most explicitly 'Afrocentric' descriptions, models of analysis explicitly or implicitly, knowingly or unknowingly, refer" to "categories and conceptual systems which depend on a Western epistemological order," as if African beliefs and African endogenous systems of thought such as Tutuola's are "unthinkable and cannot be made explicit within the framework of their own rationality" or "epistemological locus" (Mudimbe 1988: x).

If African scholars just as Mudimbe have so eloquently identified and articulated the problem which pushed Amos Tutuola to dare to write a novel, even as he was fully aware he was ill-equipped in terms of the tools of the trade in a Eurocentric sense of what a novel ought to be, how come very few of these insights have been translated into a programme of action? Why does it sound as if we African scholars, academics and intellectuals have contented ourselves with diagnosis? Why do we appear in permanent flight from the African universe of Tutuola, and to be knocking incessantly on the doors of Eurocentric legitimating instances for knowledge, even though few appear to be listening to us with any significant degree of interest and accommodation? In many regards, we are not dissimilar to the beautiful young woman in Tutuola's *The Palm-Wine Drinkard*, who is bent on running away from all the suitors with which she is familiar, until she finds herself in the dangerous hands of a man (the Skull), whose status of "the complete gentleman" has far less to it than meets the eye. Though research on and in Africa has shaped the disciplines and convictions of a supposedly universal truth (Bates et al. 1993: xiii–xiv), the quest for such universality has meant the marginalisation of African possibilities even by African practitioners of the disciplines. The outcome has been nothing short of an epistemological imperialism that has facilitated both a colonial intellectual hegemony and the silencing of Africans even in the study of Africa (Ake 1979; Copans 1990: 305-395; Zeleza 1997; Obenga 2001; Nnaemeka 2005; Oyewumi 2005; Nabudare 2006; Mama 2007; Lauer and Anyidoho 2012a, 2012b; Ndlovu-Gatsheni 2013a, 2013b), making of African intellectuals outsiders in their own land and on their own issues (Ngugi wa Thiong'o 2005), and about their own stories. It has also turned African intellectuals into disdainful and snobbish compatriots of their fellow Africans whom they label and dismiss as embarrassingly trapped in the universe of primitive magic and superstitious beliefs, such as proudly depicted by Tutuola in his books.

The colonial epistemological order has survived on the continent more because it suits the purposes of the agents of (neo)colonialism than because of its relevance to understanding African situations. Those who run educational programmes informed by this epistemological order are seldom tolerant of challenge, stimulation, provocation and competing perspectives at any level. They protect their intellectual spots jealously, and are ready to deflate all "saboteurs" and "subversives." They want their programmes to go on without disturbance. They select as trainers and lecturers or accept, engage and sponsor only research and scholarship that confirm their basic assumptions and convictions. But as protests by African students and occasionally by some academic staff of African institutions of higher education show, African universities, academics and researchers have the responsibility to challenge such unfounded assumptions based on vested interests, hidden agendas or the *habitus* of colonial hierarchies of humanity and human agency.

Most accounts of African cultures and experiences have been generated from the insensitive position of power and quest for convergence and homogeneity. Explicit or implicit in these accounts is the assumption that African societies should reproduce colonial institutions and European ideals regardless of feasibility or contextual differences. Few researchers of Africa, even in African universities, have questioned enough the theories, concepts and basic assumptions informed by the dominant colonial epistemology in which they seem to be stuck. Many would ridicule any suggestion as that which I am making in this book that Amos Tutuola and the universe of his stories has something serious to offer epistemological debates. To them, epistemology is something that comes pre-packaged in books written elsewhere and suited to the contexts of the societies for which they are written. The tendency has been for African intellectuals and academics to conform to a world conceived without them, and to celebrate the status of superior-inferiors in such a world (Chinweizu 1987; Mafeje 1998: 26-29; Lauer and Anyidoho 2012a, 2012b; Ndlovu-Gatsheni 2013a, 2013b). As the example of Tutuola's universe shows, missing or inadequately provided for are perspectives of majorities with vibrant but untold stories and rich traditions of meaning- and sense-making. The dominant colonial epistemological order is thus deprived. It is littered with defective accounts of communities recounted by others in texts without contexts, and often with a condescending and patronising tone. And when someone remotely steeped in such contexts opts or dares to suggest that they can tell the story of the hunt from their own perspective, the clampdown by the self-appointed instances of legitimation is often sharp, hard and brutishly without compunction.

Legitimately and meaningfully enlivening accounts of Africa entails paying more attention to the popular epistemologies from which ordinary people draw on a daily basis, and the ways they situate themselves in relationship to others within these epistemologies. Considering and treating the everyday life of social spaces as bona fide research sites entails, inter alia, taking the popular, the historical and the ethnographic seriously, and emphasising interdependence and conviviality within and between disciplines, and among disciplinary practitioners across geographies, gender, generational, class and racial divisions. It means creating links of conversations, collaboration and co-production with interlocutors outside of the academy and the professional circles of academics and scholars. It also means encouraging "a meaningful dialogue" between these epistemologies and "modern science," both in their old and new forms (Devisch 2002, 2007; Devisch and Nyamnjoh 2011; Ramose 2003, 2004, 2010, 2014; Jansen 2011: 31-153; Lauer and Anyidoho 2012a, 2012b; Werbner 2015). However, because the popular epistemologies in question have been actively discouraged and delegitimised since colonial encounters, not least by African intellectuals themselves, there is need to revalorise them and the multitudes shaping and sharing them. Systematic and critical non-prescriptive research into these silent epistemologies of unheard majorities will benefit significantly from Tutuola and his writings.

Epistemological recognition and conviviality entail moving from assumptions to empirical substantiation of claims about Africa. Hence the importance of questions such as: Who are these ordinary people? What do they do for their living? What is the nature of their epistemologies? Where do Africans, brought up under and practising the colonial epistemology, position themselves? How ready are the elite to be led by unheard majorities subjected to elitist discourses? Until the elite know what these epistemologies *actually are*, they would not know where and how, or with whom, to dialogue. Like Tutuola's narrators in *The Palm-Wine Drinkard* and *The Wild Hunter in the Bush of the Ghosts* who both have to fight from the belly of a hungry ghost that swallows them, the angel of studying ordinary Africans in a relevant and meaningful way may well be in the belly of the beast, just as the beast may well be in the belly of the angel. On this as on many related issues, Tutuola's creative imagination offers interesting insights.

Domestication as a dialogical epistemological shift can only begin to take shape if research by Africans critical of conventional wisdom in academia is greeted with recognition rather than censorship, caricature or derision (Obenga 2001: 49-66). And African scholars have in turn to disabuse themselves of the shame and embarrassment they tend to feel towards popular African ways of life, concepts of reality and belief systems which have suffered long histories of caricature and dismissal as a result of unequal encounters with Europe. Only by creating space for African scholarship based on Africa as a unit of analysis in its own right could scholars begin to correct prevalent situations whereby much is known of what African states, societies, economies and individuals "*are not*" but very little of what "*they actually are*" (Emphasis in original, Mbembe 2000a: 21, 2001: 9). Accepting the research agendas of African scholars sensitive to and immersed in popular epistemologies may not just be "a matter of ecumenism or goodwill," but also the beginnings of conversations that could enrich and enliven scholarship globally (Appadurai 1999: 235-237). Forging such mutuality, in a spirit of partnership and interdependence, would help re-energise African scholars and allow for building genuinely international and democratic communities of researchers.

Global conversations and cooperation among universities and scholars are a starting point in a long journey of equalisation and recognition of marginalised epistemologies and dimensions of scientific inquiry. But any global restructuring of power relations in scholarship can only begin to be meaningful to ordinary Africans through educational institutions and curricula and pedagogies in touch and in tune with their predicaments. In this connection, while organisations such as the Council for the Development of Social Science Research in Africa (CODESRIA) are making worthwhile contributions, much systematic, sustained, critical, rethinking and practice remains to be done. Nearly four decades ago Fonlon (1978) made a plea for African universities as spaces for genuine intellectuals dedicated to the common weal. For African researchers and their host universities, to contribute towards a genuine, multifaceted liberation of the continent and its peoples, they ought to start by joining their people in a careful rethinking of African concerns and priorities, and educational approaches (Copans 1990, 1993; Ramose 2003, 2004, 2010, 2014; Zeleza and Olukoshi 2004a, 2004b; Mama 2007; Lauer and Anyidoho 2012a 2012b; Ndlovu-Gatsheni 2013a, 2013b).

The need to rethink and endogenise has for long been the clarion call (Mama and Hamilton, 2003: 35), with Mamdani (1993: 19) asking for the rooting of African universities in African soil, and Mafeje (1988: 8) for a move away from "received theory or contrived universalism," to "intimate knowledge of the dynamics of African culture[s] in ... contemporary setting[s]." Such "endogenisation," Crossman argues, cannot take place within the colonial model of education, and therefore "should not only imply a freedom from dominant narratives and their methodologies but also the capacity for original and critical intellectual production by means of relatively autonomous research and educational institutions, methodologies, perspectives and choice of subject matter" (Crossman 2004: 323-324; see also Crossman and Devisch 2002; Okere et al. 2005).

As with popular epistemologies, the way forward is to encourage carefully thought through research, which from inception brings out endogenous African methodologies and perspectives. And one cannot assume methodologies and perspectives are African simply because those doing the research and the thinking *proclaim* themselves African or *look* African. As Obioma Nnaemeka argues, "insiders can also be alienated from their own culture," and "A Western-educated African who teaches African culture also speaks from a position of alienation which may not necessarily be as profound as that of the outsider" (Nnaemeka 2005: 57). The likes of Tutuola are waiting in the wings, keen to contribute to recalibrated conversations and inclusive epistemological orders in Africa and African universities, and beyond.

Hope for the future of education in Africa depends on providing for the creative processes of cultural endogenisation popular with ordinary Africans even as African scholars continue to cooperate and converse with intellectuals around the world. For scholars and writers such as Ngugi wa Thiong'o (2005) not to be "intellectual outsiders" in their own universities, insightful scrutiny of current curricula is needed. What are the origins? What assumptions underlie the content? What practicability and outcome? Through greater reconnection with and adaptation to local, national and regional socio-cultural contexts, African universities might overcome functional and philosophical difficulties and make themselves more relevant to the needs of the countries and communities of peoples they serve (Boulaga 2014[1977]; Crossman and Devisch 1999, 2002; Crossman 2004; Zeleza and Olukoshi 2004a; Olukoshi and Zeleza 2004; Devisch 2007; Mama 2007; Lauer and Anyidoho 2012a, 2012b; Ndlovu-Gatsheni 2013a, 2013b). These needs include some of those to whom Tutuola had a lifelong devotion, at much personal cost in insults and criticism. Initiatives for reconnecting universities to lived life and embedding research in African communities should be encouraged. This, however, is easier stated than done, especially when many an African academic and intellectual are all too eager to pay such initiatives little more than lip service. I can well imagine Amos Tutuola laughing sardonically at such lip service, a gourd of palm-wine in hand, from the Deads' Town, judging from the catalogue of negativities with which he was greeted when he dared to write and publish precisely about such forgotten or sidestepped African cultural values and worldviews.

The possibility of serious recalibration beyond lip service is evidenced by research and/or critical thinking – ranging from the "Négritude" of Senghor (1977), "Afrocentrism" of scholars such as Molife Kete Asante (2003) and Marimba Ani (1994), and Dani Wadaba Nabudare's (2006) "Afrokology," to Sabelo Ndlovu-Gatsheni's (2013a, 2013b) "Coloniality-Decoloniality," through philosophy (Boulaga 2014[1977]; Appiah 1992; Eze 1997; Hountondji 1980[1976], 2002, 2007; Masolo 2010; Diagne 2013), popular culture (Barber 1997; Cooper 1998; Rooney 2000; Sutherland-Addy and Diaw 2005; Edman 2010), religion (Ela 1986[1980]; Boulaga 1984[1981]; Olupona 2004; Bongmba 2012; Adogame et al. 2013; Soyinka 2013; Echtler and Ukah 2015), history, legal and political processes (Ake 1979, 2000; Amadiume 1987; Mamdani 1996; Falola and Jennings 2002; Comaroff and Comaroff 2006), and gender relations and identities (Amadiume 1987, 1997;

Imam et al. 1997; Nnaemeka 2005; Oyewumi 2005; Sutherland-Addy and Diaw 2005; Mama 2007).

What is needed, however, is not so much pointing to isolated individuals perceived to be doing "the right thing" but to a critical mass of scholars and non-scholars networking and working together strategically towards achieving the valorisation of marginalised humanity and the creative diversity of being African. In the quest to replant and endogenise education in and about Africa, through the critical rethinking of curriculum, the work of Paulus Gerdes of Mozambique calling for cross-disciplinary conversations and joint initiatives between natural and social scientists is instructive. Gerdes (1999, 2007, 2008; Djebbar and Gerdes 2007) has researched and published on mathematics, geometry and logic long practised by ordinary Africans in productive and decorative activities like mat and basket weaving, ceramics and sculpting, and in riddles and storytelling, and often illustrated by design patterns drawn on the ground and reflected in infinitely complex and varied dance steps, drum rhythms and melodies. Equally instructive is research into endogenous notions of time and calendars, ecological knowledge, farming, fishing and pastoral techniques, taxonomic knowledge in fauna and flora, pharmacopoeias and medical aetiologies, and diverse traditions of healthcare.

If this encouraging evidence of budding recalibration were to be accelerated and proliferated in scholarly circles along with a systematic exploration and harnessing of insights from the likes of Tutuola, there is hope that Africa can be party in a global conversation on knowledge-making on its own epistemological and methodological terms, with the interests and concerns of ordinary Africans carefully negotiated, navigated and blended with those of the elite, in the African tradition of accommodation and appropriation. Popular epistemologies and methodologies, systematically researched and consolidated into publicly accessible repertoires, can provide inspiration and understanding for scholarly and popular endeavours. The systematic integration of conflicting and complementary epistemologies will create space for scholarship and perspectives of all persuasions. Epistemological conviviality and interconnection are possible precisely in light of the spirit of tolerance for which Africans are renowned, and in recognition that there are no final answers to perplexing questions in a dynamic world.

Notes

[1] I can't help but share with the reader the following reaction by Professor Ntonghanwah Forcheh of the University of Botswana, upon reading this in an earlier draft of this book:

> Not necessarily. It's a fact that there is a place called Buea. I am standing in Kumba and wish to go to Buea. If I insist that existence of Buea means one best way of getting to Buea from Kumba, then I may never get there even though indeed there is Buea. The presence or absence of Buea can not be evidenced by one best way of getting there. Most things are multi-dimensional and multivariate. I presume the essence of the critic is that many schools of thought fail to accept the existence of the other.

[2] See Anonymous review of Tutuola's *Simbi and the Satyr of the Dark Jungle* in *The Times Literary Supplement*, October 21, 1955 (reprinted in Lindfors 1975: 77).
[3] See Sanya Osha, "Tributaries of Afrobeat/s,"
http://www.3ammagazine.com/3am/tributaries-of-afrobeats,
accessed 2 December 2016.
[4] *Song of Lawino* was first composed in Acholi couplets in 1956 and published in English in 1966 (Currey 2008: 98).
[5] See Paul Gilroy and Rosemary Bechler, "Paul Gilroy in search of a not necessarily safe starting point... A conversation about university education today that rearranges some of the deckchairs on the Titanic,"
https://www.opendemocracy.net/paul-gilroy-rosemary-bechler/paul-gilroy-in-search-of-not-very-safe-starting-point, accessed 31 May 2016.

Chapter Three

Tutuola and the Extravagant Illusion of Completeness

This chapter provides more illustration on Tutuola's main contribution to rethinking the world in light of the centrality of the colonial epistemic order as discussed. This regards incompleteness as our fundamental ontological status. According to this ontology, the world is an intricate universe of incompleteness, interconnections, interdependencies and conviviality. The chapter also further builds more on the idea of 'convivial scholarship' as the preoccupation of the frontier scholar in this endeavour of re-imagination.

There are two powerful illustrations (among many others) in this chapter regarding this theme of incompleteness. Firstly, we have the image of the Skull, who borrows different body parts to become a complete gentleman in order to win the affection of a beautiful woman. The potency the Skull's agency is able to achieve depends on the recognition of debt and indebtedness as normal. Freedom as absolute independence and completeness is therefore an illusion. The Skull is an example par excellence of our status as "composite beings". To denounce this status in pursuit of absolute autonomy is to alienate oneself from this essence, leading to a social death. The second illustration of incompleteness has to do with Tutuola's creative appropriation of the English language. His understanding of English is incomplete, but this does not diminish his ability as a story teller. In fact, it exemplifies the convivial themes brought out in this book. It is a case of Yoruba being influenced by English and vice versa. Both mobilising one another to the effect of story-telling.

While we see this alternative ontology in Tutuola's work, we are also reminded of the colonial epistemology and its lack of nuance. The dualism we see at play is that of traditionalism versus modernism and is evident in the contentious and largely disparaging reception to Tutuola's work at the local, especially, and international level. Among some Nigerians, Tutuola was seen as an embarrassment, as he undermined aspirations to Western modernity with his tales of Africa and Africans as superstitious, primitive and savage. On the other hand, Western fascination with Tutuola's novels often entailed discussing the author and his work by appealing to a familiar colonial rhetoric which infantilises Africans while painting them as superstitious primitives stuck in the barbarism and darkness of a distant past. In the colonial rhetoric, there is space for both admonishment and fascination with Tutuola, but for the wrong reasons.

Finally, this chapter builds on the proposed strategy of rethinking and departing from the dominant colonial epistemological order. Recognizing and celebrating our ontological incompleteness, the currency of conviviality should be spent constructively in the academic supermarket. The frontier anthropologist could explore the complementarity between fiction and ethnography. Ethnographic novels such as Tutuola's allow for greater attention to complexity and nuance and are underpinned by the general message of cross-disciplinary work which celebrates incompletes and conviviality because on their own, disciplines are incomplete. Like the skull, the extent of their potency is determined by borrowing body parts from other disciplines. This is a call for disciplines, individuals and collectives, to, in recognition of their incompleteness, adopt a disposition toward inclusivity and accommodation in being, becoming and meaning-making.

The writings of Amos Tutuola provide insights to enable scholars to question in a more commanding and substantiated fashion the sweeping assumptions and belittling implications in the colonial epistemological order. Thanks to his struggles to get published, his works and the controversies surrounding them, and his equivocal experience as a writer, Tutuola enhances understanding of the nature and implications of colonial conquest and its zero-sum games of absolute winners and absolute losers. His works and their controversial reception provide substance to the argument that the completeness dramatized by champions of the dominant colonial epistemological order is possible and achievable only through the force of the coloniser borrowing without acknowledgement, dispossession with impunity, and debasement in the name of a contrived universalism claimed by a rather parochial civilisation and a phoney civilising mission. Tutuola made this evident through the stories he told uncompromisingly and by way of his own personal experiences as a writer who was initially persuaded to seek fulfilment through shared values and a common humanity by writing and hunting for a publisher for his novels. Even though this made him an object of ridicule by critics, home and away, each for their own reason – why the visibility he craved was not for the likes of him and not for the universes of perceived savagery and primitive superstitions that everyone seeking Eurocentric modernity was afflicted by and escaping from – Tutuola never relented. In place of rigid dichotomies in thought, claim and practice of identities and belonging as Yoruba and African, Tutuola, through the adventures and exploits of his quest-heroes and narrators, recommends a life and relationships of ambiguity, ambivalence and consciousness of debt and being indebted as integral to being and becoming in a universe of conviviality and interconnections among things natural, human and supernatural.

This chapter explores Tutuola's credentials as a postmodernist writer in how he draws attention to the marginalised though popular cosmologies and ontologies of Africa, and in his insistent reminder to his readers that no civilisation is worth pursuing if founded entirely on borrowing without acknowledgement and on the violence of arrogance and ignorance. Put differently, a civilisation in which there is no provision for imperfection or incompleteness is delirious and delusional. The chapter reiterates and substantiates the argument that Tutuola's stories – unlike similar stories often qualified as "magical realism" written by "magical realists" – are not simply fantasy and voyages of an imagination gone wild primarily intended for entertainment. They are stories inspired by shared cosmologies and ontologies common in oral traditions and folktales across Africa, and often needing no magical imagination to unfold and to be told.

The chapter also discusses ways in which Tutuola's deeply ethnographic stories could richly complement often impoverished anthropological accounts of Africa – accounts that claim a relationship with and inspiration from Cartesian rationalism and scientism that practising anthropologists do not usually demonstrate beyond lip service (Nyamnjoh 2015a). Africa remains a continent where anthropology enjoys little popularity among academics and scholars, and where outsider narratives of African realities are often nonchalantly unsympathetic to the nuanced complexities of Tutuola-like cosmologies and ontologies. This situation calls for the re-interpretation of the works of first-generation African colonial and postcolonial-period novelists, writing in European and indigenous African languages, as ethnographic accounts of African perspectives, reactions and resilience to unequal encounters with European ambitions of conquest and borrowing without acknowledgement.

How then did Tutuola go about making a case for an intricate universe of incompleteness, interconnections, interdependencies and conviviality, despite the resolute effort of modernising Africans? How did he defy the attacks orchestrated by such modernising Africans and their European champions who were keen to define and confine as stuck in a long dark past the cosmologies and ontologies of the Yoruba and Africa of his lived experiences and creative imagination?

Tutuola's stories have a typical narrative pattern. Writing in 1970, Bernth Lindfors, the American literary scholar who has devoted the most systematic and thorough attention to researching and publishing on Amos Tutuola and his writing, highlighted the characteristic narrative pattern of Tutuola's novels as follows:

> All six of Tutuola's longer works follow a similar narrative pattern. A hero (or heroine) with supernatural powers or access to supernatural assistance sets out on a journey in quest of something important and suffers incredible hardships before successfully accomplishing his mission. Invariably he ventures into unearthly realms, performs arduous tasks, fights with fearsome monsters, endures cruel tortures, and narrowly escapes death. Sometimes he is accompanied by a relative or by loyal companions; sometimes he wanders alone. But he always survives his ordeals, attains his objective, and usually emerges from his nightmarish experiences a wiser, wealthier man. His story is told in an unorthodox but curiously expressive idiom which is nearly as unpredictable as the bizarre adventures he undergoes in outlandish fantasy worlds (Lindfors 1970: 308).

The six works Lindfors had analysed before reaching his conclusion were: *The Palm-Wine Drinkard* (1952); *My Life in the Bush of Ghosts* (1954); *Simbi and the Satyr of the Dark Jungle* (1955); *The Brave African Huntress* (1958); *Feather Woman of the Jungle* (1962); and *Ajaiyi and His Inherited Poverty* (1967). Tutuola's publications subsequent to Lindfors' characterisation – comprising, by Faber and Faber in London: *The Witch-Herbalist of the Remote Town* (1981); *Pauper, Brawler and Slanderer* (1987); and *The Village Witch Doctor and Other Stories* (1990), and by Three Continents Press in Washington, DC, *The Wild Hunter in the Bush of the Ghosts* (1989[1982]) – maintained the same pattern, even if with slight variations (Owomoyela 1997). *Yoruba Folktales* (1986), published by Ibadan University Press, is Tutuola's only publication by a Nigerian publisher, and, according to Owomoyela, told in a "practically flawless" English language "that is markedly different from the 'young English' that is a Tutuola hallmark" (Owomoyela 1997: 874). Although first published only in 1982, *The Wild Hunter in the Bush of the Ghosts* was written in 1948, and should, as Lindfors argues in his foreword to the 1989 edition of the novel, be considered as Tutuola's "initial venture into a written mode of storytelling" and "his first attempt at writing a long narrative for publication" (Lindfors 1989: iii). As Lindfors explains in his foreword, Tutuola was invited by Three Continents Press in 1983 – during a visit "to the United States to participate in the International Writers' Workshop at the University of Iowa" to rework *The Wild Hunter in the Bush of the Ghosts* "for wider circulation" barely a year after publication (Lindfors 1989: iii). The reworking entailed going "through the typescript of the original version carefully, correcting obvious errors and restructuring several episodes" (Lindfors 1989: iii). Lindfors adds, "I was asked to lend a hand in the revision and to supervise computerized typesetting of the final text. So what is being presented here is basically the same old Wild Hunter in more modern dress," a transformation "achieved by means of the latest technological miracles," which Lindfors believes "is very much in keeping with the spirit of the story" (Lindfors 1989: iii).

Tutuola's novels may be pure fantasy and voyages of the heightened imagination into never-never lands of magic, marvels and monsters, but, as Lindfors observes, "the beings and doings in this fantasy world are not entirely unfamiliar," common as they are to oral traditions and folktales across Africa and the world in general (Lindfors 1970: 312; Eldred Jones, reprinted in Lindfors 1975[1966]). This is precisely the reason why, although Tutuola's "dream world" is "peopled as it is by creatures an imaginative child might create," his creative imagination, unlike the creative powers of the average child which are dulled, blurred and eventually lost by the impact of adultness, has stayed on (Nigerian correspondent, *West Africa*,[1] May 1, 1954, reproduced in Lindfors 1975: 37). This speaks of a creative and a fantasy fiction that is firmly grounded on popular ideas of reality that are more or less second nature to Tutuola.

To Wole Soyinka, a fellow Yoruba storyteller from his Abeokuta hometown, Tutuola was "primarily ... a storyteller in the best Yoruba tradition, pushing the bounds of credibility higher and higher and sustaining it by sheer adroitness, by a juxtaposition of analogous experience from the familiar" (Soyinka 1963: 391). Tutuola found some fulfilment through the international recognition accorded him by his London based publisher Faber and Faber, only to be brushed aside for much of his life by fellow Nigerians seeking completeness of their own under a Eurocentric index of modernity. Lindfors (1999a) provides a detailed, well researched and well documented account of the convoluted trajectory taken by Tutuola's manuscript before eventually, quite accidentally, surfacing at Faber and Faber. According to Lindfors, Faber and Faber received the manuscript of Tutuola's first novel from The United Society for Christian Literature Lutterworth Press (to which Tutuola had initially submitted it to be considered for publication) on February 20, 1951, and published *The Palm-Wine Drinkard* on May 2, 1952. Grove Press in the US published the same book in 1953. In 1955 translated editions of the book were published in French, German, Italian and Serbo-Croatian, making Tutuola the first Nigerian author to win international recognition and acclaim, even though he started writing because he was bored with little to do in his job as a messenger and could be considered "a writer almost by accident" (Lindfors 1970: 307). As a Nigerian correspondent for the *West Africa* magazine put it in a May 1 1954 profile of Tutuola, "To free his mind from the boredom of clock-watching he reverted to an almost forgotten childhood habit of story-telling" (reproduced in Lindfors 1975: 36; see also Eric Larrabee, reprinted in Lindfors 1975: 13).

Although Tutuola had wished that his prospective publisher "will correct my WRONG ENGLISH"[2] and even "alter the story itself if possible" (Lindfors 1999a: 117), Faber and Faber were hesitant to alter his English and story. In a letter to him, they said:

> ...we agree that your English is not always conventional English as written in this country, but for that very reason we think it would be a great pity to make it conform to all the rules of grammar and spelling. Just as no one but a West African could have had such a strange tale to tell, so your manner of writing it has a charm of its own. We propose therefore that our reader should go through the manuscript before it is set up in type, correcting what are evidently copying errors, accidental omissions, confusions or inconsistencies, but leaving intact all those expressions which, though strictly speaking erroneous, are more graphic than the correct expressions would be. You can depend upon it that we have the success of the book at heart, and we hope you will be content to leave the matter to our judgement. (Faber and Faber letter quoted in Lindfors 1999a: 118).

So Faber and Faber let pass Tutuola's "broken or Pidgin English" for which "He received a great deal of criticism from Nigerian literary critics" once his book was published (Achebe 2012: 113). In fact, Faber and Faber did not as much as change the title from "The Palm-Wine Drinkard" to "The Palm-Wine Drinker," preferring to leave as was, "one of the original words invented by the remarkable author." They also decided against an introduction to the book, preferring "to let it burst upon an astonished world unheralded and unrecommended" (Peter du Sautoy of Faber and Faber, quoted in Lindfors 1999a: 126). In a letter responding to an American editor at Norton publishers, who among many others had turned the book down when approached by Faber and Faber to consider an American edition, Peter du Sautoy wrote:

> We do, of course, realise that it [*The Palm-Wine Drinkard*] is not quite as good as it ought to be, but it is the unsophisticated product of a West African mind and we felt there was nothing to be done about it except leave it alone. When I say unsophisticated, that is not altogether true, since Tutuola has been to some extent influenced by at any rate the externals of Western civilisation. It seemed to us to be an interesting example of genuine African writing and worthwhile publishing on that account. Its interest is possibly more anthropological than literary, but, apart from being in the end a little tedious, it has got a certain quality

as a piece of unusual writing (Peter du Sautoy of Faber and Faber, quoted in Lindfors (1999a: 127).

In his review shortly after publication of *The Palm-Wine Drinkard*, Arthur Calder-Marshall hailed Faber and Faber's decision not to interfere editorially with Tutuola's text in the following words:

> The publishers have done well to avoid annotating this book as if it were merely an important anthropological document. They have resisted the temptation of commissioning a surrealist artist to illustrate, for example, Wife and Husband in the Hungry Creature's Stomach or the flight of the Red-people from the Red-town in the form of two red trees, all their leaves singing as human beings. They have left this strange, poetic, nightmare volume to seek for itself the staunch admirers it cannot fail to attract (Arthur Calder-Marshall, reprinted in Lindfors 1975: 10).

Whether or not it was the product of an unsophisticated West African mind as claimed by Peter du Sautoy above, publication of *The Palm-Wine Drinkard* in May 1952 was the beginning of a relationship of interdependence with Faber and Faber that would see Tutuola publish nine books with them before his death in 1997. Tutuola was well schooled in the humility occasioned by a deep understanding that in relationships of interconnection and interdependence one insists on the pursuit of completeness or absolute autonomy at one's risk and peril. In such relationships it is normal and accepted that borrowings for self-activation are what sociality and life are really about. It is normal, social, and indeed a sign of life and being alive that the Skull from the community of skulls, like a disembodied robot, borrows body parts to wear in order to rise to the status of "complete gentleman" in the eyes of the beautiful lady who had systematically turned down every suitor. Ordinarily living the life of a skull with little need for being anything else but a skull and then developing ambitions of completeness to conquer the beautiful lady enchanted with fantasies of perfection, means that the Skull has to acquire the technology it needs to take itself to that desired level of potency. Because debt and being indebted are part and parcel of life, the Skull is able to convince others to part with the body parts it needs temporarily to achieve its ends, and for a fee. Having body parts with minds of their own enhances one's chances as a hunter-gatherer of nimble-footed game and sustenance from the bush of infinite possibilities and offers one the opportunity to navigate, hunt and gather from diverse spaces. It is very convenient to live a life in which one is not always expected to act as a unified and singular being. One can strip down to the barest minimum for the barest life possible.

Tutuola was well ahead, in his thinking, of today's proliferation of transplanted body parts among humans and increasingly from animals to humans[3], prosthetics for lost body parts, as well as technologies of plastic surgery, cloning and genetical modifications of human and kindred creatures. Thanks to such technologies, Tutuola's readers today are better able to understand and relate to his ideas of being barely human, like the Skull, and working one's way to full, albeit not always necessarily, humanness, at least in terms of appearance. Today's technologies bring home better Tutuola's idea of a composite being that can inflate and deflate itself or himself or herself as need be, and whose reality is always incomplete viewed either from appearances alone or from content and consciousness entirely.

Like his barely human Skull, Tutuola, barely schooled in colonial education and its instances of legitimation, resorts to borrowing the English language of his colonisers to tell his tall Yoruba tales. Tutuola was considered a priori, as beneath human because of the perceived savageness of his mind and its primitive imagination by an African elite aspiring for full humanity by means of whitening up in the eyes of their European colonisers. Such Africans, keen to bleach themselves culturally till they were virtually white, felt that Tutuola was pulling them down and back to the status of bare or incomplete humanity of the dark caves of their dark continent that they were determined to escape.

In all three instances – the Skull, Tutuola, his Nigerian and African critic – it is evident that an autonomy or completeness that comes from borrowing is delusory. This is especially the case if one were gentleman enough to assume the responsibility of acknowledging and/or repaying the debt one owes others (even if only as a debt of gratitude for inspiration, instigation or encouragement) – in the manner the Skull returns and pays for the body parts and accoutrements he borrowed to activate his completeness as a gentleman in the eyes of those who beheld him. Tutuola, similarly, repeatedly acknowledges that his English is borrowed, and must not be mistaken for his message or used as a measure of his intelligence. Language to him is nothing more than a container, an envelope or a messenger, even if an active, lively and enlivening one. You dwell on it exclusively at the risk of losing out on the contents or the message. The story of the Skull and that of Tutuola's modest and humble attributes as a messenger, who had the audacity to tell his stories in a borrowed tongue he hardly mastered in speech and in writing, reminds us that being human is about being indebted and keeping an active memory of one's debts and of those to whom one is indebted. If one were absolutely to repay one's debts, one would have no pretensions whatsoever to lay any claim to being complete. Paying debts in quest of absolute freedom is like seeking to break the ties of sociality and relationships that make one part and parcel of a community. It amounts to a sort of decomposition, decoupling or deconglomeration of the socialness of being. Completeness as a permanent attribute of being is a total and, indeed, extravagant illusion. One is always, somehow, indebted to someone or something for being what one claims to be. To be is to be composite and a patchwork of conviviality seeking impurities.

Through the narrator and "brave hunter of the wild bush animals" (Tutuola 1981: 226) in *The Witch-Herbalist of the Remote Town* who sets out on a six-year risky journey to find a cure for his barren wife[4] from the "Witch-Herbalist who was also called the Omnipotent, Omnipresent and Omniscient Mother" (Tutuola 1981: 190)[5], and who [the narrator and brave hunter] is repeatedly deserted by two of his four partners and advisers – his "First Mind" and his "Second Mind"[6] – and had the habit of becoming powerless and "entirely paralysed with fear" (Tutuola 1981: 164) when confronted by danger[7], Tutuola urges his readers to accept imperfection as part of being human and being alive, and to privilege interdependence even when the pressure to seek absolute autonomy is overwhelming.

The Skull turned reversible complete gentleman is a cautionary tale to the effect that "Perfection is deadly, and *the will-to-perfection is a death drive* (it is, that is just what it turns out to be), and so it is paradoxically much better not to be Best, yes, thank God we have our flaws" (Rooney 2000: 85). No sooner does the memory of the narrator decide to judge, discipline and punish the First Mind and Second Mind for their failings, than their possessor realises that he cannot function without them, for:

> To sentence Mr First 'Mind' to death means to make one of the members of his Possessor's body incomplete. And to make one of the members of a body incomplete means that body will lose its true function and that may cause death to the possessor of the body. (Tutuola 1981: 276).

Similarly,

> If Mr Second 'Mind' will serve the term of six years' imprisonment, it means he has to stop the work which he is performing in the body of his Possessor for the period of six years. So as his Possessor will miss the work for that period, it may result even in death to him. (Tutuola 1981: 276).

Acknowledging, however reluctantly, that punishing the imperfect minds was not possible without punishing their possessor in equal measure, Mr. 'Memory' conceded, and the possessor was finally reunited with his two incompetent minds. And, "as soon as both my 'minds' and my 'memory' had returned to their respective positions in me, I was able to mind things, I could think and I could memorize things" (Tutuola 1981: 279). Interdependence does not require perfection. It requires recognising and learning to make do with and make the best of one's imperfections and the imperfections of those with whom one interacts. Here, Tutuola's position resonates with Sigmund Freud, who suggests that the very idea of society, culture and civilisation lies in a balance of tensions between individual aspirations towards personal happiness and the imperative to act in recognition of and in unity with the rest of humanity (Freud

1957). Freedom as completeness or independence in absolute terms is an absolute illusion.

Indeed, the Witch-Herbalist, portrayed as the closest being to perfection, derives the most satisfaction through her regular compassion and attention to the imperfections of the burdensome who travel from far and wide to consult and seek her assistance with their burdens. Of those who come to seek her assistance, there is "The Man with Eight Burdens," who would not give up despite his afflicted personal condition of being. Seen through the eyes of the narrator, when the Witch-Herbalist summoned this man to appear before her at the altar:

> ... it was a great pity that this man could not walk to the altar, because he was totally lame, the hump which was on his back or nape was as big as a mound. Again, there was a goitre on his neck which was just like a hillock. So both hump and goitre were a heavy load for him to lift himself up from the ground or floor. Not only that, big boils were all over his body and each was as big as the head of a child. His forehead was deeply dented so much that there was not any person who would like to look at it twice. Not only that, as well his nose was so compact that it was very hard for him to breathe in and out. So for this he had non-stop hiccups. More, he had one eye only, the other one had been totally blind for a number of years, and his body was also twisted.
>
> And the only one eye of this man had swelled out as when a big snail moves out from its shell. And this meant he had eight kinds of serious burdens: he was lame, he had a hump, goitre, boils, dented forehead, compact nose, non-stop hiccups and a twisted body. But No.9 burden which was 'one eye' was ruled out from being 'a serious burden'... (Tutuola 1981: 220-221).

Confessing to being "the son of evil-doers" did not stop the Witch-Herbalist from washing off the man's burdens with "vegetable decoction." As soon as this happened, "all the burdens of this man vanished immediately," and he "became a beautiful healthy gentleman," and he "was intoxicated with joy" (Tutuola 1981: 224-225).

In his introduction to the 2014 edition of *The Palm-Wine Drinkard*, Wole Soyinka observes that in Nigeria, "Amos Tutuola's first published novel was given short shrift," and that although the "hostile reception was not quite as uniform as some of the expatriate community (mostly British, and mostly academic) tried to suggest," the "general institutional attitude" to the novel and author "ranged between outright dismissal and condescension" (Soyinka 2014: v). Tutuola, especially since his death, has been described by some Nigerian writers, critics and scholars as a hero, a legend, a spellbinding visionary raconteur and a storytelling genius who fruitfully combined magic with realism in his highly imaginative, poetic, though as perceived by some grammatically limited, prose. Many of those praising Tutuola posthumously initially regarded him as "a dangerous barbarian," a disgrace to their modernist ambitions, and as someone who sought to undo their hard-earned achievements in the pursuit of Western civilisation by perpetuating conceptions of Africa as a dark continent and Nigerians as primitive peoples (Lindfors 1999b: 140).

Lindfors sums up the embarrassment felt by the Nigerian Western elite at the recognition Tutuola was receiving, especially following publication of his first two novels, thus:

> In the early nineteen-fifties such recognition must have been a great embarrassment as well, for educated Nigerians in their growing eagerness for political independence were becoming acutely conscious of their image abroad. They wanted to give an appearance of modernity, maturity, competence and sophistication, but the naïve fantasies of the Lagos messenger projected just the opposite image. Gerald Moore suggests that Tutuola aroused the antipathy of some of his countrymen by reminding them of a world from which they wanted to escape. To such readers Tutuola was a disgrace, a setback, a national calamity (Lindfors 1970: 331).

This was a charge Tutuola refuted. Asked by a journalist whether he was not concerned that people abroad might laugh at him for writing the way he did, Tutuola retorted:

Not at all. They know Nigerians are well-educated. They know Nigeria has so many educated people like Wole Soyinka, Chinua Achebe, Dr. Omotoso, Dr. Ogunbiyi and so forth. How could they because I am writing my own book be laughing at us and saying we don't know anything? Don't you see that is wrong?" (Tutuola interviewed by Mike Awoyinka, quoted in Lindfors 1999b: 143).

If Nigerians were so rigid and prescriptive that only the truly educated could write, Tutuola conjectured during an interview with Remi Adebiyi that "perhaps the reason why Nigerian government does not give me any honour or so is because of my education," regretting the fact that he was better known and accepted "in other countries than in my own country" (Tutuola in Remi Adebiyi, quoted in Lindfors 1999b: 144).

Fondly referred to by several journalists who had interviewed him as "Pa Tutuola," upon his death, Tutuola was now perceived to have transited into the role of "an honoured ancestor, an inspirational father figure to a whole generation of younger writers" (Lindfors 1999b: 135-144). Commenting on the upsurge of accolades with which Tutuola was showered following his death, Lindfors observes:

This posthumous praise-singing might have been music to Tutuola's ears had he been able to hear it, for at the outset of his career he had been subjected to abuse from Nigerian critics who felt embarrassed or annoyed by the kind of writing he did. His imperfect grasp of English, his obvious borrowing from Yoruba folktales, and his popularity in Europe and America as a naïve primitivist alienated the educated elite who dismissed his work as childish and unsophisticated. Some even accused him of plagiarizing Daniel Fagunwa's more polished 'phantasia novels' in Yoruba. It wasn't until the mid-1970s, when several prominent writers and critics (most notably Chinua Achebe) sought to reappraise his work, that Tutuola began to win a measure of respect at home. But in his later years he was virtually ignored by the indigenous literati, who perhaps viewed him as a cultural dinosaur, a throwback to an earlier era. (Lindfors 1999b: 136).

Reacting to repeated accusations levelled against Tutuola for heavily plagiarising Chief Daniel Olorunfemi Fagunwa's Yoruba language novels following publication of *The Palm-Wine Drinkard*, Stephanie Newell springs to his defence. She considers it "unfair" to accuse Tutuola of plagiarism, arguing that Tutuola's "transposition and translation of Fagunwa's material into an English format involved new and conscious decisions about content, language, and grammar, decisions which Fagunwa did not confront in the same way in his Yoruba-language work" (Newell 2006: 82). Indeed, as Newell puts it:

> Tutuola forced the English language to accommodate Yoruba syntax and subject matter alongside a multitude of clippings from English literary culture. In so doing he became a 'translator' in the most creative sense of the word, reworking Fagunwa's oral and folkloric material into English, as well as borrowing items from English literature, updating and embellishing Fagunwa's own models while also abandoning the older man's didactic Christian framework in favour of a more secular and amoral universe. Above all, then, *The Palm-Wine Drinkard* reveals the porosity and elasticity of Yoruba literature: in this confident and robust West African culture, oral and written genres are not pure, well-bounded forms but infinitely expandable rag-bags of innovations and multicultural borrowings (Newell 2006: 82).

To Newell therefore, far from being a plagiarist, Tutuola is an innovator who draws inspiration from Fagunwa and Yoruba folktales on familiar Yoruba themes and forms, and who is able to imbue "the borrowed material with his own special wit and style, updating his material to include contemporary references" (Newell 2006: 82-83). Harold Collins makes a similar argument in defence of Tutuola, arguing that complaints of plagiarism "are founded on an erroneous but widespread misconception of literary originality that equates it with novelty of theme, action, setting, and so on," and that ignores "the adapting, modifying, sophisticating, deepening, humanizing" and syncretism that Tutuola brings to bear on Yoruba folktales as a common possession of the Yoruba people (Harold R. Collins, reprinted in Lindfors 1975a[1961]: 63-64). As Nanna Schneidermann argues in relation to imitative musical performances among youth ("the karaoke generation") in Uganda, imitation, emulation, miming or copying are best understood as generative practices central for unfolding creativity and talent (Schneidermann 2014: 43-80).

Tutuola should thus be commended, argues Omolara Ogundipe-Leslie, for the use to which he has put "the genius of the Yoruba language." The greatness of Tutuola's works lies in his simple, bold or perhaps innocent ability to carry across "into his English prose the linguistic patterns and literary habits of his Yoruba language using English words as counters." Ogundipe-Leslie richly illustrates the extent to which in *The Palm-Wine Drinkard* Tutuola "is basically speaking Yoruba but using English words" (Ogundipe-Leslie 1975[1970]: 151). She draws our attention to the following example "the incantatory quality (sometimes responsible for Tutuola's breathless paragraph and sentence formations and punctuation), typical of Yoruba literary and linguistic habits:

> When I felt that these strings did not allow me to breathe and again every part of my body was bleeding too much, then I myself commanded the ropes of the yams in his garden to tight him there, and the yams in his garden to tight him there [sic], and the yam stakes should begin to beat him also. After I had said so and at the same time, all the ropes of the yams in his garden tightened him hardly, and all the yam stakes were beating him repeatedly, so when he (Death) saw that these stakes were beating him repeatedly, then he commanded the strings of the drum which tighted me to release me, and I was released at the same time. But when I saw that I was released, then I myself commanded the ropes of the yams to release him and the yam stakes ... (Tutuola 1952: 12-13, quoted in Ogundipe-Leslie 1975[1970]: 151)

A second example by Ogundipe-Leslie is of the "perculiar ring" of Tutuola's language, which, according to her, comes from "the use of Yoruba rhetoric and word-play; from the love of the word, the proverb and the gnomic saying" (Ogundipe-Leslie 1975[1970]: 151):

> My wife had said of the woman we met: 'She was not a human-being and she was not a spirit, but what was she?' She was the Red-smaller-

tree who was at the front of the bigger Red-tree, and the bigger Red-tree was the Red-king of the Red-people of the Red-town and the Red-bush and also the Red-leaves on the bigger Red-tree were the Red-people of the Red-town in the Red-bush.' (Tutuola 1952: 83, quoted in Ogundipe-Leslie 1975[1970]: 151)

In this way Tutuola, who "could never have been articulate in the Queen's English ... becomes fluent, even eloquent, in a language of his own making." By resorting to the habits of a Yoruba language with which he is familiar, Tutuola ably "overcomes the problem of linguistic alienation which plagues other Nigerian writers, some of whom have at first to wrestle with the English language, before they can begin to try to say what they mean" (Ogundipe-Leslie 1975[1970]: 151-153). Tutuola's Yoruba culture and language consciousness has, thanks to his open-minded disposition, reached out, acquired and domesticated an otherwise strange and foreign English language. Tutuola demonstrates that although "English is not Yoruba and Yoruba is not English… he will cheerfully use what he likes from each of them in the construction of his prose" (Tabron 2003: 38). In his quest to recognise and provide for interconnections and interdependence in lieu of zero-sum games of winner takes all, Tutuola opts rather to bring Yoruba and English into a conversation that is fruitful and enriching to him and the tasks he has at hand: tell his stories the way he sees fit, drawing unapologetically on his rich cultural repertoire as a man of many worlds, local and distant, Nigerian and foreign, African and beyond.

Other critics of Tutuola are firmer in their adamance. They subscribe to a hierarchy of purity in which creative license is strictly the preserve of those at the apex of linguistic excellence. It is their conviction that, to be creative in English, one must master it first, then, and only then, is one permitted artistic license with the language. They hesitate to credit Tutuola with intentional domestication of English. To them, such intentionality is only possible with postcolonial African writers whose mastery of the English language is second to none. Thus for them, if Wole Soyinka, for example – who, as Amos Tutuola himself acknowledges, "knows English like his mother tongue" and whose "writing is very beautiful"

(Tutuola, quoted in Tabron 2003: 37) – were to write the sort of English in *The Palm-Wine Drinkard*, that would truly qualify as intentional domestication. Put differently, there is something not quite right, rewarding ignorance with the benefits of creative appropriation, when the apparent creativity is quite simply the result of the writer not knowing any better. This is the point reiterated as recently as in 2013 by Leif Lorentzon, when he questions the celebration of Africanisation of English in Tutuola's writing. To Lorentzon, the "nativization" of English in *The Palm-Wine Drinkard* could not have been "intentional, as Tutuola did not have many years in school, and his English was full of flaws". If anything, it was an accidental domestication of the English language. As he puts it, "due to or thanks to – depending on how one appreciates the novel – [Tutuola's] poor schooling, has taken the nativization of English to its furthest extreme" (Lorentzon 2013: 304). Such insistence on complete mastery of English to qualify for poetic license in the language disqualifies any creativity short of that by the colonised or postcolonial elite whose anglophilia is not in question or to be questioned. It denies the unlettered incomplete masses any pretensions to the colonial language as a *lingua franca* on their own terms, even as they are claimed by that colonial language and its elected elite speakers and writers.

Notwithstanding the belated outpour of praise and lengthy editorials in national newspapers that graced Tutuola following his death, according to Charles Larson, Tutuola's "funeral was poorly attended and badly organised." Larson quotes Tunde Aremu, who attended the event, saying: "'For so great a man, at least in the world of the literati, his burial would be expected to serve as a meeting point by not only the clan of writers, but of lovers of words, critics and other patrons of the arts. However, he went away as anonymous as he lived.'" (Larson 2001: 23). His poorly attended and badly organised funeral should take nothing away from the fact that Tutuola, even as a "freak," had grown into "too sizable a freak to be ignored" in African literary circles, even by his detractors (Gerald Moore, reprinted in Lindfors 1975[1957]: 49). "Tutuola may have died, but what he left to the world lives on" (Lindfors 1999b: 140).

In view of a resurgence of nibbling at resilient colonialism in institutions of higher education across the continent (Nyamnjoh 2016; Gibson 2016; *Pax Academica* 2015), the equally compelling resilience of Tutuola and his universe deserves closer attention. He may have died physically, but like the heroes in his novels, he defies death and dying as absolutes. Like the palm-wine drinkard who says confidently, that his wife and he "could not die because we had sold our death away" (Tutuola 1952: 106) "before entering inside the white tree of the Faithful-Mother" (Tutuola 1952: 107), Tutuola can be confident that by daring to write the way he did, about what he wrote, and not relenting until he had found a publisher for his stories, he has succeeded in living on even as death – in the manner of the "hungry-creature" who was insatiable "did not stop crying 'hungry-hungry-hungry' and delighted in swallowing his victims whole (Tutuola 1952: 107-109) – might claim to have had him. In *The Wild Hunter in the Bush of the Ghosts*, the Wild Hunter encounters another ghost who "was so greedy for food that he could not go for even a second without eating something." The ghost is so desperate to have him for his dinner, that it immediately "began to scrape my body with his thick tongue, which was as sharp as sandpaper," and "Within a few minutes every part of my body was bleeding as if somebody had dragged me on rough ground" (Tutuola 1989[1982]: 41). The spirit of Tutuola's creative imagination is firmly with his readers, ready as ever, to activate them to the levels of potency they desire and to which they aspire, in the interest of divining and providing for a system of education that is truly inclusive of popular traditions of meaning making, knowledge production, being and becoming (active existence).

It is not without significance that the publisher Faber and Faber turned to "Daryll Forde, a renowned Africanist teaching in the Department of Anthropology at University College, London," as "an anthropologist familiar with the workings of the West African imagination" (Lindfors1999a: 116), for an opinion on whether Tutuola's manuscript – *The Palm-Wine Drinkard* – had "its roots in the common West African mind" (Lindfors 1999a: 116), often assumed to be savage, primitive and lacking in complexity and systematic thought (Levi-Strauss 1966). Two other anthropologists

– Mary Danielli and the Rev. Dr. Geoffrey Parrinder – also evaluated and recommended publication of Tutuola's second book, *My Life in the Bush of Ghosts*, to which Parrinder contributed an introduction (V. S. Pritchett, reprinted in Lindfors 1975: 21; Lindfors 1999a: 127). Parrinder is quoted to have said that Tutuola's stories were "genuine African myths, such as are told in countless villages round the fire or in the tropical moonlight" (Parrinder, quoted in Eric Robinson, reprinted in Lindfors 1975: 29). While according to Lindfors:

> It is perhaps significant that the decision to publish 'My Life in the Bush of Ghosts' came not long after George Braziller had bought the American rights to The Palm-Wine Drinkard for his newly formed Book Find Club and then had quickly resold them to Grove Press, who were very eager to publish more material by Tutuola and were pressing Faber and Faber to send them a copy of the typescript of 'My Life in the Bush of Ghosts' (Lindfors 1999a: 128-129).

Whether or not Faber and Faber turned to anthropologists because the books were "the unsophisticated product of a West African mind," or because "its interest is possibly more anthropological than literary," it was evident to them that the books were quite unconventional (Lindfors 1999a: 127). If the post-publication reviews of *The Palm-Wine Drinkard* and *My Life in the Bush of Ghosts* are anything to go by (see Lindfors 1975: 1-44 for some), what Western readers were looking for in an African mind were, among other things, evidence of a fantastic primitive possessed of an imagination increasingly jeopardised by Western civilisation – a mind that served as a window or mirror to the complete gentlemen and super lady ghostesses of the West, to see how far they had evolved away from their primitive origins, childlike fantasies, simple, unsophisticated and superstitious forebears (Tabron 2003: 43-53). It was commonplace then, and still very much is in the 21st century, for Africans to be "infantilised" and "almost invariably portrayed as childlike" and as "afflicted by an absence, a *lack* of the qualities that characterised the adult white male ideal of European civilization," thus ensuring that attitudes towards Africans "remained condescending" even at their "most sympathetic" (Comaroff and Comaroff 1997b: 117).

As summed up in *The Times Literary Supplement* review of Tutuola's *Feather Woman of the Jungle* – a review which regretted Tutuola's departure away from the "African mind" of his first two novels – , an African mind in the imperial and colonising eyes of the reviewer is ultimately a mind that does not respond to changing times, but that must stay faithful to the primitive savagery badly needed for the colonial project to imagine and re-imagine itself through a mythical, contrived and linear past. It is a mind entirely defined and confined by the prescriptive gaze of the colonialists, a mind that must disabuse itself of any illusions and delusions of self-fulfilment. An excerpt of the review reads:

> There had been nothing quite like them before, and the strangeness of the African subject matter, the primary colours, the mixture of sophistication, superstition, and primitivism, and above all the incantatory juggling with the English language combined to dazzle and intoxicate. Novelty-seekers, propagandists for the coloured races, professional rooters for the avant-garde-any avant-garde, anywhere and at any time—were alike delighted, and none more vociferously than the thinning ranks of the Apocalypse. (*The Times Literary Supplement*, quoted in Lindfors 1970: 332).

As far back as the early 1950s, the publisher Faber and Faber was perceptive enough to see anthropology in literature and literature in anthropology, an interconnection many an anthropologist in and of Africa is still, nearly a century later, rather reluctant to acknowledge (Nyamnjoh 2011, 2012a, 2012b, 2013a), determinedly invested in the illusory fundamentalist and evangelical games of disciplinary completeness and purity as they are. Many an anthropologist of Africa seem reluctant to disabuse themselves of the fixation with the idea that ethnography is a particular type of representation that can and should be distinguished from other representations, fiction in particular, and to be recognised specifically as the product of professional anthropologists, who, incidentally, happen to be predominantly European and North-

African. A consequence of such rigidity in West Africa, for example, was that until recently, relatively little of the ethnography of the region was written by West Africans, who took refuge from what they perceived as a racist anthropology, in disciplines such as history, sociology and philosophy (Davies and Fardon 1991). As Catherine Davies and Richard Fardon have observed, although the implications of this state of affairs was that "Representations of local forms of society from the village community to the street life of the new cities had to be sought in 'imaginative' rather than 'ethnographic' literature," the rigid "distinction in genre" meant that the "implications of this counter-literature for ethnography could be ignored." Anthropologists of the region insisted that novels should be "understood to be extended prose fiction and ethnographies extended prose facts," and that "the conventions appropriate to them differed" (Davies and Fardon 1991: 128). Yet, a closer look at debates among anthropologists would suggest that not that many anthropologists are that interested in an overly objective discipline that pays little attention to subjectivities; they frown on the idea of being merely a science, *à la* Napoleon Chagnon (Nyamnjoh 2015a).

The debate on literature as ethnography has come a long way (Baxter and Fardon 1991; Davies and Fardon 1991; Gupta and Ferguson 1997: 30-31; Harrison 2008: 109-133). Today, it is less a question of choosing between ethnography and fiction, and more a question of exploring the extent to which both are mutually enriching and complementary (Nyamnjoh 2011, 2012b). Thus, if one is interested to establish observable and measurable causation, make generalisations, explore processes of change and detect regularities in human life, a science that explains is needed much more than one which simply interprets. Many a social scientist are seldom able to establish direct causal relationships, often settling for correlations and representations informed by interpretations that are open to conversations with competing and complementary perspectives (Hall 1997). This is especially true of anthropology where the scientificity of ethnography is often more claimed than authenticated (Clifford and Marcus 1986, Clifford 1988: 21-54). If ethnography is less an explanatory than an interpretive science, it stands to benefit from being open to dialogue with other interpretations of the reality it seeks to represent (Collins and Gallinat 2010). Ethnography, as a way of recording human cultures and as a research method within anthropology, by its very nature draws on fiction (Gupta and Ferguson 1997: 29-32), and has much in common with fiction in that it is fashioned from already fashioned accounts (Geertz 2000[1973]: 15, Clifford 1988, 2003; Nyamnjoh 2011, 2012b).

In light of the ease with which ideology colludes with science in the production of ethnographies, a number of anthropologists have been preoccupied with what ethnography and fiction have in common, and how fiction could be summoned to complement ethnography in the interest of a more rounded understanding of social reality. Even Malinowski, the founding father of ethnography (participant observation or deep hanging out) and an avid consumer of fiction in the field, saw himself as a possible "Joseph Conrad of anthropology" (Gupta and Ferguson 1997: 30-31). In the twenty-first century, ethnographic fiction or "anthropological novels" may have a role in revealing the "fiction" behind multiple forms of discourses of dominance and equality, and in bending ears to hear the voices of "others" in ways that complement anthropological representations. This requires on the part of anthropologists humility and accommodation that is often hard to find among those quick to dangle claims of being or carrying themselves as though they were all rational, logical and scientific in their everyday practices and professional interactions. If undertaken by anthropologists, ethnographic fiction can indeed provide opportunities for greater involvement in "Thick Description" (Geertz 2000[1973]) and for getting away from touches of superiority that often slip into scholarly publications. Writers of fiction such as Amos Tutuola can communicate in metaphors, implying things rather than spelling them out, leaving the reader to fill in the gaps using assumptions drawn from a shared humanity. In ethnography, use of metaphors is limited as ethnographers are required to lead their audience logical step by logical step, leaving little to the imagination, not even the indescribably human (Jacobson 1991). This is all the more reason why the anthropologist, compared to Tutuola's Skull, would be more successful by acknowledging and borrowing the missing depth and metaphorical dimensions of being human and social from the writer of fiction in the context of their fieldwork, so they could qualify to lay claim to the status of a "complete gentleman" of the intellect and academy. Additionally, ethnographic novels may provide more space and scope to tackle ethical concerns with greater complexity and nuance, given that "moral judgement in the field is less a simple minded application of ethical verities than a constant, evolving negotiation of responsibility with all those involved" (MacClancy and Fuentes 2011: 10).

An encouraging number of prominent anthropologists and literary scholars are embracing the complementarity between fiction and ethnography as modes of knowledge production and communicating the human and the social (Elenore Smith Bowen [*nom de plume* of Laura Bohannan] 1964; Stoller 1989, 1997, 2002, 2008, 2016; Stoller and Olkes 1987; Barber 1991, 1995, 1997, 2008; Cruikshank 1998; Rooney 2000; Peel 2002; Newell 1996, 2006; Meyer 2003, 2006, 2009, 2010, 2015; Meyer and Moors 2006; Newell and Okome 2013; Sullivan 2006; Maynard and Cahnmann-Taylor 2010; Englund 2011, 2015a, 2015b; van Beek 2017). However, consciously navigating between fiction and anthropology and working collaboratively with storytellers in framing and theorising the social in contemporary scholarship (Cruikshank 1998) are yet to gain legitimacy and popularity in the study of Africa, where disciplinary fundamentalism continues to pay lip service to inter-, multi-, cross- and trans-disciplinary conversations and common initiatives. Such rigid disciplinary boundaries take attention away from ongoing scholarly creativity in Africa and denies students of anthropology the opportunity of exposure to the creative effervescence of socially perceptive and imaginative writers such as Amos Tutuola.

I have in the last 20 years taken up writing novels based on ethnographic insights, fed by my intellectual curiosity, research and everyday experiences of living and working in different parts of the continent of Africa. I have done so in addition to my more formal scholarly writing out of a need to discuss research in a much more complex and nuanced manner than is usually possible in disciplinary writing. More importantly, I have been driven by a desire to take the discussion of research beyond the ivory tower, to the very people whose daily predicaments are at the heart of scholarly work and in my fiction. These are the very same Africans whose marginalised and endangered life stories and lived realities under colonialism and its pretensions of cultural completeness fuelled Amos Tutuola's determination to seek representation and preservation for them in the little colonial English that was available to him at the time, refusing to be deterred by his lack of mastery of that language of power. Not even the din of accelerated and intensified ridicule by his fellow countrymen and Africans was enough to deter him from telling the stories of the continued relevance of an Africa condemned to a prehistoric past by a colonising Eurocentric modernity.

The myth of distinction between novels as "extended prose fiction" and ethnographies as "extended prose facts" highlighted by Davies and Fardon (1991: 128) in their paper on West African fiction and representation of the cultures of the region continues to be perpetuated, even as Fardon refuses to give up on highlighting the commonalities and interconnections between fiction and ethnography. Let me take this opportunity to commend the exemplary collaboration between British anthropologist Richard Fardon and French artist Sènga la Rouge (who provides artistic drawings as illustrations) around the ethnographic value of Ousmane Sembene's *Xala* or "The Curse of Impotence," a film produced in 1974, inspired by a novella by the same author, published in 1973 under the same title. The novella, as Fardon later discovered as his interest in an ethnographic reading of the film grew, "was itself based on a screenplay, or at least film treatment, written while Sembene sought the financial backing to put the film into production" (Fardon and la Rouge 2017: 12). Sembene himself, a Wolof speaking Senegalese, saw his novella, originally published in French and subsequently translated into English, and the film it inspired or that the idea of which initially inspired it as complementary and mutually enhancing his desire to reach as many audiences with his message as possible. Far from the film supplanting the novella or vice versa, Fardon sees more of an "iterative" or supplementary relationship between the two, especially in light of the fact that the "screenplay and novella were successively revised versions of one another" (Fardon and la Rouge 2017: 13). Fardon, who believes that *Xala* has something to teach his anthropology students about West African cultures and societies, and who has over the years used West African films and fiction to teach the ethnography of the region, highlights a core value of Ousmane Sembene's *Xala* as novella and film to anthropology as follows:

> Treating these two versions anthropologically, as cultural products, should have involved my contextualizing both rather than evaluating one as a more or less authentic expression of an authorial intention than the other. If I asked students to suspend disbelief in Sembene's story and characters and treat them as they might episodes and actors in an ethnographer's description, then I ought to follow this thought consistently myself. There is nothing odd in the ethnographic record about there being a pair of descriptions of the same social circumstances: one more curious about family, kinship and the networks of connections between people, the other covering much of the same ground from a narrower political viewpoint. Anthropologists have often written complementary accounts of kinship and politics (whether in the same or different books), and their readers have asked themselves whether the two perspectives fitted together without obvious contradictions. To my mind, the two versions of Xala can be treated similarly, as largely complementary ethnographies of an imagined social network in Senegal, or more narrowly its capital Dakar, in the aftermath of formal Independence from France in 1960. They do not have to be read this way, and this reading does not preclude any other, but as a 'realist project,' consistent with Sembene's Marxism, or even a 'neo-realist project,' indebted to Italian post-war cinema, Xala – in both its versions – lends itself to such a reading (Fardon and la Rouge 2017: 15-16).

What an ethnographic study of Sembene's *Xala* – as film and novella taken together –, contributes to anthropology, Fardon observes, is the need to recognise that,

> ...interpretation of different genres of locally-grounded writings can pose similar challenges: both ethnographic accounts and socially aware fictions are based on the selective and artful re-presentation of actors and events. They may not be the same, but we can still bring some of

the same techniques and curiosities to reading them (Fardon and le Rouge 2017: 17).

In this collaborative endeavour on Ousmane Sembene's phenomenal capacity to mobilise his creativity to build bridges across apparently different artistic forms, traditions and civilisations, Richard Fardon points us in the direction of the sort of creative renewal badly needed in African and Africanist anthropology – frontier conversations across disciplines and with interlocutors outside of the academy – to capture the intricacies and nuanced complexities of Africa and Africans. This is in tune with an earlier observation by Davies and Fardon, that, in "West African imaginative writing," the "biographical, historical and experiential sources of African creative literature are so richly articulated… that European evocations of African otherness might seem superfluous" (Davies and Fardon 1991: 145). Not to recognise the interconnections and interdependencies between fiction and ethnography is, like the confusionist and his victims in Tutuola's *Pauper, Brawler and Slanderer*, to insist on an exclusionary sociality that excels at the circulation of confusion, in a stubborn quest for coherence, purity and determinacy in social life in Africa and the social life of Africans (Guyer 2015a, 2015b). To think, write and speak about social categories and identities in Africa with scant regard to the lived realities of Africans in a flexible and truly inclusive manner is to be as guilty as Tutuola's Slanderer or confusionist, "the man who says whatever comes into his mind, whether accurate or not, resulting in all kinds of mismatches between the word and the world" (Guyer 2015b: 2). To study and represent Africa in a way ordinary Africans would recognise is to cultivate an intellectual predisposition to see the familiar in unlikely places and the strange in familiar circles. For, as Chinua Achebe cautions in his novel *Arrow of God*, "The world is like a mask dancing. If you want to see it well you do not stand in one place" (Achebe 1974[1964]: 46). In a subsequent essay, Achebe elaborates:

> What makes the dance and the masquerade so satisfying to the Igbo disposition is, I think, their artistic deployment of motion, of

agility, which informs the Igbo concept of existence. The masquerade (which is really an elaborated dance) not only moves spectacularly but those who want to enjoy its motion fully must follow its progress up and down the arena. This seemingly minor observation was nonetheless esteemed important enough by the Igbo to be elevated into a proverb of general application: *Ada-akwu ofu ebe enene mmuo*, 'You do not stand in one place to watch a masquerade.' You must imitate its motion (Achebe 1988: 65).

Bringing genres into conversation the way Richard Fardon does through Ousmane Sembene's *Xala* is especially important for anthropology, which remains very unpopular with African scholars (Harrison 2008:1–59; Magubane 1971; Mafeje 1998). It is yet to embrace in a serious manner the sort of decolonisation of the mind and gaze in which African writers and filmmakers have taken a commanding lead (Ngugi wa Thiong'o 1986; Barber et al. 1997; Barlet 2000[1996]; Murphy 2000; Jeyifo 2002; Plastow 2002; Gugler 2003; Tcheuyap 2005, 2011; Meyer 2015). Ethnographic research by Africans has been channelled through the outlets of other, purportedly less tainted disciplines such as African literature, African history, African religion and theology, and African philosophy.

Fiction is one of the most common vehicles used by African intellectuals to document and share "insider" accounts of their subjectivities and societies (Soyinka 1976; Fouet and Renaudeau 1976, 1980; Wren 1980; Davies and Fardon 1991; Irele 2001; Barber 1995, 1997, 2008; Rooney 2000; Newell 1996, 2006, 2017; Losambe 2005; Newell and Okome 2013; Sullivan 2006; Okolo 2007; Adebanwi 2014b; Guyer 2015a, 2015b; Fardon and la Rouge 2017), and one only needs to take a look at the titles under "The African Writers Series" by Heinemann Educational Books (Currey 2008; Achebe 2008, 2012: 52-62; Kamau and Mitambo 2016) to fathom the ethnographic richness of such production.

Indeed, one of the best "anthropological" representations of Africans' simultaneous disenchantment and fascination with colonial education and the lifestyles of sheepish mimicry and whitening up it inspired is the late Okot p'Bitek's epic poem *Song of Lawino*, to which I have referred several times already. It was first published as an

English translation from Acholi language in 1966 by East African Publisher House, and subsequently as part of the Heinemann series (Currey 2008: 88). Initially trained as an anthropologist, on his return to Uganda from the United Kingdom, p'Bitek used fiction to question the misrepresentations induced by colonial education in Africa (Pido 1997). His is a very popular text in universities across Africa, read by students of African literature, who are reluctant to embrace anthropology. But it is not a popular reading in anthropology because of its label as fiction (Nyamnjoh 2011, 2012a, 2012b).

Wale Adebanwi, in his introduction to a special issue of the *Journal of Contemporary African Studies* devoted to "the writer as social thinker" in Africa, laments the fact that "African literature has been largely ignored by students of social thought and social theory in Africa, even though social theory in Africa has received significant, if insufficient, attention from students of African literature." Even when recognised by social scientists, he argues, "a gap persists in the engagement of scholars with the works of African writers as important conveyors of intellectually elevated and elevating classic formulations." Adebanwi's special issue comprises five essays, in addition to his introduction, all seeking to make the case for greater conversation of a social theoretical nature across literature and social science on what it means to be African and human in and from Africa (Adebanwi 2014b: 407). His argument is echoed and substantiated by the various contributors to the special issue. For instance, Shiera el-Malik explores how Bessie Head's writings challenge "epistemic totalitarianism" (el-Malik 2014), while Melissa Myambo draws ontological and epistemological insights from the writings of Chinua Achebe, Ousmane Sembene and Zakes Mda (Myambo 2014), both in a manner pertinent to current clamours for decolonisation, endogenisation and contextualisation of university education on the continent. None of the contributions is on Amos Tutuola, despite his pioneering role in African literature and the epistemological relevance of his writings to thinking, researching and teaching social theory in Africa.

Most of the works of first-generation African colonial and postcolonial-period novelists constitute rich ethnographic accounts that require systematic reinterpretation to challenge the Eurocentric liberal anthropological accounts of their contemporaries (Soyinka 1976; Wren 1980; Davies and Fardon 1991; Irele 2001; Barber 1995, 1997, 2008; Rooney 2000; Newell 1996, 2006, 2017; Losambe 2005; Newell and Okome 2013; Sullivan 2006; Okolo 2007; Adebanwi 2014b; Guyer 20015a, 2015b; Fardon and la Rouge 2017). Even as liberal anthropology has championed the cause of the "native," to many an African intellectual it appears to have succeeded mostly in *talking at, talking on, and talking past but hardly talking to or with* the very Africans whose interests it purports to represent (Gupta and Ferguson 1997: 19–32; Magubane 1971; Mafeje 1998). Talking back, African scholars have denounced anthropology for its radical alterity and for talking without listening (Depelchin 2005; Harrison 2008; Mafeje 1998; Ntarangwi 2010; Ntarangwi et al. 2006; Nyamnjoh 2012a, 2013b, 2015a).

Those who openly identify with anthropology tend either to uncritically internalize discourses and debates that bring them international recognition but little local relevance or, in the manner of colonial anthropologists, rush to study their home villages as sacred, bounded entities and focus on social problems in a narrow and often insular manner (Ntarangwi et al. 2006), and with scant regard to the epistemological import of the Tutuola-like dimensions of the societies and communities they study. Some African ethnographers have identified with sociology and social history in an effort to distance themselves from anthropology (Magubane 1971, 2010; Adesina 2008; Mafeje 1998; Magubane 2000: 1–36; Osha 2013). The worry is that distancing themselves from anthropology has only taken them further away from the world of Amos Tutuola, a world that tends to be overly caricatured by micro, positivist sociologisation with its conventional and standardised recipes of objectivation and Cartesian rationalism. These concerns inform what Achille Mbembe has provocatively described as "African modes of self-writing" (Mbembe 2002), a form of articulation steeped in nativism and parochialism that keeps the continent tunnelled in the darkness of regressionism even as cosmopolitanism as a global recipe and nascent afropolitanism are celebrated (Mbembe 2010, 2013a; Balakrishnan and Mbembe 2016). Whether among anthropologists or sociologists,

Tutuola's world of nuanced complexities and interconnections is given a raw deal, as African sociologists and anthropologists are yet to radically interrogate the colonial and colonising registers and conceptual frameworks that continue to underpin their practice.

The perpetual ignoring of the likes of Tutuola aside, ethnographic accounts of Africa by Africans continue to be "invisible" in conventional anthropological circles. In opting to interpret Tutuola's writings as ethnographic accounts, I am making the case that it is possible to marry ethnography and fiction and that this was certainly an option for African intellectuals who found their realities misrepresented by the Joseph Conrads of fiction (Achebe 2000, 2012: 52-62) and anthropologists alike (Ferguson 2006; Sharp 2008; Wolfe 1999), even if this option was not always explored to satisfactory ends. Both misrepresentations could pass for what Chinua Achebe has described as "malignant fictions," which, unlike "literary fiction" or "beneficent fiction," tend to "assert their fictions as a proven fact and a way of life." To Achebe, while beneficent or literary fiction operates within the bounds of imagination, malignant fiction or superstition breaks the bounds and ravages the real world with its prejudices and presuppositions paraded as truths (Achebe 1988[1990]: 148-149). As writers, African intellectuals wanted the freedom to "write back" to the West in an attempt "to reshape the dialogue between the colonised and the coloniser" (Achebe 2012: 55; see also Currey 2008). They write, in the words of Chinua Achebe, "to help my society regain belief in itself and put away the complexes of the years of denigration and self-abasement" (Achebe 1988: 44). He writes, in other words, to teach his African readers "that their past – with all its imperfections – was not one long night of savagery from which the first Europeans acting on God's behalf delivered them" (Achebe 1988: 45).

Even then, African intellectuals have not often been in a position to write back on equal terms with non-Africans within the dominant colonial, postcolonial, and neoliberal political economy of knowledge production (Mkandawire 1997; Nyamnjoh 2004; Zeleza 1997; Lauer and Anyidoho 2012a, 2012b; Ndlovu-Gatsheni 2013a, 2013b). Under this logic of knowledge production shaped by and in turn shaping a hierarchy of purity (Amin 2004, 2009[1988]; Canagarajah 2002;

Connell 2007; Gareau 1987; Willems 2014), anthropologists at the centre enjoy a glorification that licenses them to ignore with impunity the work of their colleagues at the periphery (Gupta and Ferguson 1997: 27). What is recognised as knowledge is very much a function of the power to define and prescribe (Bourdieu 2004: 18–21; Canagarajah 2002). And should it surprise anyone that disciplinary debates are markedly uneven across physical and social geographies (Harrison 2008; Ntarangwi 2010), and across gender, class, generational, ethnic and racial divides?

Outside Africa, anthropologists are bound to be surprised by the resilience among their African colleagues of the handmaiden image of their discipline, even as, in their own debates, attention has since moved on from colonialism and colonial anthropology. They are familiar with and relish the plethora of work by mostly young (Western) Africanist anthropologists that unsettles earlier notions of bounded cultures. They are often perplexed when their African counterparts continue to delight in flogging a dead horse, an issue for over 40 years in Africa and beyond. The test of the theoretical pudding being in the practical eating, African scholars have yet to find enough ethnographic evidence to confirm the end of colonial anthropology and the logic of a world bounded by hierarchies of race, place, culture, class, gender, and generation. Proof of this is in the very fact of the uncritical internalisation of the methods, concepts and epistemological assumptions of liberal anthropology by the complaining Africans. The flexible political, cultural, and disciplinary identities they crave are not always easy to come by, as their intellectual and physical mobility continues to be policed, even as the rhetoric of the discipline at large celebrates globalization, postmodernism, inter-, multi- and trans-disciplinarity (Nyamnjoh 2012a, 2012c, 2013b, 2015a).

I embrace recent attempts to deprovincialise or decolonise Africanist anthropology by focusing on those who travel beyond the continent's borders. I also seek to draw attention to what the persistence of the handmaiden label points to the entrenchment of the perception, even among young African scholars, that today's anthropology is still largely "colonialist" and that, between African scholars and scholars of Africa, knowledge production and consumption are still bounded by hierarchies of various types. Inviting colleagues to a conversation on the ethnographic relevance of Tutuola's work is one way of re-inventing anthropology in Africa around his core epistemological contribution on incompleteness.

In this connection, I am gratified by accounts such as the following by Caroline Rooney, who compares Tutuola's narrator in the *Palm-Wine Drinkard* (and all the other books, I may add) to an ethnologist or a philosopher. Rooney writes:

> I would suggest that the narrator is like an amateur ethnologist and natural philosopher who, in traversing a worldly but unfamiliar terrain, comes across peoples, species, events and stories that he encounters in a startling manner for the first time. In other words, he encounters other beings and ways of life in the world that are foreign to him. In these encounters no presuppositions are entertained and the hero does not project his own cultural beliefs onto what he encounters, although the text is also a self-reflective one as regards the higher knowledge, including an ethical consciousness, as well as the survival tactics gained from the encounters. As regards the empirical nature of the text, the bizarre – the alien – is presented to us in a factual way with, also, very frequent factual references to the coordinates of time, space, size, speed, and so on (Rooney 2000: 82).

Equally pertinent to his ethnographic credentials is "Tutuola's constantly dramatised fascination with the other, the *stranger*," which "makes it difficult to charge his work with a cultural conservatism" (Rooney 2000: 119). Tutuola's quest-heroes are in many regards composite strangers, in their capacity to take the inside out and bring the outside in, as well as in their never ending, light-footed and open-minded quest to enhance themselves with jujus and the potent things – material, ideas and practices – of the strange people and strange creatures they encounter in the course of their journeys of a thousand dangers away from and back to their hometowns. In Tutuola's universe, the stranger is someone familiar, whom one recognises as having something one would like to acquire to enhance oneself as well as one's actions and interactions. Through his quest-heroes as border crossing strangers, Tutuola exposes a desire to bring the stranger in, and to make the stranger part and parcel of one's being – an attribute common to humans and non-humans alike. Tutuola constantly seems to be telling his readers, to look for the stranger activator in the nearby bush whenever they come across someone flexing their muscles and beating their chest at the crossroads, known as *orita* in Yoruba.

Despite these possibilities for anthropology in Africa to entertain enriching conversations and perspectives from kindred disciplines such as literature – disciplines that have found greater suffrage among Africans disillusioned by conventional liberal anthropology – anthropologists on the continent do not seem in a hurry to embrace frontier dispositions and practices. In post-apartheid South Africa, where anthropology has purportedly had the most success as a discipline (and where, paradoxically, apartheid racial categories of "white," "black," and "coloured" are just as resilient within academia as outside it), these concerns are evident, judging from an article by two "black" South African anthropologists highlighting inequalities and politicised relations within and between anthropology departments and contesting the idea of a single South African anthropology (Petrus and Bogopa 2009) and from the responses it elicited (Becker 2009; Owen 2009; van der Waal 2009). In another context, Mpilo Pearl Sithole, another "black" South African anthropologist, who holds a PhD from the University of Cambridge and was associate professor at the University of KwaZulu Natal in Durban at the time of publication of her book, complained about the domination of the peer-review process in South Africa "by scholars allied to Western models of knowledge production, who use their 'gateway' positions to marginalise and discourage African schools of thought" (2009: cover blurb). When in 2012 I initiated a debate that in hindsight would have given anthropologists in South Africa an early start on attending to the current clamours for a decolonised and transformed university education – which intensified with the #RhodesMustFall and #FeesMustFall protests of 2015/2016 (Gibson 2016; Nyamnjoh 2016) – some of the responses I got from some colleagues both formally and informally were most reactionary and ludicrously defensive (Nyamnjoh 2012a, 2012c, 2013b; Niehaus

2013; Hartnack 2013; Teppo 2013; Gordon 2013; Warnier 2013a; Osha 2013).

Lest such concerns simply be dismissed as those of black South Africans wanting to be published, promoted and facilitated in their scholarship and academic life merely because they are black, they echo larger regional and global debates on the politics of knowledge production and consumption (Amin 2004, 2009[1988]; Canagarajah 2002; Connell 2007; Gareau 1987; Harrison 2008; Ntarangwi 2010; Nyamnjoh 2004; Zeleza 1997). Equally debated in South African anthropology are competing, conflicting notions of indigeneity and ways of knowing (Green 2009; Odora Hoppers 2002). Although largely abreast of the latest theoretical trends on reflexivity and despatialisation of difference within anthropology, the dominant "white" South African anthropologists have yet to reconstruct in any remarkable way their anthropological subject or their tendency to head for the "black" and "coloured" areas, even as their teaching and writing might decry "essentialism," "radical alterity," "exoticisation," "romanticisation," and "spatialisation of difference."

Yet, as a popular proverb with African intellectuals says, "Until the lions produce their own historian, the story of the hunt will glorify only the hunter" (Achebe 2000: 73). Only when the lions and lionesses of Africa, as hunted and hunters, give their own accounts of the hunt – like the young Nigerian writer Chimamanda Ngozi Adichie's (2009) "headstrong historian" – will the study of Africa avoid what Adichie has termed "the dangers of a single story" (TED Conferences 2009), in which African hunters are inferiorised, criminalised and eliminated from the hunting scene as "poachers" by colonialists who seek to legitimate themselves as the exclusive bona fide hunters (Steinhart 2006). Until then, African scholars will continue to be more like "outsiders within," clamouring for a "reworking" of their disciplines structured in the image of dominant lone-ranger, colonising white males of Europe and North America (Harrison 2008). Even then, it is only by glimpsing the truth of the hunt from a variety of perspectives that we are able to comprehend the complexities and ambiguities of hunting and being hunted as a game of violence and violation, over which no one, however deluded, can claim to have the last word (Lindfors 1999d; Nyamnjoh 2012a).

In the game of life as with the hunt, conversations and comparison across different actors and perspectives are indeed in order. As Amos Tutuola teaches us in *The Wild Hunter in the Bush of the Ghosts*, if lions were allowed the freedom and voice to tell their story from the standpoint of their experiences, they would not only complement the account of the hunt, but come to the hunter's rescue, especially for those who hunt across borders. Imprisoned in the lion's den by the one-legged ghost, in the hope that the lions would eat him up, the hunter is spared by the lions, because, as the lions explain:

> We must not kill or eat him, because whenever we went to his town for animals and did not find any, we used to turn overselves into men and go to this hunter's house. He always treated us well. When it was dark, he allowed us to sleep in his house till the following day. He is a hunter, and we ourselves are hunters. Hunters must never kill other hunters! (Tutuola 1989[1982]: 10).

To reiterate, ethnography, as a way of recording human cultures and as a research method within anthropology, by its very nature draws on fiction (Baxter and Fardon 1991; Davies and Fardon 1991; Gupta and Ferguson 1997; Fardon 2017). Ethnography is fashioned from already fashioned accounts (Clifford 1988, 2003; Geertz 2000[1973]; Harrison 2008) just as fiction is in Africa (Davies and Fardon 1991; Barber 1997; Newell 1996, 2006; Losambe 2005; Newell and Okome 2013; Sullivan 2006; Fardon 2017). This similarity and kindredness reiterates the need for active recognition by anthropologists and literary scholars of the conviviality between fiction and ethnography in the study of Africa, and calls for greater interaction and collaboration between African and Africanist anthropologists in the manner, perhaps inadvertently, suggested by Faber and Faber when they sought the opinion of English anthropologists in the publication of an African novel on which I am leaning currently to make a case for fiction as ethnography.

Faber and Faber, a publisher created in 1929 that credits itself with a "peerless history," publishing "the best" and "keeping standards at the very highest level" (Connolly 2009: xi) and that could easily pass for a patron saint for desperate cases in view of its track record as a "high-brow" publisher in literature (Gerald Moore, reprinted in Lindfors 1975[1957]: 56), was ready to take the risk of publishing an African novel unconcerned with the grammar and values of colonial education. In the words of Tutuola who had struggled in vain to find a publisher in Nigeria, "Faber and Faber took a risk with my work. They didn't expect it would bag a lot of money or get across to the reading masses" (Larson 2001: 20). It was a risk no Nigerian publisher was willing to take, not even after Tutuola personally translated the book into Yoruba, his mother tongue (Larson 2001: 22). Judging from his critics, there was room enough in Yoruba language literature for one only – Chief Daniel Olorunfemi Fagunwa, whose Yoruba language stories Tutuola was repeatedly criticised for plagiarising. *Yoruba Folktales*, written in impeccable English and published in 1986 by Ibadan University Press, is Tutuola's only publication by a Nigeria-based publisher.

In a world steeped in colonial ambitions of dominance, where conversion was privileged over conversation and education reduced to producing "potted plants in greenhouses" (Nyamnjoh 2012c) and "complete gentlemen" and "super ladies" to borrow from Tutuola's *The Palm-Wine Drinkard* (Tutuola 1952) and *My Life in the Bush of Ghosts* (Tutuola 1954), the sort of authentic African novel sought by Faber and Faber was difficult to come by, especially among emerging elite Africans schooled to internalise, celebrate and reproduce Eurocentric modernity and its ideas of a good story well told (Soyinka 1963; Fonlon 1965, 1967; Lindfors 1970, 1999a; p'Bitek 1984[1967]; Achebe 2000, 2012: 52-62; Larson 2001: 1-25; Wenzel 2006). Examples, such as Achimota School in Ghana, established in 1927 for training African leaders, that sought a measure of domestication of colonial education by developing curricula "that took into account the sociocultural background of African students while trying to provide an education on a par with that available at English public schools" (Yamada 2009: 29) were rare. The desired outcome of producing African graduates equipped with Western intellectual attitudes and African sympathies did not always materialise due to the tensions between assimilation and adaptation. As Shoko Yamada concludes, there was far more westernisation than keeping students "African in sympathy" at Achimota School, if only because culturally and technologically the "school [was] filled with facilities, artefacts and activities of the best quality by European standards" (Yamada 2009: 55) [8].

A manuscript of "naïve poetry" – by "a true primitive" (Selden Rodman, reprinted in Lindfors 1975: 15), barely literate lowly paid messenger in the Department of Labour in Lagos and a man of humble rural beginnings[9] – "written in English but not an English of this world" in an "unschooled but oddly expressive" style (Eric Larrabee, reprinted in Lindfors 1975: 11) or, in an "un-willed style and trance-like narrative" (Selden Rodman, reprinted in Lindfors 1975: 15), about African forests, magic, gods, spirits and superstition (Larson 2001: 1-4), – was perfect and the closest reflection of an authentic African mind, if ever there was one (Lindfors 1970, 1999a).

To V. S. Pritchett, Tutuola's endless fancy controlled by Yoruba folklore, ably gives his readers a guided tour "back thousands of years to the first terrors of human nature," with a voice that "is like the beginning to man on earth, man emerging, wounded and growing" (V. S. Pritchett, reprinted in Lindfors 1975: 23). Eric Larrabee notes, "*The Palm-Wine Drinkard* may not be, indeed, a product of genius, but it is certainly that of an unusual talent, seeking to express itself in spite of unusual obstacles" (Eric Larrabee, reprinted in Lindfors 1975: 12-13). Writing in *The New Yorker*, Anthony West recognised "the lack of inhibition in an uncorrupted innocence" as Tutuola's principal strength but characterised Tutuola's style as "naïve and barbaric" and noted that through Tutuola's writing, "One catches a glimpse of the very beginning of literature, that moment when writing at last seizes and pins down the myths and legends of an analphabetic culture" (Anthony West, reprinted in Lindfors 1975: 17). Writing in *West Africa* in February 1954 following the publication of *My Life in the Bush of Ghosts*, Eric Robinson considers Tutuola's "frightening, monstrous and vigorous world" as "the true macabre energy of Africa" (Eric Robinson, reprinted in Lindfors 1975: 30). "Scratch the surface of these statements and we find disturbing parallels to Joseph Conrad's *Heart of Darkness*" (Larson 2001: 5). *Semper aliquid novi ex Africa* – from Africa always something new, the Romans used to say. To many an African critic of Tutuola, the very fact that his exotic stories in what some considered atrocious grammar and fractured English had made their way into print was evidence that Tutuola was "encouraging a useless, impractical mythical way of thinking, of leading West African literature up a blind alley, and of providing the supercilious westerner with an excuse for continuing to patronize the allegedly superstitious Nigerian" (Harold R. Collins, reprinted in Lindfors 1975a[1961]: 59). He was serving as an excuse for Europeans to project "an image of Africa as uncouth, primitive and barbaric" (Lindfors 1975: xiii).

Tutuola himself challenges the idea of a single authentic African mind in *The Witch-Herbalist of the Remote Town*. In this 1981 novel of his, Tutuola equips his quest-narrator with, in psychoanalytic terms, a First and a Second Mind, the former pruned to misleading him, and the latter reputed for having his best interests at heart. In addition to the two minds, there is a Memory and a Supreme Second, all intended to guide him through his perilous journey to the Remote Town of the omniscient and omnipotent Witch-Herbalist and back (Tutuola 1981: 16-26). Indeed, it could be argued, as Gerald Moore did in a review article published in 1957 on Tutuola as "a Nigerian visionary," that, in *The Palm-Wine Drinkard*, "the Drinkard's adventure is not merely a journey into the eternal African bush, but equally a journey into the racial imagination, into the sub-conscious, into the Spirit World that everywhere co-exists and even overlaps with the world of waking 'reality'" (Gerald Moore, reprinted in Lindfors 1975[1957]: 49). Put differently, it is a journey into making a compelling case for reuniting different aspects of reality, regrettably divided by an overly simplified idea of science that has tended to shy away from popular questions of *what* and *why* beyond the obvious realms of direct rational, logical and physically observable causality.

Breaking through as an African writer with a creative imagination that defied categorisation even as it was firmly grounded in Yoruba cosmology and reality of infinite interconnections did not come easily for Tutuola, within and beyond the Nigeria of his day, caught in the throes of a parochial and missionary Eurocentric modernity (Lindfors 1970, 1999a; Larson 2001; Achebe 2000; Wenzel 2006). Yet nowadays, ghosts and haunting attracts the attention of contemporary cultural theorists – with books such as *The Spectralities*

Reader (Blanco and Peeren 2013), containing contributions that include a republication of Achille Mbembe's 2003 article based on Tutuola's *The Palm-Wine Drinkard* and *My Life in the Bush of Ghosts*. Thus, in the 21st century, even as African anthropologists and sociologists continue to dismissively study the supernatural dimensions of African societies from social problem perspectives and seldom as an epistemic cosmology and ontology, Tutuola's universe of interconnections between the human and the bush of ghosts, the visible and invisible, nature, culture and supernature continues to haunt and terrorise Africa's epistemologically impoverished scholarship with yearnings for critical attention and redemption.

Tutuola's ghosts are too present and too prominent to be ignored. Even the Eurocentric elite cannot ignore them for 24 hours, reason why these elite are Cartesian rationalists by day and Tutuolan in the company of ghostly attractions at night. And for good reason. Tutuola's *My Life in the Bush of Ghosts* and *The Wild Hunter in the Bush of the Ghosts* are a veritable academy of ghosts, fanciful, varied and original in myriad ways, enough to keep every fancy and fantasy alive and kicking. From *My Life in the Bush of Ghosts* alone, Harold Collins shares with us a detailed but by no means exhaustive kaleidoscopic inventory of Tutuola's wealth of ghosts that include:

> … a copperish ghost, a silverish ghost, a golden ghost, handless, footless, and arm-less ghosts, naked ghosts, a smelling ghost, a "lower-ranked" ghost, prominent ghosts, a homeless ghost, a famous ghost, "burglar" ghosts, a rich ghost, a "very beautiful young ghostess," a "jocose-ghostess," "triplet" ghosts, a very short ghost, ghost children, river ghosts (sometimes called aquatic ghosts or sceptical ghosts), the Super Lady Ghostess, the Rev. Devil Ghost, and the Television-handed Ghostess (Collins 1975[1969]: 161).

Thanks to Tutuola's novels it has become commonplace to compare and contrast ghosts as an everyday reality in Africa with ghosts as extraordinary and problematic occurrences in the West (Rooney 2000; Peeren 2010). As Gerald Moore remarks with reference to the reality of ghosts in Tutuola's works:

> To the uninitiated European reader the word "ghost" is likely to be rather misleading, for the ghosts of this book [*My Life in the Bush of Ghosts*] are not the individual spirits of those who once lived on earth; they are the permanent inhabitants of the Other World, who have never lived as mortals, but who have intimate knowledge of that life and are in constant intercourse with it. At the same time, it appears that earthly witches and wizards hold their meetings among these ghosts and that it is from there that "spirit-children" are sent to dwell among men and act as agents for the ghost world (Gerald Moore, reprinted in Lindfors 1975[1957]: 53).

In 1968, E. N. Obiechina argued that Tutuola's work was a significant contribution to the formal artistic evolution from "a purely oral narrative tradition to a purely literary narrative tradition." He recognised this in Tutuola's "ability to assimilate elements peculiar to the oral tradition to elements peculiar to the literary tradition" by imposing "a literary organisation over essentially oral narrative material" (Obiechina 1975[1968]: 144). Harry Garuba agrees, noting that Tutuola's novels and creative use of English have made him the central reference point "for the transition from the oral tale to the written text and from the indigenous languages of Africa to writing in the languages of European colonialism" in "the story of the making of modern African literature"[10](see also Cooper 1998: 42). Some have identified Tutuola among other pioneer Nigerian writers such as Chinua Achebe and Gabriel Okara, who have domesticated the English language to serve as a vehicle for "the transliteration of traditional customs, beliefs and attitudes" into the "entirely new context" of "the modern reader" who, it seems, can only relate to "Nigerian traditional life" through the investigative recreational mediation of writers invested in keeping the past and its oral traditions alive (Nnamani et al. 2014: 19). To illustrate what they mean, Nnamani et al. point out that:

> In The Palm-wine Drinkard, Amos Tutuola carries out a bodily translation from Yoruba language and world view to ensure a predominantly oral tone and to reinforce the cultural value of the novel. He assembles and embellishes Yoruba folktales and shows through his

writing, the potentialities of African folklores and mythology as a vitalizing force in Nigerian Literature. Another Yoruba influence on Tutuola's language is shown in his use of proverbs and gnomic sayings, usually translated literally from the original. It has been suggested that his lack of sufficient education keeps him close to the oral tradition and subsequently affects the kind of English he uses in the novel (Nnamani et al. 2014: 21).

Through his creative appropriation of Yoruba and English languages and cultural influences in his writings, Tutuola draws the attention of his reader to incompleteness, and to the need to recognise, cherish and draw on it as a strength. In this regard, dichotomisation between tradition and modernity, and between orality and the written is highly problematic and misrepresentative of the full value of Tutuola's contribution as a frontier writer who brought tradition and modernity, nature and culture, the natural and the supernatural, orality and the written, Africa and Europe into conversation in a manner that challenged the rigid thinking of evolutionary pretentions about human encounters and progress (Soyinka 1963; Barber 1995; Tobias 1999; Newell 2006: 71-72). In *The Palm-Wine Drinkard,* for example, Tutuola is able to unleash Drum, Song and Dance to haunt his "text as the noisy and mobile residue of orality, reminding the readers of this printed book that no boundary is permanent and texts can easily become infested with noise" (Newell 2006: 71). As Sanya Osha, a Yoruba writer and academic, tells us, in Yoruba oral history, "music derived from drums ... was sacred and meant for the exaltation of gods," with each major deity enjoying its own sacred drum texts and messages.[11] Then Sango, the god of lightning and thunder decided to widen:

> ...the audience that could enjoy sacred music. Kings as well as gods began to enjoy the music produced from drums. And then kings permitted the playing of sacred music to all and sundry which was when a new concept, alujo– music meant for dancing – evolved[12]

Tutuola refused to yield to the "preference for Western epistemological paradigm" in a "blind quest for globalization, to the exclusion of indigenous and traditional episteme" that threatens African literary creativity with "sterility" (Nnamani et al. 2014: 22; see also Cooper 1998: 44-48).

Nigerian novelist and short story writer Cyprian Ekwensi argues that Tutuola's "writing was in a class of its own, because he wrote out of a poetic mind though with grammatical limitations," adding that Tutuola would not have written the same novel in the Nigeria of the 1990s (Lindfors 1999b: 137-138). Indeed, there is a marked difference, grammatically, between Tutuola's first two published novels – *The Palm-Wine Drinkard*, and *My Life in the Bush of Ghosts*, both published in the early 1950s – and his subsequent novels. Published in 1981, *The Witch-Herbalist of the Remote Town*, for example, is strikingly different, grammatically, from the first two. This is equally true of *The Wild Hunter in the Bush of the Ghosts*, published in 1989 with a Bernth Lindfors introduction, after being reworked for wider circulation (Tutuola 1989[1982]).

Driven by his determination to keep the past alive and protect his culture (to resist being forced, in the name of completeness, to choose between the ways of others and the ways of his own people, so to speak) – "I don't want the past to die. I don't want our culture to vanish" (Tutuola interviewed by Mike Awoyinfa, quoted in Lindfors 1999b: 143) –, Tutuola did not allow his lack of higher formal education and sophistication in European literary styles and canons – his incompleteness in other words – to stand in the way of his mission: "So far as I don't want our culture to fade away I don't mind about English grammar" (Tutuola interviewed by Mike Awoyinfa, quoted in Lindfors 1999b: 143).

In a related interview with P. Wauthier, quoted by Lindfors, Tutuola declares, "it seemed necessary to write down the tales of my country since they will soon all be forgotten," adding that he wanted people of other countries to read and understand Yoruba folklore and Yoruba people better (Lindfors 1970: 310). Interviewed after his death in 1997, Tutuola's first wife confirmed his love of nature and tradition thus: "my husband was a lover of nature and tradition. He was in love with animals and plants. Whenever he was on leave, he [left] the city for the village to study how animals behave. He was in harmony with the countryside… He was easily enticed to his culture which he struggled to preserve before his death" (Tutuola's first wife in Sola Balogun, quoted in Lindfors 1999b: 141). So committed is Tutuola not to give death and dying the last word vis-à-vis the people, things and values he cherishes that in the universe he depicts in his writings, death is nothing but a form of circulation of life and its varied ways and modes of manifesting itself. Similarly, life to Tutuola "look less like a black-and-white entity and more like a nebulous quantity with confusing not-quite-alive, not-quite-dead borders"[13]. Tutuola's indicators of life are not confined to ticking the boxes of capacities such as movement, respiration, sensitivity, growth, reproduction, excretion and nutrition.

If Tutuola's commitment to cultures, values, beliefs and practices he cherished was a "longing for darkness" (Beard 1975) as some of his critics, Paul Neumarkt (1975[1971]) for example, insist, it was a longing informed and justified by a deep unease with the blazing lights of colonial civilisation – lights as dazzling and blinding as the flood of light from the Flash-Eyed Mother in *My Life in the Bush of Ghosts* (Tutuola 1954: 88). If his art, regardless of what some insist was his defective English and an "acrobatic syntax" (Barlet 2000[1996]: 198), could be used to weaken the floodlights of subjugation, rejection and repression and refocus attention on Yoruba traditions and ways of life at risk of being forgotten because of their purported inferiority, irrationalism and primitivism, he will have succeeded. Aware of the corrosive and infectious nature of colonial education and its claims of superiority, Tutuola was averse to an education that stifled instead of giving creativity and imagination feathers to fly and explore the fullness of possibilities. In other words, had he sought accomplishment in the sort of mimicry and self-denigration that colonial education implanted in those who uncritically embraced it and its styles, he would probably have stifled his creative imagination. He saw his incompleteness as a blessing:

> Probably if I had more education, that might change my writing or improve it or change it to another thing people would not admire. [....] Perhaps with higher education, I might not be a popular writer. I might not write folktales. I might not take it as anything important.

I would take it as superstition and not write in that line (Tutuola interviewed by Mike Awoyinfa, quoted in Lindfors 1999b: 143).

Tutuola's sentiment is shared by Obiechina, in a review of Tutuola's writings seen through the prism of oral tradition. To Obiechina, the fact that Tutuola's education never went beyond the elementary school was "something of an advantage" because this meant that Tutuola was "much nearer to traditional society than if he were better educated," especially as, at the time Tutuola wrote his first book, cultural contact operated "mostly through education and the more highly educated are likely to be the more acculturated" (Obiechina 1975[1968]: 143). By being the lowly educated writer that he was, Tutuola was better able to immerse his writing "in the cultural consciousness of traditional Africa as embodied in cosmology, moral values and attitudes" (Obiechina 1975[1968]: 135).

This raises the question of who validates and authenticates the level of one's education in order for one to tell one's own personal story or write about one's own society and cultural conventions (Nyamnjoh 2012a, 2012c). Should a writer's skills be judged by the ability to communicate in a second language or in the language of his/her birth and upbringing? The idea of an exogenously dictated level of education somewhat denies the likes of Tutuola the ambition of telling their stories, as they are bound to fall short of the level of completeness, competency or achievement expected for one to qualify as storyteller. It also denies a particular representation of their worlds and encounters with others that only they, with their background and experience, can make possible, however modest their level of formal education and whatever their mastery or lack thereof of the styles and canons dictated by the gendarmes of literary validation. For a sense of the type of scrutiny Tutuola's writings have had to go through in this regard, see Lindfors (1970, 1999a) and Larson (2001: 1-25). Compared to Chief Daniel Olorunfemi Fagunwa, who wrote exclusively in Yoruba, and whose influence on Tutuola is undeniable (Lindfors 1970: 325-329; Cooper 1998: 42-44), by opting to share the same Yoruba stories with a wider readership by writing in English, even if not an English sanctioned by England and its Nigerian acolytes (Lindfors 1970: 331), Tutuola has probably brought more recognition and representation for Yoruba culture and folktales at the global marketplace of cultural production. In this connection, Abiola Irele, who considers Tutuola's novels as "an extension of Fagunwa's work in Yoruba" and as representing "a continuous progression from the indigenous to the European," has argued that "insofar as his language is the spontaneous recreation in English of the structures of the Yoruba language, which provides the linguistic and cultural framework of his imagination," Tutuola could be seen as an "unconscious artist" (Irele 2001: 17). Reluctance to see him as literary has led others to dismiss his work as "an 'aberrant' literary strain which represents a 'cul-de-sac in African literature'" (Neumarkt 1975[1971]: 188-189; Newell 2006: 186). Some have seen in his deviation from the predictabilities and conventionalities of the novel as prescribed, understood and practiced in the West, evidence of Tutuola's postmodernism and magic, and as pointing to his pioneer role in redefining the cannons and reality of literature globally (Cooper 1998; Rooney 2000; Newell 2006: 186-187).

Writing in defence of Tutuola, Taban Lo Liyong reminds "Teachers of English and educated Africans who pride themselves in their mastery of English" that "in creative writing grammar does not count very much" (Liyong 1975[1968]: 115), that "Art is no respecter of education," (Liyong 1975[1968]: 120), that "Each writer has his own language," and that seriously imaginative writers "Leave the search for order and meaning to the fools" (Liyong 1975[1968]: 121). To Liyong, Tutuola's African critics were victims of a colonial and colonising education that "drives out of the mind superstition, daydreaming, building of castles in the air, cultivation of yarns, and replaces them with a rational practical mind, almost devoid of imagination" (Liyong 1975[1968]: 116). He is terribly disappointed in the educated Nigerian elite who claim superiority for little else but their mastery of the English language, and have so much disdain for Tutuola's lack of grammar, that they "run the danger of disdaining" the very African mythology Tutuola worked with. To Liyong, given the importance of myth to apprehending and comprehending the world, such rejection even of Tutuola's repertoire of myths is tantamount to the colonially educated African elite cutting their very umbilical cord and disowning their mother (Liyong 1975[1968]: 118). Tongue in cheek, Liyong expresses his frustrations with Tutuola's African and especially Nigerian champions of colonial education and its superiority syndromes in these words:

> To our surprise, one day, into the hall of fame walks a primary school boy, a naughty boy, a boy who knows no grammar, almost a total villager, and he claims a seat among the immortals. What? We shout. Who are you? When were you in Achimota? Perhaps you were at Ibadan with me? Are you a *been-to?* In a land where school knowledge is extremely important, our drop-out is meticulously analysed, weighed, and found insolvent. Our analysts pull their *agbada* up and set to *jollof-*rice and *gari* and chicken legs in their university halls and blame the whole thing on Dylan Thomas, Gerald Moore, and the whole White world. "If this fellow they mumble, (not even mentioning that name, to them accursed) had been to Oxford, and had then decided to use his mother-tongue's syntax, like Okara, perhaps we could believe him. But…" (Liyong 1975[1968]: 120).

Without claiming superiority or completeness through his achievements, Tutuola – whom Taban Liyong has described as "a modern ancient, the optimistic, daring, and defiant African of yesterday" (Liyong 1975[1968]: 118) – and his English language stories complement Fagunwa and his Yoruba language writing, as two sides of the same cultural reproduction coin or cowrie. Before his death in 1963, Fagunwa had "produced five 'novels,' a collection of stories, two travel books, and a series of graded readers for schools," and "was an extremely popular author in Yorubaland" (Lindfors 1970: 324). Without any pretentions to perfection or to absolute victories, Yoruba is all the better with the complementary literary contributions of Fagunwa (who wrote mostly for an internal Yoruba readership), Tutuola (who wrote both for Yoruba but largely for a non-Yoruba readership) and writers of Yoruba origin such as Wole Soyinka who write in the sort of sophisticated English that Tutuola could only dream of, in keeping alive its storytelling traditions in a fast moving interconnected and ever more interdependent world of rooted cosmopolitanisms.

As we learn from Okot p'Bitek's *Song of Lawino*, there is little guarantee that welcoming exhortations to embrace an exogenously induced standard of education and storytelling in a foreign language in which one excels would necessarily deliver completeness. The Western educated Ocol, husband to the community educated Lawino, falls short of such completeness despite his phenomenal investments at mimicking the ways of the purported standard-bearers of modernity and its prescriptions. He does succeed in becoming a curiosity in the eyes of his wife, who tries to understand why he uncritically succumbs to serving as a mouthpiece for the untested ways, ideas and worldviews of purportedly superior others. Lawino is incredibly insightful and tolerant in her inquiry into her husband's newfound ways of being and doing, despite her scorn and her deep sense of worry. Ocol epitomizes the post-independence "modern," "progressive and civilized man," reduced to doing little more than pouring "scorn on Black people" who he says are "primitive," "ignorant, poor and diseased." The fact of his having "read extensively and widely" only alienates him from his folks, making of him little more than a hired local customs clearing officer for the white man, his ideas and his values in Africa – a sort of stranger or outsider within. He declares himself unable to live with his wife any longer, because she is "a thing," "just a village woman," "an old type" who is "no longer attractive" and "cannot distinguish between good and bad." She is "blocking his progress" and he must clear the way for Clementine, the "modern woman" he loves, and "who speaks English" (p'Bitek 1989[1966]: 14). Such betrayal and the irrelevance that comes with the uncritical internalization of colonial and colonizing yardsticks of being educated and being modern is a recurrent and well-known theme in African writing.

Like his counterparts elsewhere on the continent, an Ocol intoxicated by the palm-wine of colonial education becomes dangerous to kin and kith. He "behaves like a hen that eats its own eggs, a hen that should be imprisoned under a basket" (p'Bitek 1989[1966]: 14). Unlettered Lawino, after careful observation and analysis of her husband, laments the fact: "When my husband is reading a new book or when he is sitting in his sofa, his face covered up completely with the big newspaper," not only does he look like a corpse in a tomb, he is so silent and so viciously anti-social that he "storms like a buffalo" and "throws things" at any child who cries, saying "that children's cries and coughs disturb him!" But "what music is sweeter than the cries of children?"; "Who but a witch would like to live in a homestead where all the grown-ups are so clean after the rains, because there are no muddy fat kids to fall on their bosoms after dancing in the rains and playing in the mud?" (p'Bitek 1989[1966]: 45-51). An education that transforms people into unthinking zombies, kills their sociality, and numbs their humanity even for their own children can hardly be relevant to social reproduction, let alone social transformation. It is an education that reduces the African elite to the state of total sterile dependency which the narrator owns up to in the opening lines of Tutuola's *The Palm-Wine Drinkard*, and for which he must atone or forever perish: "I was a palm-wine drinkard since I was a boy of ten years of age. I had no other work more than to drink palm-wine in my life."

An education to hate questions is hardly one to provide answers. Ocol "has read deeply and widely" to the point of making his house "a dark forest of books," but because he is educated not to engage and not to question, and not to answer his wife's questions, but to prescribe and dictate deafly and condescendingly, his education is not relevant to African modes of fruitful self-knowledge and self-reproduction. It is a dogmatic education that makes its graduates behave like workmen whose only tool is a hammer and for whom every problem is a nail. "Ocol has lost his head in the forest of books"; "[T]he reading has killed" him "in the ways of his people." It is as if his "testicles were smashed with large books!" and he has become "a walking corpse" (p'Bitek 1989[1966]: 91-95). Little wonder that African elites not dissimilar to Ocol exhibit an "inability to fertilize thought and action in any meaningful sense" (Ajei 2007: 6), and are truly embarrassed before the mirrors with which the likes of Tutuola and Lawino surround them. But they enjoy recognition in the eyes of the white man, as "the good children," "who ask no questions, who accept everything … like the rubbish pit, like the pit-latrine which does not reject even dysentery." Ocol is liked and patted on the back by his white masters, for asking no questions, for his unconditional subservience (p'Bitek 1989[1966]: 64), and for being a veritable subservient customs clearing officer for their otherwise toxic and contraband ideas and intellectual prescriptions.

Like p'Bitek's Lawino, Tutuola on the other hand, is daringly different in just being himself. He does not mind risking shame and ridicule to stand tall in defence of the values and ways of life he was raised in and has grown to cherish. Instead of yielding to be converted by the language of his colonisers in the manner Ocol does, Tutuola creatively appropriated English to serve as a vehicle for the popularisation of his Yoruba folktales – inspired by a Yoruba ontology that, to quote Wole Soyinka, "shies away from rigid compartmentalisation," allowing for the world of the living to flow "into the ancestral domain and into the fragile world of the Unborn," as well as for a non-linear concept of time (Soyinka 2014: vii). Armed unashamedly with the "diction ... of the proletariat rather than that of the university graduate," (Armstrong 1975[1970]: 219), Tutuola decided to meet English halfway. "Tutuola took the English language and turned it upside-down, inventing new constructions and a new syntax, not so much out of ignorance (and the lack of a formal education) [but] as roughshod ownership" (Larson 2001: 11). Tutuola thus brought the English language into conversation with Yoruba folktales, the Yoruba language and Yoruba narrative traditions (Armstrong 1975[1970]).

In this regard, Afolayan has termed Tutuola's English "Yoruba English" to the extent that "it represents the expression of either Yoruba deep grammar with English surface grammar, or Yoruba systems and/or structures in English words" (Afolayan 1975[1971]: 194-195). Referring to Tutuola "as a very keen and perceptive listener and an excellent reporter,"[14] Afolayan suggests that Tutuola, in the process of writing, first organised "his Yoruba material in his Yoruba mother tongue" before proceeding to express what he had organised, "though not necessarily vocalised or visually expressed, material in English." Tutuola not only told Yoruba stories "in the traditional way," he did so "in his own personal manner" (Afolayan 1975[1971]: 205-206). To Afolayan, "although Tutuola's language in many ways represents his own inimitable personal style... his English is that of the Yoruba user, not of the average educated user but the level of present-day Secondary Class Four," or, in the case of Tutuola's earliest novel, "it is the English user with about Secondary Class Two education" (Afolayan 1975[1971]: 198-199). Opining that "Tutuola may not be fully comprehensible to any but a Yoruba-English bilingual, particularly the one who is a native speaker of Yoruba," Afolayan draws attention to the central role played by language in how Tutuola's writing was received by whom: "ironically language has been not only what recommends Tutuola to the readers whose mother tongue is English but also a barrier to his acceptance by his own people" (Afolayan 1975[1971]: 208).

If Tutuola's intention was to ensure survival for his Yoruba culture and language by telling his stories in English, his dogged determination to think and write in English the way he would think, speak and write in Yoruba (Lindfors 1970, 1999a; Larson 2001: 1-25), was a successful way of denying the English language and its universe of origin the victory it craved by seeking to transform its African enthusiasts (skulls) into complete gentlemen and complete ladies English style. To Steven Tobias, "Tutuola's use and manipulation of both language and the fantastic play pivotal and complementary roles in his formulation of a discourse of resistance" against the often deplorable dehumanisation to which he and his fellow Nigerians were subjected under British colonialism (Tobias 1999: 69). In this way, argues Tobias, Tutuola "turns the colonial power structure on its ear in an attempt to reclaim the center for himself and his culture" (Tobias 1999: 71). Larson's study of Tutuola's *The Palm-Wine Drinkard* leads him to conclude that "it is impossible not to regard Tutuola as a postmodern writer with few antecedents or authorities" (Larson 2001: 12).

While there is certainly a case of postmodernism to be made for Tutuola, it is worth bearing in mind that not everyone who questions totalising metanarratives of completeness, superiority and authority attributed to certain collectives or social categories to the detriment of others is necessarily a postmodernist. Some may question such sweeping truth claims not because of an aversion to generalisations and the possibility of universalisms, but more because such claims have been arrived at in a hurry and/or through the intended or unintended exclusion of others, their stories, histories, experiences and perspectives. To the latter, if universalism or the great unifying story of humanity is the shared aspiration, this must not be contrived at the expense of diversity, flexibility and openness. It must not be achieved by means of selective exposure and selective retention, privileging subjugation, oppression and repression.

Postmodernism in Tutuola's case particularly entailed challenging dominant Eurocentric metanarratives of completeness and autonomy that could only result in a "complete gentleman" or "westernised gentleman" according to Sunday Anozie (1975[1970]: 247) reduced to a bare skull and its diktats keeping up appearances with borrowed body parts and fineries, as do the *nouveaux riches* of African cities, who deploy their one-legged modernity to seduce and betray "young women who have rebelled against their families in the bush" (1975[1970]: 247). Such an idea of completeness is what the late Burkinabe historian Joseph Ki-Zerbo (1992) aptly captures under the title of *"la natte des autres"* (metaphorically depicting Africans reduced to the indignity of sleeping on borrowed mats, thinking borrowed thoughts and dreaming borrowed dreams), in his call for the endogenisation of knowledge production in Africa. Tutuola's postmodernism is an open and urgent invitation to a disposition and practice that seeks to remember, recognise and provide for those culturally and physically dismembered or invisibilised by narrow but dominant and asphyxiating traditions of meaning making and knowledge production. It is postmodernism that seeks to re-insert the "Removable Heads" of the "Crazy Removable-Headed Wild Man" severed and taken as trophies and as statement of individual potency by the brave hunter in Tutuola's *The Witch-Herbalist of the Remote Town* (Tutuola 1981: 88-94). Our perennial fascination with the fantasticalness of Tutuola's universe, Harry Garuba argues, comes from the "sense of reversibility ... playfulness ... toying with our expectations, troubling our knowledge systems and classificatory grids and upsetting our categories (even our tenses) for grasping the world,"[15] that it inspires in the reader. Tutuola affords Africans both the innocence and naiveté to proclaim that the kings and queens of Eurocentric modernity are naked in their new clothes, and the fantasy spaces they need to recreate and reaffirm their suspended, caricatured or frozen humanity through unequal encounters with Europe and its extensions.

Although he does not call it such, Marc Shapiro, biographer of J. K. Rowling, whom he describes as the wizard behind the Harry Potter book series, speaks of a fantasy space when he talks of "a place where just about anything can happen and usually does" (Shapiro 2004: ix). Anthropologist Birgit Meyer, who has richly documented how popular Christianity in Ghana imaginatively brings text and film into conversation in popular Ghanaian cinema (Meyer 2003, 2006, 2009, 2010, 2015; Meyer and Moors 2006), uses the expression "fantasy spaces" to refer to dangerously attractive locations, sometimes at the bottom of the ocean, conjured up by Ghanaian filmmakers, "where money and commodities are generated in exchange for sex, and sometimes blood," and as revelatory of everyday popular imaginations about global capitalism as epitomised by America, the ultimate fantasy space (Meyer 2003: 16). As a technologically mediated fantasy space, the bottom of the ocean in these films is brought home to viewers as the place "where matters relegated to the realm of the Satanic may be addressed from a voyeuristic position" (Meyer 2003: 33, 2015).

Inspired by both definitions and in view of what I know of Tutuola and his universes, by fantasy spaces, I refer to spaces and places that facilitate the activation of human imagination beyond the confines of the ordinary and the taken for granted. Such spaces need not always be physical, tangible and perceptible through the senses, and could themselves be the fruit of the highly creative imagination of those with a capacity to dream and think beyond the ordinary. They are the extraordinary possibilities of creative minds, especially in contexts where thinking the outrageous, the barely possible and the impossible and seeking to know the unknowable is highly discouraged. If not every dream is a dream out of this world, not every daydream amounts to a fantasy, and not every place or space that supports dreaming is a fantasy space. With certain dreams in certain spaces and places, one aspires for the skies with one's feet firmly on the ground. Tutuola is no ordinary daydreamer, and his fantasy spaces are no ordinary places. Through his extraordinary capacity to daydream, Tutuola provides his readers with fantasy spaces to bring into conversation essence and consciousness, structure and agency, tradition and modernity, the local and the global, Europe and Africa. In fantastic ways, his characters determine just as much as they are determined.

Tutuola admits he grew up sharing stories with schoolmates and teachers, saying how he "became a very good storyteller," who used to be given presents by his schoolmates "for telling incredible folktales" (Olayiwola Adeniji, quoted in Lindfors 1999b: 142). What is it about children and fantasy? Children are generally assumed to be inexperienced and to lack sophistication and worldliness, which explains the innocence and naiveté often associated with them. When we feed them children's stories written by adults, we tend to let our imagination go wild with unfathomable exaggerations, hyperbole, out of the ordinary experiences and surrealism, giving animals and plants human qualities and humans plant and animal qualities, and generally infusing pain and pleasure in most unlikely places and spaces, and in twisted, grisly and dazzlingly usual ways.

Roald Dahl's children's books are replete with examples in these regards. In *James and the Giant Peach*, an orphan boy escapes from his sadistic aunts into a better life of adventure, using a "gargantuan fuzzy-skinned fruit" as his "getaway vehicle." According to Hephzibah Anderson, in over 15 books, Dahl presented children with "stories bursting with gluttony and flatulence, in which wives feed their husbands worms and the young are eaten by giants and changed into mice by bald, toeless hags. Villains loom large; as mean as they are ignorant, they tower over pint-sized protagonists, twirling them around by their pigtails or banishing them to places like 'the Chokey,' Miss Trunchbull's nail-studded punishment cupboard." The assumption in these and related writings for children by adults is that children love disgusting stories, and use fantasies to know and control their imagined monsters better in order to get to master their anxieties and monsters in real life. To Anderson, Dahl's books depict children as complicated, crazy and cruel, and "a child's world ... [as not being] all sweetness and light" but as containing "shadows too – extravagant, scary, wickedly entertaining ones."[16]

Indeed, when we feed students with specially packaged larger than life stories, we turn our world of rationality and logic upside down and inside out. The universe we create for children in the stories we imagine and tell them is a universe of infinite possibilities and extended credulity, of seeking freedom from a world that is overly confining or repressive. We suggest to children through the stories we tell them that our adult world of neat dichotomies between good and bad, right and wrong, the familiar and the strange, insiders and outsiders misses the lure and allure of ambiguity, which children and the children in adults [should] find irresistible. Despite this regime of fantasy which children internalise and reproduce for as long as we consider them children, we somehow expect them to suddenly free themselves of these fantasies and the illogical and irrational world we have carefully crafted and fed them all along. We want them to suddenly inhabit a world that is supposedly governed by objectivity and Cartesian rationalism, where the subjectivities of their childhood fantasies are purportedly shackled and tightly controlled. We start telling them, once they turn adults (or when we decide they are adults), that none of these stories is actually true or believable by rational adults, and that the only people who stubbornly believe in these stories and the universes depicted in them are supposedly primitive, superstitious and backward people to be found in geographies of darkness, superstition and magic. We tell them to rise beyond their Alice in Wonderland, Peter Pan, Robin Hood and Harry Potter fantasies and face reality.

Tutuola is different. His fantasy world is as real as his world of objectively observable and rationalisable reality. And he does not see any contradiction, nor should he, in inhabiting and providing for the realities of both worlds (which he perceives and relates to as a continuum) in his life and the lives of his characters, most especially, his quest-heroes.

Tutuola's postmodernism was in writing stories that challenged such dichotomies. He invites his readers to see the mind and the body, fantasy, logic and sensory perception as all interconnected, entangled and impossible to dissociate as easily as is often suggested when we[17] urge children to grow up and to disabuse themselves of tooth fairies, Santa Claus, the Easter Bunny, leprechauns, fairy tales, children's literature (tales spun by the likes of Roald Dahl, Philip Pullman, J. K Rowling[18], Rick Riordan, etc.), children's television superstars such as Tom and Jerry, Scooby-Doo, SWAT Ceats, Sponge Bob, Ed, Ed & Eddy, Powerpuff Girls, Rocket Power, etc.

According to Hephzibah Anderson, "to write brilliantly for children, an author must retain an element of the childlike. Sometimes, that blurs into childishness." Anderson quotes Roald Dahl, a brilliant children's author, to have said that the children's author "must like simple tricks and jokes and riddles and other childish things."[19] What makes J. K. Rowling an author of good fantasy stories "in which the reader can lose himself or herself' (Shapiro 2004: ix), according to Marc Shapiro, her biographer, is to be found in her capacity "to stop being an adult and become a child who also wants to believe in the unbelievable," and to dream without relent, day and night (Shapiro 2004: 3). Rowling, in other words, succeeds in making herself "a child at heart, an adult in body," to borrow the words of one of her English adult fans (Shapiro 2004: 8). Shapiro writes:

> … Joanne Kathleen Rowling likes to dream at all hours of the day and night. She dreams of faraway lands, bigger-than-life good guys, truly evil bad guys, and likable young children who try and make sense of it all. But unlike others, she turns her dreams into reality when she sits down with pen and paper and begins to write about the adventures of Harry Potter (Shapiro 2004: 3).

Marc Shapiro further shares the following thoughts on why fantasy adventures are irresistible to children and adults alike:

> There has always been a sense of comfort in escaping into a world of fantasy. Which is why the adventures of Harry Potter are so much fun for children and adults alike. There are, quite simply, no rules in a Harry Potter book – or at least none that cannot be broken in the name of fun and adventure (Shapiro 2004: viii).

Harry Potter's popularity across generations comes from his capacity "to accept adult burdens in his life, although he is a child" (Shapiro 2004: 8) and in the fact that "He bends and breaks the rules when it suits his purposes and has all the insecurities of a normal boy or girl" (Shapiro 2004: 9).

Pre-dating publication of the first book in the Harry Potter series in 1997 by 43 years, *My Life in the Bush of Ghosts*, published in 1954, offers the account of a child protagonist fleeing the jealousy of a polygamous home and the chaos and scourge of predatory human wars and ceaseless fighting for absolute control over people and things. He magically disappears under a huge tree – the "future sign tree" –, into a fantasy world of infinite abundance of fantasy spaces. There, as a human or an earthly, he commingles with ghosts and other strange creatures. It is a world of ambiguity par excellence, one in which everything has more to it than meets the eye, where life is quite simply larger than logic, where everyone is a potential trickster or a potential victim of trickery and cunning. It is a world in which power has no permanent abode, as it appears and disappears without warning. It is a world not of certainties and certitudes, but rather, of permanent change, where everything and everyone is in flux. Bodies and minds are mutually entangled, not in a repressive way, but in a manner that increases their possibilities where everyone and everything is second guessing and seeking to outsmart the other in life's games of potency.

As Steven Tobias observes, "hyperbole, satire, and anti-logic often prove more forceful than direct assaults with realistic, customary literary weapons" in attempts to critique and reform society (Tobias 1999: 71). In this regard, Tutuola's postmodernism also teaches us how an adult whose innocence, naiveté and imagination have been tempered by domestication, discipline, encroachments and the predictabilities and precariousness of a bounded life steeped in oppressive prescriptiveness and dogma, can reconnect with or rediscover their childhood fantasies of infinite freedoms.

In Tutuola's stories, palm-wine[20] and juju (charms and spells) are key activators. When his protagonists are adults and need to feel, think, dream and act like a child again, they are able to reactivate or rekindle their fantasy worlds and spaces by drinking palm-wine and/or by using the juju in their possession. The following passage, from *The Witch-Herbalist of the Remote Town* on how the brave hunter of the Rocky Town prepares for the long and dangerous journey to see the Witch-Herbalist of the Remote Town for a cure to his wife's barrenness, captures remarkably the centrality of palm-wine and juju as great activators in Tutuola's universe and its rites of passage:

> I entered my room and I first drank one keg of the palm-wine. Then I wore my hunting dress, I wore many kinds of juju in my loin, I wore many on my neck, both on my elbows and limbs. Several others which were the skulls of snakes, birds of prey, lizards, etc. were tied on my huge cap and I put it on my head. Having dressed like that, I took my bow and the poisonous arrows. Many kinds of juju were tied on every part of the bow as well. Then I hung the bow and arrows and my long and heavy matchet on my left shoulder. Then I put the juju ring which could make a person invisible on one of my left fingers.
>
> .... Having equipped myself like that, again I drank one keg of the palm-wine. .... then I staggered from my room to the outside of the house. ....
>
> As I knelt down before the people, and as I began to shake from feet to head for the intoxication of the powers of all the juju which I wore and as well for the power of the strong palm-wine which I had drunk in the room, so they all prayed for me. After the prayer, each of the people including my mother, father, my wife, her mother and her father, hung several kinds of juju gourds all over my dresses, head, neck, breast, loin, etc. After all these juju gourds were offered, I did not waste time at all but I stood up and I started my journey immediately (Tutuola 1981: 23-24).

It is gratifying to know that however totalising a world is, there are always pockets or avenues of possibilities for re-imagining and reenchanting that world. The universe of Tutuola's stories is of a world insulated or secured by the fact of ambiguity and infinite creativity, imagination and innovation. If everything or everyone is ambiguous, they cannot easily be classified, and therefore, however complete or incomplete they perceive themselves or are perceived to be, can always spring surprises on us, just as we can surprise them. Ambiguity means that anyone is categorical at their risk and peril. Choices are not clear cut, and mediation and reconciliation are much more likely to yield results than absolute victories.

Ambiguity means that the important action is that which takes place at the crossroads, and not in the heartland where certainties are taken for granted and prescriptions and expectations of domestication, discipline, control, standardisation, routinisation and predictability are trumped over creative diversity and flexibility. Crossroads are zones of contestation and possibilities, of foreboding and hope, of re-enactments as well as of breakthroughs. Adult fantasies offer an opportunity to redeem or reclaim the lost innocence and naiveté of childhood and its capacity to subvert the taken for granted and linear ideas of time and space. In Tutuola's novels, for instance, as Charles Larson observes, "time operates in no logical manner" and "has little to do with actual blocks of time as measured" (Larson 1975[1972]: 174-175). Adult fantasies make the case for a future inspired by elements from the rear-view mirror of adulthood pressured by constant expectations to demonstrate completeness by outgrowing childhood. Adult fantasies give adults an opportunity to imagine the richness of a future inspired by the past ahead (i.e., through the eyes of children as a production and reproduction of the fantasy spaces adults once held dear themselves, when innocence and naiveté were still at their beck and call). With nonlinear ideas of time, the past is as much behind as it is ahead of the present. The child is as much the past and present of the adult as it is the future. If the past is in the present and the future and the present and the future in the past, this speaks of continuities even in apparent discontinuities, just as it speaks of the adult in the child and the child in the adult, and ultimately of the sterility of absolutely seeking to divorce fantasy from reality. Tutuola makes of fantasy and reality two sides of the same coin or cowrie. To him, "the drunkard who has forgotten his poverty and sorrow," "comes back to his usual sadness as soon as he is conscious" (Tutuola 1981: 200). His message on the importance of fantasy and the need to be open to the possibility of other dimensions and realities is clear. This openness in itself is basic and vital to understanding our constant incompleteness. Tutuola's postmodernism, in sum, is a call to reunite and celebrate the interconnections and interdependencies between fantasy and reality by recognising and providing for urgent and necessary conversations and conviviality between essence and consciousness.

Africa's infinite capacity to accommodate even when not accommodated, and the persistence of popular epistemologies despite colonialism and its Eurocentric logic of conversion are evidence of the postmodern spirit of the continent as depicted in

Tutuola's novels. It is indicative of a profound maturity with reference to relativism and acceptance of difference. Tutuola's quest was seeking to be published, to share his creative imagination in conversation with Yoruba folktales, to use and appropriate the English language to activate himself and his people through stories, and to employ Yoruba as well, navigating between languages and worldviews, sharing African modes of thought in a colonial language, and promoting conviviality between different traditions and generations of being and becoming African. His focus on giving incompleteness a chance rather than embracing the extravagant illusion of completeness fuelled by spurious affirmations of superiority and autonomy speaks more to the logic of inclusion and less to that of exclusion and the violence of conquest and conversion.

Incompleteness touches on all aspects of existence or being and becoming (Fine 1993; Allen 1997; Tschemplik 2008; Howatson and Sheffield 2008), at individual as well as collective levels, and applies to humans and their relationships with non-humans. Its dimensions include relatedness, openness, enrichment, humility and action. It involves seeking out and kindling connectivities. It is predisposed to and predisposes inextricable embeddedness and entanglements. The concept of incompleteness invites reaching out across real or imagined borders to explore ways of thinking, living socially, bridging and networking to make inclusionary existence more possible. Recognising incompleteness opens the door for interdependence, active participation, and mutual fulfilment and enrichment. Incompleteness has little room even for apparently sympathetic binaries and dualisms, such as this passage from Plato's *The Symposium*, on the need for complementarity in the interest of human reproduction:

> 'After the original nature of every human being had been severed in this way, the two parts longed for each other and tried to come together again. They threw their arms around one another in close embrace, desiring to be reunited, and they began to die of hunger and general inactivity because they refused to do anything at all as separate beings. ….

> 'So it is that ever since that far-off time, love of one person for another has been inborn in human beings, and its role is to restore us to our ancient state by trying to make unity out of duality and to heal our human condition. For each of us is a mere tally of a person, one of two sides of a filleted fish, one half of an original whole. We are all continually searching for our other half.' (Plato's *The Symposium*, reprinted in Howatson and Sheffield 2008: 24).

Beyond the obvious, normalised dimensions of human sexuality and reproduction imperatives highlighted by Plato in the text above, incompleteness *à la* Tutuola compels us as humans to broaden our perspectives, embrace biological fluidities, complexities, permeabilities and dynamism, as well as the unknown and the unknowable, and to innovate socially, culturally and otherwise. This requires being open-ended, open-skinned, open-minded and flexible in identity claims and disclaimers.

Humility is the consequence of the awareness of incompleteness and the basis of a critical consciousness. To temper the feelings of inadequacy and despondency, and attitudes of passivity that could result from awareness of being incomplete, it is important to accentuate the dynamic nature of social action in awareness of incompleteness. The idea of incompleteness generates energy. It invites and compels people to reach out, to move beyond self-pity or victimhood, to be confident and courageous, even in the face of anxious uncertainty, and to embrace the wider (and fuller) world and its complexity, nuance, messiness and the promise of resiliency.

Incompleteness thus entails not only the reality but also an awareness of one's imperfections, inadequacies, transience, inexhaustibleness and infinitude. It is recognition and provision for one's lack or inadequacy of autonomy and independence. It opens up to possibilities (as opposed to confining or limiting) and allows for the unforeseen, for the unpredictability of the unfolding of life. It provides for cultivating and acting in tune with a disposition that delivers self-fulfilment as an eternal work in progress, fulfilment of which is achievable to any degree at all only through relationships with others – human and non-human alike, animate and inanimate. If we are always unfinished or unaccomplished regardless of our achievements, then we are more alert to and accommodating of the humility of doubt. Knowing that we fall short of whatever ideal and expectations propel us, makes us more open and receptive to others, things, ideas and ways of being and relating. It privileges impermanence as a fruitful process of creative renewal in communion with others. Recognising that one is not able to rely entirely on oneself, and to live a life without others – things and humans alike – is quite humbling. It speaks of the reality of being interdependent, even if we think otherwise. Acknowledging and providing for the unfinished business of being and becoming in relationship, compassion and solidarity with others – intimate and distant, known and unknown – is an acknowledgement of our incompleteness as an ordinary and everyday reality. It is a recognition of who or what we are, and what or who we not yet are or can ever be.[21] Awareness and provision for incompleteness could lead to policy decisions such as the law in the State of Hawaii in the USA, which requires all public servants to act with "Aloha." "The Law of Aloha" describes "Aloha" as "mutual regard and affection and extends warmth in caring with no obligation in return. 'Aloha' is the essence of relationships in which each person is important to every other person for collective existence. 'Aloha' means to hear what is not said, to see what cannot be seen and to know the unknowable."[22] This is music to Tutuola's ear, as he listens in from the Deads' Town, where death, it would appear, has not quite had and is most unlikely to have, the last laugh. Hopefully, the young and upcoming generations of African knowledge producers will, like the palm-wine drinkard, undertake questing journeys to the Dead's Town for an inspirational drink from Tutuola's cosmic gourd of incompleteness.

Notes

[1] *West Africa* was a weekly news magazine that was published in London, distributed and read in Nigeria and the rest of Africa (Lindfors 1975: 1).
[2] Tutuola was all too conscious that his English was limited. In an interview with Eric Larrabee following publication of The Palm-Wine Drinkard, he stated: "The

grammar is not correct at all. I made many mistakes" (Eric Larrabee, reprinted in Lindfors 1975: 14).

[3] Human heart, liver and other cells and embryos are being increasingly grown in pigs, for example, and then transplanted in humans who need the relevant body parts replaced.

[4] When his wife failed to get pregnant after four years of marriage, he decided to seek help, even from as far away as The Remote Town, which would take a risky journey of six years to attain, for "a woman or a man without even one issue" had "no respect or honour among his or her friends and neighbours" and was condemned to "live a sorrowful life throughout his or her life-time," if they failed to seek help (Tutuola 1981: 16).

[5] He declares: "I am going to the witch-mother to help me make the juju-medicine which can make my barren wife pregnant!" (Tutuola 1981: 182).

[6] The two other partners were his "Memory" and his "Supreme Second." The later "who was entirely invisible, was my guard throughout my journey" (Tutuola 1981: 25-26, 241).

[7] Danger often posed as "dangerous wild people of the wild jungle or other kinds of jungle beings" (Tutuola 1981: 46). These included the Brutal Ape (Tutuola 1981: 27-33), the Abnormal Squatting Man of the Jungle (Tutuola 1981: 34-45), the Strange Round Shadow (Tutuola 1981: 60-70), the Long-Breasted Mother of the Mountain (Tutuola 1981: 71-87), and the Crazy Removable-Headed Wild Man (Tutuola 1981: 88-94).

[8] See also the Ghanaian film *Heritage Africa* by Kwaw Ansah,
http://www.youtube.com/watch?v=mQ7kRWhRSzM (April 29, 2015).

[9] Eric Larrabee concludes his review of The Palm-Wine Drinkard with a visit to meet Tutuola and the Labour Department in Lagos:

> I went to the Labour Department later, to get him [Amos Tutuola] to sign my copy of his book, and found him sitting in a corner in his loose-fitting uniform, asleep. I had to get to him past row on row of the bespectacled Nigerians, sitting at their desks in bureaucratic self-satisfaction and palpably annoyed at the breach of decorum in a white man's calling on a messenger. He asked me what I wanted him to write and then, after signing the inscription, he said: 'I think, when you reach there, the U.S.A., you write a letter to me.' I said I would, but why did he want me to write? 'So I know you not forget me.' (Eric Larrabee, republished Lindfors 1975: 14).

[10] See Harry Garuba's "And the Book Lived Happily Ever After," in http://chimurengachronic.co.za/and-the-books-lived-happily-ever-after, accessed 11 May 2015. See also Lindfors (1970, 1999a) and Larson (2001).

[11] Sanya Osha, "Tributaries of Afrobeat/s,"
 http://www.3ammagazine.com/3am/tributaries-of-afrobeats, accessed 2 December 2016).

[12] Sanya Osha, "Tributaries of Afrobeat/s,"
 http://www.3ammagazine.com/3am/tributaries-of-afrobeats, accessed 2 December 2016).

[13] See Josh Gabbatiss, "There are over 100 definitions for life and all are wrong," http://www.bbc.com/earth/story/20170101-there-are-over-100-definitions-for-life-and-all-are-wrong, accessed 2 January 2017.

[14] This is a description that could also be applied to Lawino.
[15] See Harry Garuba's "And the Book Lived Happily Ever After," http://chimurengachronic.co.za/and-the-books-lived-happily-ever-after, accessed 11 May 2015.
[16] See Hephzibah Anderson, The Dark Side of Roald Dahl, http://www.bbc.com/culture/story/20160912-the-dark-side-of-roald-dahl, accessed 14 September 2016.
[17] "We" here refers to parents schooled in such western folklore that they "feed" their children.
[18] J. K. (Joanne Kathleen). Rowling, the globally renowned bestselling author of the Harry Potter series, has the following advice for writers of Children's books: "When you're writing a children's book, you need to be a ruthless killer" (Shapiro 2004: 188).
[19] See "The Dark Side of Roald Dahl," http://www.bbc.com/culture/story/20160912-the-dark-side-of-roald-dahl, accessed 14 September 2016.
[20] For readers unfamiliar with what palm-wine is, see definition and detailed discussion in Chapter Seven. There are also many useful videos formulations on YouTube on the harvest and consumption of palm-wine in different parts of the world. See also Jean-Pierre Warnier (2007: 166-167) and (Ritzenthaler and Ritzenthaler 1962: 80-81) for detailed and meticulous descriptions of the harvesting and consumption of raffia palm-wine in the Cameroon Grassfields, with especial focus on Mankon and Bafut.
[21] In a conversation with mathematician Manil Suri, a fellow resident at the Rockefeller Bellagio Center on September 2, 2016 (for which I am most grateful), he drew my attention to what is known in Mathematics as "Goedel's Incompleteness Theorem." He so kindly followed up our conversation by sending me a link to "Goedel's Theorem for Dummies." Accordingly, Goedel's Incompleteness Theorem highlights the limits of provability. It states that there are always mathematical truths that are not knowable because they are not provable mathematically. The Theorem makes a distinction between mathematical truth and mathematical proof. "Truth is about the way things are; proof is about what we can know to be true." See http://www.numbersleuth.org/trends/goedels-theorem-for-dummies, accessed 3 September 2016. See also http://plato.stanford.edu/entries/goedel-incompleteness, accessed 3 September 2016. If even within the narrow confines of our disciplinary axioms claims of completeness through provability are an impossibility, how much more impossible is it to prove completeness across competing disciplines, categories, backgrounds, lived experiences, and universes that do not necessarily share the same basic assumptions, perspectives, cannons, dogmas, and worldviews?
[22] See Hawaii Revised Statutes Division 1. Government § 5-7.5 – See more at: http://codes.findlaw.com/hi/division-1-government/hi-rev-st-sect-5-7-5.html#sthash.2nMtv8Hn.dpuf, accessed 7 September 2016. I am most grateful to Paula Daniels of the Center for Good Food Purchasing, Los Angeles, USA and fellow resident at the Rockefeller Bellagio Center, for drawing my attention to "The Law of Aloha" on 6 September 2016.

Chapter Four

Keeping Alive Popular Ideas of Reality

This chapter builds on a few already established features of Tutuola's work to argue that Tutuola can be described as a post-modernist. This claim is illustrated by presenting Tutuola as someone who disrupts the Eurocentric index of modernity, especially its pretensions as standard bearer and its posture of universalism. In this chapter therefore, we see recurring claims that (i) Eurocentric epistemologies are limited in their inflexible dualisms (ii) Tutuola's representation of endogenous African universes offers endless possibilities characterised by fluidity and ambiguities.

Tutuola's depiction of endogenous African universes and the possibilities within these universes challenge the Eurocentric order – its ontology and epistemology characterised by unsophisticated dualisms and a general lack of nuance. Another illustration is his creative appropriation of the English language to tell African stories from an African perspective. This is symbolic of Tutuola's attitude toward European modernity, a claim which is made by comparing Tutuola to Okot p'Bitek. Both authors do not reject the values internal to modernity in their entirety. Rather, they seek the freedom to interact with modernity on their own terms, in full control of how and when they oscillate between adoption and adaptation. This disposition is therefore a rejection of colonial modernity's efforts to pigeonhole the world and its inhabitants. It is a rejection of colonial modernity's pretension as guardians of history and monopoly of creativity and innovation.

This chapter is evidently symbolic. The pedestal upon which Tutuola is placed stands in contradistinction to the Eurocentric African elite. While Tutuola benefits from an imagination that offers endless possibilities as we see in his representation of African universes and systems of thought, this elite dialectically gives up freedom and autonomy by uncritically accepting Eurocentric modernity, or at best, paying lip service to the relevance of African traditions of knowledge and of being modern. Tutuola's character (in full control of the extent to which he adopts/adapts/preserves vis-à-vis European modernity – guided by the knowledge of when and how these responses are possible), as embodied in his work and epitomised by his quest-heroes and -heroines is a disposition the frontier academic should emulate, cultivate and disseminate. So far, therefore, we have seen two interrelated strategies in departing from the colonial epistemological order: convivial scholarship as instantiated in the example of ethnographic novels, and in the cultivation of appropriate and relevant virtues, attitudes and mindsets. Lastly, it is worth reiterating that Tutuola's work defies categorisation, and that to describe him as an unconscious postmodernist is merely to point to the richness and relevance of his work to discussions and debates of which he may never have been aware. This is one more proof that one does not need to be a professional academic or scholar to influence and shape debates in the academy.

If Amos Tutuola was an incidental writer, he was no less of an accidental intellectual and an accidental postmodernist at that. This chapter explores Tutuola's credentials as an unconscious postmodernist, through his resolute refusal to live a lie by sacrificing the rich complexities of the Yoruba universe of which he was a part. He refused his culture to be disqualified and defined out of circulation by a Eurocentric index of modernity, just as he resisted to be treated as a relic fighting to keep alive a forgotten and inconsequential past. By taking time and making an effort to depict the popular articulations of reality as honestly as he knew them, Tutuola was able to reveal that the future was much more to be found in the impurities of blending and blended encounters with diversity, reaching out, embracing and bridging over dichotomies and difference, and facing up to the challenge that there is often much more or much less to things than meets the eye. In the lives of Tutuola's nimble-footed, border crossing, adventurous quest-narrators, it is understood that transgression and contamination are experienced and indeed, welcome, and that investing in rituals of purification is a sterile venture. He recognised and provided for the fact that the world and its inhabitants are both fathomable and unfathomable, knowable and unknowable, complete and incomplete. Tutuola's world, to borrow from his compatriot Chinua Achebe, was very much like a dancing masquerade, the truth of which was dynamic and constantly on the move, needing nimble-footedness to appraise and keep track of. It is a world where essences are as important as consciousness, envelops as significant as their contents, and messengers as relevant as the messages they carry and deliver. In terms of epistemological encounters, Tutuola's idea of knowledge and knowing is one of complementarities and synthesis of traditions of knowledge and knowledge-making informed by a deep immersion into and mastery of the multiple worlds to which humans, as dancing masquerades, are bound to belong by the very fact of their mobility and dynamism, enhanced by technologies or jujus drawn from these worlds and creatively blended together in novel ways (Anozie 1975[1970]; Armstrong 1975[1970]).

It is little wonder therefore, that Tutuola's work often defies categorisation in conventional terms. Experts find his works "as difficult to pin down as the monsters he writes about," as they tend to "violate … prevailing notions of propriety," both in terms of Africa and the Eurocentric colonial index of modernity seeking to co-opt and impose itself (Priebe 1975[1974]: 266). This, as Richard Priebe argues, makes of Tutuola "a riddler" who "cannot be second-guessed, for he is always creating his own grammar," and spinning his readers "into a world where the impossible is always possible." As a riddler, Tutuola "generates confusion, transgresses propriety, and inverts" perceptions of the physical world that may be seen as real and normal elsewhere but fall short of his sense of popular ideas and ideals of reality with which he is familiar (Priebe 1975[1974]: 266-267).

Tutuola's postmodernism did not limit itself to the deconstruction and creative appropriation of the English language. Nor was Tutuola fundamentalist and exclusionary in his clamour to protect Yoruba culture and provide for "decolonising the mind" (Ngugi 1986) of his fellow Africans through the stories he was determined to share. The recognition and representation he craved were for worldviews and human conditions all too often endangered by the dominance of "a single story" (TED Conferences 2009; Achebe 2000, 2012: 52-61); Nyamnjoh 2004b; Currey 2008; Kamau and Mitambo 2016). A major concern of the time Tutuola was writing in the late 1940s and early 1950s "was the absence of the African voice" (Achebe 2012: 53). To those overly eager to proliferate the world with their monologues, single stories and metanarratives of completeness, Tutuola was keen to remind them, in the words of Achebe, that "every community has enough firewood in its own forests for all the cooking it needs to do" (Achebe 2000: 7), and that "no man should enter his house through another man's gate" (Achebe 2000: 17).

Along with his compatriot Chinua Achebe, whose first novel, *Things Fall Apart*, was published in 1958, Tutuola paved the way for African writers "to challenge stereotypes, myths, and the image" of Africans and their continent, by "effectively telling the African story from an African perspective – in full earshot of the world" (Achebe 2012: 53). To achieve this purpose, both writers decided to use the coloniser's language, "altered sufficiently to bear the weight of an African creative aesthetic, infused with elements of the African literary tradition" (Achebe 2012: 55).[1] Tutuola was sufficiently grounded in the workings of the world not to be conscious that the drunkard who forgets his poverty and sorrow "comes back to his usual sadness as soon as he is conscious" (Tutuola 1981: 200). He wanted recognition and representation for the forgotten or marginalised values of his Yoruba community not in exclusion of but in conversation with the new ways of being and becoming which the modern elite craved. This, he achieved, by seeking "to bring life back into art by bringing art into life, so that the two can hold a conversation" (Achebe 2012: 56). According to Achebe, Tutuola put this vitality to work in the writing of *The Palm-Wine Drinkard*. The result was a story in which:

> There is no attempt to draw a line between what is permissible and what is not, what is possible and what is not possible, what is new and what is old. In a story that is set in the distant past you suddenly see a telephone, a car, a bishop – all kinds of things that don't seem to tie in. But in fact what you have is the whole life of the community, not just the community of humans but the community of ancestors, the animal world, of trees, and so on. Everything plays a part (Achebe 2012: 57).

Amos Tutuola's Yoruba are not dissimilar in their complexity and dynamism to Achebe's Igbo, who "believe that art, religion, everything, the whole of life are embodied in the art of the masquerade" which is dynamic and constantly on the move, and which does not demand "undue respect for what the last generation did," because the "the Igbo people want to create these things again and again, and every generation has a chance to execute its own model of art" (Achebe 2012: 59). In such a context of creative dynamism and mobility, the worse fate that can befall a dancing mask or masquerade is – as René Devisch argues in relation to a *kholuka* circumcision mask in display at the Ethnographic Museum of Antwerp since 2011 – to be estranged and immobilised in the museum (Devisch 2017: 119-130). Both Tutuola's Yoruba and Achebe's Igbo acknowledge change as a permanent feature of being human and of human creativity. The wisdom of Achebe's words is in the importance to respect customs and traditions, just as it is important to understand that in the course of human mobility and encounters, new questions arise to which old answers are not quite suited. This might require making things up as one goes along, but an old broom, however experienced and thorough, cannot sweep with quite the same effectiveness as a new broom in a new context. Far from being an invitation to abandon the past for the present, it is rather a call to creatively blend the past with the present in the interest of the future. In tune with this wisdom, both Tutuola and Achebe have seen language and art primarily as communication tools across social categories, as democratic facilitators, and as enablers, just as much as they have used their art and language to reinforce cultural roles and norms in their worlds of unequal encounters with others, strange and familiar.

Through their creative appropriation of various influences in their lives, African and European alike, Achebe and Tutuola have successfully stressed the need for conviviality between change and continuity, individual freedom and collective interest, tradition and modernity, Africa and the rest. The stories both Tutuola and Achebe have left us challenge the assumption that a person native to a culture or a place is also necessarily native to its values or identifies themselves with those values, cultures or places to the same homogenising degree as others. Their art demonstrates that there is no essentialised Yoruba or Igbo identity as social and political encounters and transformations fashion different ways of knowing and being Yoruba and Igbo in Nigeria, Africa and the world. Being Yoruba or Igbo, far from being a hardback book with a definite introduction, body and conclusion, is always a process of becoming, best understood as flexible, fluid and full of ellipses – an unfinished and unfinishable story. Tutuola did not "turn away from the reality of life's intimidating complexity," by retreating "into the obvious, the tendency to be frightened by the richness of the world and to clutch what we always have understood." He stood firm, and sought to conquer life's mystery by battling with it (Achebe 2012: 59).

In light of this need to constantly bring art and life into conversation informed by the dynamism and nimble-footedness of cultures and those involved in them, Tutuola had much more in common with the character Lawino, in p'Bitek's *Song of Lawino*, who was disappointed by the sheepishness with which her colonially educated husband, Ocol, yielded to the embrace of the white man and his ways. Learned though Ocol was supposed to be, his effortless submission and subservience to the white man and his pretensions of completeness dashed her hopes. Instead of answering the critical questions his wife asked him, Ocol accused Lawino of "insulting him." He responded to her questions with a quarrel and looked down upon her, dismissing her questions as "a waste of time," "silly questions, typical questions from village girls," "questions of uneducated people, useless questions from untutored minds." To Ocol, colonially illiterate Lawino had "a tiny little brain" that was "not trained" and that could not "see things intelligently" or "sharply." He claims that, even if he tried to answer her questions, she would not understand what he was saying because she had "not been to school," and "a university man can only have useful talk with another university man or woman." He claims to speak a language different from hers, "so that even if he spoke to me in Acoli I would still need an interpreter." But according to Ocol, being "a primitive language" of "very few words," Acoli was "not rich enough to express his deep wisdom." Acoli was "not like the white man's language, which is rich and very beautiful, a language fitted for discussing deep thoughts." And so Lawino was forced to "swallow the questions" that burnt inside her; making her eyes "redden with frustration" and her to "tremble with anger" (p'Bitek 1989[1966]: 62-66). Lawino's frustration and anger have, in other victims of colonial education, resulted in chronic self-doubt, self-deprecation, and self-annihilation (Nyang 1994; Soyinka 1994; Nyamnjoh and Fuh 2014).

Fortunately for the world and values unlettered Lawino represents, the barely colonially educated Amos Tutuola refused to celebrate victimhood, opting instead to meet the white man and his language half way, by appropriating the latter to tell his stories, and by going into the belly of the colonial beast to seek for avenues to make his stories known. He refused to be distracted by the criticisms levelled at him and the likes of Lawino by the Ocols who had elected themselves to the status of champions of Eurocentric modernity in Africa. To be socially visible, those converted within the framework of Eurocentric modernity crave external recognition and environments over internal relevance and the protection of traditional endogenous cultures and worldviews. They internalise and reproduce irrelevance through an unjustifiable sense of superiority and priorities. They "boast in the marketplace showing off to people," instead of proving the merits of their education and the foreign values and standards they embrace through real achievements (p'Bitek 1989[1966]: 68). It is a modernity for keeping up appearances, for self-delusion and self-belittlement, and for talking without listening, all in the name of a quest for completeness (p'Bitek 1989[1966]: 12-14). Those enchanted by such modernity are often oblivious of a popular understand of "the beautiful" across Africa, as "that which is attractive because it is useful" (Tabron 2003: 67). Indeed, those who embrace colonial education fully become like slaves, doing the bidding of capricious and whimsical masters, and looking foolish before the likes of Lawino and Tutuola who have stood their ground in the face of the violence of conversion. In this connection, it is worthy of note that although Okot p'Bitek "doubted the usefulness of formal education," he was not averse to living a modern life. According to Odoch Pido, p'Bitek "did not live a traditional Acholi life"; "he drove a British-made Jaguar car and lived in Hurlingham, a posh Nairobi neighbourhood" around 1977 and enjoyed regular meetings with his colleagues in the Senior Common Room of the Nairobi University College, "where he challenged senior professors to academic duels by calling them headless, bush poets, and *jarwas* (savage tribalists)" (Pido 1997: 677-678). He was also a practising Roman Catholic who upon his death in 1982 was buried in a churchyard in his northern Uganda birthplace of Gulu.

What p'Bitek is really critical of is not a life enriched by modern technologies as such, but the ambitions of conquest that underpin colonial education and its appropriation of such modern technologies. As Lawino puts it with reference to the emasculated Ocol, "My husband's master is my husband's husband. My husband runs from place to place like a small boy, he rushes without dignity," doing the bidding of the white man. Rendered blind by the libraries of white men, Ocol has lost his dignity and authority by behaving "like a dog of the white man," lying by the door to "keep guard while waiting for leftovers" from the master's table. He has lost his "fire" and bull-like prowess and has succumbed to living on borrowed food, wearing borrowed clothes, and using his ideas, actions and behaviour "to please somebody else." He may have read extensively and deeply and can challenge the white men in his knowledge of their books and their ancestors of the intellect, but to Lawino, this has come at a great price: "the reading has killed my man, in the ways of his people. He has become a stump. He abuses all things Acoli; he says the ways of black people are black" (p'Bitek 1989[1966]: 91-96). Lawino reminds Ocol that if he has chosen the path of passive and sterile subservience, let him not, in frustration, "shout at me because I know the customs of our people," customs that make him feel so desperately inferior to the white man (p'Bitek 1989[1966]: 46). In this connection, Lawino and Tutuola are singing from the same hymnal. They both do not totally reject the white man's customs, but they would like the freedom to be themselves and engage with the white man and his ways on their own terms, with full dignity, selectively adopting and adapting as they see fit, and as dictated by their needs and aspirations.

To Lawino and Tutuola, colonial education and modernity must not be made to behave as if they have the monopoly of creativity and innovation, and of good traditions. Both are keen to show that the ways of their ancestors are good and solid with roots that reach deep into the soil, and that their customs are neither hollow nor thin, nor easily breakable or blown away by the winds. They refuse to yield to colonial education and its African converts, who insist on despising the ancestral customs and worldview of the communities on which they write, in favour of foreign customs little understood, admired or desired (p'Bitek 1989[1966]: 19).

Neglected, insulted and abused, Lawino reminds her husband without relent that no education makes sense if it turns one against one's people and against the ways of one's ancestors: "Listen Ocol, my friend, the ways of your ancestors are good, their customs are solid and not hollow. They are not thin, not easily breakable. They cannot be blown away by the winds, because their roots reach deep into the soil" (p'Bitek 1989[1966]: 19). Closely entangled with ideology and hegemony as colonial education is, it leaves little room for critical thinking even as it celebrates Cartesian rationalism and the competence of science as the only universally valid way of seeking knowledge. The result, quite paradoxically, is an emphasis on doing rather than thinking, and all attempts at serious questioning and exploration of alternatives are rationalised away by the dominant voices of mimicry, conformism, myopia, and "stupid stubbornness" (p'Bitek 1989[1966]: 95-98). Instead of seeing themselves as the problem, Ocol and the likes are all too ready to name and shame the likes of Lawino and Tutuola as dangerous barbarians who risk turning the clock back on Africa's pilgrimage to the apex of Eurocentric modernity and its ideologies of completeness.

Determined to whiten up in quest of Eurocentric modernity, Ocol and his likes spare no effort to dramatize the backwardness of the Lawinos and Tutuolas who argue that the pursuit of European modernity need not entail throwing the baby of African ways of life out with the bathwater of their purported backwardness. In his response to criticism by Lawino, Ocol insists, stubbornly, and with the pseudo power of a castrated bull: "Woman, shut up! Pack your things and go!" Like someone blinded to the fetters and mimicry that have violated his humanity and authority, Ocol compares Lawino's criticism to "the mad bragging of a defeated general," "the pointless defiance of the condemned," "rotting buffalo left behind by fleeing poachers," and "sour sweet," among other negative representations to depict her backwardness and the "blackness, deep, deep fathomless darkness" that "is Africa" to him. He has no time for the "idle giant basking in the sun, sleeping, snoring, twitching in dreams" that is Africa – "diseased with a chronic illness, choking with black ignorance, chained to the rock of poverty," "stuck in the stagnant muds of superstitions" – and cannot understand "why I was born black." He promises annihilation for everything Lawino stands for, everything African: "Put in detention all the preachers of Negritude" and "To the gallows with all the Professors of Anthropology, and teachers of African History, a bonfire we'll make to their works, we'll destroy all their anthologies of African literature and close down all the schools of African Studies." It is imperative, he argues with categorical zeal, to "smash all these mirrors that I may not see the blackness of the past from which I came." If independence means an excuse to reinvent the past, then such "uhuru" must never come to pass (p'Bitek 1984[1967]: 121-151).

It is this Eurocentric African elite so eloquently depicted in p'Bitek's *Song of Lawino*, which Tutuola challenges with his fantastical stories told in an English of his own. Like Lawino, Tutuola simply refuses to give up on such a powerful elite who are determined to free themselves of everything African, everything he and the likes of Lawino are so deeply immersed in, shaped by, proud of and committed to. If Lawino invested in singing a song to remind her husband of what he was losing by uncritically embracing Eurocentric modernity as a winner takes all, Tutuola systematically provided thick ethnographic accounts of the African universes and their systems of thought and representation, which the Europhiles were determinedly running away from in their quest to become complete gentlemen and ladies of Europe in Africa. These universes he depicts are not bounded, frozen, backward, simple and unambiguous the way Africa's Eurocentric enthusiasts and their European instructors would want Tutuola and Lawino to believe. Far from being stuck in the past, Amos Tutuola was one of the most futuristic intellectuals that Africa has ever had.

Tutuola's contestation of untested abstractions, metanarratives and the essentialism of bounded identities, dualisms and dichotomies introduced a relativism that predated the postmodern turn in the social sciences (Rosenau 1992), a turn which in anthropology was exemplified by texts such as *Writing Culture* (Clifford and Marcus 1986). An ethnographic reading of Tutuola challenges anthropologists and other social scientists to renegotiate taken-for-granted ideas and inventions of Africa and its social realities in favour of mobility, flexibility, fluidity, flux, complexity and nuance. The nimble-footed, boundary-crossing mobility of Tutuola's characters as negotiators and navigators of myriad identity margins and their consciousness introduces a nuanced complexity in the interconnections between outsiders and insiders in anthropological knowledge production that endorses and legitimises conversations, co-implication and co-production informed by *etic* and *emic* perspectives as two sides of the same coin or cowrie. In his stories, the status of a stranger is no one's monopoly, just as being an insider is eternally a work in progress. In this regard, Tutuola's fiction would pass the test of ethnographic fiction by a "native" non-anthropologist, of the sort discussed by Gupta and Ferguson (1997: 30-31). The fact that anthropological practice in Africa is still steeped in problematic colonial assumptions, essentialisms, and confused and confusing commitments (Nyamnjoh 2012a, 2015a) makes Tutuola a very important interlocutor for vital conversations on the future of anthropology on the continent, especially at a time of renewed clamours for decolonisation and transformation of curricula and knowledge production across universities in Africa – the 2015/2016 #RhodesMustFall and #FeesMustFall student protests in South Africa being good cases in point (Gibson 2016; Nyamnjoh 2016).

Tutuola's novels and short stories offer comprehensive depictions of African endogenous universes in a manner and with a profundity that only a native or an insider can achieve. Both reality and the universe are imbued with endless possibilities of being and becoming, thanks to the multiplicity of consciousness available to inhabit them. Things, words, deeds and beings are always incomplete, not because of absences but because of their possibilities. Faced with inadequacies, we, every now and then, invest hope, interpretation and mediation in those claiming the status of seers and frontier beings, in those imbued with larger than life clairvoyance and capacity to straddle worlds, navigate, negotiate and reconcile chasms. With the potency they avail us, we are able to activate ourselves to mitigate the inadequacies of the five senses, so that we too might perceive what is ordinarily lost to us in terms of the fullness and complexity of reality. Mediators or interpreters are multidimensional in their perception, because of their capacity to see, feel, hear, smell and taste things that are ordinarily beyond sight, feeling, hearing, smelling and tasting. They navigate and negotiate the crossroads and intersections of existence, pushing boundaries and challenging orthodoxies. This is amply illustrated with relevant excerpts from his novels in what follows, especially in Chapter Six, which deals with activation, potency and efficacy in Tutuola's universe.

As variously illustrated throughout this book, Tutuola's is a universe where life is larger than logic, and where the logic and reality of sensory perception are constantly challenged. Like a postmodern theorist (Rosenau 1992) of incompleteness, Tutuola invites us to perceive things as ambiguous and interlinked and to factor ambiguity and interconnections into how we relate to the world and the hierarchies we would like to claim or contest therein. No condition is permanent in this universe, not even the unity of being often insisted upon by certain philosophies and traditions of knowledge in scholarship. Only the permanence of change is unconditional. Natural, human and supernatural structures are just as subject to the whims and caprices of changing times and the shifting forms of the beings, things, words and deeds they seek to tame. Even time is far from linear and chronological. Everyone and everything is malleable and flexible, from humans and their anatomies, to animals and plants, gods, ghosts and spirits. Anything can be anything. People and things adopt different forms and manifest themselves differently according to context and necessity. Something transformed can regain the state that preceded its transformation. A thing can double itself, and the double becomes the thing and the thing the double. A shadow is not always only a shadow, just as a thing is not always only a thing. Masters are servants and servants are masters. Humbling ambiguity is the order of the day. Gods are humans and humans are gods. Spirits assume human forms, and humans can transform themselves into spirits, animals and plants. Sometimes a creature combines multiple forms of being – half-human and half-animal or half-plant, half-god, half-ghost, half-spirit, half-male or half-female, etc. – and assumes the consciousness akin to each form, even as it retains the consciousness of its form of origin to facilitate reverting. It is a universe of agency ad infinitum, one in which structures exist only to the extent that they can be humbled by the agency of those who make structures possible. Agency or the capacity to act efficaciously is not a birthmark or permanence but something to be discovered, cultivated, nurtured, activated and reactivated to different degrees of potency through relationships with others, things and humans alike. Context matters. Even nature and the supernatural are sensitive to context, and, like chameleons, are expected to collaborate with the consciousness that possesses it. Power is fluid, and so is weakness. Both change hands without warning. Woe betides those who invest too heavily on appearances in a nimble-footed world where signs are permanently scrambled and logic forever wrong-footed. Tutuola's universe of tales defies the currency of Cartesian rationalism and its dualistic ambitions of dominance (Nyamnjoh 2015b: 3-6).

As broached elsewhere (Nyamnjoh 2015b, 2015d), there is more and less to bodies than meets the eye, just as there is much more and much less to what strikes us in things or facets of things. When doubles mimic or parody in convincing ways, what reason is there to argue against a thing and its double being two sides of the same coin or cowrie? While surfaces are obviously important and often suffice for many ends and purposes, delving beneath appearances and digging deep into the roots of things is critical for understanding eternally nuanced and ever-shifting complexities of being and becoming. Delving deep makes impossibilities possible, just as it makes the possible impossible. Being and becoming as works in progress require borrowings, enchantment and enhancements to render them beautiful and acceptable. It is this capacity to enable and disable simultaneously that makes absence present and presence absent in certain places and spaces, private and public alike. Particular contexts challenge us in particular ways to heighten or lower the bar and threshold of acceptability and tolerability.

This capacity, Mbembe (2003) argues, is most unsettling to a fundamentally dualistic assumption in Western thought that "every life is singular." Hence: "the impossibility for a single and same thing, or a single and same being, to have several different origins or to exist simultaneously in different places and under different signs"

(Mbembe 2003: 3). It is through a simultaneous recognition of one's capacity to act on others as well as to bear the actions of others in time and space that subjectivity is made possible (Nyamnjoh 2015b, 2015d). This is in tune with the Foucauldian recognition that – technologies of self-cultivation notwithstanding (Martin et al. 1988) – no being is self-built, that every single being is the result of billions of actions of other beings that have converged in producing a subject and shaping it while making it possible for the subject in question to take itself as the object of its own actions (Foucault 1975), and thus, the self-managing, self-made individual of neoliberal and neo-Kantian Western thought is a complete delusion (Warnier 2013b: 101-105). Tutuola's bodies have meaning only to the extent that and in the manner in which they are harnessed, in full or as organs (Mbembe 2003: 17). As active and activating vehicles, containers or envelopes (Warnier 1993a, 1993b, 2006, 2007, 2009, 2013c; Salpeteur and Warnier 2013), bodies are malleable, amenable to being compressed, contorted and extended, dissected, dismembered and remembered, branded, visibilised and invisiblised, valued and devalued.

Auras and essences are as much attributes of the parts as they are of the whole, just as the part is in the whole and the whole in the part. What seems more important than the forms bodies take is the consciousness which inhabits bodies and body parts. Even when a body is seemingly palpably the same and contiguous, the consciousness that inhabits it may be fluid and flexible, pointing to a reality that impoverishes fixations with fixities, permanence and stability. The human body can assume the consciousness of an ordinary human just as it can that of a god, a spirit, death, a curious creature from the wild bushes or the endless forests, as well as it can project its own consciousness onto a plant, an animal, air or whatever other element of nature is available and handy. Tutuola's is a universe in which being a quest-hero requires being a composite – amenable to shifting bodily shapes and with the capacity for presence in simultaneous multiplicities, in familiar and unfamiliar ways, compressing and expanding time and space as need arises. Bodies and forms are never complete. They are open-ended malleable vessels to be appropriated by consciousness in its multiplicity. Bodies provide for hearts and minds to intermingle, accommodating the dreams and hopes of both, and mitigating the propensity of the one to outrace the other. Bodies are melting pots of possibilities and amenable to being melted by possibilities (Amadiume 1987, 1997; Bourdieu 1990; Butler 1990, 1993; Foucault 1988; Mauss 1973; Martin et al. 1988; Scheper-Hughes and Lock 1987; Shilling 2012[1993]; Lock and Farquhar 2007; Sanders 2008; Warnier 1993a, 1993b; 2006, 2007, 2009, 2013c; Salpeteur and Warnier 2013; Devisch 2017). Similarly, sameness is emphasised through border crossing and unbounding and fusing identities. The supernatural is quite simply natural. Gods, death, spirits and the curious and terrible creatures of the bushes and forests take on human nature and forms of settlement, just as humans develop the supernatural attributes of these ordinarily invisible forces in their lives (Abega 2000). Being so intricately entangled and even mangled up, nature, culture and supernature feed off one another, in ways that make it impossible to fathom one without the others. They co-produce and co-implicate one another, and are each present in the other even when apparently defiant of the ordinary senses to perceive and authenticate their existence with Cartesian rationalist certitude and certainty.

Notes

[1] Following Achebe's death on March 21 2013, *The Economist* remarked that as a novelist, Achebe:

> … saw himself as part of the great Western canon. The titles of his books saluted his heroes: "Things Fall Apart," from Yeats, and "No Longer at Ease," in homage to T. S. Eliot. At school he had once been punished for asking a boy, in Ibo, to pass the soap. Despite that humiliation, he liked writing in English. "I feel the English language will be able to carry the weight of my Africa experience," he declared in 1965. It would have to be a different English, though, "still in full communion with its ancestral home, but altered to suit its new African surroundings."
>
> www.economist.com/news/obituary/21574453-chinua-achebe-africas-greatest-storyteller-died-march-21st-aged-82-chinua-achebe, accessed 28 August 2013.

Chapter Five

The Palm-Wine Drinkard and the Challenge of Dichotomies

This chapter explores further the salience and implications of recognising and providing for interconnections in Tutuola's universe and cosmology. It examines the reality Tutuola accords to things we associate with death and death-like ghosts. It illustrates how Tutuola challenges the dichotomy between real and unreal, and how he bridges worlds and words such as invisible, inexplicable and impossible. In other words, it brings out the message that what is real is not always that which is accessible to sensory perception or makes cognitive sense. Tutuola's universe is a glimpse of a paradise of infinite possibilities, one into which entry is predicated upon repenting from the sinful sheepishness of a colonial epistemological order, its impositions and propensity to cultivate mimics. If we unshackle ourselves from an uncritical embrace of Eurocentric modernity, who knows the endless possibilities that await us.

The discussion involves the image of the Skull, as a continuation of what was broached in chapter four. It further illustrates Tutuola's post-modernism. On the one hand, it refutes the ontological nature of personhood (the self as a single unitary action). The fact of our incompleteness often attracts ambiguities because the inevitable composite nature of one's being means that there is always more to something and someone than meets the eye. This is why the Skull can also possibly represent the hollowness of a Western modernity. Western modernity is the skull that has refused and continues to refuse acknowledging its incompleteness, and by extension its composite nature. In this connection, Tutuola's discussion of life and death as being in constant circulation is very instructive about the need for mutual activation through indebtedness and the acknowledgement of debt. Not only does this make death and dying a process and not an event, it also means that death and life are constantly changing places in a world of perpetual impermanence. Life and death, like Siamese twins, are eternally interconnected and interdependent. So much so that even when life and death meet in the Deads' Town (as in the case of the palm-wine drinkard and his palm-wine tapster), it is not like a meeting of dichotomies but a blending of possibilities. Tutuola's universe is one in which anything, anyone and any reality can be any reality, anyone and anything, interchangeably.

The arguments in the preceding chapters around popular understandings of reality, and the need to keep them alive and integrated into more conclusive epistemologies require further substantiation from Tutuola's writings and universe. To substantiate the claims and arguments in Chapter Four on the limits of dichotomies and the imperative to recognise and provide for the interconnections, interdependencies and flexibility evident in how Tutuola understands the world and weaves together his stories, the current chapter takes a closer look at The Palm-Wine Drinkard (Tutuola 1952), his first published, most well-known and most reviewed novel.*

As half-spirit and half-human, the palm-wine drinkard's needs and deeds are no ordinary needs and deeds. The exceptionally dependent child of a wealthy father – "the richest man in our town" (Tutuola 1952: 7) – he had a supernatural appetite for palm-wine, an appetite which could only – or should I say, barely – be satisfied by a nine square mile farm of 560,000 palm trees. Being the richest man, his father could afford to pander to the unusual appetites of his bizarre son – the eldest of eight children, and the only one who substituted hard work with palm-wine drinking. The father recruits an equally exceptional palm-wine tapster to cater full-time for the appetite of his son. This creates a perfect balance: for the drinkard to qualify to "do no other work more than to drink palm-wine … from morning till night and from night till morning" since the age of ten requires an opposite or a complement in the person of "an expert palm-wine tapster" who "had no other work more than to tap palm-wine every day" (Tutuola 1952: 7). To be absolutely independent of work, the drinkard requires absolute dependence on the work of the tapster.

For fifteen years the narrator pleasures himself with a superabundance of palm-wine dutifully delivered by his devoted tapster. He drinks along with many a fair-weather friend, but when his father and tapster die suddenly and the generous supply of palm-wine dries up, his drinking partners turn their backs on him.

He becomes very lonely, sad and vulnerable, like a child doubly orphaned by losing both its biological and foster parents. Encouraged by the legendary belief that the dead are alive in the world of the living even if "in the Deads' Town" (Tutuola 1952: 96), the palm-wine drinkard sets out to track down his dead palm-wine tapster, who, in the perspective of the drinkard, had no business dying. How can those who are there to make a life of superabundant pleasures possible die?

Once on his quest, the narrator who names himself "father of the gods who could do everything in this world" (Tutuola 1952: 10), is quite ordinarily extraordinary in his capacity to collapse the boundaries between master and servant, nature and culture, village and town, home and bushes, human and supernatural, plausible and implausible, rational and superstitious, primitive and civilised, Africa and the West, etc. Not only is the palm-wine drinkard a composite of the natural and supernatural, he and the world he inhabits provide for infinite shifts between categories through flexibility and fluidity in bodies and a capacity to be anything and to take any form, even the form of air, while maintaining one's consciousness. He ably extends and activates himself thanks to the juju, spells, charms or power containing substances he carries along with him in his journey and quest for his dead tapster. In the course of his journey, he is challenged to perform many an extraordinary feat, including selling his death and leasing his fear, using a combination of his juju and cunning (Armstrong 1975[1970]: 218-219; Anozie 1975[1970]: 242).

Bushes (forests or jungles) are ambivalent places and spaces of the highest order. As we gather from many of Tutuola's books, they are places to run into seeking refuge from the terror of the community of humans, as much as they are places to escape from when one falls foul of the evil beings that inhabit them. In addition to the obvious examples of the narrators in *The Palm-Wine Drinkard* and *My Life in the Bush of Ghosts*, who are in and out of forests for various reasons, there is also the example of the youth and his younger sister in *Ajaiyi and His Inherited Poverty* (Tutuola 1967). Forests attract as much as they repel, and are as inspiring of hope and possibilities as they are dangerous and foreboding.

One can never be too prepared for a journey into or through the forest, just as the forest can never cease to spring surprises on those who live in villages and towns, distant and near. Africans have learnt to cultivate relationships of tenuous symbiosis with the forest and its magic of infinite ambivalences, taking advantage of the forest when this is possible, and seeking refuge from the forest and its dangers as they see fit (Turnbull 1961; Laburthe-Tolra 1981, 1985; Abega 1987, 2000). The bushes and forests in Tutuola's books are thus both a reality and an inviting metaphor of encounters and relationships between the familiar and the unfamiliar, the sacred and the profane, culture and nature, the human and the supernature, African and Europe, the visible and the invisible, etc.

Speaking of the skulls in the endless forest, Tutuola writes of his narrator, the palm-wine drinkard: "I had changed myself into air, they could not trace me out again, but I was looking at them" (Tutuola 1952: 27). The fact of having taken the form of air and its consciousness did not result in him losing consciousness as human. In another instance, confronted by a big river he ordinarily could not cross by foot or by swimming, he commands his juju acquired from "a kind spirit" to activate himself to acquire the form and consciousness of a canoe, while maintaining his consciousness of a human being, and is thus able to transport his wife and himself across the big river, before regaining his human form of origin (Tutuola 1952: 39). Similarly, the narrator transforms himself into a pebble to escape the dangerous dance of the mountain-creatures. "I myself had changed into a flat pebble and was throwing myself along the way to my home town" (Tutuola 1952: 117).

Confronted by the "hungry-creature" who "could not satisfy with any food in this world" and who could eat up the world's entire stock of food and "he would be still feeling hungry as if he had not tasted anything for a year" (Tutuola 1952: 108) – a perfect metaphor for colonialism and imperialism if ever one was needed –, the palm-wine drinkard, to prevent his wife from being swallowed alive by the "hungry-creature," "performed one of my jujus and it changed my wife and our loads to a wooden-doll and I put it in my pocket" (Tutuola 1952: 108).

Although this did not stop the "hungry-creature" from swallowing the wooden-doll and him as well, the palm-wine drinkard, once in the stomach of the creature, commanded his "juju which changed the wooden-doll back to my wife, gun, egg, cutlass and loads at once." Then he was able to load his gun, which he fired into the stomach of the hungry creature and cutting the stomach with his cutlass, was able to free his wife and himself, and to escape (Tutuola 1952: 109-110). What a metaphor for seeking liberation from the belly of the imperial and colonial beast!

Similarly, a mere Skull from a hole in the heart of the dark, endless forest can, as the barest form of life that it is, activate itself, however temporarily, into a "beautiful 'complete' gentleman," "tall and stout," "dressed with the finest and most costly clothes," and with "all the parts of his body ... completed" (Tutuola 1952: 18), by borrowing or renting body parts from others to enhance himself and his efficacy for the market. In its borrowed body parts and costly clothes, the Skull vibrates with such divine beauty that it instantly enchants women and men alike. Indeed, so beautiful was he that in a battlefield an "enemy would not kill him or capture him and if bombers saw him in a town which was to be bombed, they would not throw bombs on his presence, and if they did throw it, the bomb itself would not explode" (Tutuola 1952: 25). That was the promise of his borrowed beauty, if only the Skull could afford not to be gentleman enough by refusing to honour his word and his debts to those who had so generously loaned him the body parts and fineries to be more than a Skull for just a while. Those who can afford to borrow without paying back or acknowledging their debts, and who also refuse to service those debts, might claim autonomy and boast about being self-made, but they know, deep down, that there is a lot less to them than meets the eye.

In *The Palm-Wine Drinkard*, the passages that most illustrate the flexibility and fluidity of bodies as attachable and detachable containers, and the proliferation of consciousness which inhabits them, are those which describe how a mere Skull came to be a complete gentleman. This is done by borrowing body parts and costly clothes to enable him to attend the famous market of a town where the beautiful daughter of the famous head of the town has turned down every suitor imaginable. The lady is described in the following terms:

> This lady was very beautiful as an angel but no man could convince her for marriage. So, one day she went to the market on a market-day as she was doing before, or to sell her articles as usual; on that market-day, she saw a curious creature in the market, but she did not know where the man came from and never knew him before (Tutuola 1952: 18).

She was instantly charmed by this "beautiful 'complete' gentleman ... dressed with the finest and most costly clothes" (Tutuola 1952: 18). Indeed, "all the parts of his body were completed"; he was both tall and stout, and had he "been an article or an animal for sale, he would be sold at least for £2000 (two thousand pounds)" (Tutuola 1952: 18). The more he ignored the lady, the more she felt attracted to him. She "left her articles unsold" and "began to watch the movements of the complete gentleman about in the market" (Tutuola 1952: 18). When the market day ended and people were returning to their various destinations, the lady followed the complete gentlemen, despite his repeatedly "telling her to go back, or not to follow him" (Tutuola 1952: 19). She "did not listen to what he was telling her, and when the complete gentleman had tired of telling her not to follow him or to go back to her town, he left her to follow him." (Tutuola 1952: 19). Roughly twelve miles away from the market, at a crossroads, "they left the road on which they were travelling and started to travel inside an endless forest in which only all the terrible creatures were living." (Tutuola 1952: 19). As meeting points of and with deities influencing the affairs of humans in Tutuola's universe, crossroads and junctions are privileged locations for summoning the intervention of relevant deities with jujus and ritual sacrifices. Crossroads and junctions are as much places and spaces of hope and reassurance as they are zones of diminishing prospects.

Thus, as they branch off the main road at the crossroads, the lady's fantasies turn into her worst nightmare, as she begins the journey of discovery that there is much less to her prince charming than meets the eye. Her complete gentleman begins the process of self-deactivation by returning and paying the rental for "the hired parts of his body to the owners" (Tutuola 1952: 20) who had so generously lent them to him, so he could pass for what he was not. "When he reached where he hired the left foot, he pulled it out, he gave it to the owner and paid him" (Tutuola 1952: 20), and continued his journey. And "when they reached the place where he hired the right foot, he pulled it out and gave it to the owner and paid for the rentage" (Tutuola 1952: 20). Both feet gone, the complete gentleman "began to crawl along on the ground" (Tutuola 1952: 20). Frightened at what was unfolding before her eyes, as her illusion of a complete gentleman evaporated, "that lady wanted to go back to her town or her father," but the now not so complete gentleman would not let her.

This is like a metaphor for the uncritical embrace of Eurocentric modernity and its promise of completeness by Africans such as Ocol of p'Bitek's *Song of Lawino*, only to discover beyond the crossroads, like the beautiful lady enchanted by Tutuola's "complete gentleman," that there is a lot less to Eurocentric modernity than meets the eye. It is also a metaphor for what happens when one insists on completeness that is out of this world and that requires diminishing and debasing others for one to claim fulfilment. It is what would happen if one absolutely had to pay all of one's debts in order to free oneself from any form of sociality possible. Because a human being is a social being, one's humanity is by necessity a composite of all the interconnections and relationships of intertwinement, entanglements and even manglement that one has cultivated and internalised. It is impossible – indeed a contradiction – for one to claim absolute freedoms or autonomy without the prospect of self-deactivation. To make this point, Tutuola details in all its minuteness the deactivation of the complete gentleman that he has constructed.

Thus, when "they reached where he hired the belly, ribs, chest, etc. ... he pulled them out and gave them to the owner and paid for the rentage" (Tutuola 1952: 20). Left with "only the head and both arms with neck," the complete gentleman could not crawl any more, and resorted to "jumping on as a bull-frog" (Tutuola 1952: 20). Overwhelmed by fear and forbidden from returning home to her father, the lady fainted. When he had plucked off, returned and paid for both hired arms, as well as his hired neck, the "complete gentleman was reduced to head and when they reached where he hired the skin and flesh which covered the head, he returned them, and paid to the owner," reducing himself to a disembodied "Skull" (Tutuola 1952: 20-21). As a Skull, "he could jump a mile to the second before coming down" (Tutuola 1952: 22), so whenever the lady attempted to run away, "he hastily ran to her front and stopped her as a log of wood" (Tutuola 1952: 22). They got to his house, which was a hole under the ground; "there were only Skulls living in that hole" (Tutuola 1952: 22). Once home, the Skull "tied a single Cowrie on the neck of this lady with a kind of rope," "gave her a large frog on which she sat as a stool," and then "he gave a whistle to a Skull of his kind to keep watch on this lady whenever she wanted to run away" (Tutuola 1952: 22). She would remain under their watch until eventually released by the palm-wine drinker narrator, "father of the gods who could do everything in this world" (Tutuola 1952: .23-31).

This is a tale of the horrors and futilities of an insensitive insistence on completeness, independence or autonomy that can only be achieved by sacrificing sociality and living in total solitude. Spirits and gods in touch with humanity feel and behave the same as humans. Those humans with the gift of clairvoyance, like the narrator, can seek to outmanoeuvre others with their trickery but are not entirely self-sufficient, however large their supply of cunning, juju, spells and charms. As Lindfors rightly remarks, even though the palm-wine drinkard "is part-trickster, part-magician, part-superman, he cannot over-come every adversary or extricate himself from every difficult situation; supernatural helpers have to come to his assistance from time to time" (Lindfors 1970: 312). In an interconnected world of interdependence, even an initially unlikely hero, like the palm-wine drinkard, can acquire the tools for self-activation beyond their personal juju, through relying on natural and supernatural others. In this connection, Lindfors writes, "The unpromising hero who had set out on his quest with limited powers and purely selfish ambitions becomes in the end a miracle worker, the savior and benefactor of all mankind. He changes, in other words, from a typical folktale hero into a typical epic hero" (Lindfors 1970: 312).

The story is also, Steven Tobias notes, a metaphor for the hollowness of Western modernity used to dazzle Africans in colonial times. In this story of the Skull and the beautiful lady, writes Tobias,

> ... Tutuola suggests that although Western ideas and projects might at first seem tempting and attractive, these things ultimately prove little more than a deceptive facade. Once stripped away they reveal the true underlying structures of colonialism: death and enslavement. Through this tale Tutuola hints at the way in which colonial and, subsequently, postcolonial socioeconomic systems serve to chain their African victims to money and other seemingly positive trappings while simultaneously trying to remove their ability to voice resistance (Tobias 1999: 72).

In other words, if only the West could recognise the debts it owes others, and if ever it was to be gentleman enough to pay back and return all the body parts it has borrowed from other worlds, other civilisations and modernities to activate itself to the superiority or completeness it claims, its dazzling civilisation and modernity would be reduced to a mere skull and a bare existence. In the case of Africa, such debt would have to include the reality of unequal encounters that have resulted in the harvesting of African labour and resources abundantly in slavery and colonialism at different points in time (Rodney 2012[1972]; Chinweizu 1987 [1975]; Plumelle-Uribe 2001; Bwemba-Bong 2005; Lovejoy 2011; Eltis 2000; Eltis and Richardson 2008). It would require as well recognition of the silences in African history and for the West to acknowledge, account and compensate for its excesses in Africa (Depelchin 2005, 2011; Diop 1991; Obenga 2004; Mentan 2010a, 2010b; Nyamnjoh 2015c).

When the skull – that is watching the captured lady whom the narrator, on his "regenerative adventure" (Achebe 1988[1990]: 144), sets out to find and bring back to her father – falls asleep and thus is not in a position to blow the whistle and alert the other skulls, the narrator is able to change himself back from a lizard into a man to speak to the lady, who is seated "on a bull-frog with a single cowrie tied on her neck" (Tutuola 1952: 26). And even when the cowrie on the lady's neck "made a curious noise" that alerted the skulls, he had "changed" or "dissolved himself into air" before a cowrie could be tied around his neck as well (Tutuola 1952: 27). By tying the cowries round the neck of their victims, the skulls were able "to reduce the power of any human being" and "also to make a person dumb" (Tutuola 1952: 27). Again, I see this as a metaphor for the disempowering and dumbing effects of the cowries of Eurocentric modernity on its hostages. When the narrator finally snatched the lady away and started fleeing with the skulls chasing him through the forest, "rolling on the ground like large stones and also humming with terrible noise," he "changed the lady into a kitten and put her inside my pocket and changed myself to a very small bird" [a sparrow] (Tutuola 1952: 28).

The narrator of *The Palm-Wine Drinkard* constantly employs the ruse of the magician and the trickster that his juju make possible to activate his potency to bring into fruitful conversation the visible and invisible dimensions of his world, thereby averting fundamentalist ambitions of dominance. Being a subject calls for the unrelenting quest to enhance one's potency depleted in previous interactions. Power is seldom permanent. Like game it is to be stalked and harnessed in the context of particular relationships and interactions. If power were to be rigidly the prerogative of the gods, the spirits, ghosts, the invisible world, human leaders or the community of skulls, there would be no end to the vulnerabilities of ordinary humans and their world of appearances.

The narrator, as quest-hero, is half-spirit and half-human, hence his frontier credentials as someone who belongs everywhere and nowhere in particular. He is a veritable cosmopolitan crossroads creature in constant navigation, negotiation and conversation with dichotomies and boundaries in the interest of interdependence and conviviality. As quest-hero, the narrator's "cosmopolitanism and absolute freedom from physical constraints enable him to move freely through the rigidly partitioned" towns and bushes, where the inhabitants, humans and non-humans alike, "know the extent of their own territory and do not violate the territorial integrity of their neighbours," even as it is precisely in not respecting such rigid boundaries that the narrator as quest-hero stands a chance of fulfilling his quest. His boundary crossing makes him stand out as "an outsider in the new communities where his adventures take him. He is suspected and feared because, as a stranger, he is reputed to have a malignant and potentially dangerous influence over the well-being of the indigenous community" (Obiechina 1975[1968]: 128-129]). His is an example of how to navigate and negotiate the challenge of straddling myriad identity margins in favour of a life and world beyond dichotomies (Edwards 1975[1974]: 258; Mudimbe-Boyi 2002).

To die in life and live in death is part of the flexibility characteristic of Tutuola's universe. Dying biologically might suggest that one has come to the end of one's life in the world and that one is expected to disappear for good. But as Gabriel Rockhill[1] reminds us in his reflection on "Why We Never Die," one does not need to subscribe to eternal transcendence to recognise that biological death is not the end of life, and that, even biologically, we never really die. To him, the numerous dimensions of our existence each live according to different times. Biologically, he argues, death is an everyday occurrence, with different people doing it to different rhythms. As he puts it, death is "a constitutive feature of the unfolding of biological life." Even then, existence does not cease after biological death "as the material components of our bodies mix and mingle in different ways with the cosmos." Equally resistant to death are the "artifacts that we have produced," ranging "from our physical imprint on the world to objects we have made." Psychosocially, we also survive biological death through "the impact that we have had – for better or worse – on all of the people around us," given that in the fact of living "we trace a wake in the world." This means "our immanent lives are actually never simply our own."[2] Hence his conclusion:

> Authentic existence is perhaps less about boldly confronting the inevitable reality of our own finitude than about recognizing and cultivating the multiple dimensions of our lives. Some of these can never truly die because they do not belong only to us. They carry on in the physical world, in the material and cultural vestiges we leave, as well as in the psychological and social effects we have on those around us. (Gabriel Rockhill).[3]

Of *The Palm-Wine Drinkard*, Caroline Rooney recognises a similar impermanence of death when she observes, of the Skull turned complete gentleman through borrowings of body parts which ultimately have to be returned to those who own them:

> ...a shuttling between living and dying where death is not the *final* form. Rather, out of a minimal form of existence new life is woven in an increasing combination of forms or body parts until a final or complete form is attained. Once this has been attained, this final stage of a life form, there can only be a process of decomposition towards re-composition because at no point can there be a cessation of life which is a necessarily ongoing process. Here, this process of decomposition and potential re-composition is closely *observed* and thus the vital stages of it (Rooney 2000: 84).

If death is a process and not an event, it is a process on which there are far more questions, even in modern science, than definitive answers.[4] In Tutuola's universe, Death is a form of circulation and not a matter of permanent severance of links with life and the living.

One is dead to a particular context, as a way of becoming alive to prospective new contexts. Death is a form of adventure and exploration of the infinitudes of life. Death and dying are processes in gradations and by degrees. There seems to be no end to dying, just as there is no end to living. People who die reappear elsewhere and are again available for death. There is no such thing as an ordinary mortal, just as there is no such thing as the fully dead. Death and dying are as much a reality for gods, spirits, ghosts and death itself, as they are for humans. Mbembe has likened Death to the currency of life, given its central role as the value and means of exchange in Tutuola's universe (Mbembe 2003: 16). Death might be extraordinarily frightening, but it also is very ordinary and often outmanoeuvred by its victims. Not only does Death assume human proportions, it exudes ordinary human propensities and frailties when it does. Death in human proportions has a house and a yam farm, and must cultivate, consume and ensure and assure a healthy lifestyle to stay alive and away from self-cannibalisation (Tutuola 1952: 11-16). Even the dead of the Deads' Town are extraordinarily ordinary in their humanness – eating and drinking and indulging in the sociality and practices of the alives, even as they train and qualify to behave like the dead, which includes walking backwards (Tutuola 1952: 96-102). The gods are no different; not only do they look and act human, they are quite simply ordinary, just like any human.

The head of the town with the famous market asks the palm-wine drinkard to free his daughter from the terrible curious creature who borrowed body parts and fancy clothes to transform himself into a complete gentleman. In the Deads' Town – where the palm wine drinkard eventually locates his dead tapster, "BAITY," after a ten-year search – where it is "forbidden for alives to come," (Tutuola 1952: 96), alives are nonetheless tolerated. In terms of material culture and sociality, things are not that different between the world of the alives and the Deads' Town. Whatever difference there is in the Deads' Town is scarcely skin deep, as one can train and qualify as "a full dead man," as did the tapster following his death

(Tutuola 1952: 100). Despite forbidding alives from living there, the Deads' Town is very accommodating and equalising, as "both white and black deads" are living there (Tutuola 1952: 100).

The culture of gifts and gifting is the same: "he [tapster] told me that he could not follow me back to my town again, because a dead man could not live with alives ... and said that he would give me anything that I liked in the Deads' Town." (Tutuola 1952: 100). As a parting present, the tapster gives him an egg, telling him "to keep it as safely as gold" upon his return home. The tapster told him "the use of the egg was to give me anything that I wanted in this world and if I wanted to use it, I must put it in a big bowl of water, then I would mention the name of anything that I wanted" (Tutuola 1952: 101). With a magic egg the drinkard could very well conjure up magic palm-wine to continue with his old habits of pleasure without effort, if he so chose.

If that was his thinking, he was overtaken by events when he returned home. This egg becomes handy when the palm-wine drinkard returns to his famine stricken hometown, where millions had died of hunger and parents were even killing their children for food (Tutuola 1952: 118). "I commanded the egg to produce food and drinks... I saw that the room had become full of varieties of food and drinks, so we ate and drank to our satisfaction" (Tutuola 1952: 120). Soon, as "the news of the wonderful egg was spreading from town to town and from village to village" (Tutuola 1952: 120), so did people come from far and wide to be fed. And "everyone of them who had not eaten for a year, ate and drank to his or her satisfaction" (Tutuola 1952: 121). "I even commanded the egg to produce a lot of money and it produced it at once" (Tutuola 1952: 121). One day, after eating to their satisfaction as usual, the crowd began to play and wrestle with each other "until the egg was mistakenly smashed" (Tutuola 1952: 122). From that point, instead of producing food and drinks in abundance when commanded, "it produced only millions of leather-whips," which it used to flog the people who had assembled to be fed as usual (Tutuola 1952: 123). And when there was no one left to flog, the whips gathered themselves together, transformed into an egg and disappeared (Tutuola 1952: 124).

Indeed, the sameness between the alives and the dead of the Deads' Town is so striking it begs the question: what business do the dead have living at all, and curiously, like the alives? Even more perplexing is the fact of Death itself, living as a human being, among the alives, until he, the narrator, "brought Death out from his house," upon the request of a god turned man, thereby rendering Death forever with "no permanent place to dwell or stay," and since then, "we are hearing his name about in the world" (Tutuola 1952: 16).

Armed with and doubly activated by the potency of his "native juju" and his father's (Tutuola 1952: 9), the narrator was able to neutralise his vulnerability and keep the company of gods, spirits and the wild animals of the thick bushes and forests he traversed. With his native juju he could transform or project himself into a bird, fly about and overhear conversations, and seek answers to questions to prove that he could live up to his name of "father of the gods who could do everything in this world" (Tutuola 1952: 10). Chased by ghosts, he narrates how "I became a big bird like an aeroplane and flew away with my wife, I flew for 5 hours before I came down" (Tutuola 1952: 40). The swollen left thumb of his wife – who "did not conceive in the right part of her body as other women do" (Tutuola: 32) – gives birth to a son. The narrator details the event thus:

> When I completed three and a half years in that town [the town headed by his wife's father], I noticed that the left hand thumb of my wife was swelling out as if it was a buoy, but it did not pain her. One day, she followed me to the farm in which I was tapping the palm-wine, and to my surprise when the thumb that swelled our touched a palm-tree thorn, the thumb bust out suddenly and there we saw a male child came out of it and at the same time that the child came out from the thumb, he began to talk to us as if he was ten years of age (Tutuola 1952: 31).

Not only did the child speak, he named himself "ZURRJIR" (Tutuola 1952: 32), was "as strong as iron," drank more palm-wine than his father, could eat without satisfaction, fight a hundred men without relent and not be conquered, smash everything to pieces, "smashed all the domestic animals to death," and torture his parents the way only a spirit child could. When this "wonderful child" who was "stronger than everybody in that town ... began to burn the houses of the heads of that town to ashes," the people of the town, convinced of "his havocs and bad character," conspired with his father to "exile" his son from the town by setting the house on fire when the child was asleep (Tutuola 1952: 32-34). And that is how this scourge of a son who had terrorised the town and wreaked so much havoc in the community was burnt to ashes. From these ashes arises "a half-bodied baby" armed with a telephone voice – "he was talking with a lower voice like a telephone," and no less of a terrorist, as he tortured his parents without relent on their journey out of the town, until they were rescued by "three good creatures ... Drum, Song and Dance" (Tutuola 1952: 35-40).

This mention of a telephone and related "paraphernalia of modern life, ... such as bombs and railways" (Arthur Calder-Marshall, reprinted in Lindfors 1975: 10) attracted the following comment on "convenient features of modern civilised life" in Tutuola's supposedly imaginatively rich primitive universe by Dylan Thomas (reprinted in Lindfors, 1975: 7), whose enthusiastic endorsement of Tutuola's *The Palm-Wine Drinkard* helped launch the author's controversial celebrity notoriety:

> (There are many other convenient features of modern civilised life that crop up in the black and ancient midst of these fierce folk legends, including bombs and aeroplanes, high-heel shoes, cameras, cigarettes, guns, broken bottles, policemen.) There is, later, one harmonious interlude in the Faithful-Mother's house, or magical, technicolour night-club, in a tree that takes photographs... (Dylan Thomas, reprinted in Lindfors, 1975: 7).

Indeed, "Tutuola's easy use of the paraphernalia of modern life to give sharpness and immediacy to his imagery" (Gerald Moore, reprinted in Lindfors 1975[1957]: 52), is an indication that there is much more to his writings than the excavation and celebration of a long dark past, and that there is much more to his fantastic tales than merely a case of fantasy gone wild (Anozie 1975[1970]: 243-244). He blends traditional values and innovative ideas, things of the past and things of the present to give a sense of the dynamism of being Yoruba in a nimble-footed world of myriad encounters. By taking his readers through "the dark jungle" where "time is measured in hours and minutes as if the protagonists are carrying their pocket watches, distance is gauged in miles and business is conducted in £.s.d.," Tutuola is making a statement that Yoruba culture is dynamic and that things which at first might appear to be from elsewhere are part and parcel of "the composite culture of modern Africa" (Obiechina 1975[1968]: 142-143). Tutuola's writing is, above all, seeking to see the past in the present and bringing the present and the past into conversation towards a future that is far from linear and far from predicated on zero-sum games of violent encounters (Tabron 2003: 35-84). Thus, as Ogundipe-Leslie observes, and rightly so, Tutuola's acclaim as a good storyteller comes from his "use of his material, chosen from all and sundry, and minted to make something beautiful, new and undeniably his own" (Ogundipe-Leslie 1975[1970]: 148).

One good turn deserves another in Tutuola's universe. Those encountered by the narrator of *The Palm-Wine Drinkard* promise to help or reward him in exchange for services, often in the form of helping to resolve a challenge or predicament that defies them. He must do something first, something that often threatens his very life. For ten years spent going from town to town through bushes and forests thick and thin looking for his tapster, the narrator encountered people who "would say unless I should help them to do something, they would not tell" (Tutuola 1952: 99). This is true of the old man who is a god who sends him to fetch a bell from the blacksmith, but which he refuses to name, as a way of making the task more challenging for the narrator. Beaten at his own game, the old man challenges the narrator to capture Death and bring it to him. But when Death is indeed captured and brought, the old man and his family flee, for they never thought anyone could capture Death. If the palm-wine tapster is still alive in the Deads' Town, and if Death can itself be alive as a yam farmer busy struggling for subsistence and survival even as it kills others, this makes of Death a form of circulation and not a matter of permanent severance of links with life and the living.

Notes

[1] See Gabriel Rockhill, "Why We Never Die," http://www.nytimes.com/2016/08/29/opinion/why-we-never-die.html?_r=0, accessed 31 August 2016.
[2] See Gabriel Rockhill, "Why We Never Die," http://www.nytimes.com/2016/08/29/opinion/why-we-never-die.html?_r=0, accessed 31 August 2016.
[3] See Gabriel Rockhill, "Why We Never Die," http://www.nytimes.com/2016/08/29/opinion/why-we-never-die.html?_r=0, accessed 31 August 2016.
[4] See Zaria Gorvett, "The macabre fate of 'beating heart corpses'" http://www.bbc.com/future/story/20161103-the-macabre-fate-of-beating-heart-corpses, accessed 25 December 2016.

Chapter Six

Activation, Potency and Efficacy in Tutuola's Universe

This chapter further discusses the relevance of the ideas on self-activation, potency and efficacy inspired by Tutuola's writings to ongoing epistemological debates, especially on the sociological and anthropological study of African societies and realities. It argues that the interconnections and interdependencies Tutuola encourages his readers to see between consciousness and essence; mind, body and soul; mental and bodily functions and processes; in-body and out of body experiences; things and their doubles; body parts and bodies; self and other; us and them; here and elsewhere; people and things are most pertinent to an inclusive epistemology of infinite interconnections and interdependencies. In this regard, despite his marginal and almost non-existent formal education, Tutuola could ably stand tall and stand his ground in a scholarly, intellectual conversation on theories of knowledge, meaning and sense making with many a leading theory and theorist anywhere in the world. By way of example, this chapter brings into conversation with theories by theorists such as Marcel Mauss, Pierre Bourdieu, Michel Foucault and Jean-Pierre Warnier – each a frontier or crossroads person and thinker in their own way – illustrations from Tutuola's work on ideas of consciousness and essence as mediated through the body and its capacity, techniques and technologies for self-extension.

What is the relevance of Tutuola's ideas on self-activation, potency and efficacy to ongoing epistemological debates around the study of African societies? In a word, it is the notion of domesticated agency and flexible mobility. Tutuola is relevant to the structure-agency debate and is aligned to the view that both kinds of influences are symbiotically related. Appealing to Bourdieu, it is argued that self-activation/efficacy/potency require both rule following and improvisation. In this sense, our actions have objective and subjective influences. Freedom requires learning rules that are objectively structured but socially produced. Individual actions might be structured according to rules that seem outside of us, but the fact that this structure is socially produced means it represents our collective agency. And at the same time, individual improvisations within this structure can influence and shape these rules over time. In this we find a unity – between individual and collective; structure and agency. In this unity agency is never *absolute but domesticated. Domesticated agency is quite evident in Tutuola's writings. Individuals are characterised by ontological incompleteness (e.g. almost everyone is bodily inadequate in some way). Therefore, their agency is mediated by the relationships and artefacts (jujus, charms, spells, etc.) they are able to harness so as to achieve efficacy and potency. This incompleteness also spurs creativity and innovation in the ways one is able to use these relationships and artefacts.*

Reliance on jujus, charms, spells and clairvoyance might seem primitive and irrational, but they are part of the potency repertoire from the fact of our incompleteness. In this regard, they are not much different from the technologies of self-extension with which we are familiar (photos, computers, internet, cell phones, smart phones, mass media, social media, etc.). To go back to Chapter One, the question is not whether the agency of supernatural forces is real or unreal but rather on contemplating the nature of the role in meaning-making of belief in such forces. At the very least, it highlights the fact of our ontological incompleteness, and the fact that our bodies are flexible technical objects for self-activation. In addition, this kind of universe (prevalence of jujus and interventionist supernatural forces) is one where everything is possible. This kind of world can only be successfully understood through the cultivation of patience, and a caution towards dismissing or embracing things too easily. Finally, Tutuola's relevance for the study of Africa resides in his lack of fixation with boundaries and his commitment to genuine hybridity through the collapse of dichotomies across various categories.

This captures the theme of flexible mobility. His writings invite one to see both the possibility of genuine hybridity as well as the clumsiness that lies in obsessing over claiming and maintaining rigid boundaries. (E.g. the sacrifice of the hunter narrator and his wife because he gets pregnant at the same time as his wife, and purportedly because it is contrary for a man to conceive like a woman). It is a clumsiness with which we are familiar given today's events, especially as they produce the most obvious ironies. The immigrant status of almost all Americans in relation to their immigration attitudes and policies. The racism in telling people to go back home, when racism brought them to the place they claim as home. In South Africa, students and lecturers call for access to free decolonised education yet engage in xenophobic rhetoric and action. Furthermore, there is wilful silence on whether free decolonised education can benefit those from the arbitrary colonially constructed boundaries that are not South Africa.

In his *Techniques of the Body* first published in French in 1936 and translated and published in English 37 years later, Marcel Mauss (1973) argues that the human body is trained or educated physiologically, psychologically and sociologically to act and achieve particular ends within a given society. Thanks to such training or education at bodily adaptability, everybody acquires particular techniques or instruments of efficiency/efficacy that are internal to their bodies and suited to particular forms and attitudes within the logic of practice characteristic of a given society or social context. It is in this way that Mauss sees the body as the "first and most natural instrument" or "first and most natural technical object" or "technical means" of a human being, who must perfect such internal techniques to achieve his or her ends before looking beyond themselves for "instrumental techniques" of self-extension (Mauss 1973: 75-76).

Techniques of the body acquired through training for efficacy are necessary for habitual individual action and for social reproduction (Mauss 1973: 85). This approach to understanding the body in its complexity was very much in line with what Keith Hart has described as Mauss' "heroic aspiration" (Hart 2007: 479) to "a method for placing the whole person in society as a whole" by "pushing for a more concrete and complex approach to studying the human condition than the modern social sciences allow for" (Hart 2007: 475).

The idea of a confluence in biological/physiological, psychological and sociological self-discipline through training or education implied in Mauss' *techniques of the body* are complemented by Foucault's *technologies of the self* (Foucault 1988; Martin et al. 1988) and Bourdieu's *habitus* (Bourdieu 1990), which emphasise the same general idea of schooling (bodily, psychologically and socially) for disciplined, predictable, efficacious self-activation and self-actualisation that comes naturally without necessarily being natural. Subjects are not subjects in abstraction and do not act alone, or, as we have seen in the case of Tutuola's Skull, always as a unified and singular self. Subjects act in accordance with their particular surrounding sets of circumstances and relationships that bind them. The conscious and dynamic self is recognised through inextricable entanglements and interconnections with others – shaping and acting on others as much as being shaped and acted on by others from the world of nature, culture and supernature. Many of the examples discussed below speak to the Maussian and Foucauldian ideas of techniques and technologies of the body and the self, in ways that suggest greater recognition for the role Tutuola may have played, had he been taken seriously instead of being dismissed as a freak, in thinking and theorising the social through bodies as flexible technical objects of self-actualisation, that is as amenable to creatures of nature and supernature, as it is to humans.

Let's take a closer look at Pierre Bourdieu's *habitus* seen in relation to Tutuola's thinking. The idea of consciousness and essence in conversation and complementarity one gets from reading Tutuola could be seen as a precursor to Bourdieu's idea of *habitus*, through which consciousness brings body and mind, container and contents into conversation, mutual entanglement and manglement, co-ellaboration, co-creation and co-implication. Interpreting Bourdieu on *habitus*, Craig Calhoun argues that, not only is social action and the consciousness thereof structured, "social structure is inside each of us because we have learned from the experience of previous actions." Irrespective of whether we are aware of such embodiment or not, Calhoun continues, "We have a practical mastery of how to do things that takes into account social structures. Thus the way in which we produce our actions is already shaped to fit with and reproduce the social structures because this is what enables us to act effectively" (Calhoun 2003: 15-17). Put differently, our everyday consciousness and "very abilities to understand and choose and act have been shaped by processes of learning which are themselves objectively structured and socially produced" (Calhoun 2003: 15-17). Thus, "how we think about reality does shape what it is for us, but how we think about it is a result of what we have learned from our culture and experience, not simply a matter of free will" (Calhoun 2003: 15-17).

Consciousness as *habitus* is thus Bourdieu's insistence on a dialectic of structure and action. To Bourdieu, *habitus* is "at the basis of strategies of reproduction that tend to maintain separations, distances, and relations of order(ing), hence concurring in practice (although not consciously or deliberately) in reproducing the entire system of differences constitutive of the social order" (Bourdieu 1996: 2-3). Bourdieu's consciousness as *habitus* seeks to reconcile both the power of structure and the subjective choices that give social agents agency. In French intellectual circles, Bourdieu, like Achebe's proverb on the Igbo dancing masquerade as epitomised by Tutuola, was uncomfortable with both existentialism (spearheaded by Jean-Paul Sartre) and structuralism (best represented by Levi-Strauss). To Bourdieu, "If existentialism greatly exaggerated the role of subjective choice, structuralism neglected agency" (Calhoun 2003: 9). Bourdieu's basic position was that "social agents are fully determined and fully determinative (thereby dissolving the scholastic alternative between structure and agency)" (Wacquant 1996: xvii). In other words, the strategies of humans as social agents are never wholly determined by the objective constraints of society as the collective unconscious (*à la* Durkheim) nor exclusively determined by the subjective intentions of humans as social beings. Humans are as much products of culture and society (and the consciousness thereof) as they are producers of culture and society and consciousness. Humans are both victims (confined or determined by) and progenitors (creators) of the social rules and regulations that inform their relationships with and perspectives (consciousness) of themselves, others and the worlds. Bourdieu therefore saw social agents not simply as rule-following, but as dynamic agents who could improvise and adapt to changing circumstances that called for going beyond rules – that is, for acting strategically and interestedly, in the manner of many a narrator and quest-hero in Tutuola's tales, particularly when confronted with challenging predicaments for which they have no ready-made answers.

To Bourdieu, no culture or result of human cultivation is complete and free of internal contradictions, and therefore, no culture is structured beyond question. Like with Tutuola's universe, there is always a prospect, possibility or need for self-enhancement through encounters with others (be they human or from the worlds of nature and supernature) and their technologies of activation for greater potency and efficacy. In light of this reality, researching culture calls not merely for representing culture "simply as rules that people follow, but as the practical dispositions that enable people to improvise actions where no learned rule fits perfectly" (Calhoun 2003: 14). It encourages students of culture to cultivate nimble-minded frontier or crossroads intellectual dispositions that enables them to approach culture as a nimble-footed dancing masquerade that is best understood from different positions, different angles and different perspectives.

Bourdieu likens social life to a game by serious, deeply committed athletes, who have to reconcile the challenge of playing according to the rules while at the same time being creative and innovative enough to win, or at least, to avoid defeat. He invites students of the social to use his metaphor of game playing to understand various social situations. In every society and social context, people play different games as part and parcel of what it means to belong through relationships with others. He argues that social life requires active engagement in its games by those involved, and that it is impossible to remain neutral and detached as an insider, however marginal one's social status. Every degree of participation entails a degree of knowledge or consciousness of the social in a given context that is conditioned by one's specific location and trajectory in that social life. Since social games are played in particular social fields, and since "each field... has its own distinctive rules and stakes of play," (Calhoun 2003: 20), "Every field of social participation demands of those who enter it a kind of preconscious adherence to its way of working. This requires seeing things certain ways and not others, and this will work to the benefit of some participants more than others" (Calhoun 2003: 17-18). Just like games, social life is strategic; it calls for constant improvisation and strategic creativity with every new challenge or situation, and the extent to which we become adept at navigating and negotiating often contradictory expectations by various other social agents involved in our game, the more we could be said to have a *habitus* – which, in the metaphor of the game, would mean "the capacity ... to improvise the next move, the next play, the next shot" (Calhoun 2003: 3). "It is our desire for the stakes of the game that ensure our commitment to it. But we do not invent the games by ourselves; they are the products of history, of social struggles and earlier improvisations, and of impositions by powerful actors with the capacity to say this, and not that, is the right way" to act and interact socially (Calhoun 2003: 4).

If Bourdieu's *habitus* is akin to consciousness in significant ways, it also parts ways with those who insist that *habitus* is an essence of nature, and that those who possess it are born with it. As Craig Calhoun puts it, "We may be born with greater or lesser genetic potentials, but we are not born with a habitus. As the word suggests, this is something we acquire through repetition, like a habit, and something we know in our bodies not just our minds." (Calhoun 2003: 3). Calhoun defines *habitus* as "the embodied sensibility that makes possible structured improvisation" (Calhoun 2003: 19), or as "the meeting point between institutions and bodies" (Calhoun 2003: 20). To him: "Participation in social games is not merely a conscious choice. It is something we do prereflectively. We are, in a sense, always already involved," always "already inculcated with institutional knowledge – recognition and misrecognition" (Calhoun 2003: 19). However, to belong to the same field and play the same game according to the same rules, does not necessarily imply having an identical *habitus*. "We learn and incorporate into our habitus a sense of what we can 'reasonably' expect." (Calhoun 2003: 3).

With the interconnections between consciousness, essence and *habitus* in mind, this chapter explores the complexities of how human beings, ghosts, spirits and other creatures in Tutuola's universe of incompleteness employ techniques of the body, technologies of the self and instrumental techniques to activate themselves to the level of potency that makes efficacious action and frontier identities possible.

In Tutuola's universe, humans, far from being all powerful and imposing, must struggle hard to ensure a place for themselves. They do not exert "untrammelled authority over the rest of the universe" and must seek ways and means of enhancing themselves to keep pace with other creatures such as hostile elements, vicious monsters, ghosts, spirits and kindred supernatural beings. Fortunately for human beings, epitomised in Tutuola's stories by the quest-hero narrators, things such as juju, spells, charms and magic can make a difference by enabling the hero or heroine to change themselves into something else when hard pressed by their adversaries. Tutuola's characters employ the technique of metamorphosis extensively as a means of self-protection and as a facility to display their magical powers when confronted by other creatures with overwhelming powers. As Obiechina observes, unlike the Czech born German language writer Franz Kafka who uses metamorphosis as "a process of de-energisation, a process demonstrating the deflated state of Man when confronted with inexplicable and portentous forces," the use of metamorphosis in Tutuola's stories "reveal man as possessing the power and the ability to face up to or circumvent the menaces of those inimical forces" (Obiechina 1975[1968]: 126). Unlike proponents of the colonial and colonising epistemological export who, for ideological and hegemonic purposes believe that completeness is possible and attainable by the argument of force, even if not necessarily through the force of argument, Tutuola repeatedly makes it abundantly clear how rare it is to have someone or something without an incompleteness.

Indeed, as depicted in Tutuola's novel *The Witch-Herbalist of the Remote Town*, the kind and generous "Omnipotent, Omnipresent and Omniscient Mother" comes closest to perfection. The brave hunter narrator of the Rocky Town who visits her for medicine to cure his wife's barrenness is profuse in his praise of her. He wonders why people call her "Witch-Mother," when "she did not pray to witches but to the God Almighty." In her transcendental generosity and divineness of being, not only is she capable of helping whichever burdensome person comes to her with their burdens (Tutuola 1981: 201-229), she is also able to speak a multiplicity of languages in a multiplicity of voices, and has no need for interpreters. She is the crossroads of human convergence, exuding the highest order of humility and being. Tutuola describes her thus:

> She had various kinds of voices such as a huge voice, a light voice, a sharp voice, the voice of a baby, the voice of a girl, the voice of an old woman, the voice of a young man, the voice of an old man, the voice of a stammerer, the voice of boldness, the voice of boom, the voice of a weeping person, the voice which was amusing an which was annoying, the voice like that of a ringing bell, the voice of various kinds of birds and beasts. And she spoke and understood all kinds of

languages, of humans, beasts, birds, evil spirits, immortal beings, etc. (Tutuola 1981: 190-191).

In every other instance, the humans and non-humans portrayed in Tutuola's universe are bodily inadequate in one way or other. In some instances, one's inadequacies in some regards are compensated for in others through a natural endowment that is more than what is usually perceived to be normal or the norm. In other words, one might have an incomplete nature in one regard (be lame, crippled or without legs, or reduced to a mere skull, etc.), while in other regards be overly endowed as far as other natural attributes are concerned (be exceedingly tall, long armed, sleek headed, etc.). Someone might be blind, yet be extra gifted at hearing. In such instances the capacity to activate oneself beyond one's relative incompleteness vis-à-vis others is right there within oneself – nature compensating one for the inadequacies of one's nature. Whatever the situation or natural circumstance, all creatures explored train and educate themselves in ways of maximising the potency of their condition in tune with the context in which they find themselves. In emergency situations where a creature does not have within their repertoire of past experiences or accepted and standardised modes of functioning – where they lack the training, education or capacity to act with efficacy –, they might resort to instrumental techniques external to themselves for enhancement. In Tutuola's universe, magic, juju and other creatures come in handy in this regard. In addition to examples of activation, potency and efficacy discernible from the excerpts of *The Palm-Wine Drinkard* discussed in Chapter Five, the examples provided in the current chapter are predominantly from *My Life in the Bush of Ghosts* (Tutuola 1954). These should be read just as examples, as every single work of Tutuola's is proliferated with themes of activation, potency and efficacy.

Immobilised in the centre of the town where "she sat permanently like a stump" (Tutuola 1954: 90) – deactivated by the lack of mobility –, the Flash-Eyed Mother, as her name suggests, had

> ... eyes which were bringing out splashes of fire all the time and were used to bring out fire on the firewood whenever she wanted

to cook food and the flash of fire of these eyes was so strong that it would catch the firewood at the same moment like petrol or other inflammable spirit or gunpowder… (Tutuola 1954: 88).

She could also use her flash eyes "at night as a flood of light in lighting the whole town" (Tutuola 1954: 88). When offended by any of her short ghost servants, "both eyes would be flashing out fire on to the body who offends her, and the fire would be burning the body at the same moment as fluffy things or rags" (Tutuola 1954: 89). Indeed, her flash eyes were capable of reaching out across long distances, so she could use them "as a whip to flog any other of her offenders" (Tutuola 1954: 89) regardless of how physically far away from her they were. Her capacity to use her flash eyes to activate herself to such formidable levels of potency made her "very fearful to other creatures coming to her town without special reason" (Tutuola 1954: 89). Even His Majesty "the King of the Bush of Ghosts" could not dare to ask "Who is she?" (Tutuola 1954: 89). She was further activated and fortified by "a large mouth which could swallow an elephant uncut" (Tutuola 1954: 88), and by "millions of heads …on her body" (Tutuola 1954: 87), each of which

> … had two very short hands which were used to hold their food or anything that they want to take, … two eyes which were shinning both day and night like fireflies, one small mouth with numerous sharp teeth, the head was full of long dirty hair, two small ears like a rat's ears appeared on each side of the head (Tutuola 1954: 87).

Thus armed or compensated for the fact of her immobility, the Flash-Eyed Mother could rely on the Short Ghosts to hunt game for her and her multiplicities of heads. She also sold some of her flash eyes to others who desired to enhance themselves in similar fashion. The Flash-Eyed Mother "was selling the flash fire of her eyes to other kinds of ghosts who were coming from the various towns to buy it, and a flash was worth a heavy amount of ghosts' money" (Tutuola 1954: 95). She was thus able to make ends meet and in certain cases thrive on her flash fires despite her being immobilised at the centre of the town like a stump. The fact of selling the power of her flash eye to others speaks to the circulation of juju and magic as technologies of power in a manner similar to the economy of cults and ritual associations depicted by Ute Roschenthaler (2011) in the Cross River region of Cameroon and Nigeria, where cultural practices and worldviews have a lot in common with Tutuola's universe. It is comforting that the Flash-Eyed Mother does not pretend to claim completeness of any kind, despite her super endowments. She is very dependent and quite incapable of self-sustenance. Without the Short Ghosts to hunt obligingly for her, she would quite simply perish, in spite and perhaps because of her superabundance in body parts and body enhancements.

The circulation of juju and magic or trophies is a common theme in Tutuola's works. This, according to Gerald Moore, is in tune with "the widespread African belief that whenever a magician is overthrown his powers are immediately transferred to the conqueror" (Gerald Moore, reprinted in Lindfors 1975[1957]: 50). In *The Witch-Herbalist of the Remote Town* for example, the god of the river and his goddess wife became interested in the two removable heads the brave hunter narrator cut off as trophies after defeating the powerful Crazy Removable-Headed Wild Man of the wild jungle in two successive fights (Tutuola 1981: 88-94, 119-128). The god and goddess were ready to release the pregnant hunter and his pregnant wife, both of whom had been sacrificed to the god of the river by the people of the Rocky Town, "because I conceived like a woman"[1] (Tutuola 1981: 250) in exchange for the two removable heads. It was the goddess who asked the hunter: "Will you please give us these two 'Removable Heads'? I promise, if you give them to us, we shall treat your swelled-up belly so that it becomes as normal as before. In addition, we shall not detain you and your wife but we will send both of you back to your town." The intention of the god and goddess of the river was "to worship" the heads (Tutuola 1981: 259-260) and to use them to enhance their potency. The hunter consented, with additional requests of his own:

So I promised them that I would give them the heads provided they would treat my swelled-up belly, release all of the people of my town and allow me to take them back to my town, and allow my wife and me to stay with the god and goddess till my wife had delivered. When they agreed to all of my requests, then I gave them the two heads (Tutuola 1981: 260).

In other instances where one's nature taken together is the cause of one's incompleteness, one looks outside oneself for technologies – supernatural or otherwise – of self-activation to attain the potency one needs for efficacious action. In some such cases, it calls for reaching out and harnessing the potentialities of others through acts of dependence or interdependence. The grounded Flash-Eyed Mother relying exclusively on the Short Ghosts as her hunters for the food she needs to feed herself and all her extensions is an example in this regard. How she keeps them fettered to service in servitude is reminiscent of the classic master-slave relationship. Slaves are technology in human form as life reduced to non-living creatures or things. In *My Life in the Bush of Ghosts* where slavery is commonplace, "every slave buyer recognised slaves as non-living creatures" (Tutuola 1954: 164) to be used and abused with impunity. No sooner does the narrator return to The Future-Sign Tree after 24 years lost in the bush of ghosts, than he is captured and taken into slavery by slave traders, who eventually sell him to his own brother who comes seeking a slave to kill as sacrifice for his god (Tutuola 1954: 161-166).

In *The Palm-Wine Drinkard*, the drinkard or "father of the gods who could do everything in this world" himself, although in the apparently powerful position of a master, is almost slavishly dependent on the tapster for his endless supply of palm-wine. Indeed, the dependence is so much so that "The 'work' of drinking palm wine becomes impossible without the tapster, yet the dead tapster cannot return to the land of the living to resume his labour" (Wenzel 2006: 449) The Skull, on the other hand, who seems to have disposed of the burdens of body parts he does not need all of the time, resorts to borrowing from others the body parts – detachable and re-attachable as various parts of the body are in Tutuola's universe – it needs to activate self to the level of compositeness required to pass for a "complete gentleman" in the eyes of the girl with angelic beauty who has systematically turned down every suitor before him.

Still in other instances, the technology is beyond simple dependence or interdependence. It is a thing external to oneself, available to be activated to enable or render possible what one desires – something one can acquire, master, manage, own and share with others. Something like juju or magic, as such things are commonly known in Tutuola's writings. Thus, already protected by the potency of his repellent smell[2], the King of Smelling Ghosts of the 7th Town of Ghosts, with the added potency of his juju, is able to transform his seven-year-old victim – the narrator in *My Life in the Bush of Ghosts* – into various kinds of creatures– monkey, lion, camel, horse, cow or bull – and back, as it pleases him or depending on what services he wants rendered (Tutuola 1954: 21). The flexibility and reversibility in these transformations or adoption of various forms are well suited for a world where permanence, fixity or finitude does not always serve one's best interests. A technology that is adaptable – capable of taking the form of a monkey in one instance and that of a lion, camel, horse, cow or bull in another –, is clearly much more amenable than a technology that is permanently the one or the other of these forms. With his juju, the King of Smelling Ghosts was able to manipulate his victim – a case of using one technology to activate another technology – to assume the form and consciousness of whatever extension of self – creature or otherwise – he wanted. Thus:

> In the presence of these guests, my boss was changing me to some kinds of creatures. First of all he changed me to a monkey, then I began to climb fruit trees and pluck fruits down for them. After that he changed me to a lion, then to a horse, to a camel, to a cow or bull with horns on its head and at last to my former form (Tutuola 1954: 21).

To celebrate his good luck for bringing back a strange creature from earth, the King of Smelling Ghosts "performed a juju which changed me to a horse unexpectedly, then he put reins into my mouth and tied me on a stump with a thick rope" (Tutuola 1954: 22). Then "he mounted me" (Tutuola 1954: 22), "mercilessly" (Tutuola 1954: 23), accompanied by two of his attendants, "with whips in their hands and flogging me along in the bush" (Tutuola 1954: 23). "I felt as if he was half a ton weight" (Tutuola 1954: 23). This was a repeated occurrence as he paraded his victim like a trophy:

> ...he would mount me mercilessly and both his attendants would start to flog me in such a way that all the ghosts and ghostesses of that town would shout at me as a thief. But if they shouted at me like that my boss would jump and kick me mercilessly, with gladness in the presence of these bystanders until he would leave that town (Tutuola 1954: 23).

As a horse, the earthly person was fed guinea corn (which he could eat) and leaves, which "I was unable to eat ... as I am not really a horse" (Tutuola 1954: 24), and offered urine mixed with limestone to drink, which is what the smelling ghosts drank, as "ordinary water" was "too clean for them" (Tutuola 1954: 24). As a horse, "I was all the while tied in the sun which was shining severely on me" (Tutuola 1954: 24), a burden compounded by the fact that "as I was tied in the sun all the young ghosts of this village were mounting me and getting down as if I am a tree as they were very surprised to see me as a horse" (Tutuola 1954: 24)[3]. If the King of the Smelling Ghosts needed another kind of beast of burden, he would transform his victim accordingly: "he changed me again to the form of a camel and then his sons were using me as transport to carry heavy loads to long distances of about twenty or forty miles" (Tutuola 1954: 25). The narrator could also be hired out to other ghosts by his boss "to carry loads to long distances and returning again in the evening with heavier loads" (Tutuola 1954: 25). As this account shows, it takes schooling, training and discipline to acquire the habits and techniques of the body to adapt to the functions and roles one is expected to assume when one is transformed from what one normally is into something different. Such adaptations include learning to eat, walk and behave like the animal or thing into which one has transformed oneself or been transformed.

Other Ghosts in *My Life in the Bush of Ghosts* with similar powers are the "Burglar-ghosts," who come across as frontier ghosts at the crossroads of the earthly and the ghostly communities. They burgle long-distance, navigating between the bush of ghosts and towns and villages inhabited by "earthly persons," whom they resemble the most. The Burglar-ghosts describe themselves as both earthly and not earthly –, "I am and I am not" (Tutuola 1954: 40) –, "living as earthly persons and also as ghosts" (Tutuola 1954: 43). They fall through the cracks of fixed categories and binary oppositions between ghosts and humans. They are frontier beings, as they collapse the boundaries and borders between the world of ghosts and the world of humans, through their capacity to insinuate themselves into the world and anatomies of the earthly in order to burgle them. They traffic and transact between worlds, bringing ghostly beauty in contact with the ordinary normalness of the earthly, and in turn taking earthly foods, animals and things back to the bush of ghosts for their consumption. Known as "born and die babies" among the earthly, the Burglar-ghosts go about their business of burgling the earthly by luring them with a deceptive attractiveness described as follows:

> If an earthly woman conceives we would choose one of us to go to her at night and after the woman has slept then he would use his invisible power to change himself to the good baby that the woman would be delivered of whenever it is time. But after he has driven out the good baby and entered into the woman's womb, he would remain there and when it is time the woman would deliver him instead of the good baby which had been driven out... As this inferior baby has invisible power or supernatural power, so all the money spent on him and also the sacrifices would be his own and all would be stored into a secret place with the help of his invisible power (Tutuola 1954: 41).

The Burglar-ghosts are able to accumulate material goods from the earthly thanks to their capacity to manipulate them and to prey on their vulnerabilities and love of "superior babies." No amount of resources spent to keep alive such unusually attractive babies is ever enough. Once the "born and die babies" have thoroughly depleted their victims, it is time for them to return to the bush of ghosts with their booty and bounty. In the words of the same Burglar-ghost as above:

> ... after the woman has spent all she has and become poor, then one night he would pretend as if he has died, so the woman who bore him as a superior baby, her family and other sympathisers would be saying thus: 'Ah! That fine baby dies,' but they do not know that he is not a superior baby. They would bury him as a dead baby, but the earthly persons do not know that he does not die but simply stops breath. But after he is buried, then he would come out of the grave at night, then he would go direct to the secret place where all the moneys and sacrifices as sheep, goats, pigeons and fowls, all would be alive and are stored by his invisible power, and he would carry them to this town (Tutuola 1954: 41-42).

The Burglar-ghost who narrated this account, went on to prove his story. He disappeared to an earthly town, and returned ten months later "with bales of sewn clothes, sheep, goats, pigeons, fowls, all were still alive and moneys with all other used expensive articles"(Tutuola 1954: 44). When the Burglar-ghost displayed the bales of clothes he had brought back:

> I saw plainly many clothes which belonged to my friends and my mother in my town that were among these clothes and was also surprised to see many clothes which my mother just bought for me and my brother before the war scattered all of us (Tutuola 1954: 44).

If ever the narrator needed evidence, there it was. In the manner of the ethnographer that the narrator himself exemplified, not content with simply recounting past experiences, the Burglar-ghost had proceeded to do ten months of fieldwork and had returned to authenticate the ethnographic experience. In this regard, and as far as ethnography is concerned, the adventures of many a Tutuola narrator are long years of ethnographic immersion, some lasting for as long as seventeen years and more. His idea of ethnography is hardly of the slash and burn, in and out type. The narrator of *My Life in the Bush of Ghosts* and the Burglar-ghosts were not dissimilar to Tutuola in their ethnographic tendencies.

As his son Yinka Tutuola recounts in an interview with Jeff VanderMeer following Tutuola's death in 1997, his father was "never tired of writing and typing" up stories he collected from visits to the village. Tutuola took regular advantage of his annual leave to "travel to his village with an old Pye reel-to-reel tape recorder," where "he collected stories of all kinds," some of which he played back for entertainment of city folks, and some of which he transcribed and used for his writing projects. He made the collection of stories a social and convivial process. "At nights in the village, he would buy palm-wine to entertain his guests who would be competing to tell the best stories they could. He would record these stories till very late in the night." Tutuola "enjoyed being in the village so much," according to his son, who adds: "I think if he was not working with the government he would rather have preferred to live there among the village people – probably because of their simple ways of life." [4] Like the professional ethnographer whose life and very existence as a practitioner of anthropology is intimately tied to the field notes and transcriptions of observations, encounters and conversations in the field, Tutuola's:

> …life was just intertwined with stories– collecting, forming, writing or telling them. .…. Stories gave him so much joy that he lacked interest in many other things, like going to social parties.… When reel-to-reel tape recorders got out of fashion and were replaced with more compact cassette recorders, there was a problem. He couldn't transfer all his stories, for they were too many. He lost a great part of his collection. [5]

So when the Burglar-ghost so ably demonstrated his ethnographic acumen, it was enough to convince any doubting Thomas. The narrator, himself an ethnographer, judging from the evidence provided, evidence which shows that even his own parents were victims of the scam, was convinced by the thick description presented by the Burglar-ghost:

> And when I saw all that he brought and also my own and my brother's properties, then I believed his story which he told me before he went away (Tutuola 1954: 44).

Sometimes the humans or earthlies are able to outsmart the "born and die babies" with strong juju of their own. The narrator of *The Witch-Herbalist of the Remote Town* recounts how this happened to him:

> I am a 'born and die baby'. But I could not return to my folks again since my mother bore me last. As my father is a strong juju man, he tied me down with juju and by that I could not return to my folks again (Tutuola 1981: 65).

Eager to return to his folks though he remains, he has tried repeatedly and failed to do so:

> ...because the father and mother who bore me at this time had tied me down with their very powerful juju. Although I tried several times to outwit the juju, all my efforts failed because the juju was too powerful (Tutuola 1981: 103).

In *My Life in the Bush of Ghosts*, the "Super-lady" ghostess of the Nameless-town occupied exclusively by ghostesses is another ghost with the technology (power or Juju) to transform and revert to forms. The inhabitants of the Nameless-town are distinguished for having "been betrayed by their husbands after their marriage" (Tutuola 1954: 113). All wearing under their lower jaws "long brown moustaches which resemble that of he-goats," the ladies and women of the Nameless-town all marry each other, as "none of them could marry any male again" (Tutuola 1954: 113). The narrator first encounters the Super-lady as an antelope, who then transforms itself into "a very beautiful lady" (Tutuola 1954: 101), who requests him to marry her, confessing: "I prefer to marry an earthly person more than the other creatures" (Tutuola 1954: 102). The Super-lady's power to transform herself into anything of her choice and back was given her by her grandmother when her father and mother plotted to kill her through sacrificing her to be eaten by witches and wizards of the community of witchcraft whose meetings they presided (Tutuola 1954: 108). It was this power that saved her from being killed. She explains:

> So through this power I had the opportunity to change to an invisible bird early in the morning that my father and mother would kill me, then I packed all my belongings, after that I bade both of them invisible 'good-bye' and then I came to live permanently in this Nameless-town, which belongs only to women, and since that day I am not appearing to them personally but changing to a kind of a creature... (Tutuola 1954: 108).

With his ethnographic instinct and insistence on proof, the narrator, now "earthly husband" of the Super-lady, upon hearing of her "wonderful power to change to any form of creature," challenged her to prove herself by changing to some form at that very moment for him to see. She obliged:

> First, she became an antelope with two short horns on its head, secondly a lioness and roared at me several times so that I nearly died for fear, thirdly, a big boa constrictor which made me fear most when she was coiling round my body, especially when it opened the mouth very wide as if it wanted to swallow me, and after this a tigress and jumped on me at the same time, after this she jumped away from my head and was jumping from room to room, having stopped jumping about in the rooms and house, then without hesitation she jumped outside the town, she was chasing fowls about in the town. After ... that she changed to a lady as usual, and to my surprise she was on the same chair as before ... and also held the two fowls which she killed outside with her hands (Tutuola 1954: 109).

Interestingly, the technology for activating someone or something to assume different forms can be acquired and lost. It is not an intrinsic part of being a ghost, being human or being whatever and whoever. This is evident when the King of Smelling Ghosts transforms the narrator his victim from a camel back to his former form – an earthly person – with the intention of later transforming him into a horse to ride to the conference of ghosts, but when he forgets to hide away the technology, the victim appropriates it for his own ends:

> After he changed me to a person then he went away to take the reins which he would put into my mouth when he changed me to a horse, but as soon as he went away I saw where he hid the juju which he was using to change me to any animal or creature that he likes, so I took it and put it into my pocket so that he might not change me to anything again (Tutuola 1954: 26).

Without his juju to activate him, the King of Smelling Ghosts "has no power to change me to a horse again" (Tutuola 1954: 27). The king is impotent, all of a sudden. The captive has effectively deactivated his captor by taking away his juju. The latter can no longer lay claim to being complete, superior, in charge and invincible as he imagined and insisted when his juju was still in his possession. The captor deactivated, the captive regains some measure of potency, even if only temporarily, situational and ephemeral, as every potency in reality often is. The captive is able to unfetter himself from his confines and flee:

> I jumped right out from the bag to the ground and without hesitation I started to run away inside the bush for my life (Tutuola 1954: 27).

As the King of Smelling Ghosts chases and threatens to catch up with him, the narrator uses the juju he has stolen from the king and transforms himself into a cow. This makes him more powerful and able to run faster than the king who is overburdened with all his gear, amongst which is the boa constrictor he uses as a belt and the heavy bag "full of mosquitoes, small snakes with centipedes" (Tutuola 1954: 15) he carries around on his left shoulder. No sooner is he free of the King of Smelling Ghosts than he, still as a cow, is threatened by a hungry lion. So he starts escaping from the lion, only once again, to run himself into cow-men who are only too happy to embrace and return to the fold one of their cows that they imagined had gone missing (Tutuola 1954: 28). Unable to change back into a person, the seven year old starts his life as a cow (Tutuola 1954: 28). Subsequently, purely by chance, as he runs away from a crowd chasing him to kill as sacrifice to a god, he falls into a pond and upon seeing a reflection of himself as a cow in the water his form is changed back from cow to person (Tutuola 1954: 34-35).

There is a very similar experience by the Wild Hunter in the bush of the ghosts, who encounters a sixteen-headed ghost which he describes as follows:

> ... I looked at him with half an eye and saw that on each of his heads there was a town in which many kinds of creatures lived. Each town had a fire, tall trees, and rivers with big canoes moving about. Several wild beasts lived there as well. When I looked more closely, I saw that poisonous creatures such as snakes, scorpions, ants, etc., were living on all of his sixteen heads too. Both his palms were very hot. As I stood sweating terribly as if I was in a foundry or big boiler, he shouted at me to give him water (Tutuola 1989[1982]: 51).

When the Wild Hunter is taken captive by the sixteen-headed ghost, he swallowed a spell that turned him into a big ram, but he cannot turn back to his human form because he does not know how. The old woman who had given him the spell did not explain to him how to revert to his old form. He falls into the hands of sheep rearers who actively seek to sell him but none of their customers would buy him because he was "too lean" (Tutuola 1989[1982]: 52-54). Finally, the sheep rearers dispose of him for "seven shillings and six pence" to a woman who wanted a ram to offer as sacrifice. It turns out that the "spirit of the river" who had requested the sacrifice to be made by the woman, was none other than the same old woman who had given him the spell initially (Tutuola 1989[1982]: 56-58)[6]. She is finally able to transform him back from a ram into a human being, and to give him another kind of spell in the form of "nine grains of alligator pepper," capable of turning him into "a big bird or rain or something else" when confronted by dangerous ghosts (Tutuola 1989[1982]: 60).

There is no guarantee either, that a technology or juju, however potentially powerful, would work when one summons them to enhance one's potency. *The Witch-Herbalist of the Remote Town* is full of examples of how the narrator is disappointed by a juju just when he needs it the most to activate his potency. He sets off on a journey to seek help from the Omniscient, Omnipotent and Omnipresent Mother Witch-Herbalist of the Remote Town, "to help me make the juju-medicine which can make my barren wife pregnant" (Tutuola 1981: 182). Although he shakes from feet to head from "the intoxication of the powers of all the juju which I wore" like "juju gourds all over my dresses, head, neck, breast, loin, etc." as he sets off on his journey (Tutuola 1981: 24), he is occasionally confronted with instances where his juju does not work, for one reason or other. In one instance, "I tried to transform myself into another form so that I might run away for my life. But my juju which could do so did not work this time, because I had not enough time to recite the incantation which could make it effective." Faced with this failure or disappointment, "I continued to use my matchet with all my power. Again, my matchet could not reduce their [that of the wild children in the wild jungle] power all" (Tutuola 1981: 67-68). Similarly, like with computers (desktops or laptops) and cell phones (basic or smart), and other mobile devices (tablet, iPad), arming oneself with a "First Mind," a "Second Mind," a "Memory" and a "Supreme Second" the way the hunter and narrator from Rocky Town does, is no guarantee that these would not freeze or deactivate themselves just when one needs them the most. Despite the fact that his first and second minds are his partners and advisers, and are supposed to keep him company at all times, they repeatedly desert him when he is in danger and needs them to advise him. Such desertions are dutifully recorded by his memory, "as an offence for which they would be punished" (Tutuola 1981: 129), and indeed, they are both tried and sanctioned in the end (Tutuola 1981: 270-279).

The idea that power is something that comes and goes, often without warning, seems the only constant. Could this account for the disposition to take the outside in that is so overwhelmingly present in Tutuola's stories? However powerful a person is, he or she is always seeking to enhance themselves with extended body parts and extra senses on the one hand, and technologies and juju on the other. One cannot be too sure, so one must never rest on one's laurels. Complacency is a dangerous thing in a world of impermanence, where there is always more or less to things and people than meets the eye. If one loses one's head in a fight the way the Removable-Headed Wild Man in *The Witch-Herbalist of the Remote Town* does, one could borrow the "head of a rhinoceros" to continue chasing the person who has snatched one's head (Tutuola 1981: 119-120), even if only to be rendered powerless yet again, when the second head is also snatched in the fight that ensues with the snatcher (Tutuola 1981: 125). Being indebted to others is seen as normal and as a lubricant to life and any claim to achievement in general, provided one openly acknowledges one's debts to others, human and non-human alike.

In the spirit of interconnections and interdependence, life, sociality, encounters and relationships with others are all about charging, discharging and recharging. One can only stay permanently charged if one is in splendid isolation, disconnected, aloof and inactive. Even then, one's charge risks leaking or wasting away (draining itself out unproductively) and with that, one's life eventually. To be social and in relationship and interaction with others, requires and simultaneously makes possible actively charging, discharging and recharging oneself as well as the others involved. Discharging within relationships is not a wasteful exercise as it entails charging others (energy expended is not necessarily energy depleted), just as recharging entails drawing from the charge of (or being energised by) others. It is a symbiotic relationship of constant circulation of charge, discharge and recharge. As long as one loses one's charge to others in a social relationship, that cannot be considered as sterile leakage or wastefulness.

The universe depicted by Tutuola calls for patience, observation, getting used to, and interactions with and deep conversations with those one encounters (people, things and creatures natural and supernatural alike, animate and inanimate) to discover the sameness or complementarity that lodges beneath a veneer of difference. Tutuola invites us to be cautious in our instinctive tendency – occasioned and protected by sensory perceptions – to define and confine as different or as similar just by looking at the surface of phenomena, realities, things and persons. He cautions against rushing to change or embrace what we barely understand and what has barely understood us. Tutuola's universe schools his readers to see the stranger in the family and the family in the stranger. Anything can be anything because of the impossibility of permanence beyond the capacity to change ad infinitum. Repeatedly, we are urged to provide for there being simultaneously much more and much less to things than meets our senses.

It is thus not surprising that 18 years into being lost in the bush of ghosts, the earthly person, our narrator in *My Life in the Bush of Ghosts*, who would end up spending a total of 24 years with ghosts, goes native, anthropologically speaking. Having married twice to ghostesses, had a "half earthly and half ghost" son, kept the company of various ghosts across over 18 towns of the bush of ghosts, the earthly person is able to pass for "a real ghost" (Tutuola 1954: 150), speaking the language of the ghosts and behaving generally like one of them. He recounts how after the breakup of his second marriage to the Super-lady ghostess, he roams about in the bush day and night and nobody can identify him as earthly and therefore a stranger or an outsider to the community of ghosts. He had "become a full ghost and was doing everything that ghosts are doing and also speaking the language of ghosts fluently as if I was born in the bush of ghosts" (Tutuola 1954: 128). His ghostly abilities, fluencies and propensities meant that "I was always protected from uncountable merciless ghosts as it was hard for some of them to believe that I am an earthly person" (Tutuola 1954: 128). Indeed, his familiarity with the ways of ghosts and being a ghost had become so convincing that "a ghost friend of mine taught me the art of magic, because he did not know that I am an earthly person at that time" (Tutuola 1954: 150).

Certain technologies and knowledge reserved for insiders and those at the heartland can be acquired through dedicated effort by those who start their journey as outsiders and eventually ease into their host communities and ideologies. Some identity fundamentalists might still insist that these are not quite insiders, that their claimed conversions are contested or ephemeral, and continue to treat and relate to them as "outsiders within" (Harrison 2008) or as "outside the fold" (Viswanathan 1998). But that is to assume that there is an essential and only way and level of being an insider, which is by blood, the pure undiluted blood of an ancestry of insiders without a history of outsiderness, however remote, in the purity of the bloodline of their heartland (Ignatieff 1993; Geschiere 2009).

Armed with his new magical powers, the earthly person and narrator now convincingly an insider was able to change himself into different types of animals and things, depending on what he needed to activate his potency in order to attain his ends in given situations. In one instance we see him in competition with a ghost magician trying to outsmart each other in a frenzy of transformations into myriad forms. This is when he refuses to share the proceeds that came as reward following a competition in magic. He recounts that when he refused to share the gifts with his competitor, the ghost magician, the latter "changed to a poisonous snake" (Tutuola 1954: 151) and "wanted to bite me to death" (Tutuola 1954: 151). In reaction, he immediately used his own magical power and "changed to a long stick ... and started to beat him repeatedly" (Tutuola 1954: 151).

Driven nearly to death by the pain of the beating, the ghost magician "changed from the snake to a great fire and burnt this stick to ashes, after that he started to burn me too" (Tutuola 1954: 151). In turn the narrator "changed to rain" (Tutuola 1954: 151) and "quenched him at once" (Tutuola 1954: 151). Refusing to give up, the ghost magician used his powers to transform "the place that I stood to become a deep well" (Tutuola 1954: 151) and to make "rain to be raining into the well while I was inside" (Tutuola 1954: 151). The well rapidly became full of water. Before the ghost magician could close the door of the well, the narrator changed himself into a big fish and attempted to swim out. But when the ghost magician saw the fish, he changed into a crocodile, jumped into the well and came to swallow him. Before the crocodile could swallow, "I changed to a bird and also changed the gifts to a single palm fruit, I held it with my beak and then flew out of the well straight to the 18th town" (Tutuola 1954: 151- 152). Quickly, the ghost magician "changed himself again to a big hawk" and chased him about in the sky. Afraid that the hawk was catching up with him, the narrator changed himself to "air and blew within a second to a distance which a person could not travel on foot for thirty years" (Tutuola 1954: 152).

This feat did not deter the ghost magician, as the latter mobilised his magic and appeared where the narrator was heading well before the narrator arrived. Now face to face, they struggled for long, at the end of which, "I shared the gifts into two parts, I gave him a part, but he insisted to take the whole" (Tutuola 1954: 152). Reluctantly, "I gave him all." (Tutuola 1954: 152).

This was just a temporary surrender, however, as the earthly person transformed himself into air again, anticipated the ghost magician to where he was headed, killed an animal and buried it neck down in a hole he had dug near the road. When the ghost magician saw the head of the animal, he concluded the animal had planted itself deliberately on the side of the road because it wanted his gifts. He started throwing the gifts at the animal one by one, until he had no gift left on him. Later, the earthly competitor came and retrieved all the gifts from the animal's head (Tutuola 1954: 152-153).

As the earthly person is desperately seeking his way out of the bush of ghosts, his family members back in his home town are equally preoccupied with finding him, and have not given up despite his prolonged absence. They resort to another type of technology to assist them. To keep alive in him memories of home, his family secures the services of a fortune teller and his "Invisible Missive Magnetic Juju" (Tutuola 1954: 148), renowned for its capacity to "bring a lost person back to home from an unknown place" (Tutuola 1954: 148), however faraway it may be, "with or without the will of the lost person" (Tutuola 1954: 148). The force of this magnetic juju makes him dream of home repeatedly (Tutuola 1954: 147). In the end, he is delivered back home under the very same "future sign tree" where his journey into the bush of ghosts began 24 years earlier (Tutuola 1954: 160). This delivery is made possible by the powers of a "Television-handed ghostess," in recognition for his having cured her of her sores. Pleased to have been cured, the Television-handed ghostess asks him to look at her open palm. And as soon as he does, he finds himself, all of a sudden, under the exact same tree where he disappeared 24 years ago, much to his utter surprise (Tutuola 1954: 160).

Reviewing *My Life in the Bush of Ghosts* in March 1954, barely following its publication, V. S. Pritchett, noting the possible interest of the book to psychoanalysts and anthropologists remarked:

> Tutuola has never seen television; odd that he has imagined the nasty, crumbling, decaying texture of the television pictures (V. S. Pritchett, reprinted in Lindfors 1975: 22).

Venturing into Tutuola's bush of ghosts is almost always a journey of a thousand dangers from which only the quest-heroes, and an exceptional few others, ever return. Of the eight hunters who vanish into the bush of ghosts in Tutuola's very first novel – a novel written in 1948 but only published for the first time in 1982 – only the Wild Hunter named Joseph Adday, and another hunter, are able to survive decades lost, wandering and tortured by wicked mischievous ghosts in the supernatural bush. The six others perish for their sins, as they are retained by the Devil, who has the habit of telling his followers that on Judgement Day: "you and I shall wear fire like clothes, but I alone shall wear the crown of fire … because I am your father and king!" (Tutuola 1989[1982]: 102).

The Wild Hunter, who eventually escapes from the punitive bureaucracy and claws of His Majesty the Devil, King of the Fifth town of the Bush of the Ghosts – where he lived with his father, mother, aunts and cousin named Death (Tutuola 1989[1982]: 96-97), by pretending that he and two other supposed "Devil's-helpers" were going "to heaven to lure several angels of God to him" (Tutuola 1989[1982]: 105), describes the bush of the ghosts upon returning to his hometown as follows:

> …the Bush of the Ghosts was the reserved bush in which both ghosts and spirits of the dead were living as if in their own town.

...though this bush seemed just like an ordinary bush, indeed it was not. Once one entered it, it was not easy to find a way out. One could not travel to the end of it; that was as impossible as it would be for a mosquito to travel around the whole world without perishing (Tutuola 1989[1982]: 125).

A consequence of getting lost for many years in the bush of ghosts is that, even for those who survive the ordeal and return to their home town, they realise that so much has changed, just as they themselves are seen to have changed so much, often beyond recognition, as the following passage demonstrates:

Our parents and the other people of our town could not recognize us any more. Many of them had died, and many were so old that they had even forgotten our names. A few of them remembered us faintly when we described ourselves to them. Some said that they thought we were no longer alive. They asked us about the rest of the hunters, and we told them that the first, second, fourth, fifth, sixth and seventh hunters were in the custody of His Majesty the Devil whose palace was in the fifth town of the ghosts. We explained that the sixth hunter followed us on our journey to heaven but his head sprouted four horns in the 'Valley of Sinners'. These horns got hooked in the walls of the Valley, and he perished there because he was a sinner (Tutuola 1989[1982]: 124-125).

No blessing to or activation of our earthly person lost in the bush of ghosts comes without a curse. When recognised as a god who benefits and feeds from the sumptuous sacrifices brought to him, the blood of the animals slaughtered in his honour and poured on him also attracts thousands of flies which literally cover him (Tutuola 1954: 61). No sooner is he married and has a "half ghostess and half earthly person" son (Tutuola 1954: 126) with the Super-lady ghostess than is he driven away from the Nameless-town after four years of staying with her for daring to suggest, even as a joke, that "earthly people are superior to the ghosts and ghostesses or all other creatures" (Tutuola 1954: 127). Invested in completeness as both he as an earthly person and the Super-lady as ghostess are, they each celebrate their natures and communities of origin as the one best way of being and indulge themselves in absolutism, conquest and conversion. Little wonder that both the Super-lady and her earthly husband find their "half ghostess and half earthly person" son incomplete and irritating:

> Within six months that he was born he had grown up to the height of four feet and some inches. He could do everything in the house. But the worst part of it is that whenever I talked to him to do something, he would do it in the half method that ghosts are doing all their things and then in the half method that the earthly persons are doing everything. So I hated him for this habit, because I wanted him to do everything completely in the method that the earthly persons are doing everything and also his mother hated him for the half method that he was doing everything, because she wanted him to do everything in the full way that ghosts are doing their own things. She wanted him to be acting as a full ghost as herself and I myself wanted him to be acting as a full earthly person as I am (Tutuola 1954:.126-127).

To the parents, being a "half ghostess and half earthly person" was already confusion enough. Insisting on doing everything by half was taking things beyond the bounds of conventional sociality in their respective ghostly and earthly communities. It was as if their son was inviting them to live their lives permanently at the crossroads, exposed to the daily realities of confusion and contradictions of a no-man's land of hybridity and cosmopolitanism gone berserk. The parents failed to see their son as the screen upon which to project the hopes and ambitions of their marriage. By refusing to recognise their "half and half" offspring as a skilful straddler and successful negotiator of ghostly and earthly identity margins, the parents were denying themselves the potential enrichment to their lives of their bridge-builder son. Such rigid expectations of exclusionary claims not only denied their "half and half" son the benefits of his hybridity and frontierness of being, it affected their love for one another, and within four years of their marriage, they could hardly stand each other anymore. Little wonder that the superiority the narrator attempted to claim for the earthly persons in a joke was interpreted as no joking matter by the Super-lady. It was the last straw in their exclusionary logic of belonging and delusions of completeness. With both parents, there was little disposition towards a consciousness of inclusivity, interconnection and interdependence, which their half and half son embodied. They proved themselves unable to spread the benefits and shrink the burdens of marriage. Within their logic of completeness, no half measures are tolerated, not even in the name of love. Hybridity or borderline disposition and consciousness are ferociously denied and violated, and those who claim it in earnest are made to feel beleaguered and guilty of violating the standardised, routinized and predictable code of normalcy.

This is an important and repeated theme in Tutuola's writings. In *The Witch-Herbalist of the Remote Town* for instance, no one in the Rocky Town hesitates to sacrifice the brave hunter narrator and his wife to the god of the river, when he gets pregnant at the same time as his wife, after eating some of the soup prepared by the Witch-Herbalist to cure the wife of her barrenness. The reason advanced for sacrificing both of them was that: "it was contrary for a man to conceive like a woman and that it was very bad luck for the people in the town" when the man in question was also the son of "their chief priest and pagan of the gods" (Tutuola 1981: 246). Tutuola invites us to contemplate such rigid determination against compromise even when nature has yielded to most unlikely conversations across binary oppositions and dichotomies.

Chinua Achebe recognises that boundaries are a key theme in Tutuola's writing. In their adventures, Tutuola's narrator quest-heroes, who cross boundaries at much personal risk and peril, serve as a mirror to how obsessive humans and non-humans alike are with claiming and maintaining boundaries. Through his excessive consumption of palm-wine and by doing little else to earn a living, the palm-wine drinkard could be seen as having "an appetite which knows no limit or boundary" in a world where pleasure and work are expected to be carefully balanced. Thus the concept of boundaries could be applied to the jurisdiction of work and play thus:

> Because the Drinkard's appetite knows no limit or boundary, he takes and takes without giving and allows play not just to transgress but wholly and totally to overrun the territory of work. His ordeal in the jungle of correction changes him from a social parasite to a leader and a teacher whose abiding gift to his people is to create the condition in which they can overcome want and reliance on magic, and return to the arts of agriculture and husbandry (Achebe 1988: 111).

Repeatedly, the reader is made to understand that all creatures are expected to scrupulously respect boundaries, and to stay within the confines of the boundaries of their community of origin. In certain cases, the boundaries are erected in time and not in space, with certain things confined to the day time, and others to night time (Achebe 1988: 108-110). Tutuola, Achebe points out, seems to be suggesting that even in a jungle, the forest or the bush,

> ...where everything seems possible and lawlessness might have seemed quite natural, there is yet a law of jurisdiction which sets a limit to the activity of even the most unpredictable of its rampaging demons. Because no monster however powerful is allowed a free run of the place, anarchy is held – precariously, but held – at bay, so that a traveller who perseveres can progress from one completed task to the domain of another and in the end achieve progressively the creative, moral purpose in the extraordinary but by no means arbitrary universe of Tutuola's story (Achebe 1988: 110).

According to Achebe, boundaries in Tutuola's universe also imply "a duality of jurisdictions both of which must be honoured if there is to be order in the world," with Tutuola suggesting that "promise and fulfilment constitute one such duality, for a promise is no less than a pledge for future work, a solemn undertaking to work later if you can play now." Hence, "Tutuola never allows a broken promise to go unpunished" (Achebe 1988: 110-111).

Given this fixation with boundaries, the challenges of genuine hybridity or life as a frontier being collapsing dichotomies across various categories, social and otherwise, remain firmly with us even in the 21st century, and as a recurrent theme in African fiction

(Losambe 2005; Nyamnjoh 2013a, 2013c; Fishkin et al. 2014). In a world where social order and rigid boundaries are determined to make prisoners of all those who fall through the cracks of arbitrary social categories, and who are perceived as dangerous because they are different and/or reluctant to be domesticated by the gendarmes of social control, genuine hybridity is pure confusion and those who claim or promote it are confusionists (Guyer 2015a, 2015b).

There is much more to Tutuola's bush of ghosts than simply a case of an imagination gone wild, or merely the figments of an African trapped in primitive traditions with little relevance to the modern world. Within the framework of confusion and confusionism discussed by Guyer in relation to the Slanderer in Tutuola's *Pauper, Brawler and Slanderer*, and as evidence of the resonance Tutuola's work has with 21st century debates on gender and sexuality, in an April (10-16) 2015 article in the *Mail &Guardian* titled "Genderqueer: Existing outside the binary"[7], Demelza Bush, a twenty eight year old South African does not identify herself with the conventional binary gender categories, despite having the obvious sexual attributes —"breasts" and "vagina" for example – that would lead some other to categorise her as a woman. She defines herself as falling through these binaries: "I'm not a woman. But I'm not a man either." She sees herself as "genderqueer," just like the "half and half" of the union between an earthly father and a ghostess mother who is neither wholly earthly nor completely ghostly, but a mixture of both. She writes:

> As I have grown older, I have become less confused. When I was a child, I was a tomboy. When I was 14, I realised I was a lesbian. By my mid-20s, I knew I didn't like the term lesbian, so I began using the all encompassing term 'queer'.
>
> It has taken me 28 years to get to 'what' I am now: I am genderqueer. I am queer. Genderqueer. Gender nonconformist. I don't identify as male or female. Just me.
>
> Genderqueer is a label for people who don't fit into boxes.
>
> One definition of genderqueer is: 'Denoting or relating to a person who does not subscribe to conventional gender distinctions, but

identifies with neither, both, or a combination of male and female genders.'

Society's preoccupation with binary categories means that genderqueerness unsettles people. They get uncomfortable when they can't figure you out. They don't know how to read you. They don't know how to treat you. And it leaves them with a sense of discomfort. And fear.

Even though I am completely comfortable with who I am, the rest of the world isn't. Often when I shop in the men's section or walk into the women's bathroom, I am looked at as if I am a freak.[8]

Far from using the realisation and recognition of herself as "genderqueer" to proclaim her completeness, Demelza details instead how she has relied on her mother – despite the "initial horror" of the latter "at finding her little girl trying to urinate like a boy" – who has been supportive, kind and unconditional in her love. She has also relied on the boy's and men's sections to shop for toys, clothes and other gender specific consumer items. Falling through rigid gender categories and having the courage to declare her being "gender queer" is more a statement of freedom to pursue interdependence and a frontier existence than a celebration of independence and the discovery of a purported true self. Frontier beings like Demelza are only too aware that human agency is neither an imaginary meal nor a meal served unaccompanied. Its existence is recognised in action and interactions in an ambiguous world of intricate entanglements and infinite possibilities.

Tutuola's universe of incompleteness provides a framework for recognising and providing for the interconnections and interdependencies of intersexness. Within Tutuola's framework of incompleteness, instead of labelling and dismissing as a social headache and an embarrassment a person like Uganda's 47 year old "intersex" Kaggwa who was compelled to choose between being Julia or being Julius, humans are invited to contemplate and accommodate gender and sexual complexities and nuance. In Tutuola's universe there is little room for treating intersexness as a curse or as source of ridicule. Indeed, in Tutuola's realm, doctors would not spend valuable time conducting tests to determine whether intersex people are more inclined to being male or female but rather recognise how we are all intersex to some degree, drawing sometimes on the male in us and sometimes on the female, to activate ourselves as we see fit. Yet, as the BBC report on Kaggwa suggests, this is exactly what doctors are called upon to do in the 21st century.[9] Such obsession with binaries is evident in this passage:

> Intersex people are born with a mixture of male and female sex characteristics. To determine the sex of an intersex child doctors try to work out what happened during the baby's development. They check the body's DNA containers, the chromosomes, to see whether the child is genetically female or male. They see if the baby has ovaries or testes, and whether they have a womb or not. They also test the hormones the body is producing and try to determine how the baby's genitals may develop. Test results can be on a scale between male or female. According to the United Nations, the condition affects up to 1.7% of the world's population (see BBC, "Becoming Julius: Growing up intersex in Uganda," http://www.bbc.com/news/world-africa-39053828, accessed 26 February 2017).

Despite Tutuola's pacesetting accounts of same sex relationships in *My Life in the Bush of Ghosts,* of the possibility of men becoming pregnant just like women in *The Witch-Herbalist of the Remote Town*, and the womb capable of outsourcing a pregnancy to the thumb in *The Palm-Wine Drinkard*, these themes are yet to find suffrage in African literature in any open and significant way. Even when they are broached, the tendency is to shroud such sexual ambiguities, fluidities or flexibilities in secrecy. As Aretha Phiri puts it in relation to a short story by Chimamanda Ngozi Adichie and a novel by J. M Coetzee:

> Not coincidentally, J. M. Coetzee's controversial novel *Disgrace* remains silent on the sexual violation of the lesbian character, Lucy, while Chimamanda Ngozi Adichie's provocative short story, 'On Monday of last week,' merely alludes to the possibility of a same-sex relationship. Inflected by race, ethnicity and gender, these authors' inexplicit addressing of these concerns fundamentally interrogates and politicises – with different effect – non-normative, queer subjectivities while

offering spaces for reimagining subjective states and prospects. Read comparatively, both texts deploy silence as an aesthetic of queerness that functions to reflect and subvert global national attitudes to subjective 'otherness' and to render 'absences' louder than 'presences' (Phiri 2015: 155).

Prioritising essentialisms to the detriment of incompleteness, conviviality and consciousness is the curse of a world that overly emphasises regressive exclusionary logics of claiming and denying belonging through the rigidity of borders and boundaries. In his novel *Half a Life*, set in Britain, India and Portuguese Africa, V. S. Naipaul (2001) points to similar essentialist notions of culture, identity and belonging which imply that not even encounters and marriage shall bring together what rigid cultural and social geographies in abstraction have put asunder. Persons who cultivate relationships across race, class and caste are treated with condescension and disdain; and so are their offspring, whose worlds are "half-and-half" and who are not credited with more than "half a life," regardless of their personal desires, experiences and frontier existence. They feel like pawns in someone else's game, as if they were forced to live the lives of others and to bear identities imposed by authorities with ambitions of dominance. As "half-and-halfs" they live with the idea of a great disaster about to happen. They are not sure what this disaster is going to be, whether it is going to be local or worldwide, but they feel it is going to do away with their security and sense of freedom. This makes them overly sensitive to the need to prove themselves, often with an arrogance that attracts envy from those who see themselves as "full lives" bounded to a world of certainties and certitudes in which their power and privilege are not in doubt. It is a world Tutuola knows only too well, one he was committed to challenging all his life as a writer, as the travails, trials, tribulations and triumphs of his quest-heroes richly evidence.

Like Demelza's and the stories narrated by Naipaul in *Half a Life*, Tutuola's stories constitute an ontological epistemological order where "confusion is always in circulation" despite its perceived threats to established sociality and in spite of the wars waged against it (Guyer 2015a: 71). It is an epistemological order in which the sense of sight and physical evidence have not assumed the same centrality, dominance and dictatorship evident in the colonial epistemological order and its hierarchies of perceptual faculties (Stoller and Olkes 1987; Stoller 1989, 1997; Van Dijk and Pels 1996). In this epistemological order, one can be blinded by sight and sighted by blindness (Lindfors 1999d; Nyamnjoh 2012a), just as one does not need to be physically complete or physically present to act efficaciously.

In view of incompleteness as an ordinary way of being human or being anything in the universe, Tutuola makes no secret of his deep discomfort with absolutes and absolutisms. The complementariness of cunning and magic to an otherwise bare and modest life is a significant attribute of Tutuola's universe and its conciliatory system of knowledge and being. The palm-wine drinkard and his wife are able to sell their death and lend out their fear in order not to care about death or fear anymore, before they entered the big white tree, gateway into the big beautiful town of "Faithful-Mother" (Tutuola 1952: 67). Similarly, body organs can downsize and outsource their responsibilities to others, in the manner of the womb of the palm-wine drinkard's wife downsizing and outsourcing a pregnancy to her left thumb.

It is an epistemological order in which the mind and the heart are interconnected, interdependent and in permanent interchange, and within which neither claims superiority nor attributes inferiority in abstraction. Bodies and senses are minded, just as minds and consciousness are embodied and amenable to sensory perception. Tutuola invites his readers to question dualistic assumptions about reality and scholarship, inspired by: "the opposition between the affective and the cognitive, the subject and the object, appearance and essence, reason and passion, the corporeal and the ideal, the human and the animal, reality and representation, the one and the multiple," that tend to favour thinking which: "privileges above all the ability to reason (*argumentation* and *deliberation*) and the will to power, giving short shrift to the ability to feel, to remember, and to imagine"(Mbembe 2003: 2, emphasis in original; see also Mbembe 1997: 152).

In Tutuola's stories, fantasies and fantasising, dreaming and imagining are presented as normal facets of being, not something reserved for children or those with an arrested sense of a life of committed service, responsibility and rational choice. To dismiss as childish, simple-minded, unschooled, barbaric or superstitious the fruit of an active and fertile imagination like Tutuola's is to subscribe to a prescriptive one-dimensionalism that does little justice to inclusionary popular perceptions and understanding of reality informed by multiple ways of being sensitive to the richness of an ever unfolding humanity. Instead, Tutuola, in his investment in fantasies and memories, invites his readers to pay particular attention to the complexity, inclusiveness, humility, and multidimensionality of human existence.

In reading Tutuola, the real is not only what is observable or what makes cognitive sense; it is also the invisible, the emotional, the sentimental, the intuitive and the inexplicable. These popular ideas of knowing and knowledge challenge dualistic approaches to reality. They question the centrality accorded the mind and reason to the detriment of other modes of knowing with a more collaborative role for mind, reason, heart and related mediators of knowledge. They suggest a world larger than its material realities, where matter is not as fixed as assumed in dualistic rationality. Instead, they focus on what is possible and not just on what exists made apparent by human sensory perception and reason. Furthermore, they embrace the supernatural, and emphasise the interconnection of everyone and everything. Readers are introduced to a world of flux, where structure is a temporary manifestation of what is otherwise a flow of constant change. It is a universe of self-consciously incomplete beings, constantly in need of activation, potency and enhancement through relationships with incomplete others and by means of embodied and external technologies.

Put differently, Tutuola's is a universe where autonomy or independence, claimed absolutely, is an extravagant illusion which in the hands of those with ambitions of dominance provides spurious justification for coercive violence and control over humans, resources and nature. With Tutuola, readers learn to appreciate the fact that everyone and everything is always in the process of becoming, that in this regard, one fails as often as one succeeds. There is no standardised or routinized way of being anything. To be a human subject is not a given to be deduced from the assumption of a thinking, calculating, rational self. We fulfil or jeopardise our humanity action and events in and around which we interact with others, human, part human and/or non-humans. In this regard, being human or anything for that matter, may or may not come to existence, is fragile, and never achieved or to be taken as a given.

Things are not always what they appear to be, however obvious they appear to be. Our humanity is very much dependent on how it is acted out through relationships with other actors, accessible through sensory perceptions or otherwise. Being human is thus contingent, and always incomplete. Humans never achieve completion. We are all but predictable. This humbles any philosophy of being and becoming based on grand narratives, linear progression and teleological assumptions. It reminds us, in our fascination with and exploration of existence, not to conflate containers with their contents, however accustomed we are at associating particular contents with specific containers. Just as we are urged not to confine contents to containers, we are invited to prioritise consciousness even as we take essence seriously.

Notes

[1] When the narrator mistakenly ate from the soup specially prepared by the Witch-Herbalist to be eaten only by his barren wife so she could become pregnant, he became pregnant as well. People in Rocky Town started laughing at him: "This is the first time we see that the wife and her husband have conceived together! But we shall wait and see how the husband will deliver his own pregnancy" (Tutuola 1981: 244-245). Such general skepticism about pregnant men is also expressed towards transgender men who are pregnant or would love to get pregnant, according to a BBC report (see "If I ever get pregnant, I won't be an 'expectant mother'," http://www.bbc.com/news/magazine-38831313, accessed 3 February 2017).

[2] In *The Wild Hunter in the Bush of the Ghosts*, Tutuola makes us understand that earthly people smell differently from ghosts, who wave their hands across their faces, trying to avoid breathing in the smell of an earthly person when they meet one (Tutuola 1989[1982]: 9). In his first encounters with ghosts in the First Town of Ghosts, the Wild Hunter observes, "It was then that I saw clearly that all the buildings were beautiful but the ghostly inhabitants were very dirty and were

smelling just like decaying dead bodies" (Tutuola 1989[1982]: 21). The ghosts he encountered had the tendency to assume that "all earthly people all over the world were ... thieves" (Tutuola 1989[1982]: 9).

[3] For a parallel example of how the wild hunter in the bush of the ghosts is used and abused as a horse for three years by his captor, the ghost who "carried a fire with big flames on his head," and his networks of clients, see Tutuola (1989[1982]: 23-32)

[4] Yinka Tutuola, interviewed by Jeff VanderMeer, http://weirdfictionreview.com/2013/01/amos-tutuola-an-interview-with-yinka-tutuola-by-jeff-vandermeer, accessed 1 November 2016.

[5] Yinka Tutuola, interviewed by Jeff VanderMeer, http://weirdfictionreview.com/2013/01/amos-tutuola-an-interview-with-yinka-tutuola-by-jeff-vandermeer, accessed 1 November 2016.

[6] This old woman – spirit of the river – lived at the bottom of the river, which "was a big town and all the houses there were built entirely with glass" (Tutuola 1989[1982]: 58).

[7] http://mg.co.za/article/2015-04-10-00-i-am-genderqueer-comfortable-with-my-identity-at-last, accessed 13 April 2015.

[8] http://mg.co.za/article/2015-04-10-00-i-am-genderqueer-comfortable-with-my-identity-at-last, accessed 13 April 2015.

[9] See "Becoming Julius: Growing up intersex in Uganda," http://www.bbc.com/news/world-africa-39053828, accessed 26 February 2017.

Chapter Seven

Tutuola in Conversation with the Cameroon Grassfields and Beyond

This chapter seeks to further substantiate the argument that the universes of Tutuola's creative imagination are grounded ones, shared across Africa. To consider it pure fantasy and as the work of an overly imaginative mind would be to miss out on the fact that Africans in their vast majority share similar cosmologies and act in tune with related ontologies. The chapter brings into conversation Tutuola's bush of ghosts and his universe of interconnections between the worlds of logic and sensory perception and the world of beliefs and practices that are larger than an overly simplified and reductionist idea of knowledge and the knowable. This, it does, by drawing on ethnographies of palm-wine, intimacy and conviviality, Msa and Nyongo, bushfalling and bushfallers from the Cameroonian Grassfields, as well as on rumours of occult practices related to power, sex and consumerism by some modern Eurocentric cultural and political elite. These are realities and practices which resonant in significant ways with Tutuola's flexible and fluid representations of personhood, being and becoming through cunning, trickery and jujus or related technologies of activation and extension of agency. The chapter provides illustration on how Cameroonians seek to balance between aspirations for independence and relationships of dependency, by stressing the need for a negotiated belonging through building bridges of conviviality linking home and exile, utopia and dystopia.

The chapter explores the insistence – both in Tutuola's universe and in the ethnographies of economies of intimacy in Cameroon and Africa at large – on inclusivity and the need to acknowledge, recognise and provide for debt and indebtedness as a normal way of being human through relationships with others. For the Skull to seek to enhance itself with the organs, cells and tissues of others obtained by illegal means, under duress and without due compensation or any intention of returning the body parts is downrightly deceitful and not worthy of any pretensions to completeness or autonomy. The chapter challenges the global circulation of a Eurocentric index of modernity and humanity that distils and propagates the ideology of the West as the pinnacle and most complete of human achievements. It questions the tendency to place the West, taken uncritically as a homogenous entity or bounded unit, as the summit of a universal civilisation arrived at more through the argument of force and not by the force of argument. The assumed superiority of the West, the chapter argues, is the result of borrowing without acknowledgement, dispossession without restitution, and debasement, appropriation and commodification of others without compunction and with impunity. If the West is compared to Tutuola's Skull in The Palm-Wine Drinkard, it can only claim completeness as a gentleman through a stubborn refusal to acknowledge its status as a composite being, made up of borrowed body parts, which have to be kept in circulation so others can continue to access and use them in activating themselves to the levels of potency needed to attain their own ends. For the West to deny the rest of humanity access to what it so generously lent to the West at different epochs in history to attain the compositeness of passing for a complete gentlemen or civilisation, is to live a lie and to force feed others such a lie through systematic brutality and caricature of the complex, nuanced, interconnected and interdependent realities of the world and its inhabitants.

The chapter draws on Cameroonian examples to argue that the narrow insistence on individual rights, freedoms and aspirations in scholarly and general discussions of realities in Africa, has impaired understanding of the sort of interconnectedness of peoples, cultures and societies suggested by Tutuola. Discussions that refuse to see individuals as products, melting-pots and creative manipulators or jugglers of multiple identities and myriad interconnections are hardly a reflection of the sort of Yoruba and Africa that Tutuola writes about and that, as argued throughout this book, should be brought back into the equation of considerations on knowledge production and consumption on the continent. Reductionist thinking produces scholarship that defines and confines Africans in tune with the logic and expectations of rigid micro sociological categories perfected elsewhere and imported and applied with little sensitivity to the local context shaped by universes similar to Tutuola's. Imported Eurocentric social science discourses on development and democracy tend to recognise individuals and nation-states as real, while either ignoring the existence of intermediate communities, or treating these as backsliding on the long march towards Eurocentric modernity. To pick and choose in a manner that overly simplifies and caricatures an otherwise complex and intricate reality is to force ordinary Africans in their vast majority to live the Dr. Jekyll and Mr. Hyde lie of their colonially educated elite.

As discernible from Tutuola's universe, discussing agency and development in Africa demands careful scrutiny of individual and collective cultural identities. Tutuola's wisdom suggests that indigenous African ideas of freedom need to feed into the current sterility of the dominant colonial and colonising Eurocentric epistemological export on the continent. In Tutuola's universe, there is nothing wrong in seeing and treating the individual as a child of the community, as someone allowed to pursue his or her needs, but not greed. As the life stories of his various narrators and quest-heroes demonstrate, there is need to harness individual creativity, abilities and powers, so that the individuals themselves may be acknowledged and provided for by their communities. Agency in Tutuola's universe has meaning only as domesticated agency, by which is meant agency that stresses negotiation, interconnectedness and harmony between individual interests and group expectations, and between humans and non-humans. In other words, with domesticated agency, the freedom to pursue individual or group goals exists within a socially predetermined framework that emphasises conviviality with collective interests while simultaneously allowing for individual creativity and self-fulfilment. Social visibility or notability derives from being interconnected with others in a communion of interests, values, ideals and ontologies. Repeatedly, Tutuola demonstrates through the challenging adventures and experiences of his narrators and other characters that, given life's vicissitudes, it pays to be modest about personal success and measured in one's ambitions of completeness and dominance.

As Obiechina puts it, in the world of folktales in which Tutuola inserts his narrators as quest-heroes:

> The triumphant hero sees himself as a member of a community whose well-being and survival are also his own. Even though he recognised himself as an individual with an individual destiny, he is also aware that he cannot work out that destiny outside the framework of his community. The concern of the community becomes his concern and his egocentricity is strongly tempered with altruism (Obiechina 1975[1968]: 132).

Within this logic and practice of interconnections and interdependence, Tutuola's quest-heroes are thus able to draw strength from their community and in turn to help sustain the community through their individual contributions. They are only too aware that for their "personal achievements" to be worthwhile, these "must be linked to the over-all well-being of the community." It is always a case of the careful balance between individual aspirations and collective interests in Tutuola's universe. Individual freedom of action and free expression of individuality are not in question. It is always a case of "awareness of individual destiny within a larger, more inclusive communal destiny" (Obiechina 1975[1968]: 132-133). As Obiechina puts it:

> Of necessity, the hold which the community has over the individual cannot be so constrictive that the expression of his individuality is completely frustrated; the individual cannot be so individualistic in his outlook that he regards his interests as entirely independent of those of the community within which he lives. Either case would have inevitably led to the complete impoverishment of both (Obiechina 1975[1968]: 132).

As garnered in Tutuola's various accounts and especially through the adventures and exploits of his narrators as quest-heroes, domesticated agency makes possible for the collectivity to share the responsibility of success and the consequences of failure with the active and creative individual, thereby easing the pressure on individuals to prove themselves in a world of ever-diminishing opportunities and often unfathomable challenges. Domesticated agency does not deny individuals the freedom to associate or to be self-reliant, imaginative, creative and innovative or to pursue independent action. Rather it puts a premium on interactions and interdependence as insurance against the risk of dependence and solitude, where the impermanence of autonomy and independence is all too real.

Achievement is devoid of social meaning if not pursued within, as part of, and on behalf of a group of people who recognise and are able to react to that achievement. For only by making their successes collective can individuals, heroes and ordinaries alike, make their failures a collective concern as well. Such domestication emphasizes negotiation, concession and conviviality over maximization of pursuits by individuals or by particular groups in contexts of plurality and diversity. Appreciation should be reserved and room created for excellence, especially for individuals who demonstrate how well they are ready to engage with collective interests. Individuals who refuse to work towards enhancing their community are those most likely to be denied the public space to articulate their personal desires, and, to become part of the fold again, as evidenced by the epic adventures of the palm-wine drinkard, must undertake to atone for their failings (Obiechina 1975[1968]; Anozie 1975[1970]).

Faced with the vicissitudes, temporality or transience of personal success in the context of African modernity dictated by Eurocentric indicators of success, even the most achieving and cosmopolitan or diasporic of individuals hesitates to sever links with kin entirely by dramatizing completeness *à la* Tutuola's "the complete gentleman." For what use is completeness or success that is possible only with the death of sociality and the deadening of the humanity of others? Those of them who are not completely swept off their feet by such delusory expectations of completeness strive instead to make their home village or hometown part of their successes and good fortunes in the world beyond, so that, in return, the community will help them in times of individual failure and misfortune. Like with Tutuola's heroic hunters (e.g. *The Wild Hunter in the Bush of the Ghosts* and the Brave Hunter of the Rocky Town in *The Witch-Herbalist of the Remote Town*), the city and the "world out there" are perceived as hunting grounds; the home village or hometown is the place to return to at the end of the day. Investing in one's home village or hometown is generally seen as the best insurance policy, and a sign of ultimate success, for it guarantees survival even when one has lost everything in the city, and secures and manifests success in satisfying obligations (Nyamnjoh 2000). Thus, although successful urbanites may not permanently return to or retire in their home villages or hometowns, most remain in constant contact with them, and some wish to be buried or re-buried in such places of birth and childhood memories (Geschiere and Nyamnjoh 2000). Even those who have no ties with home village or hometown kin and are almost permanently trapped in urban spaces or in "the bush" (as in that which isn't home, regardless of whether better or less developed in comparative terms) often reproduce the home village or hometown and localist styles in subtle and imaginative ways where they are trapped. The example of the seven year old narrator in Tutuola's *My Life in the Bush of Ghosts*, who refuses to give up his earthly ways even as he is opening to going native in ghostly fashion, is quite telling in this connection. No one, it seems, is too cosmopolitan to be local as well, and no one is too disconnected to be interconnected and interdependent with others, home and away.

By way of ethnographic illustrations outside of Tutuola's novels, the current chapter draws striking parallels to Tutuola's universe from the Grassfields region of Cameroon (Nyamnjoh 2001, 2005a, for details of what follows) and beyond, where the bush of ghosts is both a reality and a fantasy, familiar and distant and where hunting as reality and metaphor is not confined to hunters and the hunted in the conventional sense (Nyamnjoh 2011). Like the rest of West and Central Africa, in many parts of Cameroon, palm-wine is a prominent lubricant and mediator of myriad forms of conviviality and sociality: celebration of birth, marriage, circumcision and succession, funerals, divination, libation, ritual and communication with ancestors and the dead (Butake 1990; Che 1993; Warnier 1993b, 2007; Notué and Triaca, 2005; Awasom 2010).

Palm-wine is a cloudy, whitish, sweet alcoholic drink made by fermenting the sugary sap from any of a variety of palm trees. Due to its very short shelf-life, there is a tendency to consume palm-wine as soon as it is harvested. The pressure to consume palm-wine while it is still fresh comes largely from its uncontrolled, rapid fermentation process (Chandrasekhar et al. 2012: 33). It is "consumed in a variety of flavours, varying from sweet unfermented to sour, fermented and vinegary." Palm-wine is very common throughout West and Central Africa and is known by various local names. With the right yeasting, temperature and processing conditions, palm-wine can be fermented into an alcoholic beverage with a longer shelf-life than is currently the case. Drinking huge quantities of palm-wine, especially at an advanced stage of fermentation, could result in intoxication, hallucination and delirium. With such ingredients, it is quite understandable how palm-wine could be a good lubricant to the wheels of the fertile imagination of a good storyteller in good company. It is thus very plausible, as Tutuola admitted, that *The Palm-Wine Drinkard* was inspired by an old man on his father's farm, whom he used to listen to, in a half dreamy state as a result of drinking too much palm-wine, tell stories of palm-wine drinking (Arthur Calder-Marshall, reprinted in Lindfors 1975: 9; see also Eric Larrabee, reprinted in Lindfors 1975: 13).

In Cameroon, palm-wine has a rich variety of generic names, among which are *white mimbo, mbuh, matutu* and *matango*. Among the Beti of the central and south regions, it is popularly known as *medjock melen*, while in the Grassfields, the common appellation is *muluh*. When fermented and distilled into a spirit, palm-wine takes the form of *afofo* in the northwest and southwest regions, and *odontol*, in the central and south regions of Cameroon. It is mostly drunk directly, but in some parts of the country palm-wine is mixed with honey and/or the barks of special trees with medicinal properties considered to be more effective taken together. Palm-wine is harvested either from the oil palm tree – felled or standing – or from the raffia palm tree, which grows in swampy or wet areas nearby a stream or river (Che 1993). In the Cameroon Grassfields, the most common type of palm-wine is harvested from the raffia palm tree – *Raphia farinifera*. Jean-Pierre Warnier gives a detailed description of the harvesting and consumption of raffia palm-wine in Mankon, where large quantities of "raffia wine are a necessity in all gatherings, funerals, rites of hospitality, meetings, meals, etc.," and where "Vast quantities are produced, traded and consumed" (Warnier 2007: 166-167). Writing in 1962, Robert and Pat Ritzenthaler, who also provide a rich description of how palm-wine is collected (1962: 80-81), remarked the following about the use of palm-wine for religious, ceremonial and everyday purposes in Bafut:

> Palm wine, used by men, women, and children for religious and ceremonial purposes and as a staple drink at nearly every meal, is consumed in prodigious quantities. Wine from the oil palm is considered to be the choicest, while that from the raffia-palm is inferior

and is never drunk until it has been boiled. Palm wine has the consistency of water and is cloudy white in color. It is rich in iron and in its unfermented state is taken as a health drink by some Europeans. Apparently there is no problem of parasites. Due to its high sugar content it ferments rapidly; a corked calabash of it set in the sun for a few hours will have the alcoholic content of a strong beer (Robert and Pat Ritzenthaler 1962: 80).

Indeed, in many a village throughout Cameroon, it is commonplace for those notables who own palm trees (raffia, oil or both) or can afford to buy palm-wine to sit and drink palm-wine with the chief of the village "on special days as a sign of fidelity, homage and togetherness," while those who have migrated to towns and cities seek to recreate "the typical village evening scene of togetherness and relaxation … around palm wine joints (Awasom 2010: 206), and perhaps also dancing along to palm-wine music or palm-wine inspired music such as the Bottle Dance. Awasom writes on how palm-wine consumption joints during British colonial Cameroon served as model public spheres or spaces and arenas where men and women congregated to drink leisurely, socialise, exchange news and information, opine on public and current affairs, and reach important decisions that touched on their daily lives as migrants in colonial townships (Awasom 2010). Due to the importance of palm-wine in the transactional sociality of everyday life, oil and raffia palm trees are almost everywhere domesticated, for ease of access for the tapping of palm-wine. One cannot afford to depend too much on the wild for something so important on a daily basis (Che 1993).

What is not domesticated to the same degree as palm trees belongs to the bush and the forest. Even then, in Cameroon, bushes and forests are veritable crossroads and frontier zones between the natural world, human society and the supernatural world of ancestral and related spirits. They are sacred and symbolic meeting points between humans and spirits, nature and culture, human agency and the agency of other creatures, visible and invisible, friendly and wild, big and small. As such, bushes and forests are both places and spaces of hope and co-existence of human and other beings (Mawere 2015; Abega 1987, 2000), as they are of danger and foreboding. They are likely to inspire as much fantasies of peace and harmony as they are likely to threaten, unleash terror and frustrate the aspirations of those seeking sustenance and refuge in them (Laburthe-Tolra 1981, 1985; Abega 1987, 2000). It is to the bushes and forests that the kings and princes of the Cameroon Grassfields go to get inspiration for their masquerades and cult associations – inspiration which is translated into and reflected by masquerades that appear half-human and half-animal, half-bird or half other wild creatures of the forest and the bushes – as frontier and crossroads institutions capable of bridging the divide between the cultural, the natural and the supernature, and between the living and their departed ancestors (Abega 2000). Indeed, it is striking the extent to which the universe (of the alives and the deads) Tutuola depicts in *The Palm-Wine Drinkard* resonates with notions of conviviality, interconnections and interdependence between the visible and the invisible prevalent in Cameroon, and that has preponderantly been studied under the unfortunate and unsettling theme of "witchcraft and sorcery" (Rowlands and Warnier 1988; Ardener 1996; Geschiere 1997; Nyamnjoh 2001) as preponderantly destructive attributes of African societies. As Peter Geschiere has argued abundantly, an idea of "witchcraft," if witchcraft it must be, reduced to making a meal of the flesh of others misses the point of accusations and counter-accusations of and by those with real or imagined access to magical, supernatural and occult powers (Geschiere 1995, 1997, 2013).

The emphasis on the negativity of so-called witchcraft and sorcery has tended to de-emphasise the epistemological potential of belief systems and practices that refuse to caricature reality through resorting to easy dichotomies between ways of being and knowing by means of sensory perception and other forms of being and knowing that are not easily reducible to the senses and linear conceptions of time and space. If Tutuola's fantastical sense of time and space were to be more than merely a figment of his fertile imagination, as is indeed the case, given how grounded in popular and widely shared ideas of reality his stories are (Anozie 1975[1970]; Armstrong 1975[1970]; Neumarkt 1975[1971]), what does recognising this do to reading and understanding Tutuola? Even more importantly, in what way does or should such recognition influence the study and representation of Yoruba and the many other African societies where, despite resilient colonial education and its arsenal of condescension vis-à-vis popular cosmologies, ontologies and beliefs in intricate interconnections between the nature, the humanly cultivated and the supernatural, ordinary people have persistently refused to sing a requiem for their being and becoming through their very own creative imagination? Put differently, is the only world possible and recognisable in the ivory towers of universities as kingdoms and queendoms of knowledge production and consumption *merely* one in which everything is reduced to rational thought, reductionist and deductive logic and what lends itself to measurable chronologies through the naked senses and their instrumentalisation? What do we make of those who sincerely believe, organise themselves and relate to one another and to distant others with the understanding that there is much more to life than logic, and much more to people, things and indeed the world than our senses are able to bring home to us?

If one does not simply dismiss or explain it under the label of witchcraft, magic, occult or superstition, the proliferation of unusual or unnatural happenings in Tutuola's novels suddenly takes on a whole new meaning epistemologically. Take Tutuola's idea of time and space, for instance. As Charles Larson observes, to Tutuola, time is not simply chronological and linear. Time is something to be measured less in blocks and more in human values and human achievements. This gives a whole new perspective on what at face value might appear as nothing more than an exaggerated idea of time in Tutuola's stories. What does it mean, beyond merely claiming the impossibility, for Tutuola to write emphatically about the vast distances that his heroes, heroines and other characters "are capable of covering in very limited periods of time in spite of the fact that in many cases there are no roads or pathways from one place to another"? If we are not simply to dismiss Tutuola's capacity to merge time and space in a manner that results in surrealistic possibilities where "the physical aspects of the environment divide, alter, and coalesce into new forms," what would we make of, for example, a termites' house changing into a market while the palm-wine drinkard and his wife are sleeping nearby? (Larson 1975[1972]: 175-176). The answer, I cannot stress enough, is that universities as places and spaces of knowledge production and consumption have been impoverished by the systematic imposition of a colonial and colonising Eurocentric tradition of knowledge in an African context with a rich repertoire of complementary popular traditions of knowledge that, unfortunately, are labelled as primitive, superstitious and irrational, and relegated to the margins.

Tutuola's universe is larger than the creativity of his hyper imagination. It is a widely shared universe across Africa. The fact that Africa's colonially educated elite still appear so hostile to such a universe in their sanitised disembedded and sterile so-called scientific or rational discourses, is just added evidence of how thickly embedded (or should I say stuck) beyond consciousness these elite remain in Tutuola's universe. They would rather, as the example of rumours about elite Cameroonians and their associations with the occult below demonstrate, in the double lives they lead, be Robert Louis Stevenson's Dr Jekyll (rational, modern and civilised) by day and Mr Hyde (savage, and violently malevolent) at night than display the boldness and confidence of Amos Tutuola, in pointing out that the colonial modernity of which they are so hotly in pursuit is not the dazzling "complete gentleman" of human civilisation that it appears to be.

While the stories and universe depicted by Tutuola are familiar across Africa – even if unfortunately often misrepresented and dismissed as witchcraft, the occult or primitive superstitions –, of particular resonance are the flexible and fluid representations of reality and personhood that parallels *Msa* and related notions prevalent in the Grassfields of Cameroon (Nyamnjoh 2001). This I would like to highlight here, in conversation with Tutuola and his universe.

Msa is also an omnipresent mysterious world of beauty, abundance, marvels and infinite possibilities, inhabited by very wicked, hostile, vicious and exploitative people known among the Bum, increasingly influenced by Christianity and its lexicon, as devils (*deblisu*). The equivalent in Tutuola's universe would be the ghosts and ghostesses of the bush of ghosts, and all the mysterious creatures of the various towns often traversed by his narrators in their journeys of many dangers. Indeed, the wild hunter in the bush of ghosts is surprised to find out that the bush of ghosts "was the dwelling place of Satan, who was driven away from heaven by God" (Tutuola 1989[1982]: 18) and that "the reverend" in the church of ghosts "was the Devil himself" (Tutuola 1989[1982]: 30). As a fantasy space, *Msa* is visible only to the "cunning" who alone can visit it anytime, anywhere, and who can conjure it up to appear for the innocent to glimpse and be dazzled by its lure and allure. *Msa* has a way of luring its victims, first with fantasies and marvels (utopia), then with the harsh reality of exploitation and contradictions (dystopia). Here is how Beben Ktteh of Fonfuka in Bum puts it in an excerpt of an interview I had with him, about *Msa* as an ambivalent and ambiguous fantasy space:

> At *Msa*, you are first shown only the good, the fantastic, the marvellous. This normally attracts you. Then you are trapped and caught. And you die. It is after death that you are shown the bad and distasteful aspect of it. .... After your death, you are enslaved completely: you are ill-treated, overworked, discriminated against ... Sometimes its inhabitants use you as a pillow on their beds, ask you to work on their farms, to carry water for them, wash their dishes and so on. And you do all this work when their own children and themselves do just nothing (Beben Ktteh, quoted in Nyamnjoh 2001: 45).

The discussion of *Msa* which follows is intended to emphasize the importance of comparative studies of African worlds heavily altered and ultimately disadvantaged by the persistence of colonial education and blind adherence to the dualisms of Eurocentric modernity in African scholarship and scholarship on Africa. *Msa* is a world beyond the immediate and the familiar. Like the world of Tutuola's narrators, *Msa* is perceived as a mysterious world of abundance and infinite possibilities, but which is occupied by very wicked ghosts who generally forbid earthly people from coming to their towns. As Tutuola depicts in T*he Wild Hunter in the Bush of the Ghosts*, "any earthly people who dared come there would perish or perhaps be turned into ghosts" (1989[1982]: 24) or reduced to beasts of burden to be ridden "around the bush like a horse" mercilessly:

"If I tired or slowed down, he was so wicked that he did not allow me to rest even for one second, but he flogged me instead." (Tutuola 1989[1982]: 27). As a beast of burden, the hunter's tortures knew no bounds. He could be rented to others for a fee, harnessed under the scorching sun where he perspired nonstop, and kept in an undersized "stable … so small that I was unable to stand upright or to move here and there so I remained always on my knees" (Tutuola 1989[1982]: 28). When he was not merely fed grass as food for the horse that he was, the hunter was fed "remnants of rice and many other useless kinds of food that the ghosts had rejected." Indeed, even the water they gave him "was very sour" (Tutuola 1989[1982]: 30). When the wicked ghosts were not ridding him around with impunity, the hunter's owner – the ghost who "carried a fire with big flames on his head," and his networks of clients, would harness him by putting "a rope around my neck" and tying "it to a tree," and by putting "a saddle on my back so I would be ready for another ridding" (Tutuola 1989[1982]: 27).

For those who venture to *Msa* or the bush of ghosts and survive the wickedness and supra exploitation by ghosts, these places or spaces could become a source of potency, capable of activating their inhabitants in myriad ways to attain their dreams. The wild hunter in the bush of the ghosts, for example, is encouraged to "marry a woman with two heads and six breasts," so he could turn into a ghost "after thirty years and then I would never die" (Tutuola 1989[1982]: 42). The prospect of citizenship in the bush of the ghosts through marriage is indeed tempting, for earthly people were otherwise reduced to beasts of burden, to be exploited and ill-treated without relent by their ghostly captors (Tutuola 1989[1982]: 24-32).

Some people in the Cameroon Grassfields visit *Msa* for money, some for intelligence, some for opportunity as a blanket pursuit, and some for abundance in things desired. *Msa* has productive and destructive dimensions, and is often difficult to fathom or predict. It is in the nature and dealings of *Msa* and its inhabitants to be ambiguous and capricious, and to wrong-foot those who use their cunning and trickery to seek their attention and assistance. *Msa* compresses time and space, and can be conjured to appear instantaneously, in the manner and capacity of the "Television-handed ghostess" to project the reality of the hometown of the earthly narrator in *My Life in the Bush of Ghosts*. Just like with *Msa*, Tutuola shows us how the bush of ghosts can be accessed simply by sitting under a tree (Tutuola 1954: 160) or by climbing up one (Tutuola 1989[1982]: 16-17), falling asleep and waking up to find oneself entangled in a whole new world.

From the accounts of the seven other hunters trapped in the bush of the ghosts along with the Wild Hunter in *The Wild Hunter in the Bush of the Ghosts*, we gather other ways of accessing the bush of ghosts to include: climbing on an elephant mistaken for a log of wood and being carried by it into the bush; being led to the bush by a dog that had turned into a giant; an only son being forcefully carried into the bush by his jealous sisters; being pounced upon and taken to the bush by a strange bird after shooting it; being blown into the bush by a strong breeze; being carried into the bush by malevolent, stealing spirits; and being carried into the bush by the wild animals in one's dream (Tutuola 1989[1982]: 82-89). Those fortunate enough to survive and escape the bush of ghosts have vacated it mysteriously with the assistance of two women: by watching the palm of a "Television-handed ghostess" (Tutuola 1954: 160); and by going through a door opened by "Miss Victoria Juliana," born in South Africa in 1803 to a father and mother who "came from an unknown land and settled in South Africa in the year 1800" (Tutuola 1989[1982]: 67) – "she opened the door of a room and told us to enter it with our belongings. To our surprise, we had hardly entered that room when we found ourselves back at the place on earth we had left when we were youths" (Tutuola 1989[1982]: 124).

Msa has the godlike propensity for presence in simultaneous multiplicity. Like the wirelessly delivered internet of today, *Msa* can be conjured up and accessed from anywhere – at home, in rivers, bushes and forests – and it can be made visible by cunning, clever or trickster individuals such as the narrator of *The Palm-Wine Drinkard* or that of *My Life in the Bush of Ghosts*. *Msa* is an ambiguous and ambivalent world of beauty, abundance and marvels, where everything can be found and anything is possible. It is inhabited by its own people who look no different from ordinary people, but who are actually spirits and ghosts. The people of *Msa* live in even better houses, just like Tutuola's ghosts in *The Wild Hunter in the Bush of the Ghosts*, who may be "very dirty" and "smelling just like decaying dead bodies," but all their "buildings were beautiful" (Tutuola 1989[1982]: 21). The inhabitants of *Msa* speak the respective languages of the localities where they belong and/or are conjured to appear. *Msa* can be found everywhere in the world. Its inhabitants are understood to be generally wicked, hostile and vicious; they are terrible curious creatures and spirits of the sort depicted by Tutuola in *The Wild Hunter in the Bush of the Ghosts*, *The Palm-Wine Drinkard* and *My Life in the Bush of Ghosts*.

Like with Tutuola's bush of ghosts, there is indeed much more to *Msa* than meets the eye or logic. Only tricksters and clairvoyants have the capacity and ambiguity to activate themselves to the potency required to visit *Msa* anytime, anywhere, and to fortify themselves enough to be able to frequent, without permanently jeopardising themselves, the bushes and the endless forests occupied by spirits, ghosts and terrible curious creatures like the Skull. Personal success and accumulation of material wealth that cannot be accounted for by tangible evidence of investment in work, effort and productivity tend to be associated with *Msa* and its ambiguities (Rowlands 1995; Warnier 1993a). In such situations, curiosities arise and blend. Interconnections between work and leisure, production and consumption, enrichment and exploitation, economies of intimacy and market economies, which have been associated with Tutuola and his universe (Wenzel 2006), become apparent. The same is true of *Msa* (Nyamnjoh 2001; Geschiere and Nyamnjoh 1998, 2000; Geschiere 2013) and the solidarities it inspires through philosophies of inclusive success (Nyamnjoh 2015c). Both *Msa* and Tutuola's universe of interconnections and co-implication resonate with Gogo Breeze's radio world of kinship built around a moral authority of mutual dependence between workers and employers in contemporary Zambia. Like a Tutuola quest-hero, Harri Englund's radio Gogo [Grandfather] is able to use the multivocality made possible by radio to encourage boundary-crossing in the negotiation of moral dilemmas and the cultivation of moral sympathies (Englund 2015a, 2015b).

Villains who delight in inflating themselves by deflating others, when they want something valuable, seek to activate themselves by taking their victims to *Msa* to be debased, tethered like goats and used as such – a manner not dissimilar to how the Wild Hunter discussed above is treated(1989[1982]: 24-30), or how the narrator in *My Life in the Bush of Ghosts* is repeatedly dehumanised and exploited by his captor, the King of Smelling Ghosts of the 7th Town of Ghosts (Tutuola 1954: 21). *Msa* is like a market, complete with traders and buyers. It is like a bazaar where many come but few are rewarded, and where there is often much less or much more to people and to things than meets the eyes. To get what one desires, one must bargain and pay for it, even though one can never really be sure of what one gets as things always come wrapped, mislabelled or in ambiguous packages. The only currency or unit of exchange in *Msa* is human beings, variously referred to as "goat" or "fowl," when converted by the tricksters who seek to use them to do business in *Msa*. Villains or tricksters at *Msa*, like the narrator in *The Palm-Wine Drinkard*, can only get what they want after completing payment or a transaction. Nothing sacrificed, nothing gained. Villains who fail to honour their debts must pay with their lives. The number of "fowls" or "goats" to be paid, once agreed upon, cannot be revoked or rescinded. A contract or an agreement is absolutely binding. This is why, while at *Msa*, the more sensible "Sly" or trickster, is hesitant to enter into a contract or to indebt themselves with reckless abandon. Caution is strongly advised, in how visitors at *Msa* negotiate and navigate its delicate and dangerous intricacies.

People also believe that anything that comes from *Msa* multiplies and proliferates. If it is destruction, it comes in abundance, and if it happens to be positive and constructive, the ramifications are felt and celebrated far and wide. *Msa* is, above all, an ambivalent place of ambiguities – where good and bad, pleasure and pain, construction and destruction co-exist in intricately entangled superabundance. *Msa* also suggests a place that is highly unpredictable, and where signs are scrambled as nothing is ever what it seems. Death and dying are as commonplace as they are impermanent. In *Msa*, the desires to build and to destroy are two sides of the cowrie of life. There is more goodness than one can imagine, and more evil than the imagination can grasp. Good and bad are mutually entangled at *Msa*, and no one can have one without the other. Evil is enveloped in goodness and goodness in evil, and one often gets more than one sees or bargains for. At *Msa* it is everyone for themselves and the Devil for all. Interdependence, interconnectedness and intersubjectivity seem to threaten the very existence of *Msa*; which is founded on greed and the selfish and single-minded pursuit of self-interest. Hence the violent opposition by the inhabitants of *Msa* to conviviality between those it charms and the communities they inhabit.

Msa is strikingly like the Deads' Town, which refuses to have anything to do with the alives and the places they inhabit, unless as Death gone wild, to turn the backs of its victims among the alives to their kin and communities by "killing"[1] them in the thousands. The narrator of *The Palm-Wine Drinkard* recounts: "As we were going on this road, we met over a thousand deads who were just going to the Deads' Town" (Tutuola 1952: 101). Not only were the deads "very annoyed to see alives" whom they hated, "These deads were not talking to one another at all" (Tutuola 1952: 101). When they appeared to talk, it was not in plain words but murmurs. "They always seemed as if they were mourning, their eyes would be very wild and brown and everyone of them wore white clothes without a single stain" (Tutuola 1952: 102). The ubiquity of Death and its devastations are well captured by "about 400 dead babies" marching to the Deads' Town with "sticks in their hands," beating up with the sticks and frightening the narrator and his wife into the bushes (Tutuola 1952: 102). On Yoruba consciousness, Ogundipe-Leslie remarks that "Death is not a thing of horror and the worlds of the living and the dead are co-extensive," adding that among the Yoruba, "dead babies are the most cruel of all the dead" due to high infant death-rate and their emotional toll on parents, as evidenced by the phenomenon of the "born and die" babies (Ogundipe-Leslie 1975[1970]: 149). Even when apparently blessed with the gift of a magic egg with promises that the use of the egg would satisfy every desire imaginable of the palm-wine drinkard (Tutuola 1952: 101), the egg soon becomes overwhelmed by greed and degenerates into "hordes of magical leather whips which he then sets loose on the crowds that gather demanding to be fed" (Wenzel 2006: 451).

Tutuola's dead are analogous to the zombies of *Msa*, who are only dead enough to slave away in the interest of those who have implanted them at *Msa* (Nyamnjoh 2001, 2005a). The surest and safest way to benefit from *Msa* without becoming trapped by its evils is to be a wise and humble person freed of ambitions of personal enrichment, and by choosing not to belong fully to *Msa* but to act as a bridge and mediator of the two worlds. Domesticating one's connections with *Msa* is the surest way of survival for *Msa*, those it enchants and their kith and kin. Just like the narrator of *The Palm-Wine Drinkard* who benefits from the gift of a precious egg that can answer his every wish, so too is *Msa* known to reward those who engage it with wisdom and prudence.

As a fantasy space replete with ambivalence and ambiguity, *Msa* also has much in common with Tutuola's bush of ghosts, with its capacity to materialise all of a sudden, like an act of magic. The power to appear, disappear and reappear mysteriously characterises both universes. Just as the seven year old narrator of *My Life in the Bush of Ghosts* suddenly disappears under the "future sign tree" where his 24 year journey of mysterious encounters into the bush of ghosts begins (Tutuola 1954: 160), unsuspecting children are also known to be lured to *Msa* by their trickster mates or by adult villains practiced in the ways of *Msa*. There, the children could be enslaved for long periods or cursed with incurable afflictions by the demanding and callous indifference of their overbearing overlords.

Msa and the bush of ghosts have in common the reality of what Tutuola has described as "born to die babies" in several of his stories. These babies are unlike normal babies, as they have a life as adult ghosts elsewhere in the bush of ghosts or *Msa*, and only assume the form of babies with intention to dispossess, exploit, defraud and impoverish their supposed earthly parents. "Born to die babies" who do not permanently return to the bush of ghosts because they have been "tied … down with a powerful juju" – such as the hunter narrator of *The Witch-Herbalist of the Remote Town* (Tutuola 1981: 97) – develop a frontier disposition and consciousness, armed with the composite earthly and ghostly crossroads characteristics, and enjoy the prospects, possibilities and repertoires of self-activation available to them as negotiators and navigators of myriad identity margins. In the case of the hunter of the Rocky Town, once he eats of "The Fruit-Tree Of Great Ordeal," he is able to reactivate his attributes as a "born and die baby" (Tutuola 1981: 97), since he could not go to the town of the "Born and Die Baby" without changing his "mortal body to the immortal body of the 'born and die baby'" (Tutuola 1981: 111). The hunter's breast opens up and he emerges as a "born and die baby," leaving his adult body fresh butt lifeless under the tree, and continues his journey into the town of the "Born and Die Baby" (Tutuola 1981: 97). When he no longer needs to function as a "born and die baby," the hunter returns to the spot where he left his "mortal body" and reunites with it. This is how he describes the reunion of his baby and adult bodies:

> ...as soon as I came back to my mortal body, I saw clearly how this my body was split from the breast down to the lowest part of my stomach. Then as soon as it parted to left and right, I became as little as a day-old baby. Then without hesitation, I walked from the ground to my splitting stomach, and as soon as I lay down flat in the split as if one lay on the bed, the immortal body of the 'born and die baby' in which I was, disappeared unexpectedly. As soon as it disappeared, my stomach closed back. I became alive completely (Tutuola 1981: 111).

Ideas of personhood common in the Cameroon Grassfields are instructive to an understanding of the cosmology, ontology and epistemological possibilities of beliefs in *Msa* and related universes such as depicted by Tutuola. If we take the ethnic group of Bum from which I hail as a case in point, their categorisation of people resonates remarkably with Tutuola's and his universe. Most people in Bum believe and act in recognition of the understanding that everyone is either born with "clairvoyance" (*seba* = two eyes) or "innocence" (*seimok* = one eye). The "clairvoyant" has the ability (sing. *fintini*; plur. *fintitu*) to see and do beyond the capability of the innocent. Clairvoyants are clever(manipulative and slippery) (sing. *wutatoffana* = person of sense; plur. *ghetatoffana*), the innocent short-sighted, incapable and, at times, foolish. "To see" (*yen*), when used to distinguish between the clairvoyant and the innocent, means the ability to perceive even the invisible and the intangible. The former sees (*yenalo*), and the latter sees not (*yenawi*).

A clairvoyant might be associated either with *Awung* or *Msa*. *Awung* (pl. *uwung*) are further subdivided into: wise person (sing. *awungadzunga* = good *awung*; pl. *uwungudzungu*); and sorcerer (sing. *awungabe* = bad *awung*; pl: *uwungube*). *Msa* or cunning (sing. *wutamsa* = person of *Msa*; pl. *ghetamsala*) is subdivided into: sly (sing. *wutamsamdzung* = good person of *Msa*; pl. *ghetamsamdzunga*); and villain (sing. *wutamsamba* = bad person of *Msa*; pl. *ghetamsambe*). The innocent comprise: medium (sing. *wut-ni-toffotu* = person with intelligence; pl. *gheta-ni-toffotu*); and inept (sing. *ayung, ngwo, mumu* = person capable of nothing great; pl: *wuyung, wungwo, wumumu*). *Awung* is identifiable mainly through words and action. Sorcerers, seen as jealous and destructive, "eat" or deplete their victims mysteriously. Their victims must be kin, as they are expected to prove intimacy, and it is dangerous to victimise strangers. Sorcerers can enhance their clairvoyance with medicine or magic (juju in Tutuola terms) that protects them against fellow sorcerers and against diviners, with whom relations are of mutual fear and distrust. If sorcerers seek to sever links with kin and cultivate alternative solidarities among themselves, diviners play a mediating role in that they straddle the worlds of kinship and sorcery.

The personal success and independence *Msa* appears to offer is ultimately illusory; so, also, is the semblance of a new solidarity and a counter-community it creates in individuals by encouraging them to sacrifice kin and traditional alliances. When the chips are down, *Msa*'s true ethos – greed and callous indifference – comes to the fore and individuals are expected to make the ultimate sacrifice of their own lives. The surest and safest relationship with *Msa* is not in the permanent severing of links with kin, but rather in the negotiated belonging which the "wise" and the "sly" epitomise: building bridges of conviviality linking home and exile, utopia and dystopia.

It is hard to resist seeing *Msa* as analogous to modern capitalism as exemplified by *Whiteman Kontri*, especially when experienced on the periphery. While local beliefs in *Msa* predate the transatlantic slave trade, and communication between the Grassfields and the coastal regions predates colonialism and plantation agriculture, current narratives on sorcery and the occult in the Grassfields are heavily coloured by the symbols and associations of capitalism. True, *Msa* cannot be explained by the impact of capitalism alone, but it cannot be explained without it. It is not an accident that *Msa* is also closely associated with plantation agriculture in regions of the country where able-bodied men have traditionally, since colonial times, disappeared to slave away in plantations, with some never returning at all or coming home too old to be recognised by those who grew up or aged in their absence.

It is possible to see *Msa* as a statement against endangering moral community and against the colonial and capitalism's illusion of the autonomous individual and the permanence of personal success. Like colonialism and capitalism, *Msa*, when undomesticated, brings power and opportunities to only a few – those with the clairvoyance and greed to indulge in them. The unharnessed pursuit of *Msa* enhances self-seeking individuals at the expense of family and community. But such success is merely an illusion, because, like colonialism and consumer capitalism, *Msa* is seemingly an eternal cycle of indebtedness, manipulation, zombification and the never-ending search for fulfilment. The appetites it brings only grow stronger, and those who yield to its allure are instantly trapped and ultimately consumed, but not before consuming their own and others' sociality. *Msa* is simultaneously an aspiration, a relationship and a location, which to most Cameroonians are best embodied in "*Whiteman Kontri*" (Europe and North America mainly).

Nyongo is another force to consider along with *Msa* and Tutuola's bush of ghosts, given how popular this force also is in the imaginary of coastal and Grassfields peoples of Cameroon. *Nyongo* is a dynamic, flexible, fluid and common form of potency. Those who possess and use it privilege zombification of their victims over instant gratification through instant and total death. One is accused of *Nyongo* when he or she is perceived to have appropriated or attempted to appropriate the life essence of another person, occasioning a sudden and often mysterious "temporary" death – akin to the death of the "born and die babies" common in Tutuola's works and universe. It is claimed that those capable of *Nyongo* benefit from the afflicted by harnessing the abilities of the latter to slave for them as zombies in an invisible world after their presumed death. *Nyongo* also refers to the mysterious invisible place(s) where victims of fierce greed – *Nyongo* – are said to be slaving away, visible mostly to slave drivers or to those who have consigned them to slavery. Others can only see them if activated by the clairvoyance, magic, spells and charms or juju which Tutuola often refers to in his depiction of similar mysterious universes. As Edwin Ardener observed when he first encountered this form of potency among the Bakweri in the coastal part of Cameroon in the 1950s, "it is believed that a person possessing it [*Nyongo*] is able to kill others, especially his own relatives, and to use their bodies to work for him in an invisible town on Mount Kupe in Bakossi country" (Ardener, [1960] 1996, p. 216). In this instance, as in Tutuola's *The Palm-Wine Drinkard* and *My Life in the Bush of Ghosts* – in both of which "an economic analysis of resource extraction and labour relations" is embedded (Wenzel 2006: 249) –, we find the dead and the alive, the ghostly and the earthly, entangled in networks of production, consumption and exploitation, working and going about the business of keeping the flow of life in ways both obvious and fantastical.

If dead people can work and afford the living with magical solutions to material realities, theirs must be a soft form of death, not the presumed violent and total death that comes with the graphic and violent images of clairvoyance and its potencies as dystopia. It is death by degree, and dying as a process of infinity. With *Nyongo*, there is a strong association between "dying children and the ownership" of property (the sort of personal wealth and accumulation that stalls social reproduction) akin to the "modern conveniences" which the Bakweri, as depicted by Edwin Ardener, associated with the *Nyongo* people of Mount Kupe, who even had "motor lorries," a rare commodity and social symbol in colonial Cameroon (Ardener, [1970] 1996: 248-249), that could only reach Cameroon by sea and via ship. In the 1950s, "*Nyongo* people could best be recognised by their tin houses which they had been able to build with the zombie labour force of their dead [or not so dead] relatives" (Ardener, [1970] 1996: 248; see also Geschiere 1997: 146-158). Distinctively "foreign" and rare at the time, tin houses were by every indication a new status symbol that threatened the status quo and its idea of "home" and social visibility with the prospect of the rise of a new elite in tune with values from elsewhere – or the bush of ghosts, to borrow from Tutuola's universe. Hence the desperate attempts to contain the perceived dangers to social order, even if by borrowing – in the manner Tutuola did the English language or the way the Skull borrowed body parts – the regulatory institutions or juju of others, as the Bakweri did from the Obasinjom of the Banyangi in 1955 and 1956 (Ardener [1970] 1996: 250-253; Geschiere 1997: 146-151). As in *The Palm-Wine Drinkard*, a new form of economy that destabilises old certainties and predictable modes of subsistence and existence, luring away trusted tapsters, refining social hierarchies and reducing whole communities into skulls, requires active and vigorous resistance and strategies for resiliency before it spells the end of entire civilisations, social systems, ways of being and ways of life.

If in the colonial period *Nyongo* was best epitomised by the prominent, sinister Mount Kupe and the coastal region (with its vast mysterious expanse of sea water, gateway into new ways of being and belonging) as part of the fertile crescent that attracted colonial investors, slave and migrant labour from around and beyond, in postcolonial Cameroon, by contrast, rapid urbanisation has often exposed villagers to greater towns, even dazzling them with "modern conveniences" beyond the legendary allure of the invisible town and plantations beneath Mount Kupe. People continue to disappear from villages into towns as migrant labour, and from the towns within into cities abroad, seeking greener pastures and the amenities harvested from them. As with the *Nyongo* of old when mostly children were sacrificed, today it is usually the able-bodied youth who are forced by relationships of expectations and exploitation to migrate to towns and abroad as opportunity seeking labour, where they are likely to be supra-exploited to the point of being reduced to disembodied skulls or bare bones that can only be activated to bare humanity through indebting themselves with the able-bodied humanity of others.

Just like the seven year old narrator of Tutuola's *My Life in the Bush of Ghosts* returns 24 years later with little to show in terms of success, after disappearing mysteriously under the "future sign tree," in Cameroon, some victims of Nyongo return old and faded, hardly recognisable culturally and physically by anyone, because they left their villages as children and were counted for dead, and so are best related to as not belonging, ghosts back to haunt the living with disturbing memories.

Others, for various reasons, including bitterness, sheer depletion, marriage to ghost and ghostesses, new ideas of relating to places and spaces, new ideals and new ideas of home, never quite return. Once communication has dried up even beyond reactivation by the "Television-handed ghostess," they are considered dead even by those who had sacrificed them into a life of slavery as zombies in the bush of ghosts. Their enhancement by new horizons in the bush of ghosts and other centres of accumulation of modern conveniences has been achieved at the expense of active relationships with a place called home. The long spells of being away from one's home village or hometown, kith and kin, occasioned by *Nyongo*, are strikingly similar to journeys undertaken my Tutuola's narrators and quest-heroes, from the palm-wine drinkard, through the 24 year sojourn of the earthly child in the bush of ghosts, to the Brave Hunter of the Rocky Town who undertakes a six year journey to and back from the Witch Herbalist of the Remote Town.

In a world where people are enchanted by the lure and allure of consumption, with or without effort, and irrespective of whether or not the consumed is a local convenience such as palm-wine, or an exotic object such as the magical egg brought back from the Dead's Town by the palm-wine drinkard, interconnections and interdependencies – visible and invisible, far and near, natural, cultural and supernatural – become the norm, as rigid exclusionary choices are muted in favour of the balance of inclusivity. Work and pleasure, greed and servitude, life and death, realism and fantasy, presence and absence, here and there awake to conviviality (Achebe 1988: 100-112; Wenzel 2006).

The palm-wine drinkard is a propped up man with a delusory sense of independence; a man who has done nothing but drink palm-wine since the age of ten, and who is able to do so thanks mainly to the intervention of his affluent father, the richest man in his town. In the manner of a slave-owner, the father "indulges his son's outrageous appetite" by buying the services of a palm-wine tapster to slave away nonstop, day in and out, attending to his son's reckless consumption of alcohol. Achebe brands this "exploitative and socially useless work" (Achebe 1988[1990]: 103). Such indolence and frivolity on the part of the palm-wine drinkard and his uncritically supportive father, begs the question: "What happens when a man immerses himself in pleasure to the exclusion of all work; when he raises pleasure to the status of work and occupation and says in effect: 'Pleasure be thou my work!'?" (Achebe 1988[1990]: 102). Branding the extravagant dependency and exploitation without relent perpetuated by the affluent father and his pleasure-fixated son, a "social and moral offence of colossal consequence" (Achebe 1988[1990]: 103), Achebe concludes: "*The Palm-Wine Drinkard* is a rich and spectacular exploration of this gross perversion, its expiation through appropriate punishment and the offender's final restoration" (Achebe 1988[1990]: 102). The book highlights Tutuola's prioritisation of the need to "balance between play and work" (Achebe 1988[1990]: 106). As Achebe puts it:

> Tutuola's moral universe is one in which work and play in their numerous variations complement each other. The good life, he seems to say, is that in which business and pleasure, striving and repose, giving and receiving, suffering and enjoyment, punishment and reprieve, poverty and wealth, have their place, their time and their measure. We *give* work and struggle; and in the end we *take* rest and fulfilment (Achebe 1988[1990]: 103).

Such celebration of work is particularly relevant and beneficial to "a generation and a people whose heroes are no longer makers of things and ideas but spectacular and insatiable consumers" (Achebe 1988[1990]: 112). In stressing a careful balance between play and work, give and take, Tutuola is reminding his readers "that a community which lets some invisible hand do its work for it will sooner or later forfeit the harvest" to "a merciless exactor" (Achebe 1988 [1990]: 111).

Just as with Tutuola's moral universe where pleasure without effort and consumption with reckless abandon are frowned upon, and personal success at the expense of others is perceived as anti-social, central to understanding the cosmopolitan credentials of *Nyongo* is the obsession among Cameroonians with "modern conveniences" (Ardener [1970] 1996: 248-249) or "modern forms of consumerism" (Geschiere 1997: 138-139), characterised by a "proverbial" craving for "everything that is imported rather than produced locally," as the ultimate symbol of status (Warnier 1993a: 162–196), even if this is achieved at the expense of harmony with kin.

As I have argued elsewhere (Nyamnjoh 2005a), Cameroonians from the Bamenda Grassfields, pushed into the cities and the bush of ghosts of Europe and North America to seek greener pastures and modern conveniences, increasingly perceive themselves as being in and victims of *Nyongo*, thanks mainly to relatives who are exceedingly demanding in their expectations of remittances, yet who care very little for the welfare and predicaments facing their zombies abroad, where being a human with rights and dignity is a luxury few can afford in reality, and where people slaving away are reduced to a bare existence as disembodied skulls. As one of Chinua Achebe's proverbs on invisible power goes, "when we see a little bird dancing in the middle of the pathway we must know that its drummer is in the near-by bush" (Achebe (1974[1964: 40).

The Cameroonian bushfallers are the drummers or activators in the not-so-nearby bushes to dancing relatives in home villages and hometowns. The tensions engendered by this situation result in ambivalent attitudes towards home, especially among those opened to new possibilities and less taxing forms of belonging, however dim. As Harri Englund argues in relation to Pentecostal Christians in Malawi, "the cosmopolitan imagination emerges when there is unease or uncertainty about the 'home' that most immediately imposes itself upon the subject," forcing it to renegotiate a problematic belonging that is narrowly cast in geographical and biological terms, in favour of home as a set of comforting practices and relationships (Englund 2004: 296-297). Increasingly uncomfortable with unrealistic expectations from their homes of origin and feeling less than welcome in their host communities of ghosts and ghostesses, Bamenda Grassfielders abroad – like souls trapped in the bush of ghosts – employ the language of victimhood to come to terms with their predicament, while inviting others to outgrow narrow, essentialist and opportunistic notions of belonging. In this sense, they are little different from Tutuola's quest-heroes who nimble-footedly cross otherwise rigidly controlled borders, as if to make a compelling case for the virtues of cosmopolitanism between the earthly and the ghostly towns they encounter in the course of their quest. Although not an undifferentiated category, Bamenda Grassfielders abroad are thus able, through the language of *Nyongo*, to, like many a narrator or protagonist in Tutuola's stories, capture their tensions with home and host communities, using their own encounters and experiences to argue for more flexible, negotiated, relational, and realistic ideas of belonging founded less on the essence of geography and biology than on conviviality and a shared consciousness.

If *Nyongo* signifies mysterious places where modern conveniences and inconveniences co-exist in superabundance – be this "the bush of ghosts" in Tutuola's universe (where hunters "can go to hunt animals" and from which, with only a few rare exceptions, "no hunter had ever entered and returned... safely after many years of wandering" (Tutuola 1989[1982]: 124) or simply "the bush" in the eyes of "bushfalling" Cameroonians and their relations (Nyamnjoh 2005a, 2011) – Cameroon Grasssfielders have, like Tutuola's quest-heroes and heroines, increasingly discovered such places by degree through risky journeys into unfamiliar worlds, and in accordance with the possibilities availed them for self-activation by new transportation, information and communication technologies – new juju in Tutuola terms. First the motor car (lorry) activated their long distance mobility away from their home villages, towns and region to discover the infinite marvels and dangers of plantation agriculture in coastal Cameroon, thereby enriching their vocabulary with the reality of attraction and depletion embedded in concepts such as *Nyongo*.

The parallels between Tutuola's bush of ghosts, wild and strange creatures and the idea of the bush and bushfalling as near or distant places of foraging for subsistence in Cameroon are striking in their articulation of the sacred and the profane, the domesticated and the wild, home and elsewhere. They speak to the idea of sociality and its boundaries as well as its mobilities and recalibrations through encounters with others, familiar and unfamiliar, known, unknown and unknowable. Hunting is a means by which communities bring the wild, strange unknown bushes and their inhabitants into contact, conversation and communion with their worlds in the interest of life and its circulations. The hunter is the main – but not evidently the only (as Tutuola reveals through his narrators, some of whom are not professional hunters, even if every one of them is, in a way, a hunter of sorts) – agent, who makes this possible.

In Cameroon and among Cameroonians, hunting and distance farming are metaphors of choice. This is embodied in the figure of the "*bushfaller*" and the practice of "*bushfalling*." Mobile Cameroonians perceive the city and the "world out there" in the same manner that they do hunting grounds or distant farms. The home village or hometown remains, however, the ultimate conferrer of social recognition and, as with Tutuola's quest-heroes, is the place of return at the end of the day with salvationist options for the collectivity (Nyamnjoh 2011). Indeed:

> Fear of social invisibility among kith and kin compels individuals to disappear and subject themselves to the vicissitudes, whims, and caprices of worlds and forces untamed during hunting and farming expeditions into distant undomesticated lands. Such forays allow one to invest in one's home village materially and through relationships, which is generally perceived as the best insurance policy against social effacement. Fulfilling obligations also demonstrates a certain level of success and guarantees survival and recognition, even if one has lost everything in the city or abroad. Though successful urbanites or diasporic Cameroonians may not permanently return to rural areas, most remain in constant interaction with their home villages in various ways, including active participation in development initiatives and instructions to kin for their burial or reburial in the home village … Keeping in touch with and connected to the home village is measured more through relationships, attitudes, and behavior over time than through mere claims or physical presence. As mobility has accelerated, virtuality has also been enhanced through the proliferation of information and communication technologies… (Nyamnjoh 2011: 701).

With better roads and increased mobility, hunting places or bushes became less mysterious, more visible and real as predatory sites of accumulation and/or exploitation, where one slaves away without relent, and where the ultimate sacrifice of a second and final death (in other words, permanent relocation to a new, invisible and inaccessible home in the manner of the palm-wine tapster in the Dead's Town and of the seven year old narrator in the bush of ghosts) is ever looming. Still, more technological advances or juju (airplane, television, Internet, cell phone, smartphones, social media and various other technologies for presence in simultaneous multiplicity, and for absent presence) have taken *Nyongo* further afield into distant foreign lands and virtual spaces, as families and communities, in their quest for elusive completeness, sacrifice sons and daughters to forage for opportunities in the birthplaces of modern conveniences, while at the same time multiplying opportunities both for accountability and opportunism (Nyamnjoh 2005a, 2011, 2015c; Nyamnjoh HM, 2014, Tazanu 2012).

Bamenda Grassfielders abroad compare Europe and North America, which they have the habit of referring to as "*Whiteman Kontri*," to *Nyongo*, and the habit of likening themselves to victims of *Nyongo* in *Whiteman Kontri*. There is a widely shared perception of *Whiteman Kontri* as *Nyongo*. Many a Cameroonian abroad claim they are "working *Nyongo*," to refer to when they offer devalued and highly exploited labour at factories, as cleaners, maids, security guards or prostitutes, sweating and toiling round the clock, just to make ends meet, often in a context of violence and callous disregard of their dignity as humans. They see themselves in a manner not dissimilar to how Tutuola's narrator and quest-hero in the bush of ghosts complains whenever his captors, with the help of their juju, transform him into an object or a beast of burden in order to exploit him with reckless abandon. Cameroonians also use *Nyongo* to depict the excessive demands for remittances and consumer items by relations, friends and acquaintances back in their hometowns and home villages who are not always family or friends, and who do not care much about them as human beings (Nyamnjoh 2005a, 2011, 2015c; Nyamnjoh HM, 2014, Tazanu 2012).

If in the past *Nyongo* and *Msa* were easily accessible to all villains and tricksters wanting to place their zombies for effective exploitation, increasingly such access is no longer a matter of course, especially for the ultimate centres of *Nyongo* situated in *Whiteman Kontri* with its compelling allure of modern conveniences (Nyamnjoh and Page 2002; Nyamnjoh 2005a, 2011, 2015c; Nyamnjoh HM, 2014, Tazanu 2012). Huge payments beyond simply having a human victim ("fowl" or "goat") to sacrifice are required for all sorts of things, ranging from passports to plane tickets, through medical doctors with special machines rumoured to transform a person from black to white, prophets with special abilities to empower weak passports, letters of invitation or admission, visas, work permits, green cards, services of middlemen and various types of placement fees. Even when the villains and tricksters are able to come up with the payments required, there is little guarantee that things will sail through, as their zombie could always be denied a visa for one "capricious" reason or another. But the resolve to make it to or invest in *Whiteman Kontri* is phenomenal, and some use various indirections just to get their zombies there – the more the better, especially as, increasingly, not every potential zombie is zombie enough or fortunate enough to qualify to be exploited. This means that unlike in the past, not every trickster or villain with someone to zombify qualifies to access *Nyongo* and *Msa* in a lucrative manner anymore, and resorting to indirections implies that not every zombie in the bush of ghosts is going to be welcome or to have worthwhile opportunities. In the world of exploitation, many are called but few are chosen.

Unequal opportunities for zombies in the bush of ghosts speaks not only of a hierarchy of *Nyongo* and tricksters, but also of zombies, as some *Nyongo* and tricksters are more endowed with modern (in)conveniences than others, just as some zombies are more entitled than others to the consumer margins of the bush of ghosts. Similarly, not every zombie is well placed to renegotiate relations with home or realise their dream of success, comfort and freedom in the bush of ghosts. Accounts of experiences in the modern day bush of ghosts tell not only of changing attitudes to cultures of solidarity, interconnectedness and conviviality, as informed by the consumer status of zombies compared to the status of others back in home villages and hometowns, and to the status of fellow zombies in the bush. That *Whiteman Kontri* is seen and treated as *Nyongo* or the bush of ghosts by Grassfielders and other Cameroonians out there is most evident from the accusatory language of victimhood (extreme anger, deep frustration, self-pity, regret and melancholy) that they employ to describe their subjection and ultra-exploitation by forces both in their home villages and hometowns on the one hand and host communities in the bush on the other hand. In a world pregnant with rhetoric on universal human rights and global citizenship, Cameroonians in local and distant bushes cannot comprehend why everywhere the tendency remains firmly to deny them the basics in humanity and dignity. Every relationship they forge seems to dramatize their exploitation, leaving them drained and trapped like Tutuola's tapster in the Dead's Town or the earthly in the bush of ghosts.

In the past, when technologies of mobility were limited and marrying out of one's home village or hometown rare, it was commonplace to assume that *Nyongo* could not cross boundaries (epitomised often by rivers). *Nyongo* tended to be confined to intimate family circles, narrowly defined either as nuclear or extended. If tricksters were required to show proof of intimacy by removing the amulets or juju (to disarm in other words) of their potential victims, then they had to be family since family members were most likely the closest persons in the life of the individual. But with migration to plantations, cities and abroad, where individuals have had occasion to forge new intimacies with perfect strangers and at times to question the sincerity of kin, families have ceased to be the only intimate circles in the lives of mobile and migrant Grassfielders in various bushes of ghosts. Sometimes friends and intimate strangers are far more precise on the nature and whereabouts of the amulets or juju of the sons and daughters of rural families in the plantations, cities or abroad that they are most likely to succeed with them as tricksters and villains than distant families in distant home villages and hometowns. Flexible mobility has yielded multiple zones of intimacy, and by extension a less rigid notion of family. This is significant, as increasingly Grassfielders in the bush of ghosts accuse not only their immediate and extended families of having sold them to *Nyongo*, but also friends, schoolmates and others with whom they had shared their lives and spaces during their years in their home villages and towns. In Tutuola's universe as well, we have noted how mobility and border crossing leads to encounters with different others, some of which result in marriage, reproduction and the extension of the idea of family, kin and belonging.

This is what happens with the palm-wine drinkard who marries the daughter of the king of a distant town, after rescuing her from the "complete gentleman" and his cul-de-sac community of skulls in a hole at the heart of the wild bush. Similarly, the earthly child who vanishes into the bush of ghosts for twenty four years, twice marries ghostesses, and has a half-earthly and half-ghostly son with the Super-Lady Ghostess, who insists on doing everything by half. Although the insistence by this half-earthy and half-ghostly son to bridge both cultures and civilisations results, in Freudian terms, to irreconcilable discontent in the two super-egos claiming exclusionary oversight over him (Freud 1957), the possibility of genuine hybridity that he embodies is promising of a truly unshackled cosmopolitanism. The brave hunter in *The Witch-Herbalist of the Remote Town*, is a "born and die baby" who was prevented from returning to the bush of ghosts by his father's powerful juju, and who marries the daughter of his father's assistant.

Like the Ivoirians in the popular television drama *"C'est l'homme qui fait l'homme"* (Nyamnjoh 2015c), Bamenda Grassfielders abroad are under enormous pressure from kin back home to succeed, with kin seeking consumer citizenship through them, as consumer zombies planted abroad like pipelines into the refineries and reservoirs of modern conveniences. As friends or acquaintances of those abroad, they tolerate no excuses when they email, telephone (directly or via Skype, Viber, WhatsApp, Facebook, Facetime, etc.), beep, SMS or write a letter claiming delayed remittances and consumer goodies, or even when they simply demand assistance with this or that urgent project back in the home village or hometown. They are often very impatient and rushed in their approach, with a business-like demeanour that leaves little room for being pleasant or courteous. Grassfielders back home often use accusations of nonobservance of tradition as a means of extracting gifts without gratitude from relations abroad, who are perceived to be sufficiently successful in their hunting expeditions abroad, to be able to redistribute without complaining of self-impoverishment. A long list of demands by distant kin or elderly people one hardly knows is often preceded by threats of "kontri fashion go catch you" (tradition will indict you), as those back home tend to think of themselves as custodians of tradition, who should enforce the sharing of the spoils as tradition dictates.

The truly successful bushfallers who resist such calls to redistribute or extend their perceived personal success to include those left behind, risk being accused of using tradition as an excuse to keep their resources all to themselves, in the same way that they see those at home as using tradition to claim part of that success. For them, its hostility to their humanity and quest for inclusion notwithstanding, the bush of ghosts increasingly represents an alternative (however unattractive) to the dangerous expectations of their home folks. Others, who are not necessarily as successful and established, feel the same reluctance going home on holidays, even when they would very much love to spend time with friends and family back in Cameroon. The reason is the excessive demands made on their meagre resources by people who do not care that much about them as human beings, although it must be admitted that in certain cases excessive demands are provoked by the conspicuous display of wealth, material superiority and the air of achievement which "bushfallers" and "been tos" emphasize when back home on brief visits (Nyamnjoh 2005a, 2011, 2015c; Nyamnjoh HM, 2014, Tazanu 2012).

While completely deactivating ties by changing juju such as phone numbers, email and physical addresses is an option, not many want to go down that route, however pushed. Instead, most develop coping strategies aimed at lightening the burdens of expectations from home, such as appealing to the humanity of kin and friends, discouraging opportunism and adventurism, stressing reciprocity in relationships, attracting sympathy for their own personal predicaments, feigning poverty, being frank about the hardships facing them as subjected and debased creatures at the margins of citizenship and humanity, and seeking to integrate themselves significantly in the host communities through marriage, for example.

A growing number feel that relatives and friends back in their hometowns and home villages must understand that long celebrated solidarity and conviviality are at risk, should they continue to sharpen their consumer greed with callous indifference to the humanity of kin the way they do. There is little evidence that such strategies are working, but most feel the strategies would have to work in the interest of continued harmony and interconnectedness between those at home seeking the benefits of opportunities through relationships with kin desperately hunting for such opportunities in *Whiteman Kontri* or in Tutuola's bush of ghosts (Nyamnjoh 2005a, 2011, 2015c; Nyamnjoh HM, 2014, Tazanu 2012).

As we know of *Nyongo* and *Msa*, and as Diane Adesola Mafe reminds us, Tutuola's bush is as much a settled community as any human town depicted in his novels, even if the bush is "rife with nonhuman and paranormal (spirit, ghost, ghommid) settled communities." Indeed, as she observes, "Although nature is integral to the bush, buildings, villages, and even cities figure within that space as well" (Mafe 2012: 23). The bush of ghosts is as ordinary a place as it is extraordinary. It is as much an everyday reality as it is a fantasy space of ambivalences and ambiguities.

As we gather from "C'est l'homme qui fait l'homme" (Nyamnjoh 2015c), it is not often that beggars, askers or seekers are competent givers, nor are they trusting and trustworthy. Money and consumer items meant for many villagers and townspeople often end up attending to the appetites of the individuals through whom they are channelled out of the bush of ghosts who, on the expectation chain, feel more entitled than everyone else.

Tutuola's attitude to money was very insightful. His son, Yinka Tutuola, recounts an exchange he had with his father on the subject of money:

> I could well remember a time (many years ago) when he believed I spent too much on music and drinks. Instead of saying so directly, he asked me if I had any money with me right there and then. I told him I had and he asked me to bring out a note – any denomination. I

brought one out and the next question was "Who owns it?" To this I said "I, of course!" He asked me to prove it since my name was not on it. I didn't know how to prove it, so I asked "Who owns it then?" He said "Nobody!" I knew then that he wanted to teach me something in his usual humorous way, so I asked him "Explain how money I brought out of my pocket isn't mine!" After a rather long pause (he always liked being dramatic) he said "Know from today that money by itself is a long-winged bird that flies away whenever it wills, to wherever it wills; it is an illusion until it is spent on valuable things, and as such it only belongs to someone who ties it down by using it to get tangible, worthy assets having commercial value. Know that it is what you do with 'money' that is money!" I never forget the lesson![2]

Many a bushfaller feel terribly frustrated and impotent at not being able to do things directly for particular people in their home villages or hometowns, without having to pass through middlemen and middle women who, like boa constrictors, assume the status of giant compressors. Somehow, the tendency is to assume that what is earned abroad comes easily and can thus be requested and disposed of as one pleases, or that those abroad are zombies meant to toil without ceasing, just as they can be appropriated with impunity by whoever is smart enough to do so. Zombies are beneath humanity, to be used as doormats, pillows or toilet paper, and it is a contradiction in terms to treat them as if they were humans. This means that some migrants are likely to receive accusations (if these eventually filter through to them) of being rich, selfish and dead to the relationships that made them, when in fact they are doing their level best to redistribute and maintain solidarities with those who truly matter to them. Slave drivers (opportunists and adventurers, villains and tricksters) are there to ensure that the efforts of zombies shall not trickle down to those who have valued them beyond zombiehood, so that the world shall never be restructured to accommodate zombie expectations of humanity and dignity (Nyamnjoh 2005a, 2011, 2015c; Nyamnjoh HM, 2014, Tazanu 2012).

Cameroonians left behind in home villages and hometowns are said to cook up impossible businesses or projects in their heads, with no idea whatsoever where the money is going to come from. Then they go around pestering relatives and friends abroad to provide them with fabulous, mindboggling sums of money. And since they believe in keeping up consumer appearances, everybody in *Whiteman Kontri* or the bush of ghosts is considered rich enough to be approached as a source of resources. The appearance on the scene in the 1990s of instant electronic money transfer facilitators such as Western Union has made otherwise ordinary folks drunk with expectations of money. Western Union rapidly became a status symbol for those without bank accounts. It was the place to be seen receiving money, an aspiration and a dream. Those associated with Western Union, either as senders or receivers, are highly regarded, admired and envied by others. University students with multiple connections to "boyfriends" and "fiancés" abroad have measured achievement and status through the corridors of Western Union agencies and displayed the money they collect in provocative ways that only make their local male counterparts more determined to migrate as well. Whether by family, schoolmates or others, investments back in home villages and hometowns by bushfallers are often money down the drain. Few expect them, and indeed, most would find it ludicrous or an irritation, for their bushfaller kin or friends to come asking for accounts or seeking to know what dividends the investments have yielded. Sometimes even the investment capital is swallowed or simply diverted (Nyamnjoh 2005a, 2011, 2015c; Nyamnjoh HM, 2014, Tazanu 2012).

Cell phones and smartphones are among the most coveted gifts. While there may be other reasons for owning a cell phone and for their surging attraction, one important reason is to be able to track down and hold zombies accountable for the money they earn and the material goods they accumulate in the bush of ghosts. Being sometimes undocumented, a significant number of zombies in the bush of ghosts lack permanent or fixed addresses, and can best be reached through the cell phone, email, social media or fellow zombies. Few of their contacts left behind have physical or postal addresses either. In both cases, the cell phone, smartphone, Internet and social media are Godsends, though for pestered zombies it sometimes looks like the Devil's toolkit for self-extension. These technological advances in information and communication seem to have offered *Nyongo* and *Msa* as the bush of ghosts a golden opportunity and opportunism to globalize itself and its system of control, discipline and accountability, making it virtually impossible for recalcitrant or freedom seeking zombies to live in peace, out of touch, out of hand, or out of sight, even when geographically out of close proximity. Tensions over cell phones and smartphones between husbands and wives in hometowns and home villages are in certain cases worsened by the fact that children, relations and acquaintances who have migrated to distant bushes of ghosts have tended to pay greater attention to the women left behind than to the men.

Youth from the Bamenda Grassfields studying or working in distant bushes are more likely to invite their mothers to visit than they are their fathers. For one thing, mothers are more amenable to lightening the burdens of zombiehood by keeping the house, cooking, babysitting and generally employing themselves creatively round the clock in the interest of their sons and daughters slaving away. Mothers are also least likely to be impatient or bored, and in some cases where home village or hometown conjures images of infinite squabbles with husbands, co-wives, extended families and others, they are not in a hurry to return home. Mothers therefore are more likely than fathers to be zombified in turn by zombified sons and daughters in distant bushes of ghosts. Returning zombies and consumer television do little to give a nuanced or less flashy image of Europe and North America as an Eldorado. Those who tell the truth about these bushes of ghosts are least likely to be taken seriously by kin and friends seeking paradise: If lessons are learnt about what such distant bushes of ghosts truly are, this usually comes too late. It must however be emphasised that although widespread, not everyone back home embraces the consumer bandwagon with extravagant fantasies and callous indifference to the humanity of the zombies implanted in such bushes. There are kin and friends who are measured in their demands and who care about the welfare of those in the bushes of ghosts. They may be in the minority, but they are most appreciated by the toiling zombies (Nyamnjoh 2005a, 2011, 2015c; Nyamnjoh HM, 2014, Tazanu 2012).

If easy material comfort is possible mostly with and through *Nyongo* and *Msa* as the bush of ghosts, more and more Cameroonians are doing their utmost to place their zombies at such epicentres of material accumulation, in Europe and North America, in particular. This includes often aggressively forging mercantilist relationships with whites, visible and invisible. Whites who venture into Cameroon and/or cultivate relationships with Cameroonians soon realise what an astronomical price they have to pay to be recognised and accepted as acquaintances, collaborators, friends, loved ones, husbands or wives by Cameroonians, as they are made to battle with unfathomable cravings for and expectations of fulfilment of the wildest consumer fantasies for modern conveniences. One of the very first questions a white visitor is asked is about visa formalities and what he or she could do to facilitate legal or illegal passages to their home countries, generally perceived by Cameroonians as a sort of bush amenable to hunting expeditions of myriad kinds. Fantasies about these often imagined countries are more readily available and credible than their reality. Some proudly declare that they would rather be prisoners in a Western bush of ghosts than "free" in their materially impoverished and grossly mismanaged home country (Nyamnjoh and Page 2002). Whites are also immediately confronted with a deeply materialistic foundation of love and relationships, which to them is often a culture shock, coming as they do from a background of assumptions that money and material riches must not stand in the way of true love.

With modern technologies such as the plane, television, Internet, cell phone and smartphone, flexible notions of *Nyongo* and *Msa* have been globalised as families and communities sacrifice sons and daughters to forage for opportunities in distant bushes, while at the same time multiplying opportunities for accountability and, quite paradoxically, opportunism as well. Such accessibility, flexible mobility and flexible discourses on *Nyongo* and *Msa* have also engendered flexible ideas of relationships of intimacy. In their modern globalised forms, *Nyongo* and *Msa* cross boundaries and stretch the borders of intimacy with opportunities and opportunism informed by consumerism, especially as experienced at the margins of belonging and success. With these possibilities, home appears less confined by borders, as bounded ideas of being and belonging are tinkered with constantly by desperate zombies in tune with the infinite possibilities of technologies of *Nyongo* and *Msa*.

Although the potential for *Nyongo*, *Msa* and their rewards to become global have increased, access to lucrative locations for accumulation through *Nyongo* and *Msa* actually appear to diminish with rigid policing of zombies seeking belonging beyond their local bushes of ghosts or the traditional womb of geography, race, ethnicity and family. While itself not an unproblematic alternative to the tensions and expectations of home as circumscribed by geography, culture, race and ethnicity, distant bushes of ghosts in Europe and North America (thanks to the experiences of its zombies) have at least evidenced that the answer to tensions is neither in simply substituting one womb for another, but rather in seeking to deliver the child to the world where dynamic relationships with others should be the prime indicator of belonging and citizenship. Home in this sense becomes "a radically deterritorialised" reality that is possible only through relationships that mitigate the feeling of discomfort, making one feel at home even when not at home in any conventional sense (Englund 2004: 296-306). In his 24 years of roaming the bush of ghosts, the child narrator in *My Life in the Bush of Ghosts* shares with us a sense of the possibilities and challenges of such a radically deterritorialised idea of home.

Unfortunately however, the womb and bushes of Europe and North America have taught zombies the importance of dreaming with their feet firmly on the ground, thereby entrusting them with the mission of puncturing the dreams of potential zombies with little direct personal experience of this imagined utopia. Few are actually made to feel at home away from home in the bushes, *Msa* or *Nyongo* of Europe and North America, where good and bad, pleasure and pain, utopia and dystopia are all intertwined. The extent to which the stark reality of ultra-exploitation and devaluation are likely to be dissuasive is doubtful, especially as few zombies are ready to share their experiences of fierce exclusion, and even fewer are ready to believe them. No degree of dehumanization seems compelling enough to deter Cameroonians seeking a foothold in distant bushes of ghosts, and few have a choice of permanently severing links with the home village or hometown, notwithstanding their tense relations with relatives and friends out there. Increasingly, not every villain or trickster with someone to zombify qualifies to do so in a lucrative manner anymore, and resorting to indirections entails that not every zombie in the bush of ghosts is going to be welcome, to have worthwhile opportunities, or to be minimally tolerated, let alone offered the opportunity to feel at home (Nyamnjoh 2005a, 2011, 2015c; Nyamnjoh HM, 2014, Tazanu 2012).

This speaks not only of a hierarchy of *Nyongo* and *Msa*, villains and tricksters, but also of zombies, as some *Nyongo*, *Msa*, villains and tricksters are more endowed with modern opportunities and opportunism than others, just as some zombies are more entitled than others to the consumer margins of the bushes of ghosts of Europe and North America. These hierarchies demonstrate the changing attitudes to cultures of solidarity, interconnectedness and conviviality, as informed by the consumer status of zombies compared among themselves and to the status of others in their home villages and hometowns. The accusatory language of victimhood employed by zombies to describe their subjection and ultra-exploitation by forces at home and in the host countries is evidence that, to them, home is neither simply to be found "at home" or "away from home." Like all the narrators of Tutuola's many stories, they are as much at home in familiar shores as they are away from home in distant bushes, through the relationships they are able to forge and maintain in the course of their mobility, however plagued by dangers.

As mentioned earlier and demonstrated through the example of Cameroonian *Nyongo* and *Msa* above, the universes depicted by Tutuola may be condescendingly dismissed as "magic," "witchcraft," "sorcery," "superstition," "primitivism," "savagery" and "animism," but their continued resilience and attraction across Africa are hardly in doubt (Ashforth 1996, 2001; Bastian 2001; van Dijk, 2001; Moore and Sanders 2001; Geschiere 1997, 2013; Fisiy and Geschiere 2001; Mavhungu 2012; Wasserman 2010: 118-150; Werbner 2015). The attraction of these universes is not only among ordinary Africans, but also, and perhaps more tellingly, with elite Africans, especially in settings away from the scrutinising prescriptive gaze of the gendarmes of Eurocentric modernity to which they subscribe in rhetoric, at least. Although African intellectual and political elite do not readily identify with these universes and the practices they inspire in the open, they are indeed deeply entangled in them, and feel terribly inadequate and one-dimensional having to rely exclusively on the prescriptions of Cartesian rationalism and its accoutrements. Let's take a closer look at how, despite their lip service to Cartesian rationalism African intellectual and political elite continue, through their everyday practices, contribute to keeping alive and relevant African ways of knowing and knowledge production, and fending off the one-dimensionalism of resilient colonialism and the ambitions of completeness which it claims and inspires.

Here, again, are some examples from Cameroon. There are allegations of mystical connections in urban Cameroon, the veracity of which has generally been accepted. Examples of mystical happenings associated with the modern cultural and political elite, and often bordering on power, sex and consumerism, are countless. One could easily write volumes just on allegations and rumour about the invisible and political power in Cameroon. In February 1997 an oil-filled train derailed in Yaounde. It was rumoured that the indigenes, the Ewondo (of the same ethnic origin as President Biya and his closest collaborators), barred all non-indigenes from recovering for themselves any spilt oil. They reputedly claimed the oil belonged to the autochthons alone. A disaster occurred when someone inadvertently struck a match, and hundreds of people died. This, like other accidents and deaths, was also linked to the ruling Cameroon People's Democratic Movement (CPDM) party and the President, whom it was alleged usually made mystical sacrifices of ordinary militants and supporters before a major political event, which in this case was the imminent parliamentary elections scheduled for May 1997. On previous occasions, the deaths of family members (e.g. Jeanne-Irene Biya) and close collaborators of President Biya (e.g. Motaze Roger, a presidential cook, Jean Assoumou and Jean Fochive), have been connected with rumour that they had been sacrificed to occult forces so that the President could survive difficult political spells. Political survival, according to such rumours, is predicated upon human sacrifices to occult forces.

In a context where the vote has been rendered impotent by greed and ulterior motives, legitimacy has to be conferred by less visible mechanisms than formal elections. Cabinet reshuffles are always preceded by rumours of occult sacrifices, visits to fortune-tellers and occult practices. Incumbents and aspirants are said to scheme for cabinet positions, and to employ natural and occult forces to this end. Various lodges and fraternities allegedly play a major part in determining who stays and who becomes what. Among the key players are Rosicrucianism and Freemasonry, both of which are influenced and implanted from France, a major and not-so-hidden hand in Cameroonian politics. It was even rumoured that President Biya financed the construction of a Rosicrucian lodge in France, and that he moved his membership between lodges depending on his political fortunes.[3] He might be a Catholic and even an ex-seminarian whose family has been personally blessed by Pope John Paul II on two consecutive visits to Yaounde, but this does not stop him, nor apparently contradict his alleged cultivation of mystical identities and affiliations to buttress the ambiguity and ambivalence of his political power base[4].

In 1994, following a double slash in civil servants' salaries and a 50 per cent devaluation of the Franc CFA, rumours of mystical occurrences connected with sex and sexuality were commonplace – quite understandable in a country where *phallocracy* has become a dominant mode of power, and where men use wealth and office to debase and extract maximal libidinal pleasure (Mbembe 1992, 1997; Abega 1995, 2007; Ndjio 2005; Nyamnjoh 2006b, 2009). In Limbe, rumours suggested that Igbo businessmen from Nigeria were making local men's sexual organs shrink or disappear, simply by shaking hands with them. Limbe women were rumoured food for Nigerian business tycoons' penises. These stories were widely reported and widely believed. Around the same time, it was rumoured that two girls from the University of Yaounde fell victim to a foreign tycoon. Stories claimed the girls dated the man and later returned to his posh residence in Bastos, a pricy suburb of Yaounde. Rather than sleeping with the girls in the conventionally understood sense, the foreigner chose one, and allegedly transformed himself into a boaconstrictor and began to swallow her. When the other girl realised what was happening, she hastily departed and alerted the police. The police investigation supposedly revealed that this was common practice for this man. This story circulated widely in the press, on *Radio Trottoir* and by word of mouth, and was generally believed. Today, thousands of such stories about mystical boa constrictors circulate around the country. Curiously, almost twenty years later, on the morning of Saturday, 9 November 2013, a very similar rumour broke out in Buea, spread like wildfire on social media and related channels, drawing a crowd of over 10,000 people to the premises of Eta Palace Hotel, where a wealthy top state functionary had allegedly transformed himself into a boa constrictor and attempted swallowing a University of Buea female student whom he had lured to the hotel the night before for sex in exchange for cash. The police were mobilised to contain the crowd that had assembled around the hotel, elements of which were clamouring for the hotel to be burnt down.

In *Married But Available*, a novel on power wealth and consumerism inspired mainly by goings on in Cameroon, I recount similar stories. One of the informants, Mariette, tells Lilly Loveless the researcher: "It isn't uncommon for marabouts to ask people to do strange things in broad daylight or at night in order to have power, wealth or whatever they want. We live in strange times…" According to Mariette, more and more strange things are happening, as people are into all sorts of strange cults demanding occult practices. Illicit enrichment and ambitions of power and wealth through magical or occult means are pushing people to madden reality with abnormal behaviour (Nyamnjoh 2009: 332) Among the stories she shares with Lilly Loveless is the following:

> …a very rich and beautiful woman every midday drives out of town, parks her car and goes into a farm. One day three Peeping Toms follow her out of curiosity. She parks her latest Mercedes, goes onto the farm, goes under a big tree, puts out a cloth, undresses and lies down naked, her legs spread out. In a couple of minutes, a big dark smooth snake slides down graciously from the tree and enters her fully. She screams and cries with the pleasure of pain, as they make love like normal people, wriggling and giggling as she climaxes. When it is over and the snake retires, she

keels over and starts vomiting money. Then she picks up the money and her clothes, dresses up, goes happily back to her car and drives home smiling money (Nyamnjoh 2009: 332).

Mariette also relates the increasingly common phenomenon of young male prostitutes interested mainly in men, but also in women, "like a door that opens in all directions." According to her, given the high level of unemployment and the excruciating misery engineered by chronic poverty, such young men, desperate to make ends meet, have little control over their bodies, and are dictated to by those with money and the power to give value. These givers of value are "the filthy rich" who "lack the discipline that comes with wealth well-earned and well-tamed" (Nyamnjoh 2009: 333). Most of these givers of value are well-educated university graduates, just like their victims, and have superstition in common, as evidenced by their logic of practice. As Mariette puts it:

> "They are deep in superstition, believing everything their marabouts, diviners and cults tell them to do or not to do, which are usually filthy, degrading and debasing of all that is human, virtuous and civilised. The result is that the young men and women entrapped, humbled and humiliated by the money they falsely claim to be theirs, become moving lethal reservoirs of all sorts of impurities of the flesh and the soul, which is why more and more people have taken up the habit of smelling in strange ways…" (Nyamnjoh 2009: 333-334).

A very high profile illustration is worthy of note, especially in view of the fact that those most critical of Tutuola's "barbarism," "primitivism," and superstition-ridden tales of an Africa stuck in the past were purportedly Africans most steeped in Eurocentric modernity through the colonial education they had imbibed. These were supposedly Africa's leading examples of what it meant to be Cartesian rationalists, scientific in attitude and objective in one's thoughts, beliefs and deeds. In this new light, I revisit stories I have shared before simply as part of a discussion of occult practices in Cameroon.

Professor Gervais Mendo Ze, General Manager of Cameroon Radio Television (CRTV) from 1988 to 2005, for 17 years masterminded most of the manipulation that kept President Biya recycling and perfecting the insensitivities of illegitimate power. To maintain and enhance his personal and political potency, he sought power in both its visible bureaucratic, Cartesian rationalist terms as well as its invisible, mystical, nebulous dimensions. He was also at the centre of numerous rumours connecting him with straddling religions – being both a committed Catholic who propounded the virtues of the Virgin Mary (*mariologie*) on the one hand, and a Rosicrucian whose mystical totem was a boa constrictor that sucked the blood of young virgins whom he enticed with money and expensive gifts of necklaces (*serpentologie*) on the other. Rumour had it he supplemented the blood sucked out by the mysterious serpents worn around the neck by the girls he victimized with his gifts of necklaces, by drinking their menstrual blood as well. On 15 February 1999, a girl known simply as "cousine Elise" phoned the Yaounde FM94 *A Coeur Ouvert* presenter Joly Nnib Ngom to accuse "a well-placed personality of the Republic" whom she had dated for six to seven months of having given her a boa constrictor in the form of an expensive gold necklace.[5] Rumour immediately associated Mendo Ze with the girl, and matters worsened when Mendo Ze suspended the presenter of the programme. The rumour was given extensive coverage in the private press and was widely disseminated in taxis, bars and other public places. Although the presenter was eventually reinstated, the rumour persisted, and Professor Gervais Mendo Ze was nicknamed *serpentologue*, to go with *mariologue*. This was in recognition of his marriage of mysticism with Christianity as an investment in potency for efficacious action, despite, at face value, his subscription to a Eurocentric index of modernity that expected of him exclusive adherence to Cartesian rationalism (Nyamnjoh 2001: 34, 2005b: 214). Tutuola will have been bemused by such rumours, especially in light of how such Eurocentric intellectual elites are keen, in their sanitised scholarly discourses, to distance themselves from what they love to refer to as the primitive traditions and superstitious beliefs of rural and backward Africa.

In Yaounde on Christmas day 1999, four children went missing. Three days later, they were found dead in an abandoned car with their genitals cut off.[6] Rumours started that Professor Mendo Ze had hired someone to carry out the ritual killing, since he was known to traffic in human body parts (probably intended to activate the likes of Tutuola's Skull seeking the status of "complete gentleman" and "complete lady"). A few months later, Magistrate Louis Ndzie was savagely murdered in Yaounde. It was alleged that he was the one handling the file on the murdered children and had vowed to nail Mendo Ze for his occult and diabolical practices. Having failed to persuade the magistrate through his wife (with whom Mendo Ze was said to have had an affair) and with a bribe of several million Francs CFA, Mendo Ze reportedly asked the wife to hire thugs to eliminate her magistrate husband (Nyamnjoh 2001: 34, 2005b: 214).

Similar rumours and stories about mysterious traffic in human body parts and related happenings implicating Africans who straddle Eurocentric modernity and African endogenous cosmologies and belief systems are commonplace across Africa. Why is there the tendency to believe these stories without *proof*? To those who subscribe to the popular epistemological order where reality consists of the visible and the invisible, these stories make perfect sense (Sanders 2001; Bastian 2001; Ashforth 1996, 2001; Fisiy and Geschiere 2001; Wasserman 2010; Mavhungu 2012). They believe in a world where logic, reason and directly observable relationships make sense only to the extent that they provide satisfactory answers to burning questions. If and when these obvious explanations fall short, there is need to seek for answers from dimensions of reality that do not immediately lend themselves to obvious logic, obvious reason, and obvious sensory perception. It is time to explore the power of the hidden hand, manipulating and manoeuvring, unseen and unheard, defying logic and common sense, and making mincemeat of one-dimensional intellects and the epistemological shallowness which underpin them. Put differently, it is time to harken to the foresighted wisdom of Amos Tutuola to seek conviviality between the obvious logic, reason and perceptive faculties of the physical and directly observable world, and the logic of the hidden dimensions of reality. The wisdom of conviviality informed by Tutuola's universe is in the recognition that absolutes and absolutism are to be fiercely tempered because there is always simultaneously a lot more and a lot less to things than meets the eyes.

Since the early 1990s, President Biya, with the assistance of Mendo Ze and others his government – a government that has consistently boasted a very high number of intellectuals with degrees from prestigious French and English universities –, has thwarted popular aspirations for democracy. The elite have stood their ground against the Cameroonian majority, remaining insensitive to calls for change. Even when beaten in the polls, as happened in 1992, they have remained obstinate. This is not natural, and cannot be explained simply in terms of Cartesian rationalism. How can a handful of people defy the will of the majority of Cameroonians? There must be some unseen forces, a face behind the mask that imbues them with power and confidence beyond the ordinary, power and confidence that have succeeded, quite strangely, in hypnotising masses of angry, hungry and disaffected Cameroonians during a more than 30 year clamour for democracy.

In July 2000, Professor Gervais Mendo Ze even boasted that *his* CRTV journalists were *Les Lions Indomptables de l'audio-visuel*. At the 1992 presidential elections, Paul Biya presented himself as *l'homme Lion*, imbued with the physical force and ferociousness akin to the lion, with the courage and intentions of protecting Cameroon from *les marchands d'illusions*, of which the main opposition leader John Fru Ndi and his Social Democratic Front (SDF) were presented as champions by CRTV. In taxis, market places, bars, chicken-parlours and elsewhere, ordinary people saw Biya's message as a corruption of reality. He was a lion, no doubt. But his "really" mission, to borrow from Amos Tutuola, was to devastate, for five more years as president, not to save, Cameroon and her people. This alternative interpretation never made its way to national radio and television, not even through the other presidential candidates, whose campaign broadcasts were heavily monitored and censored. Jean-Jacque Ekindi, for example, a 1992 presidential candidate, who had baptised himself the foremost *chasseur du Lion* (lion hunter), had his trenchant campaign counter-offensives banned by CRTV. Crowning CRTV the "Indomitable Lion" of the broadcast media while the government was pretending to be liberalising broadcasting was a timely reminder to the information-hungry public not to take the government's rhetoric on liberalisation too seriously. Cameroon, in short, had space for only three Indomitable Lions: President Biya, the CRTV, and the national football team whose victories and fame the President and CRTV were simulating through manipulation and corruption.

This guarantees that the Indomitable Lion of politics shall appropriate the victories and fame of the Indomitable Lions of football, thanks to facilitation and manipulation by the Indomitable Lion of broadcasting. It makes it possible for government to feed the people not with facts but with opinions only, so that they remain incapable of thinking for themselves. Truth, the Indomitable Lion of politics [Biya] has never tired of affirming, comes from above and rumour from below (*la vérité vient d'en haut, la rumeur vient d'en bas*). Hence the constant exhortation for Cameroonians to take for truth everything communicated to them by CRTV and Cameroon Tribune or by writings published in honour of the system by pro-establishment academics. They are in turn to shun "untruths disseminated by certain media, with scant regard for the most elementary of journalistic ethics and at variance with the rules and means of seeking the truth." Information from any source other than these official media, "the most trustworthy and credible sources," could only be, as Paul Biya himself termed it, "insensitive and ill-intentioned people ... who want to claim an importance that they haven't got"[7]

To crown his importance as premiere vehicle of "truth from above," Mendo Ze, during his years as director of CRTV, physically located his office on the 11th floor of the CRTV production centre at Mballa II in Yaounde, and also reserved a lift for himself. In this way, his authority was practically reinforced by the feeling of physically sitting on every one of his journalists, producers and support staff. Supplemented by mystical or occult powers, he and President Biya could see themselves as metaphorically sitting on all Cameroonians, big and small, willing and reluctant. Under Biya, CRTV assumed the same dictatorial and insensitive stature that Radio Cameroon had assumed under Ahidjo. And with this came an arrogance unmitigated by ignorance on the part of politicians in high office and journalists in their service. From the public's perspective, only someone super endowed with more than meets the eye could display with impunity the arrogance and insensitivity of President

Biya and such acolytes as Mendo Ze. One requires more than ordinary political or bureaucratic power to do what they do, and get away with it. Such power is invisible and is provided by occult practices in which they indulge with the assistance of the stifling misery of their victims.

The tendency to believe in a hidden hand and a parallel manipulative mischievous world is akin to an indictment of liberal democracy and its illusions of a one and indivisible self, individual autonomy, chronological time, linear progression, and transparency. Liberal democracy and the version of development it inspires, and its promise of political, economic and cultural enrichment for all. But in reality a hidden, manipulative hand (of capital, the West and Western dominated international institutions such as the UN, WTO, etc.) determines who among the many shall be provided for through criteria that are a far cry from the objectivity and merit of Cartesian rationalism. Its rhetoric of opening up, and of abundance, is sharply contradicted by the reality of closures and of want for most of its disciples. The hidden, manipulative hand of global capital and its concerns to champion profit over people, for example, through the IMF, World Bank and national interests of Western partners, make it possible for autocracy to pay lip service to democracy and development in exchange for guaranteeing the political stability needed by investors to venture into the peripheries of global accumulation such as the dark continent with its extractive intents (Mentan 2010a, 2010b).

In exchange for having weak foreign relations, autocratic regimes like Cameroon's are afforded the ability and protection to flex their muscles within their own countries, in a perplexing and mystical manner. Hence, instead of a transparent democracy and development for ordinary people who want such things, one finds myriad ways people's rights and dignities are bargained away in exchange for regimes of enslavement and dispossession wrongly labelled as freedoms and empowerment. Cameroonians and Africans, who are well aware of this contradiction, realise that pursuing undomesticated agency is a very risky business. There is an ever-looming possibility, even for the most successful and cosmopolitan, of the sudden unexplained failure, and of having to cope alone. Hence, nearly everyone's eagerness to maintain kin networks they can turn to in times of need, even when the opportunities afforded by such networks are not without their opportunisms. Even those in the bushes of ghosts who have severed kin links entirely seek such solidarity in kin of another type: for some ruling elite, these alternative networks are provided by membership in mystical cults such as Rosicrucianism and Freemasonry. These alternative networks purport to offer them double protection: against the harmful expectations of kin in their home villages and hometowns; and against the vicissitudes or impermanence of success in the world dominated by Eurocentric modernity – the bush of ghosts *à la* Tutuola.

Whether one is entirely localist or cosmopolitan, or both, *Nyongo*, *Msa*, the occult or bush of ghosts seems always to provide solutions to otherwise insurmountable problems, both for those its variant of modernity has by-passed and for those on whom it has smiled with dubiety. The sort of uncertainties and anxieties Africans feel in life post their encounters with European colonialism and capitalism simply cannot be attended to adequately by the imported pseudo-scientific doctrine of Cartesian rationalism and empiricism alone. This, as I have argued and sought to illustrate with the works of Tutuola and additional examples from different parts of Africa, is obvious even to the most learned (in Cartesian rationalist and empiricist terms) and cosmopolitan.

Writing about Togo and Liberia, Stephen Ellis (1993, 1999: 220-280) argues that a powerful person is one who can convince others he or she controls a complex array of visible and invisible forces. For "just as a person known to have political power is presumed also to have power over the spirit world, so a person who successfully manipulates the symbols of spiritual control is assumed also to be in possession of political power" (Ellis 1993: 471). In a context where wealth, prestige and power are interconnected, impermanent, in limited supply and intensely sought after, those deluded by ambitions of completeness are likely to think that "acquiring the strength of others" mysteriously, could be a sure technique for acquiring or maintaining all three (Ellis 1999: 265). Appearances can indeed be deceptive. If the reality of politics were limited to the apparent and the transparent as prescribed by liberal democracy, there would hardly be reason to explain success or failure otherwise. In general, if people had what they merited, and merited what they had in liberal democratic terms, there would be little need for a hidden hand of any kind, real or imagined. But because nothing is what it seems, the invisible must be considered to paint a fuller picture of reality. This is Amos Tutuola's profound contribution to understanding life in Africa, be it social, political, cultural or economic. He does not settle for simple or quick fixes; he abhors superficialities, and challenges Africans to dig deep and explore the intricate entanglements of the dynamism and mobility of what it means to be African through relationships with a past, a present and a future that emphasise interconnections. He invites Africans to disabuse themselves of the colonial syndrome of xenophilia and a chronic lack of confidence in the popular wisdoms of the continent and the creative imagination of ordinary Africans.

Following the principle of simultaneous multiplicities discussed in relation to Tutuola's universe and shared across Africa through beliefs and behaviour in recognition of the existence of parallel worlds encapsulated in notions such as the ideas of *Msa* and *Nyongo*, we can understand why, for example, few conflicts make sense without understanding the role of hidden powers in everyday life. A person who wishes to harm or influence another through such mysterious powers need not bother with the victim's physical absence when something of his or hers (hair, cloth, photo or whatever) can serve as a substitute. It is also widely believed that a stranger or an outsider could borrow the face of someone more familiar to the person they wish to harm, in order to sow confusion and tension in that person's intimate circles by way of accusations and counter-accusations of possession of and seeking to harm with dangerous mysterious powers. One may be visible and physically present, at the same time that one's spirit has temporarily left the body to hunt for game in the likeness of a predator, to commit mischief, or to wreak havoc on others and their property. This speaks not only of the multi-dimensionality of life, but also of the fact that all of life's dimensions can be articulated simultaneously at various levels, visible and invisible, physically or virtually present or absent. This possibility of absence in presence and presence in absence has – as we have seen in the discussion of the reality and relationships of bushfallers in distant bushes with kin and kith in their home villages and hometowns – been enhanced and popularised by technologies of presence in simultaneous multiplicities such as the internet, cell phones and smartphones, and social media.

Popular epistemologies or ways of knowing and knowledge production informed by universes such as Tutuola's have important implications for the study of invisible and intangible dimensions of reality and rationalities that are not easily reducible to Cartesian rationalism or the exclusionary logic of reductionist science. Scholars inspired by the dominant Eurocentric epistemological order have tended to be dichotomous in their approaches to realities and belief systems that are not immediately observable through sensory perception nor provable in Cartesian rationalist terms. When not simply dismissed as superstitious beliefs and practices by primitives, beliefs and practices suggestive of an interconnection between the visible and invisible, the tangible and intangible have tended to be confined to rural or village communities where individuals are still supposedly trapped by custom and tradition. The expectation has been that once de-contaminated, disinfected, exorcised or enlightened by science through education and urbanisation, the village African should abandon, as a matter of course, his or her penchant for superstitious beliefs and practices, accusations or counter-accusations of "witchcraft," "sorcery" and the "occult," just as Europeans are *presumed* to have done, and just as the Eurocentric African intellectual and political elite often give the impression of having done. The city or town has tended to be excluded, *a priori*, from studies of such beliefs and practices. City dwellers have either been assumed to be rational, civilised and scientific in their outlook and behaviour, or the victims of witches and wizards from their backward-looking home villages. Often tantalised by such assumptions, cosmopolitan Africans have found themselves pretending to be Cartesian rationalists in public or declaration, and epistemologically autochthonous and/or endogenous in private or practice.

However, as we have seen, and as many a study have documented, the occult and the supernatural have no sacred spaces. They are as practised in urban spaces as in rural ones, as much by the most cosmopolitan as by the most localist. They may assume new forms and new uses (Geschiere 1997, 2013), but belief in invisible forces and occult practices form part of everyday life in urban Africa (Ashforth 1996, 2001; Bastian 2001; van Dijk, 2001; Moore and Sanders 2001; Geschiere 1997, 2013; Mavhungu 2012; Werbner 2015). Even a casual perusal of newspapers makes plain that the urban elite, those who publish and read these papers, are obsessed with the supernatural, the occult and the mystical, especially in the context of globalised consumerism (Comaroff and Comaroff 1999b, 1999c). In Herman Wasserman's impressive and detailed study of the upsurge of tabloid journalism and its fascination with the occult and the larger than logic dimensions of urban life in South Africa, the rise of mass-circulating tabloids and their popularity with the poor and working class black majority urbanites are indicative of a post-apartheid South Africa determined to renegotiate an ethics of inclusion and a common humanity in journalism (Wasserman 2010: 118-150).

In contemporary Africa, development is presented as the way to salvation, promising concrete and visible results; but the more it is pursued, the greater an illusion it becomes. High expectations are not matched by positive results, and disappointment grows by leaps and bounds. Development or Western-inspired modernity seems to excel in churning out "malcontents" (Comaroff and Comaroff 1993) through unilinearity and zombification, a situation that inspires as much fear, violence and frustrations as Tutuola's bush of ghosts. A world where development is promised to many, but only a few reap the rewards, is bound to baffle and disappoint. It is also bound to intensify questioning of Cartesian rationalism as a promising way of thinking. And even if the elite leadership cannot afford to ask questions openly and aggressively for fear of turning off the tap of development trickles or of being labelled "primitive," then their private lives continue to bridge the artificial chasms between science and religion, nature and culture, the individual and community.

Faced with repeated detours and derailments on the way to the Calvary of Eurocentric development and modernity, the African elite have, albeit in a muted rather than screaming fashion, opted for the more realistic and reassuring alternative of straddling the visible and invisible worlds which the popular epistemological order has always treated as complementary parts of reality, the pursuit of which any inclusive science ought to make its mission. To research this aspect of the life of African elites, one does not and should not limit one's investigation to interviews or administration of survey questionnaires. One must indulge in deep, quality, round-the-clock participant observation among these elites to see how they confront and resolve the everyday challenges that come their way, challenges posed by the multiple worlds to which they belong – worlds of often conflicting prescriptions. Nothing short of such quality participant observation conducted in collaboration with insiders of African elite circles would yield the results of African elites as part and parcel of a frontier reality and existence that is utterly uncomfortable with simple choices and simplistic dichotomies.

In this light, one can understand the widespread belief in and resilience of Tutuola-like universes and the beliefs and practices they inspire throughout Africa, not so much in terms of the inability of Africans to modernise their beliefs and rituals, but as reflecting collective preoccupations with the conflictual relationships between competing agentive forces in societies where promises of development as a technicalised and depoliticised process are certified broken dreams for all but an elite few (Ferguson 1990, 1999, 2006, 2015). The supernatural and the magical can be as much a source and resource of personal and collective power or powerlessness as it is a call for domesticated agency against various forms of exploitation, marginalisation, inequality and individualism (Ardener 1996: 243-260; Rowlands and Warnier 1988: 121-125; Warnier 1993a: 139-162; Geschiere 1997; Fisiy and Geschiere 1996: 193-197; Geschiere and Nyamnjoh 1998). Indeed, the fact that sorcery accusations usually occur between family members or kin is indicative of how much ordinary Africans cherish the solidarity of domesticated agency and how ready they are to protect it from aggression and the harmful pursuit of personal success in tune with the exclusionary logic of European colonialism and capitalism. For what use is a social system that glorifies personal success but in reality has little space for all who seek it? As this conversation between Tutuola's universe and similar universes and the beliefs and practices they inspire among Cameroonian Grassfielders has reiterated, success attainable only at the expense of others' humanity is not considered worth pursuing.

Notes

[1] As already discussed, there is no permanence in death and dying in Amos Tutuola's *Palm-Wine Drinkard*, so this is more like dying in the eyes or the world with which one is familiar, as life continues in strikingly similar ways in the Deads' Town.

[2] See Yinka Tutuola, interviewed by Jeff VanderMeer, http://weirdfictionreview.com/2013/01/amos-tutuola-an-interview-with-yinka-tutuola-by-jeff-vandermeer, accessed 1 November 2016.

[3] *Nouvelle Expression*, 15 January 1999 and 24 March 1999.

[4] Nor are such rumours just a 1990s phenomenon. See Rowlands and Warnier 1988: 128.

[5] See *La Nouvelle Expression*, No. 494, 24 March 1999, p. 5; *Le Messager*, No. 899, 7 April 1999, p. 6; *L'Anecdote*, No. 084, 6 April 1999, pp. 5-9; *Mutations*, No. 207, 1 April 1999, p. 10; *Dikalo*, No. 424, 30 March 1999, p. 3; *Perspectives Hebdo*, No. 185, 26 March 1999, pp. 2-9.

[6] See *The Herald*, No. 854, 29 December 1999, pp. 1 and 3.

[7] *Cameroon Tribune*, No. 3080, 21 September 1984.

Chapter Eight

Conclusion: Tutuola's Legacy

This chapter concludes this treatise by summarising Tutuola's legacy which is itself symbolic of the resolution between the dialectic of recognition and relevance. Recall that the challenge for the African scholar is to be locally relevant, while still achieving international recognition. The game of knowledge production and consumption exists in this form because of unequal power relations, which complicates one's willingness and ability to challenge these unequal global structures. Tutuola embodies the resolution of this contraction. As a frontier writer, he celebrated his incompleteness and spent the currency of conviviality in his telling of African stories in the colonial language. His African stories, while they may not be taken seriously by the colonial epistemological order because of its "magical realism" and incomplete assimilation of English, are nonetheless relevant to transformation and decolonization. They provide an alternative ontology in which sense and physical evidence, while not dismissed, have not taken the centrality they have within the colonial epistemology. In navigating this universe, we come to see the importance of adopting and acknowledging our domesticated agency and inherent flexible mobility. In so doing, Tutuola, like one of his narrators and quest-heroes, empowers as well as represents the marginalised ordinary Africans alienated from the global production and consumption of knowledge.

Like his narrators and quest-heroes, Tutuola is actively part and parcel of the universe that fascinates him and feeds his sense of the unexpected. In June 1997, at the age of 77, Tutuola started his own journey to the Deads' Town, proud that *The Palm-Wine Drinkard*, "an odyssey in peculiar English, which roamed about from realism to magic and back again, as in old Africa... opened the floodgates to modern West African writing" (Achebe 2000: 44-45). All his books are contributions to his mission of keeping alive and relevant African ways of knowing and knowledge production, and fending off the one-dimensionalism of resilient colonialism. His global influence has been significant, with fellow writers and with other artists. This includes his influence on musicians Brian Eno and David Byrne of Talking Heads, a New York based rock band formed in 1975, who in 1981 released a collaborative album titled *My Life in the Bush of Ghosts*, after Amos Tutuola's 1954 novel of the same name, and barely a year before publication by Three Continents Press of his very first novel, *The Wild Hunter in the Bush of the Ghost*, written in 1948. The album was described as a "pioneering work for countless styles connected to electronics, ambience and Third World music," and as integrating "sampled vocals and found sounds, African and Middle Eastern rhythms, and electronic music techniques."[1] As evidenced by the number of reviews referenced in this book, Tutuola's work has attracted significant attention by literary scholars, mostly as a pioneering source of controversy on and around African literature, and especially, on who qualifies to tell what story, how, and why, in Africa (Lindfors 1970, 1999c; Achebe 2000; Larson 2001; Nyamnjoh 2004b; Currey 2008; Kamau and Mitambo 2016).

In Nigeria, Tutuola was just an ordinary messenger, and messengers were expected by the modern colonial elite to deliver messages and not author those messages. This was especially the case with a messenger like Tutuola, who lacked "the proper academic (educational) credentials" to be considered as an artist. To many of his Nigerian critics, he was nothing but an "upstart" (Larson 2001: 6-7). When Tutuola's imagination ran away with him, and he started thinking of himself as a writer in his own right, the Nigerian literati castigated him (Lindfors 1970, 1999a; Tobias 1999; Larson 2001: 1-25). As a letter to the editor of West Africa by I. Adeagbo Akinjogbin in June 1954 shows, they did not need to have read Tutuola's books to condemn them: "Unfortunately (or perhaps fortunately) I have not read any of his two 'extraordinary books'" (I. Adeagbo Akinjogbin, reprinted in Lindfors 1975: 41). Chinua Achebe was reacting in part to Akinjogbin's 1954 criticism of Tutuola's books in total ignorance of their contents when in 2000 he wrote:

> In 1954, a minor war broke out in the pages of *West Africa*, a biweekly journal published in London, over Amos Tutuola who had just published his second novel, *My Life in the Bush of Ghosts*. A number of

Nigerian students in Britain began to write to the editor questioning the good faith of the British and the French and the Americans who were making all that to-do about a couple of books of folk tale written in bad English. One of the writers confessed he had "unfortunately (or perhaps fortunately)" not read either book, but was convinced from what he could gather about them that they had no literary value whatsoever. He was certain that Tutuola was in it just for the money, and his European admirers for the opportunity he had provided them to "confirm their concepts of Africa." (Achebe 2000: 58)

A critical reaction by a Nigerian who appears to have read Tutuola's books is worth quoting from. It is a letter to the editor of *West Africa* by Babasola Johnson, published on April 10, 1954. Johnson complains against the "glowing tributes" paid Tutuola in a review by Eric Johnson. He proceeds to show why Tutuola does not deserve such praise, in these terms:

> Now let us face facts. *Palm Wine Drinkard* should not have been published at all. The language in which it is written is foreign to West Africans and English People, or anybody for that matter. It is bad enough to attempt an African narrative in "good English," it is worse to attempt it in Mr. Tutuola's strange lingo (or, shall I say, the language of the "Deads"?). The language is not West African Patois as some think. Patois is more orderly and intelligible than the language of *The Palm Wine Drinkard*. Patois does not contain such words as "unreturnables," "weird" or such expressions as "the really road." To illustrate, you may compare the construction of the Kroo proverb – "When massa thief 'e take. When boy take 'e thief," with the construction of the simile "as flat as a football field" (Babasola Johnson, reprinted in Lindfors 1975: 31).

Johnson's letter was followed by an editor's note clarifying that while he was entitled to his opinion about the literary quality of Tutuola's books, Johnson's remark that *The Palm-Wine Drinkard* "should never have been published suggests that he thinks he is entitled to dictate to Mr. Tutuola how he should write and to the public what they should like to read" (Editor, *West Africa*, reprinted in Lindfors 1975: 32).

As Achebe notes, the shame and embarrassment felt by Nigerian students in London, such as Babasola Johnson and Adeagbo Akinjogbin, following the publication of Tutuola's first two novels were perhaps "not so much responding to anything external as from something deep inside them – a badly damaged sense of self" (Achebe 2000: 81). They were afflicted by the sort of "miseducation and forced assimilation" that produces "white minds inside Black bodies" (Hare 1991[1965]; Fanon 1967b) and slaves of definition and confinement (van Rinsum 2001; p'Bitek 1989[1966]). As Harold Collins puts it, there is reason to suspect that the educated West Africans embarrassed by Tutuola's depiction of Africa,

> ...are suffering from the kind of colonial pecksniffery, that they are hungering and thirsting after a respectability that will impress Europeans. Perhaps they are disturbed by the fear that white men – even white nonentities – may think them uncultivated, barbarous, backward, childish, inferior. The notion that foreigners should like Tutuola's ghost novels only because these novels confirm them in their stereotyped views of Africans as barbarians, is something of a giveaway on this state of mind (Harold R. Collins, reprinted in Lindfors 1975a[1961]: 69).

Achebe is in agreement when he remarks, about the said Nigerian and West African critics of Tutuola: "Their nervous confusion, the fragility of their awareness and self-esteem can only be imagined." "Wasn't it part of the syndrome which told us while I was growing up that it was more civilized to fetch water in gallon tins from Europe than with clay pots made by ourselves?" (Achebe 2000: 70). Their suspicion of the motives of Tutuola's English, French and American publishers, among others, was only compounded by reviews such as the following by Elspeth Huxley, a British author who claimed profound knowledge of Africa and Africans:

> *The Palm-Wine Drinkard* is a folk tale, full of the queer, distorted poetry, the deep and dreadfull fears, the cruelty, the obsession with death and

spirits, the macabre humour, the grotesque imagery of the African mind.

African art, if it is genuine, is never comfortable, noble or serene; perhaps for that reason it may never reach the heights – rather will it explore the depths of fear, torment and intimidation, with a relish of humour. It is possessed by spirits and the spirits are malign. (Elspeth Huxley quoted in Achebe 2000: 56).

Achebe asks a question worth reiterating *ad infinitum*, especially when a semblance of objectivity in judgement might conceal subjective interests and motives: Given her acclaimed "exceptional knowledge of African life," "how could Mrs. Huxley miss so completely the significance of Tutuola's pioneering novel *The Palm-Wine Drinkard*, dismissing it with a wave of the hand as 'the grotesque imagery of the African mind,' and with it African art in general as possessed by malign spirits? Was it a simple failure of insight or a wilful denial and repudiation of what stood before her eyes?" To Achebe, as someone "engaged in spinning stories to validate the transfer of African lands to white settlers," Mrs Huxley had grown accustomed to "playing fast and loose with the facts" of life in Africa and the lives of Africans, to the point that "she was uncomfortable whenever the rightful owner came in sight" (Achebe 2000: 68-69).

In a critical analysis of representations of Africa in English fiction from 1874 to 1939, Douglas Killam observes that most of the novels consistently "conveyed the general belief that African society, religious and political institutions are naïve, and that this primitiveness justifies the presence of the white man" with his pretensions of a "civilising mission" (Killam 1968: xi). Scant regard was paid to the fact that these stereotypical representations and their untenable morality bore "little resemblance to real Africa." As "propaganda in the guise of fiction," the novels "foisted on the reading public an incomplete picture of the total African settling" in the interest of projecting upon Africa "a Victorian code of middle-class morality" as a justification for racial aggrandisement and exploitation (Killam 1968: 170-172).

Tutuola was indeed fortunate that it was not to Mrs Elspeth Huxley or his Nigerian compatriots in London that Faber and Faber had turned to when they needed the expert advice of those purportedly familiar with the workings of the African mind and the universe he depicted in his writings. His Nigerian critics were even more incensed when Faber and Faber offered him the visibility and recognition he was seeking, and what is more, largely on his own terms – they did not edit what they saw as his defective grammar, thus recognising his right to think in Yoruba and write creatively in English. The result was a story coloured with phrases such as this: "then I changed the lady to a kitten and put her inside my pocket and changed myself to a very small bird which I could describe as a 'sparrow' in English language" (Tutuola 1952: 28). Through this rare generosity or accident of publication, relevance came closest to being bedfellows with recognition in a story of Africa. Tutuola could afford to live with the snobbery of the Nigerian intellectual elite, and he felt gratified to have had the opportunity to publish his stories the way he had written and wanted them published. His message was more important than the language in which it was conveyed. He escaped the fate of many an African writer who are edited out of their own story to conform to what others expect storytelling to be.

As an extraordinary writer – irrespective of whether "extraordinarily good, extraordinarily bad, or extraordinarily lucky," if not all three (Lindfors 1970: 333) – Tutuola is an early example of what an African storyteller, drawing on African universes and writing in a colonial language, looks like in print. "His originality set an excellent precedent for later writers who might otherwise have followed too parasitically the literary fashions of Europe" (Lindfors 1970: 333). Not only did his efforts earn him recognition and importance "as an innovator" and as "the father of experimentation in Nigerian fiction in English" (Lindfors 1970: 333), they proved as well that Africans could seek to tell their own stories on their own terms. They also spurred the more Western educated elite to seek to outdo him in telling an African story following the literary canons of the West, and in a manner that excelled at the use of grammatically correct colonial languages (Lindfors 1999c; Achebe 2000; Larson 2001; Currey 2008; Kamau and Mitambo 2016). If Tutuola could succeed in getting published by "breaking all the rules" – "He did not write 'good English'. He did not try to create realistic situations and realistic characters. He did not bother with a plot" (Lindfors 1970: 333) – this elite felt they could do much better by proving to the Western publishers and readers what good students of their languages and canons they had become. If colonialism was the game in town, they were proud to proclaim loud and clear that they had graduated with distinction into the status of superiors among inferiors.

It is doubtful the extent to which Gerald Moore can be taken seriously, when he concludes that "Tutuola's value to the rising generation of young African writers is probably that of an example rather than of a model" (Moore, reprinted in Lindfors 1975[1957]: 57). Paraphrasing Moore, Paul Neumarkt agrees that Tutuola is "far more like a fascinating cul-de-sac than the beginning of anything directly useful to other writers". He add: "Tutuola is a trapped man, trapped in the maze of his own pathogenic disturbance." To Neumarkt, Tutuola, who inhabits a world consumed by fear and terror, does little else as a writer than lead his readers deep into the cul-de-sac of "the African bush to afford them some glimpse of the weird inferno and its ghost-like inhabitants" (Neumarkt 1975[1971]: 188-189). Lindfors would agree with Moore and Neumarkt if this assessment was limited to "form and technique," although it is still early days to be categorical in the claim that Tutuola is "not the sort of writer who attracts followers or founds a school," and that he is a literary dead end since his "achievements are unique because his background, imagination and linguistic equipment are unique" (Lindfors 1970: 333).

Notwithstanding such assessments and claims of a dead end, in Nigeria and elsewhere in Africa, some writers have followed in Tutuola's footsteps, by refusing to settle for sterile mimicry. They have sought to follow Tutuola's examples by writing books that could possibly only be written by Africans, because inspired by their experiences as Africans. Achebe, for example, creatively appropriated the language of the coloniser by blending it with "African creative aesthetics, infused with elements" of the literary traditions of the Igbo community that inspired his stories. He recounts, "I borrowed proverbs from our culture and history, colloquialisms and African expressive language from the ancient griots, the worldviews, perspectives, and customs from my Igbo tradition and cosmology, and the sensibilities of everyday people" (Achebe 2012: 55). Like Tutuola, Achebe was committed to ensuring that all of Africa's stories are told, and that all must be done to fend off a contrived idea of "the world story" or "the Great story" arrived at in a rush "based simply on our knowledge of one or a few traditions" (Achebe 2012: 60-61). Like Tutuola, Achebe was committed to bringing about the death of the single story.

As a kindred spirit to Tutuola, Achebe makes a case for flexibility and humility in how we claim and articulate identities. He used his Igbo identity more as a vantage point for understanding the universal than as a fixation or a birthmark. To Achebe Igbo identity is open-ended and inclusive. His use of proverbs demonstrates that communication is a process in which meaning is multiple, layered and infinite, and where context is cardinal to understanding. Proverbs in Achebe's work also demonstrates that there is no essentialised Igbo identity as social and political encounters and transformations fashion different ways of knowing and being Igbo. Being Igbo in an interconnected world of ever increasing possibilities of encounters with other people from other places and spaces, and with other ways of seeing and doing, far from being a hardback book with a definite introduction, body and conclusion, is always a process of becoming, best understood as flexible, fluid and full of ellipses – an unfinished and unfinishable story.

As mentioned in Chapter Four, Achebe acknowledges change as a permanent feature of being Igbo and being human. While it is important to respect customs and traditions, it is just as important to understand that in the course of human mobility and encounters, new questions arise to which old answers are not quite suited. This might require making things up as one goes along, but an old broom, however experienced and thorough, cannot sweep with quite the same effectiveness as a new broom in a new context. Far from being an invitation to abandon the past for the present, it is rather a call to creatively blend the past with the present in the interest of the future. In his writings, Achebe invites his readers to contemplate the intricacies of being and belonging, through the characters he creates, for whom these are not matters with easy choices. If his public pronouncements on his own life are anything to go by, being and belonging to Achebe as an individual are no easy matters either. He recognises that his "life has been full of changes" that have shaped the way he looks at the world, and that renders complex "the meaning of existence and everything we value"[2] The challenge of being and becoming African or anything else, is not so much identifying with people, places and spaces one is familiar with, but especially with spaces, places and people one is yet to encounter or to become familiar with. Hence Achebe's call for empathy and compassion, with the argument that:

> …it's not difficult to identify with somebody like yourself, somebody next door who looks like you. What's more difficult is to identify with someone you don't see, who's very far away, who's a different colour, who eats a different kind of food. When you begin to do that then literature is really performing its wonders.[3]

In his use of proverbs in *Things Fall Apart* and his other writings, Chinua Achebe, just like Tutuola his predecessor, has left us with enough food for thought on power, politics, relationships and encounters to ensure that things do not fall apart, even when we are drunk on palm-wine harvested from Deads' Town, in our continuous quest to be and become African in an ever changing world.

Tutuola's intimate family circles were not unaffected by the criticism his father received from fellow Nigerians for daring to write what he wrote. Reflecting on his father's books after Tutuola's death, his son, Yinka Tutuola, came to his father's defence. He recounts how his father's joy at being published and achieving international renown "was almost doused by some of his academic kinsmen from West Africa, from Nigeria in particular"[4], who:

> … took it upon themselves to defend the English language more than the English and the Americans combined, and refused to see anything good in the efforts of a semi-illiterate writer (by Western standards) but an undeniable professional raconteur (by Yoruba standards). To them anything, everything, must be judged, evaluated, and recommended

only if they passed Western tests and standards. And that was a time when they were fighting Western colonialism, imperialism, culture, influence, you name it, through the writings of their novels, poems, etc.[5]

According to Yinka Tutuola, his father stood his ground, because he knew what he was doing. He explains how his father used his writing to bring Yoruba and English into conversation:

> I enjoyed all my father's books and I used to discuss them with him. I also asked questions. But as small as I was then I could easily pick on his grammar and at times I would make suggestions. Looking behind some years later I discovered that he preferred direct translation of the Yoruba words, thoughts and usage into English word-for-word, rather than using their English equivalents or expressing them the way an Englishman would do. This according to him added 'flavor to my stories.' For example, the word 'second' (a unit of time) is expressed as 'a twinkle of an eye' by the Yoruba people and this is exactly how he used it in his books. There are many examples of words like this which many thought he coined or which they attributed to his ignorance of the rules of grammar, but these kinds of expressions are the real day-to-day Yoruba way of expressing such words, thoughts, or actions. Professor Ogundipe-Leslie noted this well when she pointed out that he 'has simply and boldly (or perhaps innocently) carried across into his English prose the linguistic pattern and literary habits of his Yoruba language, using English words as counters. He is basically speaking Yoruba but using English words.' This, I think, is one of those things that made him unique among African writers. He believed folk stories, by all means, should be told choosing words that would ultimately express the original local meaning or thought, even at the expense of good grammar. This is where some went against him. But he stood his ground and many loved him for it.[6]

Abiola Irele insists that not everyone in Nigeria gave Tutuola's work "a hostile reception," and that his "work was in fact regarded with genuine admiration by the discerning part of the reading public" in Nigeria (Irele 2001: 180). Support from the likes of Achebe (2000,

2012) and Wole Soyinka (1963) notwithstanding, Tutuola's travails, not least in the hands of less discerning fellow Africans as his worst critics, are indicative of the formidably challenging hurdles facing the deeply unfinished and unfinishable story of decolonisation in a context where elite Africans, even in their clamours for transformation of higher education on the continent, are busy burning the midnight oil whitening up (Nyamnjoh 2016). It is also an example of what privileging conversations over conversion could yield in African encounters with the wider world. It speaks to the open-minded sweet-footed frontier African at the crossroads and junctions of African encounters, mediating creative conversations and subverting the regressive logic of exclusionary identities.

Tutuola's stories constitute an epistemological order where the sense of sight and physical evidence has not assumed the same centrality, dominance and dictatorship evident in the colonial epistemology and its hierarchies of perceptual faculties (Stoller 1989, 1997; van Dijk and Pels 1996). The stories invite us to question dualistic assumptions about reality and the scholarship inspired by such dualism.

In his blurb to the 1989 edition of *The Wild Hunter in the Bush of the Ghosts*, American literary scholar and leading authority on Amos Tutuola, Bernth Lindfors, refers to this text, first written for publication in 1948, as "a fitting harbinger of the rich and varied literary efflorescence to follow." Like its author, whose recognition by Nigerians and Africans trapped in the expectations of completeness inspired by the prescriptive gaze of colonial and colonising Western education and civilisation took long years in coming, *The Wild Hunter in the Bush of the Ghosts* "languished unpublished for long years and only Tutuola's occasional vague references to his 'first novel' kept the matter at all public" (Lindfors 1989: iv). To Lindfors, Amos Tutuola deserves recognition

> ...as a founding father of one of the most remarkable national literatures to emerge in an international language in the 20th century. His work deserves a place of ancestral honor in the pantheon not only of Nigerian letters but of African writing (Lindfors 1989: iv).

Lindfors' call is echoed by Wole Soyinka, who considers Tutuola as a "forerunner of Gabriel García Márquez, Ben Okri, Shahrnush Parsipur and others in the narrative style conveniently known as magical realism" (Soyinka 2014: viii), the "ability to depict reality objectively but with a magical dimension" (Hart 2007: 84), or, in the case of Tutuola's books, "the complete blending of fantasy with conventional realism," a common characteristic of the traditional African folktales he draws on (Obiechina 1975[1968]: 127). Achebe echoes Soyinka when he writes: "The beauty of his [Tutuola] tales was fantastical expression of a form of an indigenous Yoruba, therefore African, magical realism. It is important to note that his books came out several decades before the brilliant Gabriel García Márquez published his own masterpieces of Latin American literature, such as *One Hundred Years of Solitude*" (Achebe 2012: 113).

To Brenda Cooper, what magical realism achieves in Tutuolan and West African fiction is to seek:

> ...to capture the paradox of the unity of opposites; it contests polarities such as history versus magic, the precolonial past versus the post-industrial present and life versus death. Capturing such boundaries between spaces is to exist in a third space, in the fertile interstices between these extremes of time or space (Cooper 1998: 1).

Cooper is, however, ready to condone magical realism only to the extent that using the magical as a device for exploring reality is limited to when "there is a degree of critical, ironic distance from it which prevents supernatural explanations being proffered to elucidate historical processes" (Cooper 1998: 222). If "magical realism" is that which does not conform with a Eurocentric rationality (and understanding of reality as evidence-based sensory perception in time and space as chronological, concrete, linear and objective), it is clearly not an appropriate term for what the Amos Tutuola tradition of fiction offers, even if it is the current term in circulation (Cooper 1998; Bowers 2004; Wenzel 2006; Adeeko 2007; Hart 2007).[7]

That Tutuola has inspired younger generations of storytellers in "magical realism" (Cooper 1998) or the reality of a multifaceted world of presence in simultaneous multiplicities is evidenced in Ben

Okri's *The Famished Road* (1991) and *Astonishing the Gods* (1996), and also in the proliferation of Nollywood films about the place and power of the supernatural and the occult in everyday life.[8] Nigerian and other filmmakers can continue to draw inspiration from Tutuola's works with the encouragement from J. K. Rowling, the world famous English-born author of the bestselling seven volume "magical realism" Harry Potter series[9], whose first book in the series was published in 1997 (Shapiro 2004: 10), the very year Tutuola died, and who has openly expressed her amazement "at the way modern filmmaking and the wizardry of special effects had [has] succeeded in making her most imaginative notions a big screen reality" (Shapiro 2004: 166). Despite the intricacy of her stories, Rowling was pleased with how "Hollywood had captured the magic of her books and her fertile imagination" (Shapiro 2004: 197). Bringing text and film into conversation, as Richard Fardon has argued in relation to Ousmane Sembene's work, is instructive on how to bring ethnography and fiction into conversation, and as enriching as the creative innovativeness with which African writers have sought to demonstrate the dynamism and mobility of African cultures through encounters with others in history (Fardon and la Rouge 2017).

Introducing the 2014 edition of *The Palm-Wine Drinkard*, Wole Soyinka remarks that "Amos Tutuola has been enjoying a quiet but steady revival" both "within his immediate cultural environment, and across America and Europe," adding that, "[a]s long as there is a drop of wine left to tap from the West African palm tree, Amos Tutuola lives on."(2014: viii). It is a good sign, therefore, that West and Central Africa proliferate with palm trees, palm-wine joints and palm-wine music to continue to lubricate the sort of creative imagination that Tutuola can claim as his legacy. In some countries like Cameroon the palm-wine culture is sustained largely thanks to the persistence of large scale oil-palm plantation agriculture started in colonial times (Konings 2011). Could this be reason enough to hope that with the surging revival in the fortunes of Tutuola *The Palm-wine Drinkard* will soon be treated across Africa the way good palm-wine is usually treated, as needing no advertisement? And would Africans grow in their addiction to *The Palm-Wine Drinkard* that they can, as does Akuebue in Chinua Achebe's *Arrow of God*, readily affirm, with

Tutuola in mind, that "The only medicine against palm wine is the power to say no" (Achebe 1974[1964]: 98)?

As Harry Garuba argues, the very fact that Faber and Faber managed to secure an introduction from Wole Soyinka, the Yoruba Nigerian Nobel Prize-winning author, is significant because Tutuola's countrymen scoffed at the accolades this novel received from reviewers in Europe and the USA when it was first published. By getting Soyinka – one of the few Nigerian writers and intellectuals to consistently defend Tutuola and his creative imagination (Soyinka 1963) – to write this introduction, the publishers are, as it were, providing the final seal of authority that binds the initial international recognition to the belated embrace of the writer by his local constituency.[10] The blurb to the new edition of *The Palm-Wine Drinkard* says as much. It reads:

> This classic novel tells the phantasmagorical story of an alcoholic man and his search for his dead palm-wine tapster. As he travels through the land of the dead, he encounters a host of supernatural and often terrifying beings – among them the complete gentleman who returns his body parts to their owners and the insatiable hungry-creature. Mixing Yoruba folktales with what T. S. Eliot described as a 'creepy crawly imagination,' *The Palm-Wine Drinkard* is regarded as the seminal work of African literature (Blurb, 2014 edition of Tutuola's *Palm-Wine Drinkard*).

The 2014 edition is crowned with two commendations: one by Dylan Thomas – "Brief, thronged, grisly and bewitching," excerpted from his famous review published in the *Observer*, (Dylan Thomas, reprinted in Lindfors 1975: 7-8) – and another by Chinua Achebe – "Tutuola's art conceals – or rather clothes – his purpose, as all good art must do" (Achebe 1988[1990]: 101), quoted as commendation, 2014 edition of Tutuola's *Palm-Wine Drinkard*). Although there are still some Nigerian academics, some of whom are yet to read him, who consider Tutuola's *The Palm-Wine Drinkard* and other writings "childish and crude and certainly not the kind of thing a patriotic Nigerian should be exporting" abroad or teaching to university students in the country and elsewhere, Tutuola does indeed have a major contribution to make on beneficent literary fiction (Achebe 1988[1990]: 100-101) and, as I have sought to demonstrate in this book, to ongoing quests for complementary epistemological options informed by African ontologies and cosmologies, cultures and traditions of meaning making and knowledge production.

As Achebe remarks, for those who care to read even the opening lines of *The Palm-Wine Drinkard*, Tutuola's social and ethical concerns are immediately apparent. If the palm-wine drinkard had been drinking palm-wine from his childhood years, and had no other work than to drink palm-wine, this qualifies as a "life of indolent frivolity" (Achebe 1988[1990]: 106) that begs the question: "What happens when a man immerses himself in pleasure to the exclusion of all work; when he raises pleasure to the status of work and occupation and says in effect: 'Pleasure be thou my work!'?" (Achebe 1988[1990]: 102). And how does the rest of society respond to such consumerism with reckless abandon that is condoned by an affluent father – the richest man in town? Should the richest man in the community not employ his wealth better than "to indulge his son's outrageous appetite"? Could not he have used his riches better than buying the services of a tapster to slave away without relent, harvesting palm-wine, which in turn is literally poured down the drain through sterile consumption by a spoilt son and his idle fair-weather friends deprived of self-control and moderation? Achebe brands this "exploitative and socially useless work," and as a "social and moral offence of colossal consequence" (Achebe 1988[1990]: 103). To him therefore, "*The Palm-Wine Drinkard* is a rich and spectacular exploration of this gross perversion, its expiation through appropriate punishment and the offender's final restoration" (Achebe 1988[1990]: 102). Tutuola's moral universe in general is one that calls for "balance between play and work" (Achebe 1988[1990]: 106). In Achebe's estimation, a lasting legacy of Tutuola's through *The Palm-Wine Drinkard* is to be found in its celebration of work, a theme particularly relevant and beneficial to "a generation and a people whose heroes are no longer makers of things and ideas but spectacular and insatiable consumers" (Achebe 1988[1990]: 112). In stressing a careful balance between play and work, give and take, Tutuola is reminding his readers "that a community which lets some invisible hand do its work for it will sooner or later forfeit the harvest" to "a merciless exactor" (Achebe 1988 [1990]: 111).

Tutuola's gripping description of the supernatural world of his Yoruba culture and indeed other Nigerian and African cultures and subcultures can be likened to the themes of magic, spirits, superstition, death, power, authority, impermanence of life, blackmail, human betrayal, constant struggles against the forces of nature, uncertainties of life, and so on that dominated the films of a well known Yoruba filmmaker, the late Hubert Ogunde. Additionally, his novels, *The Palm-Wine Drinkard*, for example, have been adapted for the stage, and performed in Yoruba with music and dance (Mphahlele 1972[1967]: 168) since 1963, going on tour in Ghana and parts of Europe, and performing at the First Pan-African Cultural Festival in Algiers in 1969 (Lindfors 1975: 71). According to Oyekan Owomoyela, the adaptation of *The Palm-Wine Drinkard* for the stage by Kola Ogunmola benefitted from UNESCO funding and "was a spectacular success, and it played a significant role in enhancing Tutuola's reputation as an author" (Owomoyela 1997: 866). Even his contentious use of English has inspired others, such as veteran comedian Chief Zebrudaya "Alias 4:30," who became famous for using "incorrect English" in "one of the funniest of all TV comedies" series "New Masquerade," which ran from 1983-1993.[11] Appearances, of course, can be deceptive.

Everyone has a story to tell, educated in school or not, and even if it requires palm-wine induced fantasies and creative imagination, the cultural dinosaurs of Africa, prematurely extinct or made to hibernate in the limbo of the Deads' Town, must be given the opportunity to share stories others might consider "a throwback to an earlier era" (Lindfors 1999: 136). Many a less fortunate author have had their stories buried in the endless forest of bad books, stories stoned to death by publishers and critics determined to annihilate "the African mind" with exogenously induced yardsticks of art and literary appreciation. The power of fantasy and creative imagination is an open shop, there for all who frequent the market of life, with or without Death and Debt as currency. Apparently, we the sophisticated, frequent flyer intellectual elite of Africa, enchanted by the complete gentlemen of Eurocentric modernity, do not have the monopoly of lived experiences.

Back in the late 1950s, when many literary critics were quibbling over what to make of Tutuola and his peculiar brand of fiction, Gerald Moore perceptively saw him as "something much rarer and more interesting than another novelist." To Moore, Tutuola was "a visionary writer who must be seen as such if he is to be understood or effectively judged" (Gerald Moore, reprinted in Lindfors 1975[1957]: 51-52). Instead of settling for "Imitativeness" which Moore saw as "the besetting temptation of Nigerian writers" in the 1950s, Tutuola opted for "confidence" that enabled him to transform even his apparent disadvantages such as "his fragmentary English" into special virtues, that made it possible for him to tell the stories of the great imaginative life of his Yoruba people, using his command of a rich repertoire of local idioms "to create a style at once easy and energetic, naïve and daring" (Gerald Moore, reprinted in Lindfors 1975[1957]: 57).

Amos Tutuola may have been a mere messenger in the Department of Labour in Lagos and a man of humble rural beginnings, who dared to dabble into the "art" of writing, only to be labelled and dismissed as an accidental writer and as an aberration by those claiming superiority in the art of storytelling. He may have fallen short of writing the English language beyond his "acrobatic syntax," preferring instead on "adapting English to Yoruba syntax and constructions" (Barlet 2000[1996]: 198), and may have drawn significantly – some would say excessively – from the repertoire of Yoruba folktales and from the likes of Chief Daniel Olorunfemi Fagunwa. But is not being alive and finding one's way through life all about activation: activating and being activated by others, humans and non-humans alike?

Tutuola – just like the Skull briefly turned into a complete gentleman in *The Palm-Wine Drinkard* to catch the attention of the elusive bride –, to earn himself a special niche in the history of African literature, stumbles "into greatness by the sheer vigor of his imagination" (Lindfors 1975: xiv), and by having the naïve confidence to write in English, without falling "into that stilted English which so many educated African writers use" (V. S. Pritchett, reprinted in Lindfors 1975: 21). As Bernth Lindfors argues, their crudeness and unkemptness aside, Tutuola's works "possessed elemental vitality which the published writings of more sophisticated authors too often lacked. Tutuola was the naïve prodigy of African letters" (Lindfors 1975: xiv). Indeed, as Kingsley Amis observes in his review of *My Life in the Bush of Ghosts*, a review published in February 1954, shortly after publication of the novel, Tutuola presents his readers with "a severe test" of their "originality as readers" and of their ability to throw all their "preferences and preconceptions out of the window when the need arises" (Kingsley Amis, reprinted in Lindfors 1975: 26). Of *My Life in the Bush of Ghosts*, Amis writes, and this could well be extended to all of Tutuola's books,

> ...this book clearly needs repeated readings before its extraordinariness can be fully noted, let alone mastered, and there is no doubt of the size of Mr. Tutuola's talent, which makes the average 'modern novel' look jejune and vapid (Kingsley Amis, reprinted in Lindfors 1975: 26).

It is a pity that delusions of completeness and linear articulations of being human, being modern and being civilised should stand in the way of recognition of the full magnitude and depth of Tutuola's creative imagination and its importance to meaning and sense making, and to knowledge production and consumption. Paradoxically as well, even his Nigerian and fellow African critics well-schooled at the winner takes all logic of colonialism and colonial education do not seem to have fared any better – despite their phenomenal sacrifice resulting in a "badly damaged sense of self" (Achebe 2000: 81). Indeed, similar to his Nigerian critics educated at Oxford, Cambridge, London and related ivy league universities in the United Kingdom and its global outposts – whose mastery of the English language, however sophisticated, could always be faulted for its "Nigerian" or "foreign" accent by so-called "native English" speakers – Tutuola's "young English," whatever growth was apparent in it with every new story he wrote since publication of *The Palm-Wine Drinkard* in 1952, would never be enough to redeem him from the scrutinising, prescriptive and blazing floodlights of imperial Britain and its civilizational hierarchies. To some, regardless of country, geography or race, Tutuola will forever remain a barbaric primitive or at best, a "modern West African imagination ... working with a lazy freedom in the English language" (V. S. Pritchett, reprinted in Lindfors 1975: 21).

As victims of globally dominant philosophies of being and becoming based on grand narratives concocted in a hurry, linear progression and teleological assumptions, ordinary Africans immersed in popular traditions of meaning-making such as Tutuola's are denied the right to creative imagination and representation of their realities in accordance with the civilisations and universes they know best and from a more grounded and dynamic sense of an interconnected past, present and future. The interconnecting global and local hierarchies of these dominant philosophies mean that African elites schooled in a Eurocentric modernity are all too eager to label and dismiss (however hypocritically) as *traditional knowledge* the creative imagination of what their Western counterparts love to term "the African mind" – instead of creating space for the fruit of that mind as a *tradition of knowledge* (Mudimbe 1988; Ki-Zerbo 1992, 2010[1972]; Hountondji 1980[1976], 1997, 2002; Falola and Jennings 2002; Nabudare 2006; Connell 2007; Cooper and Morrell 2014; Connell et al. 2016).

The suppressed are like active volcanos; they eventually erupt. The story and universe of *The Palm-Wine Drinkard*, *My Life in the Bush of Ghosts*, *The Witch-Herbalist of the Remote Town* and all the other novels and short stories published by Tutuola before his transitioning into Dead's Town in 1997 resonate with the daily lives of Tutuola's Yoruba community (Soyinka 1963; Lindfors 1970; Barber 1995; Tobias 1999; Garuba 2003, 2013)[12] and have variants in tune with social life and cultural contexts throughout Africa (Lindfors 1970: 317-318; Anozie 1975[1970]; Armstrong 1975[1970]; Obiechina 1975[1968]). These variants often sit uncomfortably with the resilience of colonial education and its dominant epistemologies (Nyamnjoh 2001, 2012a 2012c) that are championed by dualisms and dichotomies in the Eurocentric modernity that inspired colonialism and that continue to inform how reality is defined and perceived

(Mbembe 1997, 2003). If we believe that Tutuola's universe has something to offer epistemologically, that we should not continue to dismiss or will it out of the African and global present and future merely because it makes us look and feel primitive and superstitious (and thus incomplete) in the legitimating eyes of the hegemonic variant of Eurocentric modernity, then we must invest time and scholarly energies to document (ethnographically, literarily, historically, archeologically, etc.) these universes for their epistemological significance. In particular, we must document the manner in which these popular universes privilege consciousness over essence and underscore the importance of relatedness, openness, enrichment, humility and mutually empowering action and interactions. Such documentation should be conducted not in isolation but in conversation with researchers and writers throughout the continent, as comparison is critical for theory building.

The popular epistemological order inspired by Tutuola's universe and writings is also at variance with the tendency in the colonial and colonising Eurocentric export to minimize the power of society, social structures, communal and cultural solidarities by "trumpeting instead the uncompromising autonomy of the individual, rights-bearing, physically discrete, monied, market-driven, materially inviolate human subject" (Comaroff and Comaroff 1999a: 3). It is an epistemological order that refuses to see individuals and social structures as either all powerful or all passive. Similarly, it does not see individuals and social structures as easily detachable from one another, and to be manipulated into compliance with the expectations of some purported puppet master who knows best. Tutuola's epistemological order stresses instead a mix between individual rights and interests on the one hand, and the rights and interests of groups and collectivities, on the other. There is little room in it for zero-sum games of winner takes all.

As a reject, malcontent or dreg of the palm-wine of Eurocentric modernity, and as a skilled messenger and student of his Yoruba community and the world at large, Amos Tutuola has left humanity with a fantastical epistemological option on the imperative of attending to the nuanced complexities, interconnections, interdependencies, flexibilities, fluidities, mobilities, encounters and power dynamics simultaneously shaped by and shaping considerations and characterisations such as race, place, culture, gender, generation, religion and education. African intellectuals and intellectuals the world over cannot thank Tutuola enough for distinguishing himself as a messenger despite his modest and humble status and for, in the manner of the palm-wine drinkard, carefully navigating and negotiating his journey of a thousand dangers back home from the Deads' Town, with the gift of a magic egg from his dead Tapster to re-imagine his community and humanity. Let us fill and drink from Amos Tutuola's cosmic gourd of palm-wine that we may explore and embrace the convivial imperative in African knowledge production and consumption which his writings have inspired.

Notes

[1] See https://en.wikipedia.org/wiki/My_Life_in_the_Bush_of_Ghosts_(album), accessed 30 October 2016.

[2] www.goodreads.com/author/quotes/8051.Chinua_Achebe, accessed July 21 2013

[3] www.nairaland.com/1233528/famous-quotes-prof-chinua-achebe, accessed July 23, 2013.

[4] Yinka Tutuola, interviewed by Jeff VanderMeer,
http://weirdfictionreview.com/2013/01/amos-tutuola-an-interview-with-yinka-tutuola-by-jeff-vandermeer, accessed 1 November 2016.

[5] Yinka Tutuola, interviewed by Jeff VanderMeer,
http://weirdfictionreview.com/2013/01/amos-tutuola-an-interview-with-yinka-tutuola-by-jeff-vandermeer, accessed 1 November 2016.

[6] Yinka Tutuola, interviewed by Jeff VanderMeer,
http://weirdfictionreview.com/2013/01/amos-tutuola-an-interview-with-yinka-tutuola-by-jeff-vandermeer, accessed 1 November 2016.

[7] See Onoge (1974) on the crisis of consciousness in African literature. See also Garuba (2003, 2013).

[8] See Location One. (2010), panel on Nollywood with filmmaker Zina Saro-Wiwa, film scholar Awam Amkpa, and AfricaLab founder Mahen Bonnetti and moderated by Claudia Calirman.
http://derica.tumblr.com/post/2746338774/sharon-stone-in-abuja-exhibition, accessed 2 August 2014.

⁹ Apparently the Harry Potter series made Joanne K. Rowling, who "just a few short years ago … had been a single mother living on welfare in a drafty flat" (Shapiro 2004: 217), so rich and famous that:

> In a poll conducted by *The Sunday Times*, Joanne found herself near the top of a list of the wealthiest people in England, an astounding eleven places higher than Queen Elizabeth. And in a list of Scotland's most powerful 100 people, Joanne came in at number four (Shapiro 2004: 217).

> By 2004, Rowling's first four books in the series had "sold more than 10 million copies in over a hundred different languages" (Shapiro 2004: 10). It is an irony that while African intellectuals – in their quest to catch up with the modernity and civilised realities of a world founded on science, rationality and objectivity purportedly represented by the West in their estimation – were busy criticising Amos Tutuola for daring to perpetuate images of Africa as a continent of magic, witchcraft and wizardry, Scotland, Britain and the rest of the West were busy commercialising the same beliefs and fantasies, and laughing all the way to the bank as authors and filmmakers.

¹⁰ See Harry Garuba's "And the Book Lived Happily Ever After," http://chimurengachronic.co.za/and-the-books-lived-happily-ever-after, accessed 11 May 2015.

¹¹ See https://www.naij.com/389859-photos-what-chief-zebrudaya-did-at-synagogue-church.html, accessed 30 December 2016.

¹² According to T. A. Oyesakin of Lagos State University, the stories are so common a daily reality that "By 15, a typical Yoruba child is conversant with the folktales" (cited in Lindfors 1999b: 139).

References

Abega, S. C. (1987) *L'Esana chez les Beti*, Yaounde: Editions Clé.
Abega, S. C. (1995) *Contes d'Initiation Sexuelle*, Yaounde: Editions Clé.
Abega, S. C. (2000) *Les Choses de la Forêt: Les Masques des Princes Tikar de Nditan*, Yaounde: Presse de l'UCAC.
Abega, S. C. (2007) *Les Violences Sexuelles et l'Etat au Cameroun*: Paris: Karthala.
Abu-Lughod, L. (2008), *Writing Women's Worlds: Bedouin Stories*, Berkeley: University of California Press.
Achebe, C. (1974[1964]) *Arrow of God*, Oxford: Heinemann (African Writers Series).
Achebe, C. (1988[1990]) *Hopes and Impediments: Selected Essays*, New York: Anchor Books.
Achebe, C. (2000) *Home and Exile*. New York: Anchor Books.
Achebe, C. (2012) *There was a Country: A Personal History of Biafra*, London: Allen Lane.
Adebanwi, W. (2014a) *Yorùbá Elites and Ethnic Politics in Nigeria: Obáfémi Awólówò and Corporate Agency*, Cambridge: Cambridge University Press.
Adebanwi, W. (2014b) "The Writer as Social Thinker," *Journal of Contemporary African Studies*, 32(4): 405-420.
Adeeko, A., (2007) "Specterless Spirits/Spiritless Specters: Magical Realism's Two Faces," *The European Legacy*, 12(4): 469-480.
Adesina, J.O. (2008) "Archie Mafeje and the Pursuit of Endogeny: Against Alterity and Extroversion," *African Development* 33(4): 133-152.
Adichie, C. N. (2009) "The Headstrong Historian", In: *The Thing Around Your Neck* (collection of short stories by C. N. Adichie), London: Fourth Estate, pp.198-218.
Adogame, A., Chitando, E., Bateye, B. (eds) (2013) *African Traditions in the Study of Religion, Diaspora and Gendered Societies: Essays in Honour of Jacob Kehinde Olupona*, Surrey: Ashgate Publishing Ltd.
Afolayan, A. (1975[1971]) "Language and Sources of Amos Tutuola," In: Bernth Lindfors (ed.), *Critical Perspectives on Amos Tutuola*, Boulder: Three Continents Press. Pp. 193-208.

Ajei, M. O. (2007) *Africa's Development: The Imperative of Indigenous Knowledge and Values*. (Thesis in Philosophy). University of South Africa. Available at: http://uir.unisa.ac.za/handle/10500/1266, accessed 21 March 2011.

Ake, C. (1979) *Social Science as Imperialism: A Theory of Political Development*. Ibadan: University of Ibadan Press.

Ake, C. (2000) *The Feasibility of Democracy in Africa*. Dakar: CODESRIA.

Allen, R. E. (1997) *Plato's Parmenides*, New Haven: Yale University Press.

Amadiume, I. (1987) *Male Daughters, Female Husbands: Gender and Sex in an African Society*. London: Zed.

Amadiume, I. (1997) *Reinventing Africa: Matriarchy, Religion & Culture*. London: Zed.

Amin, S. (1980) *Class and Nation: Historically and in the Current Crisis*. London: Heinemann.

Amin, S. (2004) *The Liberal Virus: Permanent War and the Americanization of the World*, New York: Monthly Review Press.

Amin, S. (2006) *Capitalism in the Age of Globalization: The Management of Contemporary Society*, London: Zed.

Amin, S. (2009[1988]) *Eurocentrism: Modernity, Religion, and Democracy. A Critique of Eurocentrism and Culturalism*, New York: Monthly Review Press.

Amin, S. (2010) *Ending the Crisis of Capitalism or Ending Capitalism?*, Oxford: Pambazuka.

Ani, M. (1994) *Yurugu: An African-Centered Critique of European Cultural Thought and Behavior*, Trenton, NJ: Africa World Press.

Anozie, S. O. (1975[1970]) "Amos Tutuola: Literature and Folklore, or the Problem of Synthesis," In: Bernth Lindfors (ed.), *Critical Perspectives on Amos Tutuola*, Boulder: Three Continents Press. Pp. 237-253.

Appadurai, A. (1999) Globalization and the research imagination. *International Social Science Journal*, 51(160): 229-238.

Appadurai, A. (2001) "Grassroots globalization and the research imagination," In: Appadurai A (ed.) *Globalization*. Durham, NC: Duke University Press, 1-21.

Appiah, K.A. (1992) *In My Father's House: Africa in the Philosophy of Culture*. Oxford: Oxford University Press.

Ardener, E. (1996) "Witchcraft, Economics and the Continuity of Belief," In: Ardener, Shirley (ed.): *Kingdom on Mount Cameroon: Studies in the History of the Cameroon Coast, 1500-1970*. Oxford: Berghahn.

Armstrong, R. P. (1975[1970]) "The Narrative and Intensive Continuity: The Palm-Wine Drinkard," In: Bernth Lindfors (ed.), *Critical Perspectives on Amos Tutuola*, Boulder: Three Continents Press. Pp. 209-235.

Asante, M. K. (2003) *Afrocentricity: The Theory of Social Change*, revised and expanded. Chicago, IL: African American Images.

Ashforth, A. (1996) "Of secrecy and the commonplace: witchcraft and power in Soweto," *Social Research* 63(4): 1183-1234.

Ashforth, A. (2001) "On living in a world with witches: everyday epistemology and spiritual insecurity in a modern African city (Soweto)," In: Moore H, Sanders T (eds) *Magical Interpretations, Material Realities: Modernity, Witchcraft and the Occult in Postcolonial Africa*, London: Routledge, 206-225.

Awasom, N. F. (2010) "The Emergence of Public Spheres in Colonial Cameroon: The Case of Palm Wine Drinking Joints as lieux de sociabilité in Bamenda Township," *Africa Development*, XXXV (1 & 2): 201-220.

Balakrishnan, S. and Mbembe, A. (2016) "Pan-African Legacies, Afropolitan Futures," *Transition*, No. 120, You Are Next (2016), pp. 28-37.

Barber, K. (1991) "Multiple Discourses in Yorùbá Oral Literature," *Bulletin of the John Rylands University Library of Manchester*, 73(3): 11-24.

Barber, K. (1995) "African-Language Literature and Postcolonial Criticism," *Research in African Literatures*, 26(4): 3-30.

Barber, K. (1997) "Introduction," In: Barber K (ed.) *Readings in African Popular Culture*, Oxford: James Currey, 1-12.

Barber, K. (2008) *The Anthropology of Texts, Persons and Publics: Oral and Written Culture in Africa and Beyond*, Cambridge: Cambridge University Press.

Barber, K. Collins, J. and Ricard, A. (1997) *West African Popular Theatre*, Oxford: James Currey.

Barlet, O. (2000[1996]) *African Cinemas: Decolonizing the Gaze*, London: Zed Books.

Bastian, M.L. (2001) "Vulture men, campus cultists and teenaged witches: modern magics in Nigerian popular media," In: Moore H, Sanders T (eds) *Magical Interpretations, Material Realities: Modernity, Witchcraft and the Occult in Postcolonial Africa*, London: Routledge, 71-96.

Bates R. Mudimbe V. Y. and O'Barr J. (1993) *Africa and the Disciplines*, Chicago, IL: University of Chicago Press.

Baxter, P.T.W. and Fardon, R. (Guest Editors) (1991) (Special Issue) Voice, Genre, Text: Anthropological Essays in Africa and Beyond, *Bulletin of the John Rylands University Library of Manchester*, 73(3).

Beard, P. (1975) *Longing for Darkness: Kamante's Tales from Out of Africa*, San Francisco: Chronicle Books.

Becker, H. (2009) "The Inequalities of South African Anthropology," *Anthropology Southern Africa*, 32(1-2):89-90.

Beebe, M. A. Kouakou, K.M. Oyeyinka B. O. and Rao M. (eds) (2003) *Africa Dot Edu: IT Opportunities and Higher Education in Africa*, New Delhi: Tata McGraw-Hill.

Behar, R. (1993) *Translated Woman: Crossing the Border with Esperanza's Story*, New York: Beacon Press.

Berger, I. (1997) "Contested boundaries: African studies approaching the millennium presidential address to the 1996 African studies association annual meeting," *African Studies Review*, 40(2): 1-14.

Blanco, M. D. P. and Peeren, E. (eds) (2013) *The Spectralities Reader: Ghosts and Haunting in Contemporary Cultural Theory*, London: Bloomsbury.

Bongmba, E. K. (ed) (2012) *The Wiley-Blackwell Companion to African Religions*, Chichester: Wiley-Blackwell Publishers.

Boulaga, F. E. (1984[1981]) *Christianity Without Fetishes: An African Critique and Recapture of Christianity*, New York: Orbis Books.

Boulaga, F. E. (2014[1977] *Muntu In Crisis: African Authenticity and Philosophy*, Trenton: Africa World Press.

Bourdieu, P. (1984) *Distinction: A social Critique of the Judgement of Taste*, Cambridge, Massachusetts: Harvard University Press.

Bourdieu, P. (1990) *The Logic of Practice*, Stanford: Stanford University Press.

Bourdieu, P. (1991) *Language and Symbolic Power*, Cambridge: Polity Press.

Bourdieu, P. (1996) *The State Nobility*, Cambridge: Polity.

Bourdieu, P. (2004) *Science of Science and Reflexivity*. Chicago, IL: University of Chicago Press.

Bowen, E.S. [*nom de plume* of Laura Bohannan] (1964) *Return to Laughter: An Anthropological Novel*, New York: Anchor Books.

Bowers, M. A. (2004) *Magic(al) Realism (The New Critical Idiom)*, London: Routledge.

Butake, B. (1990) *And Palm-Wine Will Flow*, Yaounde: SOPECAM.

Butler, J. (1990) *Gender Trouble: Feminism and the Subversion of Identity*, New York: Routledge.

Butler, J. (1993), *Bodies that Matter: On the Discursive Limits of 'Sex,'* New York: Routledge.

Bwemba-Bong, R. (2005) *Quand l'Africain Était L'Or Noir de l'Europe: L'Afrique: Actrice ou Victime de la "Traite Des Noirs"?*, Paris: Edition Menaibuc.

Cabral, A. Njinya-Mujinya, L. and Habomugisha, P. (1998) "Published or rejected? African intellectuals' scripts and foreign journals, publishers and editors," *Nordic Journal of African Studies*, 7(2): 83-94.

Calhoun, C. (2003[2000]), "Pierre Bourdieu," in: George Ritzer, (ed.) *Blackwell Companion to the Major Social Theorists*, Cambridge, MA: Blackwell, pp. 274-309.

Canagarajah, A.S. (2002) *A Geopolitics of Academic Writing*. Pittsburgh, PA: University of Pittsburgh Press.

Chandrasekhar, K. Sreevani, S. Seshapani, P. and Pramodhakumari, J. (2012) "A Review on Palm Wine," *International Journal of Research in Biological Sciences*, 2 (1): 33-38.

Che, H.C. (1993) *The Basis of the Local Wine Enterpreise: A Synthesis*, Jos: Plateau State Printing.

Chinweizu (1987[1975]) *The West and the Rest of Us: White Predators Black Slavers and the African Elite*, Lagos: Preo.

Chumbow, B. S. (2005) "The language question and national development in Africa," In: Mkandawire T (ed.) *African Intellectuals: Rethinking Politics, Language, Gender and Development.* Dakar: CODESRIA/Zed, pp. 165-192.

Chumbow, B. S. (2009) Linguistic diversity, pluralism and national development in Africa. *Africa Development* 34(2): 21-45.

Clarke, K. M. (2004) *Mapping Yorùbá Networks: Power and Agency in the Making of Transnational Communities,* Durham: Duke University Press.

Clifford, J. (1988) *The Predicament of Culture: Twentieth-Century Ethnography, Literature, and Art,* Cambridge, MA: Harvard University Press.

Clifford, J. (2003) *On the Edges of Anthropology (Interviews),* Chicago. Prickly Paradigm.

Clifford, J. and Marcus, G. E. (eds.) (1986) *Writing Culture: The Poetics and Politics of Ethnography,* Berkeley: University of California Press.

Collins, H. R. (1975a[1961]) "Founding A New National Literature: The Ghost Novels of Amos Tutuola," In: Bernth Lindfors (ed.), *Critical Perspectives on Amos Tutuola,* Boulder: Three Continents Press, pp. 59-70.

Collins, H. R. (1975b[1969]) "Tutuola's Literary Powes," In: Bernth Lindfors (ed.), *Critical Perspectives on Amos Tutuola,* Boulder: Three Continents Press, pp. 155-167.

Collins, P. and Gallinat, A. (eds) (2010) *The Ethnographic Self as Resource: Writing Memory and Experience into Ethnography,* New York: Berghahn Books.

Comaroff, J. and Comaroff, J. (1997a) "Ethnography of Africa: The usefulness of the useless," In: Grinker R. R., Steiner, C. B. (eds) *Perspectives on Africa: A Reader in Culture, History, and Representation,* Oxford: Blackwell, 689-703.

Comaroff, J. and Comaroff, J. (1997b) *Of Revelation and Revolution: The Dialectics of Modernity on a South African Frontier,* Volume Two. Chicago, IL: Chicago University Press.

Comaroff, J. and Comaroff. J. (eds) (2006) *Law and Disorder in the Postcolony.* Chicago, IL: Chicago University Press.

Comaroff, J. and Comaroff, J. L. (2009) *Ethnicity, Inc.* Scottsville: University of Kwazulu-Natal Press.

Comaroff, J. and Comaroff, J. L. (2012) *Theory from the South: Or, How Euro-America is Evolving Toward Africa*, Boulder, CO: Paradigm Publishers.

Connell, R. (2007) *Southern Theory: Social Science and the Global Dynamics of Knowledge*, Cambridge: Polity.

Connell, R. Collyer, F. Maia, J. and Morrell, R. (2016) "Towards and Global Sociology of Knowledge: Post-Colonial Realities and Intellectual Practices," *International Sociology*, DOI: 10.1177/0268580916676913, 1-17.

Connolly, J. (2009) *Faber and Faber: Eighty Years of Book Cover Design*, London: Faber and Faber.

Conrad, J. (1995) "Heart of darkness," In: Lyon, J. (ed.) *Joseph Conrad: Youth, Heart of Darkness, The End of the Tether*, London: Penguin, 45. (Original work published 1899).

Cooper, B. (1998) *Magical Realism in West African Fiction: Seeing with a Third Eye*, London: Routledge.

Cooper, B. and Morrell, R. (eds) (2014) *Africa-Centred Knowledges: Crossing Fields & Worlds*, Suffolk: James Currey.

Copans, J. (1990) *La Longue Marche de la Modernité Africaine: Savoirs, Intellectuels, Démocratie* [*The Long March of African Modernity: Knowledge, Intellectuals and Democracy*], Paris: Karthala.

Copans, J. (1993) "Intellectuels visibles, intellectuels invisibles [Visible Intellectuals, Invisible Intellectuals]," *Politique Africaine* 51: 7–25.

Crais, C. and Pamela, S. (2009) *Sara Baartman and the Hottentot Venus: A Ghost Story and a Biography*, Johannesburg: Wits University Press.

Crossman, P. (2004) "Perceptions of 'Africanisation' or 'endogenisation' at African universities: Issues and recommendations," In: Zeleza P. T., Olukoshi A (eds) *African Universities in the Twenty-First Century*. Dakar: CODESRIA, 321-340.

Crossman, P. and Devisch, R. (1999) *Endogenisation and African Universities: Initiatives and Issues in the Quest for Plurality in the Human Sciences*, Leuven: Katholieke Universiteit Leuven.

Crossman, P. and Devisch, R. (2002) "Endogenous knowledge: An anthropological perspective," In: Odora-Hoppers C (ed.) *Towards a Philosophy of Articulation: IKS and the Integration of Knowledge Systems,* Cape Town: New Africa Education Publisher, pp. 96-125.

Cruikshank, J. (1998) *The Social Life of Stories: Narrative and Knowledge in the Yukon Territory,* Lincoln: University of Nebraska Press.

Currey, J. (2008) *Africa Writes Back: The African Writers Series & the Launch of African Literature,* Oxford: James Currey.

Davies, C. and Fardon, R. (1991) "African Fictions in Representations of West African and Afro-Cuban Cultures," *Bulletin of the John Rylands University Library of Manchester,* 73(3): 125-145.

Denzer, L. (1992) "Domestic science training in colonial Yorubaland, Nigeria," In: Hansen, K. T. (ed.) *African Encounters with Domesticity,* New Brunswick, NJ: Rutgers University Press, pp. 116-139.

Depelchin, J. (2005) *Silences in African History: Between the Syndromes of Discovery and Abolition,* Dar es Salaam: Mkuki Na Nyota.

Depelchin, J. (2011) *Reclaiming African History,* Nairobi: Pambazuka.

Devisch, R. (2002) *Endogenous Knowledge Practices, Cultures and Sciences: Some Anthropological Perspectives.* Unpublished paper.

Devisch, R. (2007) "The university of Kinshasa: From Lovanium to Unikin," In: Afolayan M. O. (ed.) *Higher Education in Postcolonial Africa: Paradigms of Development, Decline and Dilemmas,* Trenton, NJ: Africa World Press, pp. 17-38.

Devisch, R. and Nyamnjoh, F. B. (eds) (2011) *The Postcolonial Turn: Re-Imagining Anthropology and Africa,* Bamenda/Leiden: Langaa RPCIG/African Studies Centre, Leiden.

Devisch, R. (2017) *Body and Affect in the Intercultural Encounter,* Bamenda/Leiden: Langaa RPCIG/African Studies Centre, Leiden.

Djebbar, A. and Gerdes, P. (2007) *Mathematics in African History and Cultures: An Annotated Bibliography.* Available at: www. Lulu.com, accessed 18 March 2011.

Diagne, S. B. (2013) *L'Encre des Savants: Réflexions sur la Philosophie en Afrique,* Dakar: CODESRIA.

Dibango, M. (in collaboration with Danielle Rouard) (1994) *Three Kilos of Coffee: An Autobiography,* Chicago, IL: University of Chicago Press.

Dieng, A. A. (2006) *Hegel et l'Afrique Noire: Hegel Était-il Raciste?*, Dakar: CODESRIA.

Diop, C. A. (1991) *Civilization or Barbarism: An Authentic Anthropology*, New York: Lawrence Hill Books.

Eagleton, T. (1991) *Ideology: An Introduction*, London: Verso.

Echtler, M. and Ukah, A. (eds) (2015) *Bourdieu in Africa: Exploring the Dynamics of Religious Fields,* Leiden: Brill.

Edman, B. (2010) *Writing Identity in the Age of Postcolonialism: Figurations of Home and Homelessness in African Poetry*, Cape Town: CASAS.

Edwards, P. (1975[1974]) "The Farm and the Wilderness in Tutuola's *The Palm-Wine Drinkard*," In: Bernth Lindfors (ed.), *Critical Perspectives on Amos Tutuola*, Boulder: Three Continents Press, pp. 255-253.

Ela, J.-M. (1986[1980]) *African Cry*, New York: Orbis Books.

Ela, J.-M. (1994) *Restituer l'Histoire aux Sociétés Africaines. Promouvoir les Sciences Sociales en Afrique Noire* [Reconstruct the History of African Societies: Promoting the Social Sciences in Black Africa], Paris: Harmattan.

Elias, N. (2000) *The Civilizing Process*, Oxford: Blackwell.

el-Malik, S. S. (2014) "Against Epistemic Totalitarianism: the Insurrectional Politics of Bessie Head," *Journal of Contemporary African Studies*, 32(4): 493-505.

Eltis, D. (2000) *The Rise of African Slavery in the Americas*, Cambridge: Cambridge University Press.

Eltis, D. and Richardson, D. (2008) *Extending the Frontiers: Essays on the New Transatlantic Slave Trade Database*, New Haven: Yale University Press.

Englund, H. (2004) "Cosmopolitanism and the devil in Malawi," *Ethnos*, 69(3): 293-316.

Englund, H. (2011) *Human Rights and African Airwaves: Mediating Equality on the Chichewa Radio*, Bloomington: Indiana University Press.

Englund, H. (2015a) "Forget the Poor Radio Kinship and Exploited Labor in Zambia," *Current Anthropology*, 56(11): S137-S145.

Englund, H. (2015b) "Multivocal morality Narrative, Sentiment, and Zambia's Radio Grandfathers," *Hau: Journal of Ethnographic Theory*, 5 (2): 251-273.

Eze, E. C. (ed) (1997) *Postcolonial African Philosophy: A Critical Reader*, Oxford: Blackwell Publishers.

Fadipe, N. A. (1970) *The Sociology of the Yoruba*, Ibadan: Ibadan University Press.

Falola, T. and Jennings, C. (eds) (2002) *Africanizing Knowledge: African Studies Across the Disciplines*, New Brunswick, NJ: Transaction.

Fanon, F. (1967a) *The Wretched of the Earth*, Harmondsworth: Penguin.

Fanon, F. (1967b) *Black Skin, White Masks*, New York: Grove.

Fardon, R. and la Rouge, S. (2017) *Learning from the Curse: Sembene's Xala*, London: Hurst Publishers.

Ferguson, J. (1990) *The Anti-Politics Machine: 'Development,' Depoliticization and Bureaucratic Power in Lesotho*, Cambridge: Cambridge University Press.

Ferguson, J. (1999) *Expectations of Modernity: Myths and Meanings of Urban Life on the Zambian Copperbelt*. Berkeley, CA: University of California Press.

Ferguson, J. (2006) *Global Shadows: Africa in the Neoliberal World Order*, Durham, NC: Duke University Press.

Ferguson, J. (2015) *Give a Man a Fish: Reflections on the New Politics of Distribution*, Durham: Duke University Press.

Fine, G. (1993) *On Ideas: Aristotle's Criticism of Plato's Theory of Forms*, Oxford: Oxford University Press.

Fishkin, B. H. Ankumah, A. T. and Ndi, B. F. (eds) (2014) *Fears, Doubts and Joys of Not Belonging*, Bamenda: Langaa RPCIG.

Fisiy, C. and Geschiere, P. (1996) "Witchcraft, violence and identity: different trajectories in postcolonial Cameroon," In: R. Werbner and T. Ranger (eds) *Postcolonial Identities in Africa*, London: Zed Books.

Fisiy, C. F. and Geschiere, P. (2001) "Witchcraft, development and paranoia in Cameroon: interactions between popular, academic and state discourse," In: Moore H, Sanders T (eds) *Magical Interpretations, Material Realities: Modernity, Witchcraft and the Occult in Postcolonial Africa*, London: Routledge, pp. 226-246.

Fonlon, B. (1965) "Idea of culture I," *ABBIA: Cameroon Cultural Review*, 11: 5-29.

Fonlon, B. (1967) "Idea of culture II," *ABBIA: Cameroon Cultural Review*, 16: 5-24.

Fonlon, B. (1978) *The Genuine Intellectual*, Yaounde: Buma Kor.

Foucault, M. (1975) *Surveiller et Punir*, Paris: Gallimard.

Foucault, M. (1988) "Technologies of the Self," In: Martin, L.H., Gutman, H. and Hutton, P. H. (eds): *Technologies of the Self: A Seminar with Michel Foucault*, Amherst: University of Massachusetts Press, pp. 16-49.

Foucault, M. (1995) *Discipline and Punish: The Birth of the Prison*, New York: Vintage Books.

Fouet, F. and Renaudeau, R. (eds) (1976) *Littérature Africaine: L'Engagement*, Dakar: Les Nouvelles Éditions Africaines.

Fouet, F. and Renaudeau, R. (eds) (1980) *Littérature Africaine: Le Déracinement*, Dakar: Les Nouvelles Éditions Africaines.

Freud, S. (1957) *Civilization and its Discontents*, London: The Hogarth Press.

Gareau, F. H. (1987) "Expansion and increasing diversification of the universe of social science," *International Social Science Journal*, 114: 595-606.

Garuba, H. (2003) "Explorations in Animist Materialism: Notes on Reading/Writing African Literature, Culture, and Society," *Public Culture*, 15(2): 261-285.

Garuba, H. (2013) "On Animism, Modernity/Colonialism and the African Order of Knowledge: Provisional Reflections," In: Green, Lesley (ed.): *Contested Ecologies: Dialogues in the South on Nature and Knowledge*, Cape Town: HSRC Press, pp. 42-51.

Geertz, C. (2000[1973]) *The Interpretation of Cultures*, New York: Basic Books.

Gerdes, P. (1999) *Geometry from Africa: Mathematical and Educational Explorations*, Washington, DC: Mathematical Association of America.

Gerdes, P. (2007) *Sona Geometry from Angola: Mathematics of an African Tradition*, Milan: Polimetrica.

Gerdes, P. (2008) *African Basketry: A Gallery of Twill-Plaited Designs and Patterns*, Available at: www. Lulu.com, accessed 16 April 2011.

Geschiere, P. (1995) *Sorcellerie et Politique en Afrique: La Viande des Autres*, Paris: Karthala.

Geschiere, P. (1997) *The Modernity of Witchcraft: Politics and the Occult in Postcolonial Africa*, Charlottesville: University of Virginia Press.

Geschiere, P. (2009) *The Perils of Belonging: Autochthony, Citizenship, and Exclusion in Africa and Europe*, Chicago, IL: University of Chicago Press.

Geschiere, P. (2013) *Witchcraft, Intimacy, and Trust: Africa in Comparison*, Chicago: University of Chicago Press.

Geschiere, P. and Nyamnjoh, F.B. (1998) "Witchcraft as an Issue in the 'Politics of Belonging': Democratization and Urban Migrants' Involvement with the Home Village," *African Studies Review*, 41 (3): 69-91.

Geschiere, P. and Nyamnjoh, F.B. (2000) "Capitalism and Autochthony: The Seesaw of Mobility and Belonging," In: "Millennium Capitalism and the Culture of Neoliberalism," *Public Culture 2000*, (eds.) Jean and John Comaroff, 12(2): 423-452.

Gibson, N. (2016) "The specter of Fanon: the student movements and the rationality of revolt in South Africa," *Social Identities*, DOI: 10.1080/13504630.2016.1219123.

Gordon, R. J. (2013) "Not Studying White, Up or Down, but Around Southern Africa: A Response to Francis Nyamnjoh," *Africa Spectrum*, 48(2): 117-121.

Grinker, R. Lubkemann, S. C. and Steiner, C. B. (eds) (2010) *Perspectives on Africa: A Reader in Culture, History, and Representations*, Oxford: Wiley-Blackwell.

Gugler, J. (2003) *African Film: Re-Imagining a Continent*, Bloomington: Indiana University Press.

Gulley, N. (1962) *Plato's Theory of Knowledge*, London: Methuen and Co. Ltd.

Gumede, W. and Dikeni, L. (eds) (2009) *The Poverty of Idea: South African Democracy and the Retreat of Intellectuals*, Johannesburg: Jacana.

Gupta, A. and Ferguson, J. (1997) "Discipline and Practice: 'The Field' as Site, Method, and Location in Anthropology," In: Gupta A, Ferguson J (eds) *Anthropological Locations: Boundaries and Grounds of a Field Science*, Berkeley, CA: University of California Press, 1-46.

Guyer, J. I. (2015a) "Response: one confusion after another: 'Slander' in Amos Tutuola's Pauper, Brawler and Slanderer (1987)," *Social Dynamics: A Journal of African Studies*, 41(1): 69-72.

Guyer, J. I. (2015b) "Introduction to the question: is confusion a form?," *Social Dynamics: A Journal of African Studies*, 41(1): 1-16.

Hall, S. (ed.) (1997) *Representation: Culture Representations and Signifying Practices*, London: Sage.

Hall, S. (2010) "Foreword," In: Anheier H and Isar R. Y. (eds) *Cultural Expression, Creativity & Innovation*, Los Angeles, CA: Sage Publications, pp. ix-xii.

Hare, N. (1991[1965]) *The Black Anglo-Saxons*, Chicago: Third World Press.

Harrison, F. V. (2008) *Outsider Within: Reworking Anthropology in the Global Age*, Urbana: University of Illinois Press.

Hart, K. (2007) "Marcel Mauss: In Pursuit of the Whole. A Review," *Comparative Studies in Society and History*, 49(2): 473-485.

Hart, S. M. (2007) "Magical Realism in the Americas: Politicised Ghosts in *One Hundred Years of Solitude*, *The House of Spirits*, and *Beloved*," In: Harold Bloom (ed), *Bloom's Modern Critical Views": Gabriel García Márquez. Updated Edition*, pp. 83-93.

Hartnack, A. (2013) "On Gaining Access: A Response to Francis Nyamnjoh's 'Blinded by Sight: Divining the Future of Anthropology in Africa,'" *Africa Spectrum*, 48(1): 107-112.

Hawking, S. W. (1988) *A Brief History of Time: From the Big Bang to Black Holes*, London: Guild.

Hountondji, P. J. (1980[1976]) *Sur la 'Philosophie Africaine'* Yaounde: Edition CLE.

Hountondji, P. J. (ed.) (1997) *Endogenous Knowledge: Research Trails*. Dakar: CODESRIA.

Hountondji, P. J. (2002) *The Struggle for Meaning: Reflections on Philosophy, Culture, and Democracy in Africa*, Athens, OH: Ohio University Press.

Hountondji, P. J. (ed) (2007) *La Rationalité, Une ou Plurielle?* Dakar: CODESRIA.

Howatson, M. C. and Sheffield, F. C. C. (eds) (2008) *Plato: The Symposium*, Cambridge: Cambridge University Press.

Hughes, A. L. (2012) "The Folly of Scientism," *The New Atlantis*, Number 37, pp.32-50.

Ignatieff, M. (1993) *Blood and Belonging: Journeys into the New Nationalism*, New York: Farrar, Straus and Giroux.

Imam, A. (1997) "Engendering African Social Sciences: An Introductory Essay," In: Imam A, Mama A, Sow F (eds) *Engendering African Social Sciences*, Dakar: CODESRIA, pp. 1-30.

Imam, A. Mama, A. and Sow, F. (eds) (1997) *Engendering African Social Sciences*, Dakar: CODESRIA.

Irele, F. A. (2001) *The African Imagination: Literature in Africa and the Black Diaspora*, Oxford: Oxford University Press.

Jacobson, D. (1991) *Reading Ethnography*, New York: SUNY.

Jansen, J. (2011) *We Need to Talk*, Northlands: Bookstorm & Pan Macmillan.

Jeater, D. (2007) *Law, Language and Science: The Invention of the 'Native Mind' in Southern Rhodesia, 1890-1930*, Portsmouth: Heinemann.

Jeyifo, B. (ed.) (2002) *Modern African Drama*, New York: W.W. Norton and Company.

Jones, E. (1975[1966]) *"The Palm Wine Drinkard:* Fourteen Years On," In: Bernth Lindfors (ed.), *Critical Perspectives on Amos Tutuola*, Boulder: Three Continents Press, pp. 109-113.

Kamau, K. and Mitambo, K. (eds) (2016) *Coming of Age. Strides in African Publishing Essays in Honour of Dr Henry Chakava at 70*, Nairobi: East African Educational Publishers.

Killam, G. D. (1968) *Africa in English Fiction: 1874-1939*, Ibadan: Ibadan University Press.

Ki-Zerbo, J. (1990) *Educate or Perish: Africa's Impasse and Prospects*, Abidjan: UNESCO/UNICEF.

Ki-Zerbo, J. (1992) "Le Developpement Clès en Tête," In: Joseph Ki-Zerbo (ed), *La Natte des Autres: Pour un Développement Endogène en Afrique* [The Key to Development, Dakar: CODESRIA, pp. 1-71.

Ki-Zerbo, J. (2003) *A Quand L'Afrique? Entretien avec René Holenstein*, Paris: Edition de l'Aube.

Ki-Zerbo, J. (2010[1972]) *Education et Développement en Afrique Cinquante Ans de Réflexion et d'Action*, Ouagadougou: Fondation pour l'Histoire et le développement endogène de l'Afrique.

Konings, P. (2011) *Crisis and Neoliberal Reforms in Africa. Civil Society and Agro-Industry in Anglophone Cameroon's Plantation Economy*, Bamenda: Langaa/ASC.

Krings, M. and Okome, O. (eds) (2013) *Global Nollywood: The Transnational Dimensions of an African Video Film Industry*, Bloomington: Indiana University Press.

Kuhn, T.S. (1970[1962]) *The Structure of Scientific Revolutions*, Chicago: The University of Chicago Press.

Laburthe-Tolra, P. (1981) *Les Seigneurs de la Forêt: Essai sur le Passé Historique, l'Organisation Sociale et les Norrnes Ethiques des Anciens Beti du Cameroun*, Paris: Publications de la Sorbonne.

Laburthe-Tolra, P. (1985) *Initiations et Sociétés au Cameroun: Essai sur la Religion Beti*, Paris. Karthala.

Larson, C.R. (1975[1972]) "Time, Space and Description: The Tutuolan World," In: Bernth Lindfors (ed.), *Critical Perspectives on Amos Tutuola*, Boulder: Three Continents Press, pp. 171-181.

Larson, CR. (2001) *The Ordeal of the African Writer*, London: Zed Books.

Lauer, H. and Anyidoho, K. (eds), (2012a) *Reclaiming the Human Sciences and Humanities through African Perspectives, Volume I*, Accra: Sub-Saharan Publishers.

Lauer, H. and Anyidoho, K. (eds), (2012b) *Reclaiming the Human Sciences and Humanities through African Perspectives, Volume II*, Accra: Sub-Saharan Publishers.

Lennon, K. (2004) "Feminist Epistemology," in: Niiniluoto, H., Sintonen, M. and Wolenski, J., (eds), *Handbook of Epistemology*, Dordrecht: Springer Science+Business Media Dordrecht, 1013-1026.

Levi-Strauss, C. (1966) *The Savage Mind*, Chicago: University of Chicago Press.

Lindfors, B. (1970) "Amos Tutuola: Debts and Assets," *Cahiers d'Études Africaines*, 10(38): 306-334.

Lindfors, B. (ed.) (1975) *Critical Perspectives on Amos Tutuola*, Boulder: Three Continents Press.

Lindfors, B. (1989) "Foreword," Amos Tutuola, *The Wild Hunter in the Bush of the Ghosts*, Washington D.C.: Three Continents Press, p. iii.

Lindfors, B. (1989) "Blurb," Amos Tutuola, *The Wild Hunter in the Bush of the Ghosts*, Washington D.C.: Three Continents Press, p. iv.

Lindfors, B. (1999a) "Amos Tutuola's Search for a Publisher," in: Lindfors, B. (sole author), *The Blind Men and the Elephant and Other Essays in Biographical Criticism*, Trenton: Africa World Press, pp. 109-133.

Lindfors, B. (1999b) "A 'Proper Farewell' to Amos Tutuola," in: Lindfors, B. (sole author), *The Blind Men and the Elephant and Other Essays in Biographical Criticism*. Trenton: Africa World Press, pp. 135-146.

Lindfors, B. (1999c) *The Blind Men and the Elephant and Other Essays in Biographical Criticism*, Trenton: Africa World Press.

Lindfors, B. (1999d) "The Blind Men and the Elephant," in: Lindfors, B. (sole author), *The Blind Men and the Elephant and Other Essays in Biographical Criticism*, Trenton: Africa World Press, pp. 1-16.

Liyong, T.L. (1975[1968]) "Tutuola, Son of Zinjanthropus" In: Bernth Lindfors (ed.), *Critical Perspectives on Amos Tutuola*, Boulder: Three Continents Press, pp. 115-122.

Lock, M. and Farquhar, J. (eds) (2007) *Beyond the Body Proper*, Durham: Duke University Press.

Lorentzon, L. (2013) "'But it will have to be a new English' A Comparative Discussion of the 'Nativization' of English among Afro- and Indo-English Authors," in: Bernth Lindfors and Geoffrey V. Davis (eds) *African Literature and Beyond: A Florilegium*, Amsterdam: Editions Rodopi. Pp. 301-315.

Losambe, L. (2005) *Borderline Movements in African Fiction*, Trenton: Africa World Press.

Lovejoy, P. E. (2011) *Transformations in Slavery: A History of Slavery in Africa (African Studies)*, Cambridge: Cambridge University Press.

Machirori, F. (2011) "Incompletely me," *Mail & Guardian*, 18 March, 45-46. Available at: http://mg.co.za/article/2011-03-18-incompletely-me, accessed 18 March 2011.

MacClancy, J. and Fuentes, A. (2011) "Centralizing Fieldwork," In: J. MacClancy and A. Fuentes, (eds.) *Centralizing Fieldwork: Critical Perspectives from Primatology, Biological and Social Anthropology*, New York: Berghahn Books, 1-26.

Maclure, R. (ed.) (1997) *Overlooked and Undervalued: A Synthesis of ERNWACA Reviews on the State of Education Research in West and Central Africa*, Support for Analysis and Research in Africa (SARA), Bamako, Mali.

Mafe, D. A. (2012) "Ghostly Girls in the 'Eerie Bush': Helen Oyeyemi's the Icarus Girl as Postcolonial Female Gothic Fiction," *Research in African Literatures*, 43(3): 21-35.

Mafeje, A. (1988) "Culture and development in Africa: The missing link," *CODESRIA Bulletin*, 1: 7-8.

Mafeje, A. (1998) "Anthropology and Independent Africans: Suicide or end of an era?," *African Sociological Review*, 2(1): 1–43.

Magubane, B. (1971) "A Critical Look at Indices Used in the Study of Social Change in Colonial Africa," *Current Anthropology*, 12(4/5): 419-445.

Magubane, B. (2010) *My Life and Times*, Scottsville: University of KwaZulu-Natal Press.

Magubane, Z. (2004) *Bringing the Empire Home: Race, Class, and Gender in Britain and Colonial South Africa*, Chicago, IL: University of Chicago Press.

Malusi, and Mpumlwana, T. (eds) (1996) *Steve Biko: I Write What I Like*, Randburg: Raven.

Mama, A. (2007) "Is it ethical to study Africa? Preliminary thoughts on scholarship and freedom," *African Studies Review*, 50(1): 1–26.

Mama, A. and Hamilton, G. (2003) *Envisioning the African University of the Future*, Nairobi: Ford Foundation.

Mamdani, M. (1990) *The Intelligentsia, the State and Social Movements: Some Reflections on Experiences in Africa*, Kampala: Centre for Basic Research.

Mamdani, M. (1993) University crisis and reform: A reflection on the African experience, *Review of African Political Economy*, 58: 7-19.

Mamdani, M. (1996) *Citizen and Subject: Contemporary Africa and the Legacy of Late Colonialism*, London: James Currey.

Mamdani, M. (1998), *When Does a Settler Become a Native? Reflections of the Colonial Roots of Citizenship in Equatorial and South Africa*, Inaugural Lecture as A.C. Jordon Professor of African Studies, University of Cape Town, 13 May, Cape Town: University of Cape Town, Department of Communication.

Mamdani, M. (2007) *Scholars in the Marketplace: The Dilemmas of Neo-Liberal Reform at Makerere University, 1989-2005*, Dakar: CODESRIA.

Mamdani, M. (2009) "African Intellectuals and Identity: Overcoming the Political Legacy of Colonialism," In: William Gumede and Leslie Dikeni (eds.), *The Poverty of Ideas: South African Democracy and the Retreat of Intellectuals*, Johannesburg: Jacana, 122-142.

Martin, L. H. Gutman, H. Hutton, P. H. (eds., 1988) *Technologies of the Self: A Seminar with Michel Foucault*, Amherst: University of Massachusetts Press.

Masolo, D. A. (2010) *Self and Community in a Changing World*, Bloomington: Indiana University Press.

Mauss, M. (1973) "Techniques of the Body," *Economy and Society*, 2(1): 70-88.

Mavhungu, K. (2012) *Witchcraft in Post-colonial Africa. Beliefs, Techniques and Containment Strategies*, Bamenda: Langaa RPCIG.

Mawere, M. (2015) *Humans, Other Beings and the Environment: Harurwa (Edible Stinkburgs) and Environmental Conservation in Southeastern Zimbabwe*, Cambridge: Cambridge Scholars Publishing.

Maynard, K. and Cahnmann-Taylor, M. (2010) "Anthropology at the Edge of Words: Where Poetry and Ethnography Meet," *Anthropology and Humanism*, 35(1): 2-19.

Mazrui, A. (1986) *The Africans: A Triple Heritage*, London: BBC.

Mazrui, A. (1994) "Development in a Multi-Cultural Context: Trends and Tensions," In: I. Serageldin and J. Taboroff, eds., *Culture and Development in Africa*, Washington D.C., The World Bank, pp. 127-136.

Mazrui, A. (2001) The African renaissance: A triple legacy of skills, values and gender. In: Saxena SC (ed.) *Africa Beyond 2000*. Delhi: Kalinga, 29–59.

Mbembe, A. (1997) "The 'Thing' and Its Double in Cameroonian Cartoons," In: Barber K (ed.) *Readings in African Popular Culture*, Oxford: James Currey.

Mbembe, A. (2000a) *De la Postcolonie: Essai sur l'Imagination Politique dans l'Afrique Contemporaine [The Postcolony: An Essay on Political Imagination in Contemporary Africa]*. Paris: Karthala.

Mbembe, A. (2000b) "African Modes of Self-Writing," *Identity Culture and Politics: An Afro-Asian Dialogue*, 2(2): 1-35.

Mbembe, A. (2002) "African Modes of Self-Writing," *Public Culture* 14(1):239-273.

Mbembe, A. (2003) "Life, Sovereignty, and Terror in the Fiction of Amos Tutuola," *Research in African Literatures*, 34(4): 1-26.

Mbembe, A. (2008) "Passages to Freedom: The Politics of Racial Reconciliation in South Africa," *Public Culture*, 20(1): 5-18.

Mbembe, A. (2010) *Sortir de la Grande Nuit: Essai sur l'Afrique Décolonisée*, Paris: La Découverte.

Mbembe, A. (2013a) *Critique de la Raison Nègre*, Paris: La Découverte.

Mbembe, A. (2013b) "*From* Life, Sovereignty, and Terror in the Fiction of Amos Tutuola," In: Blanco, M. D. P. and Peeren, E. (eds) (2013), *The Spectralities Reader: Ghosts and Haunting in Contemporary Cultural Theory*, London: Bloomsbury, pp. 131-149.

Mentan, T. (2010a) *The New World Order Ideology and Africa. Understanding and Appreciating Ambiguity, Deceit and Recapture of Decolonized Spaces*, Bamenda: Langaa.

Mentan, T. (2010b) *The State in Africa. An Analysis of Impacts of Historical Trajectories of Global Capitalist Expansion and Domination in the Continent*, Bamenda: Langaa.

Meyer, B. (2003) "Visions of Blood, Sex and Money: Fantasy Spaces in Popular Ghanaian Cinema," *Visual Anthropology*, 16(1): 15-41.

Meyer, B. (2006) "Impossible Representations: Pentecostalism, Vision, and Video Technology in Ghana," In: Meyer, B. and Moors, A (eds). (2006) *Religion, Media and the Public Sphere*, Bloomington: Indiana University Press, pp. 290-312.

Meyer, B. (eds) (2009) *Aesthetic Formations: Media, Religion, and the Senses*, New York: Palgrave Macmillan.

Meyer, B. (2010) "'There Is a Spirit in that Image': Mass-Produced Jesus Pictures and Protestant-Pentecostal Animation in Ghana," *Comparative Studies in Society and History*, 52(1): 100-130.

Meyer, B. (2015) *Sensational Movies: Video, Vision, and Christianity in Ghana*, California: University of California Press.

Meyer, B. and Moors, A. (eds). (2006) *Religion, Media and the Public Sphere*, Bloomington: Indiana University Press.

Mkandawire, T. (1997) "The social sciences in Africa: Breaking local barriers and negotiating international presence. The Bashorun MKO Abiola distinguished lecture presented to the 1996 African studies association annual meeting," *African Studies Review*, 40(2): 15-36.

Mkandawire, T. (ed.) (2005) *African Intellectuals: Rethinking Politics, Language, Gender and Development*, Dakar: CODESRIA/Zed.

Mngxitama, A. Alexander, A. and Gibson, N.C. (eds) (2008a) *Biko Lives! Contesting the Legacies of Steve Biko*, New York: Palgrave MacMillan.

Mngxitama, A. Alexander, A. and Gibson, N.C. (2008b) 'Biko lives. In: Mngxitama, A. Alexander, A. Gibson, N.C. (eds) *Biko Lives! Contesting the Legacies of Steve Biko*, New York: Palgrave MacMillan, 1-20.

Moore, G. (1975[1957]) "Amos Tutuola: A Nigerian Visionary," In: Bernth Lindfors (ed.), *Critical Perspectives on Amos Tutuola*, Boulder: Three Continents Press, pp. 50-57.

Moore, H.L and Sanders, T. (eds) (2001) *Magical Interpretations, Material Realities: Modernity, Witchcraft and the Occult in Postcolonial Africa*, London: Routledge.

Mphahlele, E. (1972[1967]) *Voices in the Whirlwind and Other Essays*, New York: Palgrave MacMillan.

Mudimbe, V. Y. (1988) *The Invention of Africa: Gnosis, Philosophy, and the Order of Knowledge*, London: James Currey.

Mudimbe-Boyi, E. (ed) (2002) *Beyond Dichotomies: Histories, Identities, Cultures, and the Challenge of Globalization*, New York: State University of New York Press.

Murphy, D. (2000) *Sembene: Imagining Alternatives in Film & Fiction*, Oxford: James Currey.

Musisi, N.B. (1992) "Colonial and missionary education: Women and domesticity in Uganda, 1900–1945," In: Hansen, K. T. (ed.) *African Encounters with Domesticity*. New Brunswick, NJ: Rutgers University Press, pp. 172-194.

Myambo, M. T. (2014) "Imagining a Dialectical African Modernity: Achebe's Ontological Hopes, Sembene's Machines, Mda's Epistemological Redness," *Journal of Contemporary African Studies*, 32(4): 457-473.

Nabudare, D. W. (2006) "Towards an Afrokology of knowledge production and regeneration," *International Journal of African Renaissance Studies,* 1(1): 7-32.

Ndi, B.F. (ed) (2015) *Secrets, Silences and Betrayals,* Bamenda: Langaa RPCIG.

Ndjio, B. (2005) "Carrefour de la Joie: Popular Deconstruction of the African Postcolonial Public Sphere," *Africa,* 75(3): 265-294.

Ndlovu-Gatsheni, S. J. (2013a) *Coloniality of Power in Postcolonial Africa: Myths of Decolonization,* Dakar: CODESRIA.

Ndlovu-Gatsheni, S. J. (2013b) *Empire, Global Coloniality and African Subjectivity,* New York: Berghahn.

Naipaul, V. S. (2001) *Half a Life.* London: Picador.

Neumarkt, P. (1975[1971]) "Amos Tutuola: Emerging African Literature," In: Bernth Lindfors (ed.), *Critical Perspectives on Amos Tutuola,* Boulder: Three Continents Press, pp. 183-192.

Newell, S. (1996) "Constructions of Nigerian Women in Popular Literatures by Men," *African Languages and Cultures,* 9(2):169–188.

Newell, S. (2006) *West African Literatures: Ways of Reading,* Oxford: Oxford University Press.

Newell, S. (ed) (2017) *Writing African Women: Gender, Popular Culture and Literature in West Africa,* London: Zed Books.

Newell, S. and Okome, O. (eds), (2013) *Popular Culture in Africa: The Episteme of the Everyday,* London: Routledge.

Ngugi wa Thiong'o, (1986) *Decolonising the Mind: The Politics of Language in African Literature,* London: James Currey.

Ngugi wa Thiong'o, (1997) "Detained: A Writer's Prison Diary," In: Grinker RR, Steiner CB (eds) *Perspectives on Africa: A Reader in Culture, History, and Representation,* Oxford: Blackwell, pp. 613-622.

Ngugi wa Thiong'o, (2005) "Europhone or African Memory: The Challenge of the Pan-Africanist Intellectual in the Era of Globalization," In: Mkandawire T (ed.) *African Intellectuals: Rethinking Politics, Language, Gender and Development,* Dakar/London: CODESRIA/Zed, pp. 155-164.

Niehaus, I. (2001) "Witchcraft in the new South Africa: from colonial superstition to postcolonial reality?," In: Moore H, Sanders T (eds) *Magical Interpretations, Material Realities: Modernity, Witchcraft and the Occult in Postcolonial Africa,* London: Routledge, 184-205.

Niehaus, I. (2013) "Anthropology and Whites in South Africa: Response to an Unreasonable Critique," *Africa Spectrum*, 48(1): 117-127.

Niiniluoto, H. Sintonen, M. and Wolenski, J. (2004) "Foreword," in: Niiniluoto, H. Sintonen, M. and Wolenski, J. (eds), *Handbook of Epistemology*, Dordrecht: Springer Science+Business Media Dordrecht, pp. vii-viii.

Nkwi, P. N. (1998) "The Status of Anthropology in Post-Independent Africa: Some Reflections on Archie Mafeje's Perceptions," *African Sociological Review*, 2(1): 57-66.

Nnaemeka, O. (2005) "Bringing African Women into the Classroom: Rethinking Pedagogy and Epistemology," In: Oyewumi, O. (ed.) *African Gender Studies: A Reader*, New York: Palgrave Macmillan, pp. 51-65.

Nnamani, U. Emejulu, O. and Amadi, A. I. (2014) "Cultural Disclaimer and Literary Sterility: Domestication of the English Language in Gabriel Okara's the Voice, Chinua Achebe's Things Fall Apart, and Amos Tutuola's the Palm Wine Drinkers," *Research on Humanities and Social Sciences*, 4(20): 18-22.

Nossal, K.R. (1998) "Tales that textbooks tell: Ethnocentricity and diversity in American introductions to international relations," Available at: http://socserv2.socsci.mcmaster.ca/~polisci/faulty/nossal/tales.htm, accessed 7 August 2001.

Notué, J. P. and Triaca, B. (2005) *Mankon: Arts, Heritage and Culture from the Mankon Kingdom*, Milan: 5 Continents Edition.

Ntarangwi, M. (2010) *Reversed Gaze: An African Ethnography of American Anthropology*, Urbana: University of Illinois Press.

Ntarangwi, M. Mills, D. and Babiker, M. (eds.) (2006) *African Anthropologies: History, Critique and Practice*, Dakar: CODESRIA.

Nwagwu, W.E. (2015) "Counterpoints about Predatory Open Access and Knowledge Publishing in Africa," *Learned Publishing*, 28(2): 114-122.

Nwagwu, W. E. and Ojemeni, O. (2015) "Penetration of Nigerian Predatory Biomedical Open Access Journals 2007-2012: A Bibliometric Study," *Learned Publishing*, 28(1): 23-34.

Nyamnjoh, F. B. (2001) "Delusions of development and the enrichment of witchcraft discourses in Cameroon," In: Moore H, Sanders T (eds) *Magical Interpretations, Material Realities: Modernity, Witchcraft and the Occult in Postcolonial Africa*, London: Routledge, 28-49.

Nyamnjoh, F.B. (2002) "'A Child is One Person's only in the Womb': Domestication, Agency and Subjectivity in the Cameroonian Grassfields," In: R. Werbner, (ed.), *Postcolonial Subjectivities in Africa*, London: Zed Books, pp. 111-138.

Nyamnjoh, F. B. (2002) "Local Attitudes Towards Citizenship and Foreigners in Botswana: An Appraisal of Recent Press Stories. *Journal of Southern African Studies,* 28(4): 751-771.

Nyamnjoh, F. B. (2004a) "A Relevant Education for African Development – Some Epistemological Considerations," *African Development,* 23(1): 161-184.

Nyamnjoh, F. B. (2004b) "From Publish or Perish to Publish and Perish: What 'Africa's 100 Best Books' Tell Us about Publishing Africa," *Journal of Asian and African Studies,* 39(5): 331-355.

Nyamnjoh, F. B. (2005a) "Images of Nyongo amongst Bamenda Grassfielders in Whiteman Kontri," *Citizenship Studies,* 9(3): 241-269.

Nyamnjoh, F. B. (2005b) *Africa's Media, Democracy and the Politics of Belonging,* London: Zed Books.

Nyamnjoh, F. B. (2006a) *Insiders and Outsiders: Citizenship and Xenophobia in Contemporary Southern Africa,* Dakar/London: CODESRIA/Zed.

Nyamnjoh, F. B. (2006b) *A Nose for Money,* Nairobi: East African Educational Publishers.

Nyamnjoh, F. B. (2007[1995]) *The Disillusioned African.* Bamenda: Langaa RPCIG.

Nyamnjoh, F. B. (2009) *Married But Available,* Bamenda: Langaa RPCIG.

Nyamnjoh, F. B. (2011) "Cameroonian Bushfalling: Negotiation of Identity and Belonging in Fiction and Ethnography," *American Ethnologist,* 38(4): 701-713.

Nyamnjoh, F. B. (2012a) "Blinded by Sight: Divining the Future of Anthropology in Africa," *Africa Spectrum,* 47(2-3): 63-92.

Nyamnjoh, F. B. (2012b) "Intimate Strangers: Connecting Fiction and Ethnography," *Alternation,* 19(1): 65-92.

Nyamnjoh, F. B. (2012c) "Potted Plants in Greenhouses: A Critical Reflection on the Resilience of Colonial Education in Africa," *Journal of Asian and African Studies,* 47(2): 129-154.

Nyamnjoh, F. B. (2013a) "Fiction and Reality of Mobility in Africa," *Citizenship Studies,* 17(6-7): 653-680.

Nyamnjoh, F. B. (2013b) "From Quibbles to Substance: A Response to Responses," *Africa Spectrum,* 48(2):127-139.

Nyamnjoh, F. B. (2013c) "The Nimbleness of Being Fulani," *Africa Today,* 59(3): 105-134.

Nyamnjoh, F. B. (2015a) "Beyond an Evangelising Public Anthropology: Science, Theory and Commitment," *Journal of Contemporary African Studies,* 33(1): 48-63.

Nyamnjoh, F. B. (2015b) "Incompleteness: Frontier Africa and the Currency of Conviviality," *Journal of Asian and African Studies,* advance online publication, DOI: 10.1177/0021909615580867, 1-18.

Nyamnjoh, F. B. (2015c) *C'est l'homme qui fait l'homme: Cul-de-Sac Ubuntu-ism in Côte d'Ivoire,* Bamenda: Langaa RPCIG.

Nyamnjoh, F. B. (2015d) "Amos Tutuola and the Elusiveness of Completeness," *Stichproben. Wiener Zeitschrift für kritische Afrikastudien,* 15(29): 1-47.

Nyamnjoh, F. B. (2016) *#RhodesMustFall. Nibbling at Resilient Colonialism in South Africa,* Bamenda: Langaa RPCIG.

Nyamnjoh, F. B. and Fuh, D. (2014) "Africans Consuming Hair, Africans Consumed by Hair," *Africa Insight,* 44(1):52-68.

Nyamnjoh, H. M. (2014) *Bridging Mobilities: ICTs Appropriation by Cameroonians in South Africa and The Netherlands,* Bamenda/Leiden: Langaa.

Nyang, S.S. (1994) "The cultural consequences of development in Africa," In: Serageldin I, Taboroff, J (eds) *Culture and Development in Africa,* Washington, DC: World Bank, 429-446.

Obenga, T. (2001) *Le Sens de la Lutte Contre l'Africanisme Eurocentriste,* Paris: Khepera/Harmattan.

Obenga, T. (2004) *African Philosophy: The Pharaonic Period: 2780-330 BC,* Popenguine: Per Ankh.

Obiechina, E.N. (1975[1968]) "Amos Tutuola and the Oral Tradition," In: Bernth Lindfors (ed.), *Critical Perspectives on Amos Tutuola*, Boulder: Three Continents Press, pp. 123-144.

Odora Hoppers, C. (ed.), (2002) *Indigenous Knowledge and the Integration of Knowledge Systems: Towards a Philosophy of Articulation*, Claremont: New Africa Education.

Ogden, C. K. and Richards, I. A. (1923) *The Meaning of Meaning: A Study of the Influence of Language upon Thought and of the Science of Symbolism*, New York: Harcourt, Brace and Company.

Oguibe, L. (2004) *The Culture Game*. Minneapolis, MN: University of Minnesota Press.

Ogundipe-Leslie, O. (1975[1970]) "The Palm-Wine Drinkard: A Reassessment of Amos Tutuola," In: Bernth Lindfors (ed.), *Critical Perspectives on Amos Tutuola*, Boulder: Three Continents Press, pp. 145-153.

Okere, K. Njoku, A. and Devisch, R. (2005) "All knowledge is first of all local knowledge: An introduction," *Africa Development*, 30(3): 1-19.

Okolo, M. S. C. (2007) *African Literature as Philosophy*, London: Zed.

Okri, B. (1991) *The Famished Road*, London: Vintage.

Okri, B. (1996) *Astonishing the Gods*, London: Weidenfeld & Nicolson History.

Okwori, J. Z. (2003) "A Dramatized Society: Representing Rituals of Human Sacrifice as Efficacious Action in Nigerian Home-Video Movies," *Journal of African Cultural Studies*, 16(1): 7-23.

Olupona, J. K. (ed) (2004) *Beyond Primitivism: Indigenous Religious Traditions and Modernity*, New York: Routledge.

Oluskoshi, A. and Zeleza, P. T. (2004) "Conclusion: The African university in the twenty-first century: Future challenges and a research agenda," In: Zeleza, P. T, Olukoshi A. (eds) *African Universities in the Twenty-First Century: Volume II: Knowledge and Society*, Dakar: CODESRIA, pp. 595-617.

Onoge, O. F. (1974) "The Crisis of Consciousness in Modern African Literature: A Survey," *Canadian Journal of African Studies*, 8(2): 385-410.

Onyejekwe, O. O. (1993) "Some disturbing trends in tertiary education in Africa," In: De Villiers I (ed.) *Southern African Conference on the Restructuring of Education*, Pretoria: HSRC, 1-7.

Osha, S. (2013) "The Value of Outsiderdom, or, Anthropology's Folly," *Africa Spectrum*, 48(1): 129-134.

Owen, J. (2009) "Commentary on Messrs Petrus and Bogopa's Commentary 'South African Anthropologies at the Crossroads: A Commentary on the Status of Anthropologies in South Africa,'" *Anthropology Southern Africa*, 32(1-2): 90.

Owomoyela, O. (1997) "Amos Tutuola," In: C. Brian Cox (ed), *African Writers*, Volume II, New York: Charles Scribner's Sons, pp.865-878.

Oyewumi, O. (ed.) (2005) *African Gender Studies: A Reader*, New York: Palgrave Macmillan.

Parsons, N. (2002) "One Body Playing ManyParts-Ie Betjouana, el Negro, and il Bosquimano," *Pula: Botswana Journal of African Studies*, 16(1): 19-29.

Pax Academica, (African Journal of Academic Freedom) (2015) Special Issue on "Student and Scholar Protests in Africa," Numbers 1 and 2, 2015.

p'Bitek, O. (1984[1967]) *Song of Lawino; Song of Ocol*, Oxford: Heinemann.

p'Bitek, O. (1989[1966]) *Song of Lawino*, Nairobi: East African Educational Publishers.

Peel, J. D. Y. (1968) A*ladura: A Religious Movement among the Yoruba*, London: Oxford University Press.

Peel, J. D. Y. (2002) "Christianity and the Logic of Nationalist Assertion in Whole Soyinka's Ìsarà," In: Maxwell, D. with Lawrie, I. (eds) *Christianity and the African Imagination: Essays in Honour of Adrian Hastings*, Leiden: Brill.

Peeren, E. (2010) "Everyday Ghosts and the Ghostly Everyday in Amos Tutuola, Ben Okri, and Achille Mbembe," In: Blanco, M. D. P. and Peeren, E. (eds), *Popular Ghosts: The Haunted Spaces of Everyday Culture*, New York: The Continuum International Publishing Group Inc., pp. 106-117.

Petrus, T. S. and Bogopa, D. (2009) "South African Anthropologies at the Crossroads: A Commentary on the Status of

Anthropologies in South Africa," *Anthropology Southern Africa,* 32(1–2): 87–88.

Phiri, A. (2015) "Queer subjectivities in J.M. Coetzee's *Disgrace* and Chimamanda Ngozi Adichie's 'On Monday of Last Week,'" *Agenda,* 29(1): 155-163.

Piaget, J. (1972) *Psychology and Epistemology: Towards a Theory of Knowledge,* Harmonsworth: Penguin Books.

Pido, J.P.O. (1997) "Okot p'Bitek," In: C. Brian Cox (ed), *African Writers,* Volume II, New York: Charles Scribner's Sons, pp.669-683.

Pityana, B. N. Ramphele, M. Mpumlwana, M. and Wilson, L. (eds) (1991) *Bounds of Possibility: The Legacy of Steve Biko & Black Consciousness,* Cape Town: David Philip.

Plastow, J. (ed.) (2002) *African Theatre: Women,* Oxford: James Currey.

Plumelle-Uribe, R. A. (2001), *La Férocité Blanche: Des Non-Blancs aux Non-Aryens, ces Génocides Occultés de 1492 à nos Jours,* Paris: Albin Michel.

Polanyi, M. and Prosch, H. (1975) *Meaning,* Chicago: The University of Chicago Press.

Prah, K. (1998) African scholars and Africanist scholarship. *CODESRIA Bulletin,* 3-4: 25-31.

Priebe, R. (1975[1974]) "Tutuola, the Riddler," In: Bernth Lindfors (ed.), *Critical Perspectives on Amos Tutuola,* Boulder: Three Continents Press, pp. 265-273.

Quijano, A. (2000) "Coloniality of power, Eurocentrism, and Latin America," *Nepantla: Views from South,* 1(3): 533-580.

Ramose, M. B. (1999) *African Philosophy Through Ubuntu,* Harare: Mond Books.

Ramose, M. B. (2003) "Transforming Education in South Africa: Paradigm Shift or Change?," *South African Journal of Higher Education,* 17(3): 137–143. Available at: www.ajol.info/index.php/sajhe/article/view/25413, accessed 5 April 2011.

Ramose, M. B. (2004) "In Search of an African Philosophy of Education" *South African Journal of Higher Education,* 18(3): 138-160.

Ramose, M. B. (2010) "Learning Inspired Education," *Caribbean Journal of Philosophy,* 2(1). Available at: http://ojs.mona.uwi.edu/index.php/cjp/article/view/2507, accessed 5 April 2011.

Ramose, M. B. (2014) "Ubuntu: Affirming a Right and Seeking Remedies in South Africa," In: Leonhard Praeg and Siphokazi Magadla (eds), *Ubuntu: Curating the Archive,* Pietermaritzburg: University of KwaZulu-Natal Press, pp.121-136.

Ritzenthaler, R. and Ritzenthaler, P. (1962) *Cameroons Village: An Ethnography of the Bafut,* Milwaukee Public Museum Publications in Anthropology 8, Milwaukee: The North American Press.

Robinson, P. (1981) *Perspectives on the Sociology of Education: An Introduction.* London: Routledge and Kegan Paul.

Rodney, W. (2012[1972]) *How Europe Underdeveloped Africa,* Dakar: CODESRIA and Pambazuka Press.

Rooney, C. (2000) *African Literature, Animism and Politics,* London: Routledge.

Rosa, M. (2014) "Theories of the South: Limits and Perspectives of an Emergent Movement in Social Sciences," *Current Sociology Review,* 62(6): 851-867.

Roschenthaler, U. (2011) *Purchasing Culture: The Dissemination of Associations in the Cross River Region of Cameroon and Nigeria,* Trenton: Africa World Press.

Rosenau, P. M. (1992) *Post-Modernism and the Social Sciences: Insights, Inroads, and Intrusions,* Princeton: Princeton University Press.

Rowlands, M. (1995) "The material culture of success: ideals and life cycles in Cameroon," In: J. Friedman (ed.) *Consumption and Identity,* London: Harwood Press.

Rowlands, M. and Warnier, J.-P. (1988) "Sorcery, Power and the Modern State in Cameroon," *Man,* 23(1): 118-132.

Ruch, E. A. and Anyanwu, K. C. (1984) *African Philosophy: An Introduction to the Main Philosophical Trends in Contemporary Africa,* Rome: Catholic Book Agency – Officium Libri Catholici.

Ruthven, K. K. (1990[1984]) *Feminist Literary Studies: An Introduction,* Cambridge: Cambridge University Press.

Rwomire, A. (1992) "Education and development: African perspectives," *Prospects,* 22(2): 227-239.

Salpeteur, M. and Warnier, J.-P. (2013) "Looking for the Effects of Bodily Organs and Substances through Vernacular Public Autopsy in Cameroon," *Critical African Studies*, 5(3): 153-174.

Sanders, T. (2001) "Save Our Skins: Structural Adjustment, Morality and the Occult in Tanzania," In: Moore H, Sanders T (eds) *Magical Interpretations, Material Realities: Modernity, Witchcraft and the Occult in Postcolonial Africa*, London: Routledge, pp. 160-183.

Sanders, T. (2003) "New Answers to Old Questions: Tradition, Modernity, and Postcoloniality. Reconsidering Witchcraft: Postcolonial Africa and Analytic (Un)Certainties," *American Anthropologist*, 105(2): 338-352.

Sanders, T. (2008) *Beyond Bodies: Rainmaking and Sense Making in Tanzania*, Toronto: University of Toronto Press.

Santos, B. S. (2014) *Epistemologies of the South: Justice against Epistemicide*, Boulder, CO: Paradigm Publishers.

Şaul, M. and Austen, R. A. (2010) (eds) *Viewing African Cinema in the Twenty-First Century: Art Films and the Nollywood Video Revolution*, Athens: Ohio University Press.

Scheper-Hughes, N. and Lock, M. M. (1987) "The Mindful Body: A Prolegomenon to Future Work in Medical Anthropology," *Medical Anthropology Quarterly, New Series*, 1(1): 6-41.

Schipper, W. J. J. (1990a) "The white man is nobody's friend: European characters in African fiction," In: Schipper, W. J. J. Idema, W. L., Leyten, H. M. (eds) *White and Black: Imagination and Cultural Confrontation (Bulletin 320)*, Amsterdam: Royal Tropical Institute, pp. 31-53.

Schipper, W. J. J. (1990b) "Homo Caudatus: Imagination and power in the field of literature," In: Schipper, W. J. J., Idema, W. L., Leyten, H. M. (eds) *White and Black: Imagination and Cultural Confrontation (Bulletin 320)*, Amsterdam: Royal Tropical Institute, 11-30.

Senghor, L.S. (1977) *Liberté 3: Négritude et Civilisation de l'Universel*, Paris: Editions du Seuil.

Shapiro, M. (2004) *J. K. Rowling: The Wizard Behind Harry Potter*, New York: St. Martin's Griffin.

Sharp, J. (2008) "Mafeje and Langa: The Start of an Intellectual's Journey," *Africa Development*, 33(4):153-167.

Shaw, R. (2001) "Cannibal transformations: colonialism and commodification in the Sierra Leone hinterland," In: Moore H, Sanders T (eds) *Magical Interpretations, Material Realities: Modernity, Witchcraft and the Occult in Postcolonial Africa*, London: Routledge, 50-70.

Shilling, C. (2012[1993]) *The Body & Social Theory*, Los Angeles: Sage.

Shweder, R.A. and LeVine, R.A. (eds) (1984) *Culture Theory: Essays on Mind, Self, and Emotion*, Cambridge: Cambridge University Press.

Sithole, M. P. (2009) *Unequal Peers, The Politics of Discourse Management in the Social Sciences*, Pretoria: Africa Institute of South Africa.

Schneidermann, N. T. (2014) *Connectionwork: Making a Name in Uganda's Music Industry*, PhD thesis, Department for Culture and Society, Faculty of Arts, Aarhus University, Denmark.

Sokal, A. and Bricmont, J. (1998) *Intellectual Impostures*, London: Profile.

Soyinka, W. (1963) "From a Common Back Cloth: A Reassessment of the African Literary Image," *The American Scholar*, 32(3): 387-396.

Soyinka, W. (1976) *Myth, Literature and the African World*, Cambridge: Cambridge University Press.

Soyinka, W. (1981) *Aké: The Years of Childhood*, London: Rex Collings.

Soyinka, W. (1990) *Ìsarà: A voyage round 'Essay'*, London: Methuen.

Soyinka, W. (1994) "Culture, memory and development," In: Serageldin I, Taboroff J (eds) *Culture and Development in Africa*. Washington, DC: World Bank, 201-218.

Soyinka, W. (2013) *Of Africa*, New Haven: Yale University Press.

Soyinka, W. (2014) "Introduction: Sea Never Dry, Wine Never Dry," In: Tutuola, Amos (author): *The Palm-Wine Drinkard and his Dead Palm-Wine Tapster in the Dead's Town*, London: Faber and Faber, v-viii.

Steinhart, E. I. (2006) *Black Poachers, White Hunters: A Social History of Hunting in Colonial Kenya*, Oxford: James Currey.

Stevenson, R. L. (1999[1886]) *Dr. Jekyll and Mr. Hyde*, Irvine, CA: Saddleback Educational Publishing.

Stoller, P. (1989) *The Taste of Ethnographic Things: The Senses in Anthropology*, Philadelphia: University of Pennsylvania Press.

Stoller, P. (1997) *Sensuous Scholarship*, Philadelphia: University of Pennsylvania Press.

Stoller, P. (2002) *Money Has No Smell: The Africanization of New York*, Chicago: Chicago University Press.

Stoller, P. (2008) *The Power of the Between: An Anthropological Odyssey*, Chicago: Chicago University Press.

Stoller, P. (2016) *The Sorcerer's Burden: The Ethnographic Saga of a Global Family*, New York: Palgrave Macmillan.

Stoller, P. and Olkes, C. (1987) *In Sorcery's Shadow: A Memoir of Apprenticeship among the Songhay of Niger*, Chicago: Chicago University Press.

Sullivan, J. (2006) "Redefining the Novel in Africa," *Research in African Literatures* 37(4):177-188.

Sutherland-Addy, E. and Diaw, A. (eds) (2005) *Women Writing Africa: West Africa and the Sahel*, New York: The Feminist Press at the City University of New York.

Tabron, J.L. (2003) *Postcolonial Literature from Three Continents: Tutuola, H.D., Ellison, and White*, New York: Peter Lang.

Taylor, C. (2007) *A Secular Age*, Cambridge Massachusetts: The Belknap Press of Harvard University Press.

Tazanu, P. M. (2012) *Being Available and Reachable. New Media and Cameroonian Transnational Sociality*, Bamenda: Langaa.

TED Conferences (2009): "Chimamanda Adichie: The Danger of a Single Story," https://www.ted.com/talks/chimamanda_adichie_the_danger_of_a_single_story, accessed 25 February, 2010.

Tcheuyap, A. (ed.) (2005) *Cinema and Social Discourse in Cameroon*, Bayreuth: Bayreuth African Studies.

Tcheuyap, A. (2011) *Postnationalist African Cinemas*, Manchester: Manchester University Press.

Teppo, A. (2013) "'Poor Whites' Do Matter, *Africa Spectrum*, 48(2): 123-126.

Tobias, S. M. (1999) "Amos Tutuola and the Colonial Carnival," *Research in African Literatures*, 30(2): 66-74.

Tschemplik, A. (2008) *Knowledge and Self-Knowledge in Plato's Theaetetus*, Plymouth: Lexington Books.

Turnball, C. M. (1961) *The Forest People*, London: The Reprint Society.

Tutuola, A. (1952) *The Palm-Wine Drinkard*, London: Faber and Faber.
Tutuola, A. (1954) *My Life in the Bush of Ghosts*, London: Faber and Faber.
Tutuola, A. (1955) *Simbi and the Satyr of the Dark Jungle*, London: Faber and Faber.
Tutuola, A. (1958) *The Brave African Huntress*, London: Faber and Faber.
Tutuola, A. (1962) *Feather Woman of the Jungle*, London: Faber and Faber.
Tutuola, A. (1967) *Ajaiyi and His Inherited Poverty*, London: Faber and Faber.
Tutuola, A. (1981) *The Witch-Herbalist of the Remote Town*, London: Faber and Faber.
Tutuola, A. (1986) *Yoruba Folktales*, Ibadan: University of Ibadan Press.
Tutuola, A. (1989 [1982]) *The Wild Hunter in the Bush of the Ghosts*, Washington D.C.: Three Continents Press.
Tutuola, A. (1987) *Pauper, Brawler and Slanderer*, London: Faber and Faber.
Tutuola, A. (1990) *The Village Witch Doctor and Other Stories*, London: Faber and Faber.
van Beek, W. E. A. (2017) *Transmission of Kapsiki-Higi Folktales over Two Generations: Tales that Come, Tales that Go*, New York: Palgrave Macmillan.
van Dijk, R. (2001) "Witchcraft and scepticism by proxy: Pentecostalism and laughter in urban Malawi," In: Moore, H. Sanders, T. (eds) *Magical Interpretations, Material Realities: Modernity, Witchcraft and the Occult in Postcolonial Africa*, London: Routledge, pp. 97–117.
van Dijk, R. and Pels, P. (1996) "Contested Authorities and the Politics of Perception: Deconstructing the Study of Religion in Africa," In: Werbner R, Ranger T (eds) *Postcolonial Identities in Africa*. London: Zed, pp. 245–270.
VanderMeer, J. (2013) "Amos Tutuola: An Interview with Yinka Tutuola,"

http://weirdfictionreview.com/2013/01/amos-tutuola-an-interview-with-yinka-tutuola-by-jeff-vandermeer/, accessed 1 November 2016.

van Rinsum, H. J. (2001) *Slaves of Definition: In Quest of the Unbeliever and the Ignoramus*, Maastricht: Shaker.

Verger, W. F. (1989) *Dílógún: Brazilian Tales of Yoruba Divination Discovered in Bahia*, Ibadan: Centre for Black and African Arts and Civilisation.

Viswanathan, G. (1998) *Outside the Fold: Conversion, Modernity, and Belief*, Princeton: Princeton University Press.

Visweswaran, K. (1994) *Fictions of Feminist Ethnography*, Minneapolis: University of Minnesota Press.

Wacquant, L. J. D. (1996) "Foreword," in: P. Bourdieu, (ed.) *The State Nobility*, Cambridge: Polity, ix-xxii.

Warnier, J.-P. (1993a) *L'Esprit d'Entreprise au Cameroun*, Paris: Karthala.

Warnier, J.-P. (1993b) "The King as a Container in the Cameroon Grassfields," *Paideuma*, 39, 303-319.

Warnier, J.-P. (2006) "Inside and Outside, Surfaces and Containers," In: C. Tilley, W. Keane, S. Kuechler, M. Rowlands, P. Spyer (eds.), *Handbook of Material Culture*, London: Sage, pp. 186-195.

Warnier, J.-P. (2007) *The Pot-King: The Body and Technologies of Power*. Leiden: Brill.

Warnier, J.-P. (2009) "Technology as Efficacious Action on Objects… and Subjects," *Journal of Material Culture*, 14(4): 413–424.

Warnier, J.-P. (2013a) "On Agnotology as Built-in Ignorance," *Africa Spectrum*, 48(1): 113-116.

Warnier, J.-P. (2013b) "Quelle Sociologie du Politique? À l'école de Weber et Foucault en Afrique," *Socio* 01: 95-108.

Warnier, J.-P. (2013c) "The Sacred King, Royal Containers, Alienable Material Contents, and Value in Contemporary Cameroon," in: Hans Peter Hahn and Hadas Weiss (eds), *Mobility, Meaning and the Transformations of Things*, Oxford: Oxbow Books., pp.50-62.

Wenzel, J. (2006) "Petro-magic-realism: toward a political ecology of Nigerian literature," *Postcolonial Studies*, 9(4): 449-464.

Werbner, R. (1996) "Introduction: Multiple identities, plural arenas," In: Werbner R, Ranger T (eds) *Postcolonial Identities in Africa*. London: Zed, 1-27.

Werbner, R. (2015) *Divination's Grasp: African Encounters with the Almost Said*, Bloomington: Indiana University Press.

Willems, W. (2014) "Provincializing Hegemonic Histories of Media and Communication Studies: Toward a Genealogy of Epistemic Resistancein Africa," *Communication Theory*, 24(4): 415-434.

Wolfe, P. (1999) *Settler Colonialism and the Transformation of Anthropology: The Politics and Poetics of an Ethnographic Event*, London: Cassell.

Wolenski, J. (2004) "The History of Epistemology," in: Niiniluoto, H., Sintonen, M. and Wolenski, J., (eds), *Handbook of Epistemology*, Dordrecht: Springer Science+Business Media Dordrecht, 3-54.

Wren, R. M. (1980) *Achebe's World: The Historical and Cultural Context of the Novels of Chinua Achebe*, Essex: Longman.

Yamada, S. (2009) "'Traditions' and Cultural Production: Character Training at the Achimota School in Colonial Ghana," *History of Education*, 38(1): 29-59.

Zeleza, P. T. (1997) *Manufacturing African Studies and Crises*, Dakar: CODESRIA.

Zeleza, P. T. and Olukoshi, A. (eds) (2004a) *African Universities in the Twenty-First Century: Volume I, Liberalisation and Internationalisation*, Dakar: CODESRIA.

Zeleza, P. T. and Olukoshi, A. (eds) (2004b) *African Universities in the Twenty-First Century: Volume II, Knowledge and Society*. Dakar: CODESRIA.